## Beyond Minimum Harmonisation

This book explains the functioning of shared competences in environmental protection by focusing on Member States interaction with the EU framework. By studying this interaction, Squintani reveals the room for improving the level of environmental protection, legal certainty, and efficiency of the system for environmental protection envisaged under the EU Treaties. Accordingly, this book makes a contribution to EU environmental law and policy, but also should be of interest to constitutional lawyers more generally and to scholars working in any field of EU policy and law in which minimum harmonisation is used. Thanks to its focus and clear, accessible prose, this book is also valuable additional reading material for environmental law courses, and to those involved in decision-making in the EU.

**Lorenzo Squintani** is Senior Lecturer in European and Economic Law at the University of Groningen. He is founder and member of the managing board of the U4 Environmental Law Network and a member of the managing boards of the European Environmental Law Forum, and of the Journal for European Environmental and Planning Law. His research and teaching interests include EU substantive law and EU environmental and climate law and he has authored several publications in the area of European environmental and climate law. Dr Squintani regularly advises Dutch, European Union, and international institutions on environmental issues.

Cambridge Studies in European Law and Policy

This series aims to produce original works which contain a critical analysis of the state of the law in particular areas of European law and to set out different perspectives and suggestions for its future development. It also aims to encourage a range of work on law, legal institutions and legal phenomena in Europe, including 'law in context' approaches. The titles in the series will be of interest to academics; policymakers, especially those who are interested in European legal, commercial and political affairs; practising lawyers, including the judiciary; and advanced law students and researchers.

Books in the Series

*The Politics of Justice in European Private Law*
Hans Micklitz

*The Transformation of EU Treaty Making: The Rise of Parliaments, Referendums and Courts Since 1950*
Dermot Hodson and Imelda Maher

*Redefining European Economic Integration*
Dariusz Adamski

*Human Rights in the Council of Europe and the European Union: Achievements, Trends and Challenges*
Steven Greer, Janneke Gerards and Rosie Slowe

*Core Socio-Economic Rights and the European Court of Human Rights*
Ingrid Leijten

*Green Trade and Fair Trade in and with the EU: Process-based Measures within the EU Legal Order*
Laurens Ankersmit

*New Labour Laws in Old Member States: Trade Union Responses to European Enlargement*
Rebecca Zahn

*The Governance of EU Fundamental Rights*
Mark Dawson

*The International Responsibility of the European Union: From Competence to Normative Control*
Andrés Delgado Casteleiro

*Frontex and Non-Refoulement: The International Responsibility of the EU*
Roberta Mungianu

*Gendering European Working Time Regimes: The Working Time Directive and the Case of Poland*
Ania Zbyszewska

*EU Renewable Electricity Law and Policy: From National Targets to a Common Market*
Tim Maxian Rusche

*European Constitutionalism*
Kaarlo Tuori

*Brokering Europe: Euro-Lawyers and the Making of a Transnational Polity*
Antoine Vauchez

*Services Liberalization in the EU and the WTO: Concepts, Standards and Regulatory Approaches*
Marcus Klamert

*Referendums and the European Union: A Comparative Enquiry*
Fernando Mendez, Mario Mendez and Vasiliki Triga

*The Allocation of Regulatory Competence in the EU Emissions Trading Scheme*
Jospehine Van Zeben

*The Eurozone Crisis: A Constitutional Analysis*
Kaarlo Tuori and
Klaus Tuori

*International Trade Disputes and EU Liability*
Anne Thies

*The Limits of Legal Reasoning and the European Court of Justice*
Gerard Conway

*New Governance and the Transformation of European Law: Coordinating EU Social Law and Policy*
Mark Dawson

*The Lisbon Treaty: A Legal and Political Analysis*
Jean-Claude Piris

*The European Union's Fight against Corruption: The Evolving Policy towards Member States and Candidate Countries*
Patrycja Szarek-Mason

*The Ethos of Europe: Values, Law and Justice in the EU*
Andrew Williams

*State and Market in European Union Law: The Public and Private Spheres of the Internal Market before the EU Courts*
Wolf Sauter and Harm Schepel

*The European Civil Code: The Way Forward*
Hugh Collins

*Ethical Dimensions of the Foreign Policy of the European Union: A Legal Appraisal*
Urfan Khaliq

*Implementing EU Pollution Control: Law and Integration*
Bettina Lange

*European Broadcasting Law and Policy*
Jackie Harrison and Lorna Woods

*The Transformation of Citizenship in the European Union: Electoral Rights and the Restructuring of Political Space*
Jo Shaw

*The Constitution for Europe: A Legal Analysis*
Jean-Claude Piris

*The European Convention on Human Rights: Achievements, Problems and Prospects*
Steven Greer

*Social Rights and Market Freedom in the European Constitution: A Labour Law Perspective*
Stefano Giubboni

*EU Enlargement and the Constitutions of Central and Eastern Europe*
Anneli Albi

# Beyond Minimum Harmonisation

## Gold-Plating and Green-Plating of European Environmental Law

Lorenzo Squintani
*University of Groningen*



CAMBRIDGE
UNIVERSITY PRESS

**CAMBRIDGE**
**UNIVERSITY PRESS**

University Printing House, Cambridge CB2 8BS, United Kingdom

One Liberty Plaza, 20th Floor, New York, NY 10006, USA

477 Williamstown Road, Port Melbourne, VIC 3207, Australia

314–321, 3rd Floor, Plot 3, Splendor Forum, Jasola District Centre, New Delhi – 110025, India

79 Anson Road, #06–04/06, Singapore 079906

Cambridge University Press is part of the University of Cambridge.

It furthers the University's mission by disseminating knowledge in the pursuit of education, learning, and research at the highest international levels of excellence.

www.cambridge.org
Information on this title: www.cambridge.org/9781108481007
DOI: 10.1017/9781108646055



First published 2019

Printed and bound in Great Britain by Clays Ltd, Elcograf S.p.A.

*A catalogue record for this publication is available from the British Library.*

*Library of Congress Cataloging-in-Publication Data*
Names: Squintani, Lorenzo, 1981- author.
Title: Beyond minimum harmonisation : gold-plating and green-plating of European environmental law / Lorenzo Squintani.
Description: Cambridge [UK] ; New York, NY : Cambridge University Press, 2019. | Series: Cambridge studies in European law and policy | Includes bibliographical references and index.
Identifiers: LCCN 2018051439 | ISBN 9781108481007 (hardback) | ISBN 9781108703703 (paperback)
Subjects: LCSH: Environmental law–European Union countries. | Environmental protection–European Union countries. | Environmental law–Economic aspects–European Union countries. | Legal certainty–European Union countries. | Economic development–European Union countries. | Environmental law–International unification. | BISAC: LAW / International.
Classification: LCC KJE6242 .S68 2019 | DDC 344.2404/6–dc23
LC record available at https://lccn.loc.gov/2018051439

ISBN 978-1-108-48100-7 Hardback

*To Laurence, for a career dedicated to developing academic talents*

# Contents

# Figures

# Tables

# Foreword

In February 2006, during my first class on European Environmental Law at the University of Amsterdam, I asked Professor Sevenster what Jan H. Jans meant in a passage in the second edition of *European Environmental Law*. In the section concerning the principles of subsidiarity and proportionality, Jans explains the problematic relationship between subsidiarity and environmental quality standards. At page 13 he states:

*On the one hand it can be said that European standard setting tends to even out competitive differences and avoids 'a race to the bottom'. On the other hand it deprives Member States of the opportunity of maintaining 'healthy' policy competition. A reasonable balance could be attained here if European environmental rules were mainly cast in the mould of minimum harmonization. This would allow the provision of a minimum level of protection throughout the Community, without depriving the Member States of the power to adopt more stringent standards for their own territory. Policy competition would then only be made impossible below the European standards.*

The reference to a 'healthy' policy competition maintained by means of minimum harmonization and the possibility of adopting more stringent standards struck a chord in me. On the one hand, probably due to my Italian origin, I was sceptical about the idea that Member States would adopt stricter standards. Do Member States adopt stricter standards? Why should they, given that stricter standards will negatively affect the competitiveness of their national industries? On the other hand, I wondered about the linkages between more stringent protective measures and 'healthy' policy competition. What is the role that stricter standards play in the development of Union environmental law? When two years later, Professor Jans hired me to conduct a Ph.D. research project to establish whether Member States do set stricter standards after minimum harmonization of environmental law, I thought that

I would finally get some answers to my own questions. I never asked Jan what he meant. I did not really need to. Writing my Ph.D. thesis has given me sufficient information to answer my questions myself. Yet, my Ph.D. was mainly aimed at gathering empirical data on the actual use of gold-plating. In this book, I expand upon such empirical data to discuss four theoretical aspects of this phenomenon. I would like to believe that, after reading this book, the reader will also be able to answer these questions.

***Lorenzo Squintani***
*Groningen, 2019*

# Series Editors' Preface

In the first days of October 2018, as this book was sent to press and this editors' preface was composed, the issue of emissions standards for cars was in the news for two reasons. On the one hand, the newspapers reported on a battle within the Council of Ministers and between the Council and the European Parliament over tougher future emissions standards – whether to introduce reductions of 30%, 35% or 40% as wished by the European Parliament. At the same time, UK newspapers reported on a reduction in car sales in September 2018 in the United Kingdom, because car manufacturers and retailers had incentivised sales in August 2018, in order to complete sales in advance of a new test on emissions coming into force at the beginning of September. In the background, the UN Intergovernmental Panel on Climate Change (IPCC) highlighted the need for urgent changes to meet the challenge of climate change, in the endeavour to reduce anticipated global warning caused by human sources to a maximum (and hopefully tolerable) of 1.5°C.

The tensions between commercial pressures and environmental standards are plain for all to see. They are examined in detail in this book, which homes in on the very important question of minimum harmonisation and the issue of what happens when Member States choose to surpass the standards that have been set in EU regulations. To that end, the author develops an important distinction between gold plating, which is focused in particular on how commercial interests operate in relation to environmental standards, and green-plating, which brings the environmental angle sharply into focus. Against the background premise that environmental measures can have a positive relationship with economic development, the overall aim is to produce a framework that enables Member States to understand when they can go beyond EU environmental measures, and with what types of measures. To that end, it will be of interest not just to scholars and students, but also to policymakers and other stakeholders, such as those working in NGOs who are interested in, and perhaps in some circumstances will contest, those types of national measures. In sum, it is an important and welcome addition to *Cambridge Studies in European Law and Policy*.

Jo Shaw
Laurence Gormley

# Abbreviations

| | |
|---|---|
| ACTAL | Advisory Board on Administrative Burdens |
| ALARA | As Low As Reasonably Achievable |
| ASSIs | Areas of Special Scientific Interest |
| AQA | Air Quality Act |
| AQO-01 | Air Quality Order 2001 |
| AQO-05 | Air Quality Order 2005 |
| BA-12 | Birds Act 1912 |
| BA-37 | Birds Act 1937 |
| BAT | Best Available Techniques |
| BATNEEC | Best Available Techniques Not Entailing Excessive Costs |
| BREF | Best available techniques REFerence |
| BRIO | Binding Rules on Installations Order |
| DEG | Dutch Emissions Guidelines |
| EMA | Environmental Management Act |
| ENVI | Committee on the Environment, Public Health and Food Safety |
| EPO | Environmental Permits Order |
| EU SCM | European Standard Cost Model |
| FFA | Flora & Fauna Act |
| GALA | General Administrative Law Act |
| GAEP | General Act on Environmental Permits |
| GRIO | General Rules on Installations Order |
| HA-54 | Hunting Act 1954 |
| HLG | High Level Group of Independent Stakeholders on Administrative Burdens |
| IPPC | Integrated Pollution Prevention and Control |
| NGOs | Non-governmental organizations |
| MNRs | Marine Nature Reserves |

| | |
|---|---|
| NCA-67 | Nature Conservation Act 1967 |
| NCA-98 | Nature Conservation Act 1998 |
| PM | Particular matt |
| SAC | Special areas of conservation |
| SCM | Standard Cost Model |
| SPA | Soil Pollution Act |
| SSSIs | Sites of special scientific interest |
| TEU | Treaty on European Union |
| TFEU | Treaty on the Functioning of the European Union |
| UK | United Kingdom |
| WA | Waste Act |
| ZLO | Zoning Law Order |

# Table of Cases

## Court of Justice of the European Union

## General Court of the European Union



## National Courts

*The Netherlands*

# Table of Legislation

## International Law



## EU Legislation

### *Primary legislation*

*Secondary legislation*

## Domestic legislation

*Italy*

Acts

*United Kingdom*

## Acts



## Statutory Instruments



*The Netherlands*

## Acts and Orders

## Besluiten



## Other



*Kamerstukken (old to new)*

## Kamerstukken II Second Chamber (Tweede Kamer)

## Kamerstukken I First Chamber (Eerste Kamer)



## Other

# Introduction

## *Minimum Harmonisation in European Environmental Law*

### I.1 Introductory Remarks

Each European car driver knows by now that his or her automobile emits more carbon dioxide than that indicated under the factory specifications. Producers and importers of passengers and commercial vehicles in Europe based these specifications on regulations promulgated by the European Union (EU).[1] Besides the cases of manifest fraud, which covered the main pages of EU journals in 2016/2016,[2] even those specifics that have been established following the rules represent only a percentage of the actual emissions produced by a vehicle. It would therefore not be unreasonable for a Member State to decide to pass national legislation going beyond the standards set by the EU legislation on this matter. However, would this be possible? Can a Member State pass stricter environmental standards than those established in Brussels in this specific case?

Similarly, greenhouse gas emissions reductions are based on EU law under the Emission Trading Scheme Directive (ETS Directive).[3] There is

[1] Regulation (EC) No 443/2009 of the European Parliament and of the Council of 23 April 2009 setting emission performance standards for new passenger cars as part of the Community's integrated approach to reduce CO2 emissions from light-duty vehicles, [2009] OJ L 140/1; and Regulation (EU) No 510/2011 of the European Parliament and of the Council of 11 May 2011 setting emission performance standards for new light commercial vehicles as part of the EU's integrated approach to reduce CO 2 emissions from light-duty vehicles, [2001] OJ L 145/1.

[2] E.g. Russell Hotten Volkswagen: The scandal explained, BBC News 10 December 2015; and Guilbert Gates How Volkswagen's 'Defeat Devices' Worked, *The New York Times*, updated March 16, 2017.

[3] Directive 2003/87/EC of the European Parliament and of the Council of 13 October 2003 establishing a scheme for greenhouse gas emission allowance trading within the Community and amending Council Directive 96/61/EC, [2003] OJ L 275/32.

general agreement that these EU standards are not sufficiently effective.[4] It would therefore not be unreasonable for a country such as the Netherlands, which is making slow progress in reducing its greenhouse gas emissions, to decide that operators of industrial installations covered by the ETS Directive shall surrender more emissions allowances for each ton of carbon dioxide emitted by those installations than required by the ETS Directive. The Netherlands could also decide to subject such operators to emission limit values, in parallel to the obligations stemming from the ETS Directive. However, industrial installations are covered by a multitude of EU environmental directives. This creates difficulties for Member States in understanding whether, what and how to pass stricter standards in this field. How then can the European Union, in accordance with its duty to cooperate sincerely with the Member States under Article 4(3) of the Treaty on European Union (TEU), provide guidance about such questions?

Moving on to the field of waste management, EU and national regulation in this field have criss-crossed one another for over forty years. Persons living in the EU have all experienced waste return systems, such as those for plastic bottles. Are such waste return systems an EU requirement or a national one? How to tell? The concept of 'Extended Producer Responsibility' underpinning return systems seems to derive from Scandinavian countries and/or Germany.[5] Yet it can now be found in many EU waste directives as well. It is now a concept existing in each of the Member States. How have national and EU law influenced one another in this field? Do national standards going beyond those of the EU in this field influence the development of waste law in Europe?

What about economic development? Higher national environmental standards inevitably come at a cost. Stricter car emissions tests or standards, if introduced by a car producing country, such as Sweden, means extra costs for car producers from that country. For example, Volvo will have to make extra investments to comply with such standards, leading to extra costs for its vehicles. This could lead to a weakening of the competitiveness of Volvo on the internal market, other than the Swedish one, in which Volvo competes with car producers not subject to the

[4] For critical remarks on this system see, e.g. Woerdman (2015), pp. 64–74 with further references; Peeters (2016), chapter 2; and Bogojevic (2016), pp. 670–687.

[5] Krämer (2011), p. 345 states that it derives from Scandinavian countries. Ezroj (2009), pp. 201–204 says that the first Extended Producer Responsibility programme in Europe was the German Packaging Ordinance introduced in 1991.

stricter Swedish standards. This could even lead to the setting up of a double production line, one for Sweden and one for the other markets. On the other hand, we should not forget what occurred once the big American car manufacturers were confronted with the economic crisis in 2008. FIAT, an Italian car manufacturer purchased around 30% of Chrysler, an American manufacturer, for zero dollar/euro.[6] Instead, FIAT paid Chrysler with green technology developed in order to comply with the EU emissions standards in this field. Could this apply also in the imaginary example of Volvo? What is the relationship between national environmental standards going beyond EU regulation and economic development? Are such standards good or bad for economy?

This book aims to answer these questions. It establishes what more stringent protective measures are, and what other kinds of national measure can be considered to go beyond EU requirements (Chapter 1). It also establishes what the relationship is between such national standards and the development of a high level of environmental protection in the European Union (Chapter 2). Legal certainty is an issue little discussed in this field, yet of pivotal importance. This book establishes a framework aimed at improving Member States' understanding of whether is possible to go beyond EU standards, what kind of measures are possible in specific cases, and how to predict whether such measures will withstand judicial review before the Court of Justice of the European Union (Court of Justice) (Chapter 3). Finally, despite its legalistic approach, this book looks also at the relationship between environmental protection and economic development. It shows that, despite growing evidence that stricter environmental standards can be beneficial to economic development, national regulatory impact assessments do not take sufficiently into account such potential benefits (Chapter 4).

After reading this book, the reader will have a better and more comprehensive understanding of the intricate set of rules that exist in Europe, at the EU and national level, in order to protect the environment. The reader will understand what the relationship is between (minimum) harmonisation of environmental standards and national measures going beyond such standards, commonly called 'gold-plating'. Accordingly, before addressing the four topics outlined above, this

[6] See joint statement by Fiat S.p.A., Chrysler LLC and Cerberus Capital Management L.P. made on 20 January 2009, in 'Fiat to take equity stake in Chrysler as alliance is announced', web article italiaspeed.com/2009 available at: www.italiaspeed.com/2009/cars/industry/01/chrysler/2001_statement.html (Accessed June 2017).

introduction continues thus, describing the concept of 'harmonisation' and the manner in which the Treaties envisage it as regards environmental protection.

## I.2 (Minimum) Harmonisation in European Environmental Law

If we consider environmental protection in Europe today,[7] we see a complex system of rules adopted by the Member States of the European Union and the European Union itself. Lawyers would say that environmental protection is a shared competence between the Union and its Member States.[8] In practice, this means that in addition to environmental measures of an exclusive national nature, there are many national environmental measures that are taken to implement Union environmental law. According to Article 3 of the Treaty on European Union (TEU),[9] the Union is tasked to work for the sustainable development of Europe based on balanced economic growth and price stability, a highly competitive social market economy, aiming at full employment and social progress, and a *high level of protection and improvement of the quality of the environment*. This task is undertaken by the Union by means of, inter alia, legislative acts – mostly directives – establishing a high level of environmental protection. This process of environmental standards setting at EU level is known as 'harmonisation'.

In the European Union, the concept of 'harmonisation' is intrinsically linked to the establishment of the internal market, i.e. an area without internal frontiers in which goods, persons, services and capital can circulate freely and in which competition is undistorted.[10] The European Economic Community (EEC) was indeed created to achieve the establishment of such a market. The Treaty of Rome of 1957 focused on two regulatory techniques to achieve this goal. The 1985 Commission White Paper on *Completing the Internal Market*[11] highlighted how, besides Treaty prohibitions on import and export barriers among the Member States (i.e. pursuing deregulation), the Commission envisaged the adoption of common EU rules, which might replace diverging national standards

[7] In this study, references to Europe should be seen as references to the European territories of the Member States of the European Union.
[8] Article 4 TFEU.
[9] For the latest consolidated version see [2016] OJ C 202/13.
[10] Article 26 TFEU in conjunction with Protocol No. 27 on the Internal Market and Competition.
[11] COM (85) 310, para. 64.

(i.e. pursuing re-regulation).[12] Harmonisation indeed reduces or even eliminates differences among national standards by establishing a new standard. The creation of such a new standard requires making choices as to the type and quality of the regulatory regime it intends to create.[13] To paraphrase Weatherill, harmonisation is a means to improve the functioning of the internal market, but where what is harmonised is diverse measures of (say) environmental policy taken at national level, the consequence of harmonisation is an EU choice about environmental policy.[14]

The making of such an EU choice is made possible by the legal bases envisaged under the Treaties. Within the context of this contribution, the most relevant ones are the current Article 114 of the Treaty on the Functioning of the European Union (TFEU)[15] on the approximation of laws, Article 192 TFEU on environmental policy, and Article 194 TFEU on energy policy. Union environmental policy and law were introduced in the Treaty only with the Single European Act.[16] Still, already before 1987, the EU legislator had harmonised environmental standards by relying on the then Articles 100 and/or 235 EEC. Article 100 EEC, despite focusing on the harmonisation of the internal market, was, for example, used to adopt Council Directive 73/404/EEC relating to detergents,[17] which had the further objective of restricting the use of non-biodegradable detergents in order to appreciably reduce pollution of the natural environment in general, and, in particular, water pollution. Similarly, Council Directive 75/716/EEC relating to the sulphur content of certain liquid fuels was adopted on this legal basis.[18] The use of this legal basis for environmental policy purposes brought Close to raise the question whether this practice constituted an abuse of the powers indicated by the 1957 Treaty.[19] A question that the Court of Justice answered negatively in two

[12] Similarly, Weatherill (2017), p. 151.
[13] Idem, p. 152.
[14] Idem, p. 153 where the word 'social' is used instead of the word 'environmental'.
[15] For the latest consolidated version see [2016] OJ C 202/47.
[16] Single European Act [1987] OJ L 169/1; For a first commentary D'Oliveira (1988), pp. 123–125; Jacobs (1988), pp. 117–122; Krämer (1987), pp. 659–688; and Vandermeersch (1987), pp. 407–429.
[17] Council Directive 73/404/EEC of 22 November 1973 on the approximation of the laws of the Member States relating to detergents, [1973] OJ L 347/51.
[18] Council Directive 75/716/EEC of 24 November 1975 on the approximation of the laws of the Member States relating to the sulphur content of certain liquid fuels, [1975] OJ L 307/22.
[19] Close (1978), pp. 461–481.

infringement procedures against Italy based on these two directives, respectively.[20] No less problematic has been the use of Article 235 EEC, which allowed the EEC to adopt measures aimed at achieving EEC goals for which no specific legal basis had been provided for in the Treaty. This residual legal basis had been used to adopt, for example, Council Directive 75/439/EEC on the disposal of waste oils,[21] the validity of which has been challenged in court, due to an alleged misuse of power.[22] The Court of Justice confirmed that this legal basis can be used to pursue environmental policy. At times, these two legal bases were used conjunctively as in the case of Council Directive 75/442/EEC on waste.[23] Also as regards the use of both provisions conjunctively, the Court of Justice concluded that this was not in breach of the attribution principle.[24] Still, it was clear that a fully-fledged environmental policy would have greatly benefitted from the addition of an ad hoc legal basis in the Treaties.

To this end, the Single European Act of 1987 added Articles 130r, 130s, and 130t to the Treaty of Rome, with Article 130s constituting a legal basis to pursue environmental protection. Several Member States feared losing their sovereignty in this sensitive policy area. Article 130t EEC (today Article 193 TFEU) served to reassure the Member States that the level of environmental protection *remains*, at least partially, a national competence, as the Union legislator can set a minimum level of protection, subject to the limitation of having to respect the Treaties.[25] Indeed, traditionally, harmonisation measures based on this provision pursue minimum harmonisation.[26]

[20] Case 91/79, *Commission of the European Communities v Italian Republic*, [1980] ECR 1099, ECLI: EU:C:1980:85 and Case 92/79, *Commission of the European Communities v Italian Republic*, [1980] ECR 01115.

[21] Council Directive 75/439/EEC of 16 June 1975 on the disposal of waste oils, [1975] OJ L 194/23.

[22] Case 240/83 *Procureur de la République v Association de défense des brûleurs d'huiles usagées (ADBHU)*, [1985] ECR 531.

[23] Council Directive 75/442/EEC of 15 July 1975 on waste, [1975] OJ L 194/39.

[24] E.g. Case 68/81, *Commission of the European Communities v Kingdom of Belgium*, [1982] ECR 153.

[25] Jacqué (1986), p. 124 states that the clause in Article 193 TFEU was one of those introduced on request of the Federal Republic of Germany,[25] with *Länder* and *Bundesrat* actually opposing the European Single Act because they feared losing competences over environmental policy (Nicolaysen (1988), p. 115). Germany insisted also on the introduction of a clause stating that the level of protection must be set at a 'high level'. Another clause thus inserted was the principle of subsidiarity.

[26] Over a 'practice of minimum harmonisation as a means of attaining environmental goals' see Jans & Vedder (2012), pp. 108–122.

Minimum harmonisation essentially means that Member States have to implement the minimum level of protection established by Union environmental measures, and additionally, they may maintain or introduce measures providing a higher level of environmental protection than that pursued by the Union legislator. To be clear, it does not mean that the level of protection of the environment must be the lowest possible one.[27] Both Article 114 and 192 TFEU aim at a high level of environmental protection. Article 37 of the Charter of Fundamental Rights confirms this approach.[28] Minimum harmonisation can hence be better associated to 'optimal' harmonisation than to 'minimal' harmonisation.[29] It is the optimal level of environmental protection given the specific circumstances of the case and the interests at stake during the negotiation process. This level need not be the highest,[30] nor the lowest, possible.

Moreover, it should be noted that the concept of 'minimum harmonisation' should not be applied to an EU measure as a whole. As indicated by Hofhuis, EU legislation can contain a mix of minimum and maximum harmonisation.[31] Which level is pursued must therefore be established at the level of each specific provision within an EU act. To this extent, indications can be found in the text of the provision under scrutiny. Words such as 'at least', 'not more than', and 'a minimum of' indicate that Member States have room to pursue a higher level of protection of the environment than that required by the provision at hand. The pursuing of minimum harmonisation can also be recognised by the use of clauses explicitly stating that stricter national standards are allowed. When such clauses are formulated with regard to the whole content of an EU measure, this means that the EU measure as a whole pursues minimum harmonisation. Even when no such indication can be read in the EU measure concerned, it is still possible that minimum harmonisation is pursued. Treaty provisions such as Article 193 TFEU does indeed state that measures based on Article 192 TFEU should not prevent Member States from maintaining or introducing more stringent protective measures.

[27] Hofhuis (2006), pp. 10 and 11.
[28] For the latest consolidated version see, [2016] OJ C 202/389.
[29] Hofhuis (2006), p. 11.
[30] Case C-233/94, *Federal Republic of Germany v European Parliament and Council of the European Union*, [1997] ECR I-2405.
[31] Hofhuis (2006), p. 11.

Chapter 1 refines the meaning of the concept 'more stringent protective measures' while Chapter 3 looks deeper at the manner in which the EU legislator indicates to the Member States the room to go beyond EU standards. Yet it should already be clarified here that going beyond EU standards does not mean derogating from EU law. Member States' actions take place under the umbrella of the so-called principle of sincere cooperation.[32] Sincere cooperation is a broad concept which encompasses a positive and a negative obligation. On the one hand, the Union and the Member States must cooperate to achieve the objectives set out in the Treaties. On the other hand, they must refrain from undertaking actions which could jeopardise the achievement of such objectives. In the context of minimum harmonisation, this means that Member States must respect the EU minimum first.

From a temporal perspective, harmonisation should not be seen as a static exercise. Developed in an official manner since 1972, EU environmental policy has reached today a body of law that encompasses most environmental issues. Soil is probably the least regulated environmental medium at EU level; nevertheless, this does not mean that harmonising measures will no longer be adopted by the EU legislator in this field. Further harmonisation or re-harmonisation is continuously pursued by the EU institutions.

## I.3 Environmental Protection: A Member States' Responsibility

The existence of a great variety of EU environmental standards could suggest that environmental protection is mainly an EU responsibility. This conclusion would be wrong. From the perspective of the environment, the above shows that environmental protection in Europe derives from the Member States' implementation of the Union minimum, from the use that Member States make of the possibility of going beyond the requirements of Union law and from the use that Member States make of their power to regulate matters not regulated by Union law. This is the essence of a system based on shared competences. It should be noted that under the principle of subsidiarity, set out in Article 5(3) TEU, the Union may act only if and insofar as the objectives of the proposed action cannot be sufficiently achieved by the Member States, either at a central level or at the regional and local level, but can rather, by reason of the scale or effects of the proposed action, be better achieved at the Union

[32] Article 4(3) TEU.

level. In essence, as stated by Krämer, Member States have to protect the environment and certain measures have to be taken by the Union.[33] Moreover, under Article 193 TFEU, Member States may adopt measures pursuing a higher level of environmental protection than that required by Union environmental legislation based on Article 192 TFEU. The Court of Justice has established that, since Member States may adopt stricter measures, Union environmental measures do not need to be based on the highest level of environmental protection that is technically possible.[34] As stated in the literature, this shows that the European system of environmental protection is based on the idea that Member States will adopt stricter measures.[35] In short, environmental protection remains primarily a Member State responsibility.

The use that Member States make of the possibility to go further than required by Union law, and the use that Member States make of their power to regulate matters not regulated by Union law, is traditionally approached from two different points of view. On the one hand, it is looked at from an environmental perspective. From this perspective, lawmakers, enforcement and judicial bodies, non-governmental organisations (NGOs) and academics consider whether national law establishes a higher level of environmental protection than that required by Union law. This practice is, in most of the cases, referred to as the Member States' power to establish *more stringent protective measures* or *more stringent measures*.[36] On the other hand, Member State actions are approached from an economic perspective. From this perspective, lawmakers, industry and – always most often – academics consider whether national law places burdens upon industry and citizens that are not required by Union law. This practice is often referred to as *gold-plating*.[37]

## I.4 Focus and Structure of the Book

In the literature, Pagh strongly criticises what he called *"the stricter" mantra*.[38] The idea that a minimal level of environmental protection at

[33] Krämer (2011), p. 440.
[34] Case C-284/95, *Safety Hi-Tech Srl*, [1998] ECR I-4301, para. 49.
[35] Jans, Squintani et al. (2009) p. 418.
[36] This concept is used also outside environmental law. See on this concept further in Chapter 1, Section 1.2.
[37] This concept is used also outside environmental law. See on this concept further in Chapter 1, Section 1.3.
[38] Pagh (2006), pp. 5–15.

Union level will be integrated with stricter national standards at the national level is misleading, most notably because it seems that Member States do not maintain or introduce national standards to provide a higher level of environmental protection.[39] In a previous publication with Anker, Purdy and De Graaf, I wrote that 'it may be argued that a 'no gold-plating' principle makes little sense as a dominating transposition principle in environmental legislation.'[40] Further, it has been argued that the decision not to adopt national environmental legislation going beyond the relevant EU measure *frustrates* the concept of Article 5 TEU and of Article 193 Treaty for the Functioning of the European Union.[41] As my co-authors and I stated in a previous publication, 'the absence of gold-plating can reverse the whole system of environmental protection under [the Treaties]'.[42] At the same time, it has long been recognised in the literature that there has been a lack of data and clarity on the legal meaning of more stringent protective measures and gold-plating, on the presence or absence of such measures and the reasons behind their presence or absence.[43] In my Ph.D. thesis I demonstrated that gold-plating is more widespread than previously thought.[44] It occurs in all environmental fields and in each Member State it is possible to identify cases of gold-plating, even in those countries which have developed policies to constrain it. Still, it confirms that there is a growing tendency not to go beyond EU standards. This growing practice can have repercussions for the functioning of the system of environmental protection as envisaged under the Treaties.

To understand better these possible repercussions, this book goes a step further. It builds upon the empirical data gathered during and after my Ph.D. thesis in order to establish a more general theory on the relationship between national and EU environmental standards. It does so by focusing on four areas of interest. First, it looks at the meaning of the concepts '*more stringent protective measures* or *more stringent measures*',

39 For example, Krämer (2011), p. 440 and Jans, Squintani et al. (2009), p. 435.
40 Anker et al. (2015), p. 43.
41 Krämer (2011), p. 440.
42 Jans, Squintani et al. (2009), p. 435.
43 To be precise, a few preliminary studies on gold-plating have been performed in the United Kingdom and in the Netherlands; see Chapter 1, Section 1.3. However, such studies did not specifically focus on environmental protection and only looked at the law as it stood at the time at which the studies were performed. Therefore, they do not provide a clear picture of the 'stricter mantra' phenomenon in environmental law.
44 Squintani (2013), chapter 9.

on the one hand, and at the concept of 'gold-plating', on the other. This analysis shows that gold-plating is a misleading concept. Accordingly, the concept of 'green-plating' is introduced. Chapter 2 analyses the relationship between green-plating and the development of EU environmental law. This analysis shows evidence of the importance of the former for the latter, strengthening the conclusion that blind national policies dogmatically constraining green-plating are hardly reconcilable with the principle of sincere cooperation under Article 4(3) TEU. Chapter 3 analyses the clarity of the manner in which the EU legislator indicates the room to go beyond EU standards, and predictability of the manner in which the Court of Justice reviews such standards if adopted. This analysis will not only indicate that there is ample room to improve legal certainty in the field of green-plating; it also indicates how such room could be exploited by developing a framework in this regard. Finally, Chapter 4 analyses the relationship between green-plating and economic development. It shows what economic considerations are used to justify refraining from gold-plating and green-plating. It also illustrates that economic consideration can in fact be used to justify green-plating. Theory and practice in this context are both analysed and used to assess the manner in which regulatory impact assessments take account of the potential beneficial effects of green-plating on economic development. The conclusion is that regulatory impacts assessments usually fail to recognise such potential benefits, confirming the misleading nature of the discussion on gold-plating taking place in the European Union. The findings from these four chapters lead to the question on whether EU law can limit Member States' bias towards gold-plating, which is discussed in the conclusions to this book.

Generally, the debate on more stringent protective measures or gold-plating is approached in the literature by focusing on Articles 191 to 193 TFEU, which specifically regulate environmental protection. Additionally, there is focus on Article 114 TFEU, which is the legal basis of Union harmonisation with the objective of the establishment and functioning of the internal market, including when these measures can contribute to environmental protection.[45] However, I will focus only on measures taken in the context of Articles 191 to 193 TFEU because previous research has shown that Member States make little use of the possibility of introducing stricter environmental standards under

[45] For example, Jans & Vedder (2012), chapter 2 and pp. 122–133.

Article 114 (4–6) TFEU.[46] In this book, the terms 'Union environmental law', 'Union environmental legislation', 'Union environmental measures' or 'Union environmental acts' refer to provisions based on Article 192 TFEU.

In order to provide a picture of the 'more stringent protective measures' and the 'gold-plating' phenomena that is unaffected by time-related factors, I will not only focus on the law as it stands today,[47] but will look at all the developments in the legal sectors analysed. This approach is also necessary because knowing why an environmental measure was there in first place is relevant to explaining why a Member State maintains a more stringent protective measure or gold-plating. Although gold-plating and more stringent protective measures can take the form of legislative acts,[48] administrative decisions[49] or judicial decisions,[50] in this book priority is given to the transposition phase, i.e. the phase of the implementation process in which EU standards are translated into national standards. This is due to the fact that explanatory memoranda and parliamentary debates provide a good insight into the reasons for pursuing, or refraining going beyond EU standards. Although some experiences from the United Kingdom play an important role in the proceedings of this book, the methodology followed in this book ensures that the data used in my analysis is, so to say, 'Brexit-proof'. In other words, this book uses individual data to establish a generalised picture the relevance of which will continue to exist even if the United Kingdom leaves the EU.

[46] De Sadeleer (2003). See also Pagh (2006), p. 6, where he notes the Commission has only granted Member States the power to permanently maintain stricter measures in eight cases, all regarding the same Directive. Similar findings can be found in, Jans, Sevenster & Janssen (2007), pp. 1368–1373 and Fleurke (2008).

[47] By today I mean the date at which I ended my empirical research, August 2012. Developments after this date are taken into consideration only incidentally.

[48] For example, Case C-2/10, *Azienda Agro-Zootecnica Franchini sarl en Eolica di Altamura Srl v Regione Puglia*, [2011] ECR I-06561 (*Windmills*).

[49] For example, Joined cases C-379/08 and C-380/08, *Raffinerie Mediterranee (ERG) SpA, Polimeri Europa SpA and Syndial SpA v Ministero dello Sviluppo economico and Others (C-379/08) and ENI SpA v Ministero Ambiente e Tutela del Territorio e del Mare and Others (C-380/08)*, [2010] ECR I-2007 (*ERG II*).

[50] For example, Case C-318/98, *Criminal Proceedings against Giancarlo Fornasar, Andrea Strizzolo, Giancarlo Toso, Lucio Mucchino, Enzo Peressutti and Sante Chiarcosso*, [2000] ECR I-4785.

# 1 Gold-Plating: A Misleading Overarching Concept

## 1.1 Introductory Remarks

Gold-plating is a widely used concept, by both politicians and scholars. It is replacing the concept of *more stringent protective measures* in discussion referring to the use that Member States make of the possibility to go beyond the requirements of Union law, and the use that Member States make of their power to regulate matters not regulated by Union law. This chapter argues that the use of the 'gold-plating' concept as an overarching concept, hence covering more stringent protective measures, is misleading.

The main reason for such a statement is presented in this chapter, firstly, in Section 1.2, by analysing the concept of 'gold-plating'. The word 'gold-plating' clearly derives from the United Kingdom, but a fascinating cross-fertilisation process taking place, in particular, between the United Kingdom and the Netherlands, has influenced this concept. The historical development of the concept of gold-plating and a comparison of the manner in which the United Kingdom, the Netherlands and the European Union approach gold-plating will bring this cross-fertilisation process to the foreground. The result of this process is a concept that focuses on economic burdens. It is business-centric, explaining the clear negative connotation that gold-plating has acquired in the societal discourse. Second, Section 3.1 analyses the concept of 'more stringent protective measures'. Despite having been introduced into the Treaty of Rome in 1987, and used in several EU measures based on what nowadays is Article 192 of the Treaty on the Functioning of the European Union ( TFEU), the meaning of this concept is still being discussed in the literature. Section 1.3 aims at ending this discussion conclusively by clarifying the constitutive requirements of the concept. The main finding that can be drawn from the analysis performed in Section 1.3 is that the concept of 'more stringent protective measures' focuses on the level of environmental protection, without disregarding other values such as the economic interests related to the creation and functioning of the internal market.

Accordingly, the stigmatisation of the 'more stringent protective measures' concept occurring from the use of 'gold-plating' as an overarching concept is unjustified. If further perpetrated it could even endanger the functioning of the system envisaged by the Treaties for the protection of the environment, as it deprives it of one of its foundations, i.e. that Member States retain the main responsibility as regards environmental protection, explained in the introduction to this book. Besides, the use of the concept of 'gold-plating' deprives the Union legislature of a catalyst for the further development of EU environmental law, as explained in Chapter 2. In view of these reasons, this chapter concludes by proposing the introduction of a new overarching concept, that of '*green-plating* '.

## 1.2 Gold-Plating: Development and Definition of a Concept

The term 'gold-plating' was first used in the United Kingdom, where it is generally understood to mean that national law places burdens on business not required by a Union measure.[1] Weatherill refers to a speech in 2001 by the Director General of the Confederation of British Industry entitled 'No more gold-plating!'[2] However, it is unclear when this term was used for the first time.[3] I found references asserting that the discussion of gold-plating started directly after the accession of the United Kingdom to the European Economic Communities in 1973.[4]

[1] Ambler, Chittenden & Obodovski (2004), p. 6.

[2] Weatherill (2005), p. 539.

[3] In Federation of Small Business, 'Better Regulation... Is better for business?' 2004, p. 20 states that the following publication should be consulted for complaints about gold-plating: Institute of Directors, *Your Business Matters* (Report from the Regional Conferences, URN 96/765) (1996) p. 9. This suggests that this term was already in use in the United Kingdom as early as in 1996.

[4] Ambler, Chittenden & Obodovski (2004), p. 5. Gold-plating has been addressed by the Government in a series of studies: Department for Trade and Industry, *Review of the Implementation and Enforcement of EC Law* (London, DTI, 1993); Cabinet Office, *Improving the Way the UK Handles European Legislation: Pilot Quality Assurance and Transposition Conference* (London, Cabinet Office, 2002); Bellis (2003); National Audit Office, *Lost in Translation? Responding to the Challenges of European Law* (2005–06 HC 26); Davidson (2006). See also Thomas & Lynch-Wood (2008), p. 180.

The origin of the concept of 'gold-plating' is indeed linked to the deregulation programmes pursued in the United Kingdom during those years, as well as in the Netherlands. As discussed in this section, the deregulation programmes in these two countries have led to the development of specific policies on gold-plating. Cross-fertilisation between these national policies refined the meaning of gold-plating, to the extent known today. Indeed, although the Netherlands and the United Kingdom are not the only Member States in which gold-plating has been officially addressed,[5] the Netherlands and the United Kingdom are the Member States in which these policies seem to be the most developed. Today, the European Union itself, via the route of the Better Regulation Agenda, has taken over the concept of gold-plating. So far, only the United Kingdom and the Netherlands define gold-plating explicitly. All other countries and the European Union simply seem to follow the lead taken by the Dutch and the UK governments.

## 1.2.1 *The United Kingdom and Gold-Plating*

### 1.2.1.1 The Development of the UK Policy on Gold-Plating

In the United Kingdom, the focus on administrative burdens (so-called *red tape*) dates back to the 1940s. However, attention to this phenomenon increased during the 1990s and the 2000s, when a series of reports – including the 'Less is More' report by the so-called Better Regulation Task Force (BRTF) and the report of the so-called Hampton Commission[6] – highlighted the status of the situation and proposed solutions. The report 'Less is More' further developed the so-called principles of good regulation (Annex B).[7] The first principle was proportionality and stated: 'Regulators should only intervene when necessary. Remedies should be appropriate to the risk posed and costs identified and minimised.' In 'Less is More' a corollary was added, stating: 'EC Directives should be transposed without gold-plating'. As we can see, this report clearly linked better regulation to gold-plating.

[5] Jans, Squintani et al. (2009), pp. 419–423. Krämer (2011), p. 440, with reference to Austria, Belgium and Germany.

[6] Better Regulation Task Force: Regulation – Less is More. Reducing Burdens, Improving Outcomes. March 2005. Hampton (2005).

[7] These principles were first set out in 1997 and then refined over time; see Federation of Small Business, Better Regulation... Is it better for business?, 2004, p. 10. (www.fsb.org.uk/docs/default-source/fsb-org-uk/policy/assets/0952-better-regulation.pdf?Status=Master&sfvrsn=1)

With the Better Regulation Action Plan in May 2005, later supported by the Legislative and Regulatory Reform Act 2006, the government carried over the advice of the BRTF and of the Hampton Commission, at least to a certain extent. In the context of gold-plating, in addition to developing a specific policy, the government established a series of advisory bodies. The Better Regulation Commission,[8] the Better Regulation Executive and the Reducing Regulation Committee perform an 'in-house' check of statutory instruments, which are delegated acts, to avoid gold-plating. In Parliament, the House of Lords Merits of Statutory Instruments Committee (Merits Committee) was appointed in 2003 with the power to subject to the attention of the House of Lords proposed statutory instruments inappropriately implementing Union legislation, which includes cases where statutory instruments introduce gold-plating.[9] These bodies have had impact on the gold-plating of environmental measures. For example, the Better Regulation Commission and the Merits Committee challenged the transposition of the Energy Performance of Buildings Directive.[10] The Directive requires an energy label for buildings that has to be renewed every ten years. The 2007 Energy Performance of Buildings Regulations required renewing the label every time a property is marketed to be sold or rented.[11] Both advisory bodies considered this provision gold-plating and asked the government not to pass it.[12]

In 2010, with the Cameron government starting its mandate, the focus on gold-plating increased. The so-called One-In/One-Out method of law-making has been introduced in the context of better regulation, meaning that no new legislative act affecting businesses can be made if an old act imposing at least equivalent administrative burdens upon business is not eliminated.[13] Moreover, extensive consultation started to establish

[8] This Commission, which replaced the Better Regulation Task Force, no longer exists.

[9] On the parliamentary control of the transposition of Union law, see Thomas & Lynch-Wood (2008), pp. 196–200.

[10] Directive 2002/91/EC of the European Parliament and of the Council on the energy performance of buildings, [2003] OJ L 1/65. This directive is based on Article 175 EC.

[11] Energy Performance of Buildings (Certificates and Inspections) (England and Wales) Regulations (SI 2007/991), Regulation 11(4). Later deleted with the Energy Performance of Buildings (Certificates and Inspections) (England and Wales) Regulations 2010 (SI 2010/1456) Regulation 2(6)(b).

[12] Better Regulation Commission, Energy Performance Certificates and Residential Properties, London BRC, 2007; and House of Lords Merits of Statutory Instruments Committee, 18th Report (2006–07 HC 92), para. 34.

[13] This technique was recommended already in 2005 by the BRTF Report 'Less is More'.

which provisions affect the life of UK citizens without being justified by the public interest. Consequently, UK environmental law underwent systematic scrutiny in 2011.[14] Measures implementing European obligations are not touched by these instruments, but gold-plating is. In March 2012, the then Environment Secretary Caroline Spelman announced that

*Environmental regulations will be made simpler and more effective while remaining as strong as ever following a review of red tape.*[15]

As regards the specific policy on gold-plating, we can distinguish two main moments of development. A first document referring to gold-plating was the 'Transposition Guide: How to Implement European Directives Effectively' of the Regulatory Impact Unit.[16] This document warned civil servants about gold-plating and defined this concept, as explained in the next section. Under this guide, any gold-plating should be justified against any costs or benefits that will arise from it.[17]

A year later, Tony Blair made a speech in which he evoked the need to end gold-plating.[18] According to Blair, gold-plating was the result of a cultural attitude of civil servants. They were overzealous in transposing Union measures into national provisions. Blair stated: 'We need to change that approach to end gold-plating of European regulations.'[19] This speech, given to the Confederation of British Industry, symbolised the starting point of UK policy on gold-plating. As noted in the 2005 Cabinet Office Transposition Guidelines, government policy on transposition is to avoid gold-plating, unless there are exceptional circumstances justified by a *strong costs/benefits* analysis and *extensive consultation* with business.[20] Any gold-plating has to be explained in a so-called Impact Assessment and in the so-called Transposition notes and needs to

[14] See www.redtapechallenge.cabinetoffice.gov.uk/home/index/ (last accessed March 2012).
[15] Statement available at www.defra.gov.uk/news/2012/03/19/red-tape-challenge/ (last accessed March 2012).
[16] Cabinet Office, Regulatory Impact Unit, Transposition Guide: How to Implement European Directives Effectively, 2003.
[17] Idem, p. 17.
[18] Thomas & Lynch-Wood (2008), p. 204, with reference to Tony Blair, Prime Minister's Speech to the Confederation of British Industry, Birmingham, 18 October 2004.
[19] Tony Blair, Prime Minister's Speech to the Confederation of British Industry, Birmingham, 18 October 2004.
[20] Regulatory Impact Unit, *Transposition guide: how to implement European directives effectively*, Cabinet Office (2005), p. 5.

receive specific clearance from a Cabinet Committee.[21] The 2005 Guidelines of the Regulatory Impact Unit of the Cabinet Office state:[22]

*From March 2005, Transposition Notes should contain an explicit comment on any over-implementation that has taken place during the transposition process. In the introduction to the Note, drafters should include one of the following statements: These regulations do what is necessary to implement the Directive, including making consequential changes to domestic legislation to ensure its coherence in the area to which they apply. [or, LS] These regulations do more than is necessary to implement the Directive in the following areas* [. . .].

This shows that gold-plating has been proceduralised. The relevance of such a proceduralisation is clear when we consider that business has already challenged national legislation introducing gold-plating in the court, without previously consulting the relevant business categories.[23]

Following the advice of the Davidson Review,[24] the UK policy was broadened also to cover existing domestic standards.[25] However, even under this second and ongoing phase, gold-plating is still allowed if justified by cost-benefit considerations and after extensive consultations with stakeholders. For example, in 2008, Thomas & Lynch-Wood reported that, during the transposition of the Energy Performance of Buildings Directive (around 2007), the government defended a case of gold-plating by stating that climate change is important enough to justify going further than European requirements.[26] The government called this case of gold-plating *green-plating*.

### 1.2.1.2 The Definition of Gold-Plating in the United Kingdom

Following the various developments of the UK policy on gold-plating, the government has been providing for an official definition of

21 Idem, p. 17.

22 Idem, Annex 1.

23 Jans, Squintani et al. (2009), p. 430 with reference to the claim brought in 2007 by the Surveyors Professional Body against the Act transposing Directive 2002/91/EC of the European Parliament and of the Council on the energy performance of buildings (Energy Performance of Buildings Directive), [2003] OJ L 1/65. This directive is based on Article 175 EC (now Article 192 TFEU). The government suspended the entry into force of the provision in question in order to avoid the legal challenge.

24 The Davidson Review (2006) makes reference to a Dutch report, showing the existence of some links between these two national policies. The report to which the Davidson Review refers is ECORYS, OpdenKamp Adviesgroep en Europa Instituut, Koppen op EG-regelgeving. Eindrapportage definitief, Rotterdam 2006.

25 *Transposition Guide 2007*, Department for Business, Enterprise and Regulatory Reform, p. 28.

26 Thomas & Lynch-Wood (2008), p. 199 with reference to Hansard HC Deb., vol. 460 col. 646 16 May 2007 (Yvette Cooper MP, Minister for Housing and Planning).

gold-plating in the Cabinet's transposition guidelines for Union legislative acts. This official document defines gold-plating as follows[27]:

*Gold-plating is when implementation goes beyond the minimum necessary to comply with a directive, by:*

- *extending the scope, adding in some way to the substantive requirement, or substituting wider UK legal terms for those used in the directive; or*
- *not taking full advantage of any derogations which keep requirements to a minimum (e.g. for certain scales of operation, or specific activities); or*
- *retaining pre-existing UK standards where they are higher than those required by the directive; or*
- *providing sanctions, enforcement mechanisms and matters such as burden of proof which are not aligned with the Macrory principles[28] (e.g. as a result of picking up the existing criminal sanctions in that area); or*
- *implementing early, before the date given in the directive. (N.B. Bringing implementation forward in the UK by a matter of weeks to coincide with a UK Common Commencement Date can be justified if it can be demonstrated that the benefit of early implementation outweighs the cost.)*

This shows that the constitutive elements of the concept of 'gold-plating' are:

a) the presence of a Union directive, although the term 'beyond' does not limit gold-plating to the scope of application of the Union measure; and
b) the presence of a more stringent regime than strictly required.

The latter requirement is not simply linked to the level of protection, but, in light of the background of this approach, it focuses also on the level of burdens.

## *1.2.2 The Netherlands and Gold-Plating*

### 1.2.2.1 The Development of the Dutch Policy on Gold-Plating

Contemporarily to the UK government, the Dutch government started focusing on administrative burdens as early as 1975, when the Ministry of Economic Affairs established a working group collaborating with business associations to simplify the fiscal and social regulatory

[27] Department for Business, Enterprise and Regulatory Reform, Transposition Guide 2007, p. 28.

[28] R. Macrory, Regulatory Justice: Making Sanctions Effective, Final Report, November 2006, available at: www.berr.gov.uk/

framework affecting small and medium enterprises.[29] In 1998 the so-called Slechte Commission,[30] also called 'Commission on Administrative Burdens', was established to assess the extent of the administrative burdens phenomenon.[31] The conclusions of the Slechte Commission were that administrative burdens had reached uncontrollable levels.[32] Following the advice of the Slechte Commission,[33] the government increased its efforts to reduce administrative burdens.[34] As regards gold-plating, in addition to developing a specific policy, the government instituted the Advisory Board on Administrative Burdens' (Actal) which,[35] since 2003, has been advising the government on cases of gold-plating.[36] It should be noted that Actal provides its advice only on an ad hoc basis since it has limited staff and budget.[37] Actal sets its own agenda.[38] A clear example of the influence of this body on gold-plating in the field of environmental law is provided by the case of the proposal in 2007 on a reporting duty on biomass for energy purposes, which never reached the Dutch Parliament due to the negative advice of Actal, and which explicitly stated that such a proposal was in contrast with the Dutch policy on gold-plating.[39]

29 Arendsen (2008), p. 134 with reference to Nijsen, *Dansen met de Octopus*, Een bestuurskundige visie op informatieverplichtingen van het bedrijfsleven in de sociale rechtsstaat, Uitgeverij Eburon, Delft, 2003.
30 The chairman of the commission, J. Slechte, was a former senior executive at Shell: Voermans (2001), p. 225.
31 Arendsen (2008), p. 137.
32 Commissie Administratieve Lasten, *Regels zonder overlast*, Eindrapport van de Commissie Administratieve Lasten, The Hague, 25 November 1999.
33 Arendsen (2008), pp. 139–140.
34 Proceedings of the Second Chamber of the States General, Kamerstukken II 1999/2000 24 036, nr. 148.
35 Initially established on the basis of Besluit van 30 maart 2000, houdende instelling van een Adviescollege toetsing administratieve lasten, Stb. 2000, 162, later amended, and not established on the basis of Besluit van 17 februari 2006 tot instelling van een Adviescollege toetsing administratieve lasten 2006, Stb. 2006, 138, finally amended by Stb. 2008, 259. This body will be further described in Section 1.2.4, below.
36 For example, Advies van 10 januari 2002 concerning the incineration of waste, RL/ML/2002/009.
37 Voermans (2001), p. 226.
38 The *modus operandi* of Actal is described at www.actal.nl.
39 Actal annual report 2007, p. 22. Actal considered that the legislative proposal introduced obligations not foreseen by Directive 2001/77/EC of the European Parliament and of the Council of 27 September 2001 on the promotion of electricity produced from renewable energy sources in the internal electricity market, [2001] OJ L 283/33 and Directive 2003/30/EC of the European Parliament and of the Council of 8 May 2003 on the promotion of the use of biofuels or other renewable fuels for transport, [2003] OJ

The Netherlands has indeed a specific policy on gold-plating. As regards this specific policy, (so far) we can distinguish four main moments of development. It was formulated in the Government Coalition Agreement of 2003.[40] The coalition agreement stated that the relationship between economic interests and environmental protection, which had been forgotten, needed to be re-established. On the one hand, green technologies and green taxes would be encouraged, while on the other hand, the Netherlands would be active at the Union level to increase the level of environmental protection. At the same time, the Netherlands would not introduce new rules going further than required, unless a specific Dutch problem required a specific Dutch solution.

As clearly indicated in the coalition agreement, the Dutch policy on gold-plating aims to take into account economic considerations when protecting the environment. However, only new cases of gold-plating were to be avoided. The *second* phase started around 2004–2005, when the policy was extended to any field of law and covered existing cases of gold-plating.[41] Moreover, the policy was refined: gold-plating had to be avoided, unless a *specific* and *significant* Dutch interest required otherwise. In this second phase, the significance criterion has been added to the specificity criterion. These two formulations share reference to a 'no gold-plating, unless' regime. Therefore, gold-plating remains possible. The *third* phase started with the Government Coalition Agreement of October 2010. According to this agreement, gold-plating will be 'tracked down and eliminated'.[42] The jargon used by the government shows the increased aversion of the Dutch government to gold-plating. The 'unless a specific and significant Dutch interest requires otherwise' clause is no longer there. The coalition agreement seems to have changed the political regime applied to gold-plating from 'no gold-plating, unless' to 'no gold-plating, regardless'. In 2011, the government even changed the Dutch Lawmaking Guidelines (in Dutch: *Aanwijzingen voor de regelgeving*)

L 123/42. Actal's Opinion was not published due to the fact that the legislative proposal was not published either.

[40] See the Government Coalition Agreement of 2003, *Hoofdlijnenakkord voor het kabinet CDA, VVD, D66*, 16 May 2003, p. 12.

[41] Written Cabinet Statement to Industry 2004 (in the original Dutch: *Industriebrief hart voor de industrie*), Proceedings of the Second Chamber of the States General, Kamerstukken II, 2005/2006, 29 515, nr. 143 and 151. Later also Written Cabinet Statement to Parliament dd. 2 November 2007, reference number OI/O/7130085.

[42] See Government Coalition Agreement of 30 September 2010, Freedom and Responsibility (*Vrijheid en verantwoordelijkheid*), pp. 13 and 14.

to explicitly refer to the Dutch policy on gold-plating.[43] Guideline 331 states that transposition should be limited to what is strictly necessary. Until 2011, this guideline was only concerned with avoiding delays. It was inserted after a series of major delays in the transposition of directives. These cases originated in the tendency to link the transposition of directives to reform of the subject covered by the relevant Union measures.[44] Today, this provision serves also to avoid affecting the competitive position of Dutch industry, as indicated in the explanatory note to Guideline 331. In 2012, during the preliminary phase of agreeing a proposal for an act regulating environmental and spatial matters conjunctively, the government stated that gold-plating in legal terms is now rare in the field of environmental and spatial law.[45] With the so-called Rutte II government, the fourth and current phase of Dutch policy on gold-plating started in autumn of 2012. This phase is characterised by uncertainty about the government attitude towards gold-plating. Indeed, there is no reference to gold-plating in the government agreement.[46] At the same time, the section of the agreement concerning nature conservation reports that Dutch nature conservation law will, where relevant, be brought into line with the level of protection required by the Birds Directive[47] and the Habitats Directive[48] and other regulations.[49] This duly occurred in 2016 with the introduction of the new Nature Protection Act (*Wet Natuurbescherming*) in January 2016.[50] This act eliminated almost all cases of gold-plating which still existed in this field of environmental protection after the many reforms that had already taken place following the introduction of the Dutch policy on gold-plating.[51] The

[43] Prime Minister Circular of 18 November 1992, last amended by Prime Minister's Order, Minister of the Interior, 1 April 2011, nr. 310225, houdende vaststelling van de negende wijziging van de Aanwijzingen voor de regelgeving, Stcrt. 2001, nr. 6602.

[44] For a discussion on the timely implementation of Union directives, see Polak (1990), p. 194.

[45] Letter from the Minister for the Environment and Infrastructure, Schultz van Haegen, of 9 March 2012 'Stelselwijziging Omgevingsrecht', reference number IENM/BSK-2012/21699, p. 21.

[46] Government Coalition Agreement of 29 October 2012, VVD–PvdA, '*Bruggen slaan*'.

[47] Council Directive 79/409/EEC of 2 April 1979 on the conservation of wild birds, [1979] OJ L 103/1. Now recast by Directive 2009/147/EC of the European Parliament and of the Council of 30 November 2009 on the conservation of wild birds, [2010] OJ L 20/7.

[48] Council Directive 92/43/EEC of 21 May 1992 on the conservation of natural habitats and of wild fauna and flora, [1992] OJ L 206/7.

[49] Government Coalition Agreement of 29 October 2012, VVD–PvdA, '*Bruggen slaan*', p. 38.

[50] Staatsblaad 2016, nr. 34.

[51] Squintani & Zijlmans (2013).

government agreement for the so-called Rutte III government, started in autumn 2017, follows this less defined approach. It simply states that gold-plating will be kept to a minimum.[52]

#### 1.2.2.2 The Definition of Gold-Plating in the Netherlands

In the Netherlands, gold-plating is referred to by the terms '*nationale koppen*' or '*lastenluwe implementatie*', which can be translated as *national toppings* and *burden neutral implementation*, respectively.[53] The Dutch government has not defined the term 'national topping' itself, but has adopted the definition provided in three studies: the so-called ECORYS report[54] and the Europa Instituut en Asser Instituut report[55] first, and the Deloitte Study[56] later. These reports were commissioned to determine whether Dutch law imposed obligations upon individuals that were not required by Union law.[57] The ECORYS report defined a national topping as:

*A measure which, in the presence of a Union directive which has been correctly implemented in the Netherlands, goes further than the minimum requirement if the directive pursued minimum harmonisation or, if the directive pursued total harmonisation, a measure that aims at the top of the space left by the directive or that introduces stricter standards than other Member States do where the directive allowed discretion as regards certain aspects of its implementation.*[58]

[52] Government Coalition Agreement of 10 October 2017, VVD–CDA-D66-CristenUnie, '*Vertrouwen in de Toekomst*', p. 44.

[53] ECORYS, OpdenKamp Adviesgroep en Europa Instituut, *Koppen op EG-regelgeving. Eindrapportage definitief*, Rotterdam 2006; see also Europa Instituut en Asser Instituut, National Koppen op EG-regelgeving. *Tweede ronde van meldingen van het bedrijfsleven over 'koppen' in de Nederlandse wet- en regelgeving, juridisch bekeken*, Leiden 2007. For 'burden neutral implementation' see Deloitte Consulting BV, Onderzoek naar lastenluwe implementatie van Europese regelgeving, Augustus 2013, available as attachment to Proceedings of the Second Chamber of the States General, Kamerstukken II 2012/13 29 362, nr. 224.

[54] ECORYS, OpdenKamp Adviesgroep en Europa Instituut, *Koppen op EG-regelgeving. Eindrapportage definitief*, Rotterdam 2006.

[55] Europa Instituut en Asser Instituut, National Koppen op EG-regelgeving. *Tweede ronde van meldingen van het bedrijfsleven over 'koppen' in de Nederlandse wet- en regelgeving, juridisch bekeken*, Leiden 2007. This definition is also followed in the literature, for example Vogelezang-Stoute et al. (2009), pp. 34–35 and Dijkman, De Jonge & Post (2011), pp. 3–4.

[56] Deloitte Consulting BV, Onderzoek naar lastenluwe implementatie van Europese regelgeving, Augustus 2013, available as attachment to Proceedings of the Second Chamber of the States General, Kamerstukken II 2012/13 29 362, nr. 224 (Deloitte Study).

[57] Proceedings of the Second Chamber of the States General, Kamerstukken II 2006/07, 29 515 and 29 826, nr. 222, pp. 2 and 3.

[58] ECORYS report, p. 15. This is a liberal translation. The original text states: 'In dit onderzoek wordt het begrip nationale kop als volgt gedefinieerd: Er sprake is van een

A passage from the Europa Instituut en Asser Instituut report indicates that the definition of national toppings provided in the ECORYS report was overly linked to the concepts of minimum and total harmonisation.[59] Accordingly, the Europa Instituut en Asser Instituut report tried to make the definition more functional by defining national toppings as:[60]

*Cases where the Netherlands, through the correct implementation of Union directives, and in some case regulations, goes further than what is strictly necessary to implement the relevant Union directives.*[61]

The most important innovation of this definition is that it also covers cases where the Netherlands did not use a derogation clause. Although this classification provides for a better understanding of the concept of 'national topping', there is some incongruence among the various categories.[62] In August 2013, Deloitte published a study on whether the Netherlands has implemented certain Union measures in a burden-neutral manner. In this study, the concept of 'burden-neutral implementation' is defined as:

*Dutch law implements Union measures with as few burdens as possible for the business addressed by the Union measure at hand. This means that the Dutch legislator makes use of the room allowed under the EU measure concerned to reduce burdens for business and avoids adopting additional measures leading to extra burdens for business. Burdens are defined as administrative costs, compliance costs, enforcement costs, restrictions and the costs deriving from long procedures.*[63]

EG-richtlijn; Nederland deze heeft geïmplementeerd; Dit een correcte implementatie betreft; Deze implementatie a) bij minimumharmonisatie boven de minimumnorm van de richtlijn uitgaat; b) bij totale harmonisatie aan de bovenkant van de bandbreedte zit of bij gebruik van de beoordelingsvrijheid die de richtlijn biedt, stelt strengere normen dan andere lidstaten.'

59 Europa Instituut en Asser Instituut report, p. 7.

60 Idem, p. 8.

61 This is a liberal translation. The original text states: 'Er is sprake van een nationale kop indien: er sprake is van een EG-richtlijn (of een EG-Verordening die nog nadere uitvoering van de lidstaten vereist; Nederland deze heeft omgezet in nationaal recht; dit een correcte omzetting betreft; de Nederlandse regelgeving verder gaat dan gezien de Europese Richtlijn strikt genomen noodzakelijk is.'

62 Stoop (2012), p. 233.

63 This is a liberal translation. The original text states: 'De Nederlandse wetgever implementeert EU-regelgeving met zo min mogelijk lasten voor de, door de richtlijn geadresseerde, bedrijven. Dit betekent dat de wetgever daarbij gebruikmaakt van beleidsruimte die het mogelijk maakt de lasten voor bedrijven te beperken en nalaat om aanvullende verplichtingen op te leggen die leiden tot extra lasten voor bedrijven. Lasten

The Deloitte Study also defined the concept of 'burdens' as:

- Costs deriving from the obligation to deliver information to public authorities ('administrative costs');
- Costs deriving from substantive obligations ('compliance costs');
- Costs suffered by business to comply with the information and substantive obligation deriving from the enforcement of legal provisions ('enforcement costs');
- Extra requirements by service providers or enforcement authorities, differences in national regulations which place Dutch businesses at a competitive disadvantage with businesses from other Member States, complex division of power between and within public authorities, etc. (so-called restrictions).[64]

The main innovation of this definition is the strict link between the concept of 'burden-neutral implementation' and the personal scope of application of the Union measure concerned. The new definition seems to exclude cases in which the Netherlands regulates natural and legal persons not covered by the Union measure at hand. More generally, 'burden-neutral implementation' underlines that when more options are available to comply with Union law, the least burdensome one should be chosen.

In September 2013, the Dutch government seemed to have accepted this definition of 'burden-neutral implementation'.[65] However, in November 2013, a written answer by the Ministry of Infrastructure and Environment to questions posed by the Dutch Parliament, in which the cases of gold-plating existing in the Netherlands in the fields of agriculture, nature conservation and fishery were discussed, made use of the definition introduced by the Europa Instituut en Asser Instituut report.[66] Neither the explanatory note to the proposal for the reform of nature

worden gedefinieerd als administratieve lasten, nalevingskosten, toezichtlasten, belemmeringen kosten verbonden met lange procedures.'

64 Deloitte Study, p. 4.

65 Proceedings of the Second Chamber of the States General, Kamerstukken II 2012/13 29 362, nr. 224, pp. 16 and 17

66 Here, reference is made to the answer as such and to the memo attached to it, see Proceedings of the Second Chamber of the States General, Kamerstukken II 2013/14, *Aanhangsel van de handelingen* 442. The Dutch government had accepted the definition introduced by the Europa Instituut en Asser Instituut report in 2007, Proceedings of the Second Chamber of the States General, Kamerstukken II 2006/07, 29 515 and 29 826, nr. 222, pp. 2 and 3.

conservation law,[67] nor the explanatory note to the proposal for the reform of the whole of Dutch environmental legislation (the Environment and Planning Act)[68] make an explicit reference to the concepts of 'national topping' or 'burden-neutral implementation'. In the latter document, it is only referred to the policy of not going beyond what is required by Union measures.[69] Yet, the reform of nature conservation law, culminated in the emanation of the Nature Conservation Act in 2016, treated all national measures, going beyond the Birds Directive and Habitats Directive in the same manner, regardless of whether they fell within or outside the scope of application of such EU acts. In the government agreement of 2017, the term 'national topping' is used explicitly.[70] At the moment of writing this chapter, it is unclear which definition the Dutch government follows. Looking at the approach followed under the Nature Conservation Act in 2016 and under the Environment and Planning Act, there seems to be little practical difference in the manner in which the Dutch government looks at the concept of 'national topping' and that of 'burden-neutral implementation'. On the basis of these reports and of parliamentary documents referring to 'national toppings', the concept of 'national topping' covers cases where:

- Dutch law establishes stricter standards than those established by a Union measure
- The Netherlands does not take advantage of derogation clauses in a Union measure
- The goals of the Union measure are implemented earlier than required and this creates more burdens for industry
- The enforcement of the level of protection is stricter than that required by a Union measure explicitly regulating the enforcement regime

[67] Here reference is made to the explanatory memorandum of the amended proposal, published in June 2014, Proceedings of the Second Chamber of the States General, Kamerstukken II 2013/14, 33 348, nr. 5.

[68] Proceedings of the Second Chamber of the States General, Kamerstukken II 2013/14, 33 962, nr. 3. The expression 'more burden neutral' (*lastenluwer*) is used once without further specification. The Environment and Planning Act was adopted on 23 March 2016, *Wet van 23 maart 2016, houdende regels over het beschermen en benutten van de fysieke leefomgeving (Omgevingswet)* Stb 2016 nr. 156.

[69] Proceedings of the Second Chamber of the States General, Kamerstukken II 2013/14, 33 962, nr. 3, p. 36.

[70] Government Coalition Agreement of 10 October 2017, VVD–CDA-D66-CristenUnie, '*Vertrouwen in de Toekomst*', p. 44.

- The Netherlands expands the field of application beyond the scope of a Union measure
- Dutch law interprets concepts left vague by the Union more stringently than required, or
- Dutch law adopts more stringent means or instruments to achieve a Union goal than is strictly necessary.[71]

An additional aspect of a national topping is that the measure concerned must affect the competitive position of Dutch companies. This requirement is based on economic considerations that, however, the two reports mentioned above did not consider as being a constitutive requirement of national toppings.[72] The concept of 'burden-neutral implementation' covers these same measures with the uncertainty concerning cases in which the Netherlands regulates natural and legal persons not covered by the Union measure at hand. Given the great similarities between these two concepts it possible to conclude that in order to qualify as a 'national topping' or 'burden-neutral implementation' in the Dutch context, the following aspects are relevant:

a) the presence of a Union directive;
b) a correct implementation thereof; and
c) the presence of a regime which is more stringent than strictly necessary.

The latter requirement is not simply linked to the level of protection, but, in light of the background of this approach, it focuses also on the levels of burden.

### 1.2.3 *The European Union and Gold-Plating: The Union Better Regulation Policy*

As opposed to the United Kingdom and the Netherlands, the European Union does not have a definition of gold-plating. However, it does have a policy stemming from Member States' actions, which also concerns gold-

[71] The Europa Instituut en Asser Instituut report does not classify this case as a case of national topping, Europa Instituut en Asser Instituut report, p. 14. However, the parliamentary discussions in the context of air quality law and nature conservation show that this aspect also falls within the concept of 'national topping'; for example, Letter of the Secretary of State for Economic Affairs, Agriculture and Innovation, Henk Bleker, to the Dutch House of Representatives of 14 September 2011. See further, infra, in this section.

[72] For example, ECORYS report, p. 14.

plating. Member States' actions aiming at reducing regulatory burdens did not only focus on national legislation. At the Union level, several Member States, including the United Kingdom and the Netherlands, expressed their concerns about the burdens flowing from Union law.[73] In response to these concerns, the European Union has launched a comprehensive better regulation strategy, following the Interinstitutional Agreement on Better Law-Making in 2003,[74] in the context of the Lisbon Strategy. This policy aims to simplify and improve existing regulation, to better design new regulation and to reinforce the respect and the effectiveness of the rules. Two important aspects of the Better Regulation policy are the simplification of the regulatory framework on the one hand and the reduction of administrative costs on the other.[75] In the context of simplification, the Commission has stated that:

[. . .] *layers of 'gold-plating' erode the simplifying effect of EU rules.*[76]

Gold-plating plays a role in the better regulation policy. According to the Commission, gold-plating affects both transposition and implementation of Union law, and the quality of national and regional regulation. In the context of reducing the administrative costs, the Commission developed a model, the so-called European Standard Cost Model (EU SCM), which is based on the Dutch SCM, but which specifically takes account of gold-plating.[77] According to the Commission, it is important to establish who is responsible for administrative costs. It should be noted that the Commission did not consider a specific field of Union law. The positions expressed above do not concern environmental regulation in particular.

In its activities the Commission is assisted by an advisory body, the 'High Level Group of Independent Stakeholders on Administrative

[73] Haythornthwaite (2007), p. 21.

[74] Published in [2003] OJ C 321.

[75] Administrative costs are the sum of 'business costs', which are those costs not linked to regulations, and 'administrative burdens', which are a specific kind of regulatory burden representing the costs that business incurs to provide information to public authorities and which would not otherwise be incurred. See Commission Working Document, Measuring administrative costs and reducing administrative burdens in the European Union, COM(2006) 691 final, in particular Section 1.2. Administrative costs are categorised into: *Category A*, burdens from International and European law; *Category B*, burdens from International and European Law as implemented in a national legal order; *Category C* burdens from national law.

[76] Commission Working Document – Second progress report on the strategy for simplifying the regulatory environment, COM(2008) 33 final, 30 January 2008, p. 10.

[77] COM(2006) 691 final, pp. 6 and 7.

Burdens' (HLG).[78] This group delivered an opinion on gold-plating in the context of environment law in April 2009.[79] This opinion focused attention on the administrative burdens created by five environmental legislative acts[80] and concluded that 8% of the administrative burdens from the acts analysed was due to gold-plating.[81] Although the HLG recognised that this figure is considerably lower than expected and that shared responsibilities means that Member States are allowed to maintain or introduce gold-plating,[82] it concluded that 8% is a substantial amount and that therefore the Commission should request the Member States to investigate to what extent these additional obligations are creating an unnecessary burden and can be reduced or removed without affecting the effectiveness of national implementation of the Union legislation.[83]

The position of the Commission brought gold-plating to the attention of the European Parliament and the Council. In a resolution dated 4 September 2007, the European Parliament stated that it:

> [...] *deplores Member States' practice of 'gold-plating', and calls upon the Commission to investigate what further measures might be taken to prevent it, including the introduction of a right of direct action for citizens.*[84]

As we can see, in this document, the European Parliament did not just make a simple statement; it also indicated specific measures to prevent

[78] Established by Commission Decision C(2007) 4063.

[79] This opinion is available at: http://ec.europa.eu/enterprise/policies/better-regulation/administrative-burdens/high-level-group/index_en.htm (last accessed March 2012).

[80] These five measures are: 1) Directive 2003/105/EC of the European Parliament and of the Council of 16 December 2003 amending Council Directive 96/82/EC on the control of major accident hazards involving dangerous substances, [2003] OJ L 345/97 (Seveso II); 2) Regulation (EC) No 1013/2006 of the European Parliament and of the Council of 14 June 2006 on shipments of waste, [2006] OJ L 190/1; 3) Council Directive 96/61/EC of 24 September 1996 concerning integrated pollution prevention and control, [1996] OJ L 257/26; 4) Directive 2002/96/EC of the European Parliament and of the Council of 27 January 2003 on waste electrical and electronic equipment (WEEE), [2003] OJ L 37/24; 5) Directive 2000/53/EC of the European Parliament and of the Council of 18 September 2000 on end-of life vehicles, [2000] OJ L 269/34.

[81] HLG April 2009 Opinion, pp. 2 and 6. The burdens from gold-plating were estimated to cost EUR 58 million.

[82] Idem, pp. 2–4. The HLG Opinion shows that the gold-plating of environmental measures counts for not more than 0.048% of the total burdens deriving from Union law.

[83] Idem, pp. 6 and 7.

[84] European Parliament resolution of 4 September 2007 on Better Regulation in the European Union (2007/2095(INI)).

gold-plating.[85] Finally, the Council stated in a resolution of 4 December 2007 that it:

> [. . .] *invites the Member States to keep under review the options and discretions implemented in their legislation, limit their use (wherever possible) and report to the Commission on these findings.*[86]

The position of the Council is more nuanced than that of the Commission and of the European Parliament. However, it is remarkable that these three Union institutions have expressed a negative opinion on gold-plating. In 2009 the Commission reported that, in the field covered by a selection of environmental measures, there were 135 national obligations to provide information not required by Union law against the 1178 obligations to provide information required by the Union environmental measures analysed.[87] Remarkably, the Commission did not recommend actions to limit gold-plating. In addition, in the 2010 Commission Communication 'Smart Regulation in the European Union', the Commission simply stated that it will investigate further the issue of gold-plating.[88] This seems a milder position than that previously expressed.

### 1.2.4 *Cross-Fertilisation of Gold-Plating Policies and Definitions*

The description in Sections 1.2.1, 1.2.2 and 1.2.3 reveals a certain degree of convergence in the content and temporal development of the Dutch, UK and Union policies. This is of course not a coincidence. At the Union level, the Dutch Presidency in 2004 characterised its mandate by focusing on better regulation. I argue that the Commission's attention to gold-plating could be seen as a reaction to Member States' allegations that Union law creates excessive burdens. The EU SCM refined the Dutch SCM to tackle gold-plating in order to establish who is responsible for the

[85] A similar position was stated by the European Parliament in: European Parliament resolution on the implementation, consequences and impact of the internal market legislation in force (2004/2224(INI)); and European Parliament resolution of 21 October 2008 on 'better law-making 2006' pursuant to Article 9 of the Protocol on the application of the principles of subsidiarity and proportionality (2008/2045(INI)).

[86] 2836th Economic and Financial Affairs Council meeting – Brussels, 4 December 2007, Press Release.

[87] Commission working document, Reducing administrative burdens in the European Union – 2008 progress report and 2009 outlook, COM(2009) 16, Annex II. This statement is based on the HLG opinion presented above.

[88] COM(2010) 543.

administrative burdens.[89] It is therefore understandable that the Commission's attention to gold-plating appears diminished in its 2010 Communication, given that the HLG highlighted that gold-plating accounts for only 8% of the total burdens linked to Union legislation. The Commission had probably hoped for a higher figure in order to be able to reciprocate the allegation of increasing administrative burdens to the Member States.

In the United Kingdom, the Netherlands was adopted as a model for the United Kingdom to refine its policy on better regulation, especially as regards its focus, inter alia, on gold-plating. At the request of the UK government, the 'Less is More' report reviewed the main characteristics of the Dutch system and suggested following the Dutch example.[90] As regards gold-plating, the report states:

*European legislation makes it harder to meet any national burden reduction target than would be the case were all laws to be created nationally, but the Dutch believe that they can achieve their target despite European legislation. [. . .] By reforming the domestic application of Directives, including removing any domestic additions to the core EU requirements, we could unilaterally reduce some aspects of the Administrative Burden, without the need for renegotiation at a European level. [. . .]*

Moreover, Actal served as an inspiration for the Better Regulation Committee and the Better Regulation Executive.[91]

The comparison with the Netherlands in the 'Less is More' report is a symbol of the comparative approach adopted by these two countries with respect to better regulation in general and gold-plating in particular. Such a comparative approach explains the many similarities between these two countries in their policies on the reduction of administrative burdens and as regards the specific policies on gold-plating. Hence, it should not come to a surprise that also the official definitions of gold-plating in these two county coincide.

To a large extent, the concepts used in the Netherlands and the United Kingdom are synonyms. Compared to the Dutch definition of national topping or burden neutral implementation, the only element lacking in the UK definition of gold-plating is that national law must correctly

[89] COM(2006) 691 final, pp. 6 and 7.

[90] Better Regulation Task Force: Regulation – Less is More. Reducing Burdens, Improving Outcomes. March 2005, pp. 4–6 and Annex C.

[91] The BRTF based its advice to set up advisory bodies to serve the better regulation agenda on Actal, Better Regulation Task Force: Regulation – Less is More. Reducing Burdens, Improving Outcomes. March 2005, Annex C.

implement a directive. However, as regards the concept of 'gold-plating' this aspect can be inferred from the fact that the definition of gold-plating is located in the Government's transposition guidelines. These guidelines aim at the correct implementation of Union law.[92] Moreover, even if the UK Government's transposition guidelines only focus on the transposition phase, it can be argued that the concept of 'gold-plating' also covers administrative and judicial measures, since from the point of view of industry, it does not matter what the legal nature of the act generating extra burdens is. Even from a temporal development of the definitions, there are similarities. In both countries, gold-plating initially focused on new cases. Around 2004 to 2005 in the Netherlands and in 2006 in the United Kingdom, the definitions were extended to cover existing standards. Finally, both countries followed 'not unless' regimes until 2010.

However, there are differences. Most importantly, the United Kingdom proceduralises gold-plating by requiring a costs/benefits analysis to be inserted in the Impact Assessments and by requiring extensive consultations with stakeholders. In the Netherlands, Actal provides advices on an ad hoc basis and consultations with stakeholder are held in some cases. However, there is no clear and systematic procedure to discuss gold-plating as exists in the United Kingdom. With the 2010 elections and the respective installations of the Cameron government in the United Kingdom and the Rutte government in the Netherlands, the differences increased. The Netherlands introduced a strong *political* ban on gold-plating where no exception seemed politically acceptable, at least officially. The United Kingdom, on the other hand, still allows gold-plating. Today, such differences seem to have been reduced once again.

As regards the differences between the national policies on gold-plating and the Union policy on gold-plating, the main difference is surely, that at Union level, gold-plating is still anchored in the Better Regulation policy. Gold-plating is taken into consideration due to its alleged effects on simplification and administrative burdens. This could explain why DG XI does not mention gold-plating in any of its documents. At a national level, gold-plating is mostly considered for its alleged negative effects on economic development and competitiveness. Today, the administrative burden dimension is only of secondary importance; in other words, gold-plating is rejected as such at the national level.

92 See also the first sentence of the definition referring to 'what is necessary to comply with a directive'.

Despite this difference between national and Union policies on gold-plating, it is striking to see that the concept of 'gold-plating' has an overwhelming negative connotation at both national and Union level. This finding can only be understood by considering, as shown above, the strict linkage between gold-plating policies and better regulation agendas at national and EU level. These agendas have been developed by politicians in order to give attention to views expressed by one part of society, and one alone: business. Gold-plating is a business-centric concept, as reflected in the constitutive elements of this concept here presented.

### 1.2.5 *Refinement and Further Developments of the Concept of 'Gold-Plating'*

In the period 2003–2006, a series of refinements of this concept appeared in the literature. A first distinction was made between *absolute* and *relative* gold-plating. The former means that national law goes further than required by Union law, while the latter means that national law transposes Union law more stringently than other Member States do.[93] In the Netherlands, another distinction was made between *ex-ante* and *ex-post* national toppings.[94] *Ex-ante* national toppings are where the national legislator maintains a measure which goes beyond what is required. On the other hand, *ex-post* national toppings are cases where the legislator introduces a new measure. As discussed above, in the United Kingdom, the concept of gold-plating covered pre-existing standards from 2006/2007.[95] Furthermore, UK authors distinguish between *justified* and *unjustified* or *unnecessary* gold-plating.[96] To this extent, gold-plating is justified only if the net benefits for the UK economy are higher than the costs.[97] Another refinement is that between *voluntary* and *inadvertent* gold-plating. Inadvertent gold-plating means that the gold-plating was not motivated or justified in consultation and through costs/benefits analyses, or that past justifications no longer suffice.[98] Finally, a particular kind of gold-plating created in the United Kingdom concerns an alleged tendency to force the Union legislator to pass legislation that would

93 Ambler, Chittenden & Obodovski (2004), p. 6.
94 Jans, Squintani et al. (2009).
95 This was recommended in the Davidson (2006), p. 77, Recommendation No. 11. This recommendation was carried over in the Department for Business, Enterprise & Regulatory Reform, Transposition Guide 2007.
96 Davidson (2006), p. 12.
97 Ibidem.
98 Ibidem.

otherwise have not been passed,[99] especially in cases where UK legislation had been passed shortly before the enactment of the offending Union measure.[100] Such a Member State is called *prime* or *first mover* and the results of its action are considered gold-plating.[101]

In addition to the concept of 'gold-plating', the concepts of *over-implementation* and *over-elaboration* are discussed in the United Kingdom. Over-elaboration was a term frequently used in the period 2003–2006.[102] It means that the terminology used in a Union measure is adapted to the terminology used in a national legal system.[103] If a UK transposition act requires more words than the Union act in question, UK writers complain of over-elaboration or gold-plating.[104] These two terms are used as synonyms. Although the debate on over-elaboration has not yet ended, today, this term is no longer regarded as a synonym. Over-implementation is also often referred to as a synonym of gold-plating.[105] However, this concept is broader. It covers gold-plating, *double banking* – i.e. failing to streamline the overlap between legislation in force at national and Union level – and *regulatory creep* – i.e. uncertainty concerning regulation and guidelines and over-enforcement.[106]

Among scholars, the term 'gold-plating' reached Union-wide attention thanks to the works of academics such as Weatherill, who in 2005 wrote an article on the factors broadening or limiting the impact of the Europeanisation of laws through harmonisation, referring to national legislative *spillovers* as gold-plating.[107] For Weatherill, when a national legislator applies a Union measure to a field falling outside the Union measure's material or personal reach, it creates gold-plating.[108] Today, Union institutions use this term as well.[109] However, they do not specify

[99] Ambler, Chittenden & Obodovski (2004), p. 6.

[100] Davidson (2006), p. 78.

[101] The UK approach in the context of the IPPC Directive and the ETS Directive has been referred to as an example of this tendency, Davidson (2006), p. 78.

[102] Stephen (2004), p. 10 with reference to Bellis (2003) See also TPA Review of October 2008, Brussels or Whitehall: Locating the source of the UK's regulatory burden.

[103] Ambler, Chittenden & Obodovski (2004).

[104] Stephen (2004), p. 10.

[105] Cabinet Office Transposition Guide 2003, p. 12.

[106] Davidson (2006), p. 12.

[107] Weatherill (2005), pp. 538–541.

[108] Idem, p. 539. This practice is also called '*voluntary harmonisation*'.

[109] For example, Commission Working Document – Second progress report on the strategy for simplifying the regulatory environment, COM(2008) 33 final, 30 January 2008, p. 10; and European Parliament resolution of 4 September 2007 on Better Regulation in the European Union (2007/2095(INI) ). The Union policy on gold-plating is further discussed in Chapter 3.

what they mean by gold-plating. Recently, we can also encounter the concept of 'gold-plating' in other Member States. For example, in 2009 Burmeister & Staebe published an article on the limits of gold-plating during the transposition of Union directives in Germany.[110] In this article they distinguish between *real* gold-plating and *false* gold-plating. The former refers to cases where national law establishes stricter requirements than those required by a Union directive, while the latter refers to cases where national law applies the regime established by a Union directive to a field falling outside that covered by the directive itself.[111]

### Further Developments: Spillovers and 'Related' Measures

In both the Netherlands and the United Kingdom, there seems to be a tendency to extend the discussion on gold-plating to the whole of the national law regulating matters not regulated by Union law. In 2011, the Cameron government started reviewing the whole of UK environmental law in the light of the so-called Red Tape Challenge.[112] In this context, all measures not required by Union law had to be justified in order to be maintained.[113] Although from a terminological perspective the Government still distinguishes between *red taping* and 'gold-plating', the approach applied is comparable. As regards the Netherlands, between 2010 and 2013 it seemed that the Dutch government even considered measures falling outside the scope of application of Union law, but which were related to a topic regulated by the Union legislator, as 'gold-plating'.[114] Despite the fact that today this does no longer seems to be the case,[115] it is clear that there is a tendency in the Netherlands and the United Kingdom to place a growing number of national measures not required by Union law at the same level. Whether in the UK this trend will continue is unclear at the moment, due to Brexit.

110 Burmeister & Staebe (2009). For Belgium (Wallonia), see Misonne (2011).

111 Burmeister & Staebe (2009), pp. 445–446.

112 Red tape means regulatory burden. See the dedicated website: www.redtapechallenge.cabinetoffice.gov.uk/home/index/ (accessed November 2011).

113 The *Red Tape Challenge* website distinguishes legislation not required by Union law with a Union Jack flag. Those required by Union law are indicated by an EU flag.

114 Brief Henk Bleker, Staatssecretaris EL&I aan de Tweede Kamer, *Aanpak Natura 2000*, (2011), no. 230499, 10. Squintani & Zijlmans (2013) 161.

115 This statement is based on the definition of burden neutral implementation discussed above and on the overview of existing cases of national toppings in the field of nature conservation available in Proceedings of the Second Chamber of the States General, Kamerstukken II 2013/14, *Aanhangsel van de handelingen* 442.

Within the context of this book, I will consider two kinds of national measures falling outside the scope of Union environmental measures, as falling within the concept of 'gold-plating'. First, so-called national *spill-overs*, which concern measures where the legal regime of a Union environmental measure is applied to cases falling outside the scope of the Union measure concerned.[116] For example, the IPPC Directive covered only certain big industrial installations.[117] National measures applying the regime required by the IPPC Directive to small and medium industrial installations are *spillovers* and will be considered as 'gold-plating' in this book.

Second, cases where national law regulates matters which, although falling outside the scope of application of Union environmental law, are *related* to a Union environmental measure, will also be considered as 'gold-plating'. For example, the Habitats Directive applies only to habitats with a Community interest.[118] National measures protecting nature reserves without Community interest can be considered to be measures related to the subject matter of the Habitats Directive, but not covered by such a directive.

## 1.3 More Stringent Protective Measures: A Definition

As written in the introduction to this book, Union environmental policy and law were introduced in the Treaty only with the Single European Act. Several Member States feared losing their sovereignty in a sensitive policy area. Article 130t EEC (today Article 193 TFEU) served to reassure the Member States that the level of environmental protection *remains* a national competence, at least partially, as the Union legislator can set a minimum level of protection, and subject to the limitation of having to respect the Treaties.[119] This is the background in which the concept of

[116] On this concept see, for example, Weatherill (2005). This practice is also called '*voluntary harmonisation*'.

[117] Council Directive 96/61/EC of 24 September 1996 concerning integrated pollution prevention and control, [1996] OJ L 257/26. Codified by Directive 2008/1/EC of the European Parliament and of the Council of 15 January 2008 concerning integrated pollution prevention and control (Codified version), [2008] OJ L 24/8.

[118] Article 1 in conjunction with, in particular, Article 2 of the Directive.

[119] Jacqué (1986), p. 124 states that the clause in Article 193 TFEU was one of those introduced on request of the Federal Republic of Germany, with *Länder* and *Bundesrat* actually opposing the European Single Act because they feared losing competences over environmental policy (Nicolaysen [1988], p. 115). Germany insisted also on the introduction of a clause stating that the level of protection must be set at a 'high level'. Another clause thus inserted was the principle of subsidiarity.

'more stringent protective measures' was introduced in the environmental field by the first sentence of nowadays Article 193 TFEU stating:

*The protective measures adopted pursuant to Article 192 shall not prevent any Member State from maintaining or introducing more stringent protective measures.*

A closer look at the first sentence of Article 193 TFEU reveals that this provision introduces the concept of 'more stringent protective measures' by means of an obligation 'not to prevent the adoption of more stringent protective measures'. This obligation is linked to the measures taken pursuant to Article 192 TFEU. Therefore, the addressee of this obligation is the Union legislator.[120] The Union legislator is not allowed to take measures restricting Member States from adopting more stringent protective measures. This conclusion cannot be challenged, as argued in the literature, by noting that Article 193 TFEU does not include a clause stating that measures taken pursuant Article 192 TFEU must establish minimum requirements, as Article 153(2) TFEU does.[121] The absence of such a clause does not change the nature of the first sentence of Article 193 TFEU. It is an obligation 'not to prevent Member States', and thus it can only be regarded as addressing the Union legislator.

Despite the elapse of thirty years, scholars have not yet agreed about the meaning of this provision. The following three positions have been taken:

a) Measures based on Article 192 TFEU must always pursue minimum harmonisation, and therefore more stringent protective measures of the Member States cannot be prohibited;
b) Measures based on Article 192 TFEU may pursue total harmonisation, but more stringent protective measures by the Member States are still allowed under Article 193 TFEU; and
c) More stringent protective measures are not allowed if a measure based on Article192 TFEU pursues total harmonisation.

The prevailing doctrine holds that Article 193 TFEU has a fundamental legal value, meaning that Member State competence to adopt more stringent protective measures cannot be restricted.[122] For some of these authors, Union secondary environmental law must always pursue

[120] Similarly, Wagner (2000), pp. 102 and 103, Lenz & Borchardt (eds.) (2003), p. 1765 and Trüe (2005), p. 145. Cf. Hofhuis (2006), p. 46.
[121] For example, Hofhuis (2006), pp. 45 and 46.
[122] Mainly, Winter (2000a), p. 380 Winter (2000b), p. 666.

minimum harmonisation.[123] If Union environmental measures pursue total harmonisation, then they are in violation of Article 193 TFEU and can be annulled.[124] The main argument is that secondary law cannot violate primary law.[125] This line of thought refers to the *Fornasar* case and the *Deponiezweckverband Eiterköpfe* case for confirmation.[126] Both cases relate to waste management. Italian and German law, respectively, went beyond what was required by the relevant Union directives. The Court of Justice determined whether this was allowed by stating that the Community rules do not seek to effect *complete* harmonisation in the area of the environment. Another argument used is that Union measures based on Article 192 TFEU aim to achieve the environmental objectives of Article 191(2) TFEU. A prohibition to maintain or introduce more stringent protective measures would be in contrast with the legal basis of the European environmental measure concerned.[127] Jans & Vedder criticise this argument in light of Case C-64/09, *Commission v France*,[128] in which the Court of Justice confirmed that measures based on Article 192 TFEU may also pursue non-environmental objectives, which may restrict Member States from adopting more stringent protective measures.[129]

A second group of academics agrees that Member States can always take more stringent protective measures, but argue that although Article 193 TFEU does not exclude total harmonisation, Member States are still allowed to take or maintain more stringent measures under Article 193 TFEU.[130] Their main argument is, again, that secondary law cannot restrict primary law. Moreover, according to Winter, Article 193 TFEU would have hardly any significance at all if applied only to minimum harmonisation. If a directive pursues minimum harmonisation, more stringent measures can already be taken in the directive itself, with no need to rely on Article 193 TFEU.[131]

[123] For example, Wagner (2000), pp. 102–103.
[124] Van Ooik (1999), p. 307.
[125] Idem, p. 307.
[126] Case C-318/98, *Criminal Proceedings against Giancarlo Fornasar, Andrea Strizzolo, Giancarlo Toso, Lucio Mucchino, Enzo Peressutti and Sante Chiarcosso*, [2000] ECR I-4785, para. 46; and Case C-06/03, *Deponiezweckverband Eiterköpfe v Land Rheinland-Pfalz* [2005] ECR I-2753, para. 27.
[127] This argument is reported by Jans & Vedder (2012), p. 119.
[128] Ibidem.
[129] Case C-64/09, *European Commission v French Republic*, [2010] ECR I-3283.
[130] Sevenster (1992), pp.297–303.
[131] Winter (1998) and Winter (2000b), p. 666 and B.W. Wegener, Answers to the Questionnaire redacted in the context of the Avosetta meeting of February 2009 in Monção, Portugal, available at www.avosetta.org

Finally, a minoritarian group of academics argue that Article 193 TFEU does not prevent the Union legislator from adopting total harmonisation measures, and that as consequence, Member States are not allowed to take more stringent measures that go beyond the level of harmonisation achieved. This view is firstly based on the argument that Article 193 TFEU is simply a codification of the legal practice at the time when the predecessor of Article 193 TFEU was inserted in the Treaty. It did not, thus, aim at restricting the powers of the Union legislator.[132] The idea of a simple codification process is, however, difficult to reconcile with what was stated at the beginning of this section, namely that Article 130t EEC was established to reassure those Member States who stood to lose sovereign rights in this policy area. Jans & Vedder also argue that total harmonisation is possible because Article 193 TFEU cannot be interpreted as granting the Member States the power unilaterally and without the ex ante supervision of the Commission to disregard standards set by the Union legislator.[133] According to Jans & Vedder, this seems strange, particularly in view of the procedure set out in paragraphs 4 to 6 of Article 114 TFEU.[134] Jans & Vedder also claim that total harmonisation is possible under Article 192 TFEU on the basis of paragraph 61 of the *Deponiezweckverband Eiterköpfe* case,[135] stating that it is Union law that governs the competence of the national legislators with regard to the introduction of more stringent protective measures.[136] To this extent, Jans & Vedder conclude:[137]

> [...] *how can the competence of the Member States to take more stringent environmental measures be 'governed' by European law, if the European legislature is not granted such competences* [to restrict Member States competence to introduce more stringent measures, LS]?

In the 2012 edition of *European Environmental Law*, Jans & Vedder reinforced their position by reference to the *ERG-II* case,[138] in which national law was unable to rely on Article 16 of the Environmental Liability Directive,[139] which is similarly worded to Article 193 TFEU,

[132] Krämer (1987), pp. 677–678; Jans (1989), p. 232, where he refers to *codification of the practice*; Jans (1991), p. 26; and Jans & Vedder (2008), p. 108.

[133] Jans & Vedder (2012), p. 119.

[134] Ibidem.

[135] Case C-06/03, *Deponiezweckverband Eiterköpfe v Land Rheinland-Pfalz* [2005] ECR I-2753.

[136] Jans & Vedder (2008), p. 110.

[137] Ibidem.

[138] Idem, p. 121.

[139] Directive 2004/35/CE of the European Parliament and of the Council of 21 April 2004 on environmental liability with regard to the prevention and remedying of environmental damage, [2004] OJ L 143/56.

because it was in contrast with the goal and the legal framework of the Directive.[140] Jans & Vedder conclude:[141]

*As appears from this judgment, a Member State cannot rely on a 'more stringent measure' clause in a directive if this is incompatible with the explicit content of the directive itself. There is no reason why this judgment cannot be applied by analogy to Article 193 TFEU.*

Hofhuis agrees that total harmonisation is possible under Article 192 TFEU, but follows a different route. In particular, this author relies on the Opinion of Advocate General Cosmas in the *Fornasar* Case,[142] in which the Advocate General stated:[143]

*35 Article 130t of the EC Treaty specifically implements, in the context of environmental protection, the principle of subsidiarity, which governs Community policy in this field.*

The principle of subsidiarity regulates the application of the competences established in the light of the principle of conferred powers,[144] and constitutes a limit to Union actions in the fields of shared competences.[145] It was inserted into the Treaty with the Single European Act,[146] and, until the Maastricht Treaty, it was enshrined in Article 130r(4) EEC, hence applied only within the context of environmental policy and law.[147] This principle leaves great discretion to the European Union.[148] As indicated by Konstadinides, the subsidiarity principle reflects the reluctance of the Union institutions and Member States to limit their freedom of action.[149] Consequently, this could explain why Hofhuis considers that Article 193 TFEU does not preclude total harmonisation.[150]

140 Joined cases C-379/08 and C-380/08, *Raffinerie Mediterranee (ERG) SpA, Polimeri Europa SpA and Syndial SpA v Ministero dello Sviluppo economico and Others (C-379/08) and ENI SpA v Ministero Ambiente e Tutela del Territorio e del Mare and Others (C-380/08)*, [2010] ECR I-2007 (*ERG II*), paras. 65–67.

141 Jans & Vedder (2012), p. 121.

142 Hofhuis (2006), p. 54.

143 Opinion of the Advocate General Cosmas in Case C-318/98, *Criminal Proceedings against Giancarlo Fornasar, Andrea Strizzolo, Giancarlo Toso, Lucio Mucchino, Enzo Peressutti and Sante Chiarcosso*, [2000] ECR I-4785, para. 35.

144 Van Ooik (1999), p. 44.

145 Cf. Lenaerts & Van Nuffel (2005), p. 104.

146 Single European Act [1987] OJ L 169/1.

147 Originally, it was formulated in more general terms, Lenaerts (1994), pp. 858–865.

148 Konstadinides (2009), p. 121, referring to D. Wyatt, Examination of the Witnesses (Questions 1–19), House of Lords Select Committee on European Union (7 December, 2004).

149 Konstadinides (2009), p. 121.

150 Hofhuis (2006), p. 54.

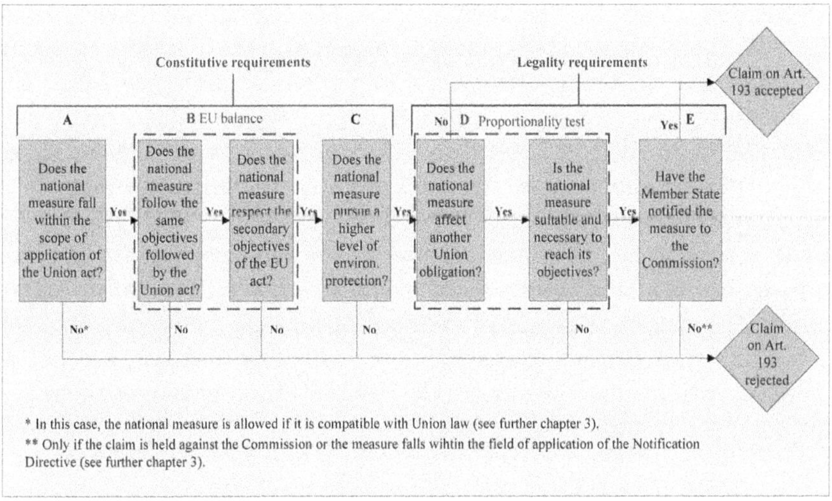


Figure 1.1 The steps to rely successfully on Article 193 TFEU

I postulate that a middle ground between these three views is possible. Such a middle ground becomes evident by looking at the constitutive requirements of more stringent protective measures. As further discussed in the following sections, these grounds can be reduced to the following three, interconnected, requirements:

a) Falling within the field of application of a measure based on Article 192 TFEU;
b) Staying within the boundaries of the EU balance between environmental and non-environmental objectives; and
c) Pursuing a higher goal or establishing a stricter means.

Together with the legality requirements discussed in Chapter 3, these requirements infer the steps that Member States need to comply with to rely successfully on Article 193 TFEU. Figure 1.1 provides a schematic overview of these steps.

Accordingly, I argue that Article 193 TFEU precludes the EU legislature from impeding the Member States to maintain or adopt more stringent protective measures, as also sustained by the majoritarian view presented above. In order to claim fulfilment of the first sentence of Article 4(3) TEU, the EU legislature must respect this duty – clearly spelled out in Article 193 TFEU – when adopting measures based on Article 192 TFEU. Yet not all national measures aiming at a higher level of environmental protection than that pursued by the EU legislation under Article 192 TFEU can be considered more stringent protective measures within the meaning of Article 193 TFEU. Only when national law fulfils the constitutive requirements evincible from the wording of Article 193 TFEU and the case law of the Court of Justice, can Member States rely on the concept of more stringent protective measure in a way which is compatible with the third sentence of Article 4(3) TEU. This means that, as argued by the minoritarian view, the content of measures based on Article 192 TFEU limits Member States' power to establish unilaterally the height of the level of protection of the environment. Such limitations, as further discussed in the following sections, are not in conflict with primary law as Article 193 TFEU itself envisages them.

### 1.3.1 *Falling within the Field of Application of a Measure Based on Article 192 TFEU*

As shown by the first sentence of Article 193 TFEU, the Treaty links the concept of 'more stringent protective measures' to protective measures adopted on the basis of Article 192 TFEU. This means that more stringent protective measures based on provisions other than Article 192 TFEU are not covered by Article 193 TFEU. As stated by Jans & Vedder, Article 193 TFEU cannot be used to adopt protective measures taken pursuant to Treaty provisions, such as Articles 114, 207 or 43 TFEU.[151]

Moreover, since Article 193 TFEU refers to the generic concept of a 'measure' based on Article 192 TFEU, I agree with Krämer that it does not matter whether the measure adopted under Article 192 TFEU is a regulation, directive or decision. It is also not relevant which decision-making procedure is followed (Art. 192(1) or 192(2) TFEU).[152] Kromarek suggests that environmental action programmes are also covered by this concept.[153] Moreover, the concept of 'measure' also covers international environmental agreements concluded by the European Union.[154] Under Article 191 TFEU, the Union has the objective of promoting measures at the international level to deal with regional or worldwide environmental problems, and in particular to combat climate change. The legal basis of the opening negotiations of the decisions, providing negotiating directives, authorising the signing and concluding of international agreements

151 Jans & Vedder (2012), p. 114.
152 Krämer (2011), p. 114.
153 Kromarek (1988), p. 84.
154 Similarly, Krämer (2011), p. 114.

is Article 192 TFEU.[155] Under Article 216(2) TFEU, once an international agreement has been concluded by the Union, its provisions are binding upon its Member States as a matter of Union law.[156] When Member States are a party to such international agreements as well, these are so-called [environmental] mixed agreements. As indicated in the *Demirel* case,[157] the provisions of mixed agreements are Union obligations for the Member States insofar as they fall within the scope of Union competences.[158] Under Union law, they are measures adopted under Article 192 TFEU.

Article 192 TFEU allows the Union legislator to enact legislation to achieve the objectives referred to in Article 191 TFEU. Among the objectives listed, there is an objective of *preserving*, *protecting* and *improving* the quality of the environment. The reference only to '*protective* measures' in Article 193 TFEU caused academics to wonder whether Article 193 TFEU also covers measures aimed at 'preserving and improving'.[159] According to Krämer, this is the case because a clear distinction between these objectives cannot be drawn.[160] I agree with Krämer on this point: it is indeed difficult to state whether, for example, measures aiming at preventing environmental damage under the so-called Environmental Liability Directive should be considered as measures for preserving or protecting the environment. The concept 'protective measures' under Article 193 TFEU seems sufficiently broad also to cover preserving and improving measures.

From the above, we can conclude that the *first* constitutive requirement of a more stringent protective measure is that it must fall within the field of application of a Union measure based on Article 192 TFEU. This, however, raises questions about what the field of application of a Union environmental measure is, something which is not easy to establish at times.[161]

155 For example, Council Decision 2002/628/EC authorising the conclusion of the Convention on Biological Diversity Council Decision of 25 June 2002 concerning the conclusion, on behalf of the European Community, of the Cartagena Protocol on Biosafety, [2002] OJ L 201/48.

156 Van Rossem (2012), p. 66. See also Case C-104/81, *Hauptzollamt Mainz v C.A. Kupferberg & Cie KG a.A.*, [1982] ECR 3641, para. 13.

157 Case C-12/86, *Meryem Demirel v Stadt Schwäbisch Gmünd*, [1987] ECR 3719.

158 Van Rossem (2012), p. 70 with reference to Case C-459/03, *Commission of the European Communities v Ireland*, [2006] ECR I-4635 (*Mox Plant*).

159 Krämer (2011), p. 114.

160 Ibidem.

161 Jans & Vedder (2012), p. 98.

The scope of a Union environmental measure must be assessed on the basis of an analysis of the personal, material, geographical and temporal scope of a specific measure. Sometimes, a Union environmental measure explicitly states that it does not cover a certain matter. If a national measure regulates these matters, then the Court of Justice does not consider it as being a more stringent protective measure. For example, this has been stated in the *ERG* case concerning the Environmental Liability Directive.[162] This Directive applies to certain cases of environmental damage. The Directive explicitly states that, inter alia, it does not apply to damages caused by actions that ended before 30 April 2007.[163] An Italian measure seemed also to apply to damages caused by actions that ended before 30 April 2007, with the issue being whether this was compatible with the Directive. During the dispute, it was claimed that the Italian measure was a more stringent measure under Article 16 of the Directive, which is worded similarly to Article 193 TFEU. The Court of Justice approached the case by clarifying that damage caused by actions that ended before 30 April 2007 was a matter governed by national law in compliance with the rules of the Treaty and without prejudice to other secondary legislation.[164] In this case, the Court of Justice assessed the claim based on the concept 'more stringent measure' only to the extent that the Italian measure applied to damages caused by actions that ended after 30 April 2007. Since Article 16 of the Directive is worded similarly to Article 193 TFEU, I see no reason why the rule established in this judgment should not apply to measures adopted under Article 193 TFEU.

The scope of application of a Union environmental measure is also influenced by the objectives of the measure concerned. Its objectives are usually stated in the regulation or directive itself. For example, the Habitats Directive aims at contributing to ensuring biodiversity through the conservation of natural habitats and of wild fauna and flora in the European territory of the Member States to which the Treaty applies (Article 2). Accordingly, national measures aiming at protecting the beautiful natural scenery of a certain habitat cannot be viewed as measures falling within the scope of the Habitats Directive. It should be noted

[162] Case C-378/08, *Raffinerie Mediterranee (ERG) SpA, Polimeri Europa SpA and Syndial SpA v Ministero dello Sviluppo economico and Others*, [2010] ECR I-1919 (*ERG*).

[163] See Article 17 of the Environmental Liability Directive.

[164] Case C-378/08, *Raffinerie Mediterranee (ERG) SpA, Polimeri Europa SpA and Syndial SpA v Ministero dello Sviluppo economico and Others*, [2010] ECR I-1919 (*ERG*), paras. 44 and 59.

that the analysis of the objective of a Union legislative act should take into account all the values that were taken into consideration while establishing the Union act,[165] including those that were implicit.

Despite some unclarity, a national measure extending the legal regime established for a part of the subject matter of a Union environmental measure to another part of that subject matter constitutes a more stringent protective measure. Indeed, it is relevant to note that Article 193 TFEU refers to the concept of 'measure' as a whole. This approach seems to be confirmed in the *Nationale Raad van Dierenkwekers en Liefhebbers* case.[166] In this case, the Court of Justice was called upon to decide whether a national prohibition on importing, holding or trading in mammals listed under Annexes B, C and D to the EU regulation implementing the Convention on International Trade in Endangered Species of Wild Fauna and flora (CITES)[167] could be justified. The Regulation only applies this regime to mammals listed under Annex A. The Court of Justice responded that:

> *As regards, specifically, the prohibition on the commercial use of specimens of species in Annex B to Regulation No 338/97, the Court has already held that that prohibition constitutes a more stringent measure for the purposes of Article 176 EC* [today Article 193 TFEU, LS] *(*Tridon, paragraph 49*). That is also true as regards specimens of species in Annexes C and D to that regulation, as the regulation does not contain any specific provision laying down a general prohibition on their commercial use.*[168]

The Court continued by stating that the same findings are all the more compelling as regards specimens of species which are not covered by Regulation (EC) No 338/97, as there has been no adoption of any harmonisation measure at the Union level prohibiting their commercial use. Accordingly, the Court of Justice correctly relied on Article 193 TFEU, despite the fact that the commercial use of the species in question in the main proceeding had not been prohibited at the Union level, because

165 Holwerda (2011), p. 45.

166 Case C-219/07, *Nationale Raad van Dierenkwekers en Liefhebbers VZW and Andibel VZW v Belgische Staat*, [2008] ECR I-4475. The reasoning in the *Nationale Raad van Dierenkwekers en Liefhebbers* case was confirmed in Case C-100/08, *Commission of the European Communities v Kingdom of Belgium*, [2009] ECR I-140 summary publication, para. 67 of the Dutch version of this judgment, which is available in full only in Dutch and French.

167 Council Regulation (EC) No 338/97 of 9 December 1996 on the protection of species of wild fauna and flora by regulating trade therein, [1997] OJ L 61/1.

168 Case C-219/07, *Nationale Raad van Dierenkwekers en Liefhebbers VZW and Andibel VZW v Belgische Staat*, [2008] ECR I-4475, para 19.

these species are covered by the CITES Regulation. Indeed, Article 1 of the Regulation refers to all species of wild flora and fauna.

A consequence stemming from this requirement is that a national measure must be of the same *type* as the EU measure at hand in order to fall under Article 193 TFEU. Indeed, if the EU legislator has regulated one specific kind of measure, the other measures must be considered as not having been regulated and hence as falling under national law. Reliance on Article 193 TFEU in such cases is not only unnecessary, but also impossible due to the lack of a benchmark. Of course, there are cases in which, despite regulating only one specific kind of measure, the EU legislator intended to regulate other kinds of measures as well, by simply precluding them. This consideration is particularly important in regard to the emissions trading system (ETS) Directive. By establishing a cap-and-trade system to achieve cost-effectiveness, it can be argued that the EU legislator intended to exclude all other types of measures to reduce greenhouse gas emissions from the installations covered by the ETS Directive. The manner in which the EU legislator has regulated the relationship with the, nowadays, Industrial Emissions Directive,[169] shows the relevance of this statement. Indeed, the ETS Directive excludes the applicability of permit requirements limiting CO2 emissions as regards installations covered by both Directives.[170] If the cap-and-trade instrument serves to achieve, next to a reduction of greenhouse gases, cost-effectiveness,[171] the introduction of instruments regulating greenhouse gases from ETS installations other than cap-and-trade, can hardly be considered to respect the balance established by the EU legislature, which is the second constitutive requirement as discussed in the next section.[172]

### 1.3.2 *Staying within the Boundaries of the EU Balance between Environmental and Non-Environmental Objectives*

Article 193 TFEU only covers 'more stringent' protective measures. Accordingly, one should determine when a national measure is 'more stringent' than the protective measures taken pursuant to Article 192

[169] Directive 2010/75/EU of the European Parliament and of the Council of 24 November 2010 on industrial emissions (integrated pollution prevention and control), [2010] OJ L334/17.

[170] Article 9(1) of the IE Directive. On this topic, Squintani, Holwerda & De Graaf (2012), pp. 67–88.

[171] Article 1 of the ETS Directive.

[172] Squintani, Holwerda & De Graaf (2012), pp. 67–88.

TFEU. In this context, there is nowadays little discussion in the literature that national law must follow the same objectives as the Union measure based on Article 192 TFEU in respect of which the national legislator wants to introduce stricter standards.[173] Given that, under the principle of conferral,[174] measures based on Article 192 TFEU must follow, as their main objective,[175] the goals indicated under Article 191 TFEU, i.e. environmental protection, this means that the national measure relying on Article 193 TFEU must pursue the same environmental objective as the Union measure at hand.[176] The German *Deponiezweckverband Eiterköpfe* case illustrates this point.[177]

This case concerns four national requirements that were alleged to be more stringent than required by the so-called Landfill Directive.[178] The first and the third requirements were linked to the goal of the Directive. As regards the first requirement, German law established a stricter reduction target for organic waste remaining in waste accepted in landfill than that required by Article 5(2) of the Directive. The Court of Justice stated that such a measure clearly pursues the same objectives as the Directive (paragraph 38). As regards the third requirement, German law regulated biodegradable and non-biodegradable organic waste, while Article 5(1) and (2) of the Directive covered only biodegradable waste. In addition, in this case the Court of Justice responded that the German measure in question pursued the same objectives as the Directive. After having established that the national measures pursued the same objectives as the Directive, the Court of Justice concluded that they *constituted* a more stringent protective measure – a reinforced (*verstärkte*) protective measure in the original German version of the judgment – for the purpose of Article 193 TFEU (then Article 176 EC). In this case, the Court of Justice seems to interpret the German version – and by doing so also the French (*renforcée*) and the Italian (*rinforzata*) versions – of Article 193

173 In the past, the requirement of 'following the same direction' and 'being of the same type' were contested by Sevenster, who in 1992 stated that goal and type are not requirements imposed by Article 193 TFEU (then Article 130t EEC), but by the proportionality principle, Sevenster (1992), p. 285.

174 Article 5(1 and 2) TEU.

175 For example, the seminal judgments in Case C-300/89, *Commission of the European Communities v Council of the European Communities*, [1991] ECR I-2867 and Joined Cases C-164/97 and C-165/97, *European Parliament v Council of the European Union*, [1999] ECR I-1139.

176 See also Krämer (2011), p. 115.

177 Case C-6/03, *Deponiezweckverband Eiterköpfe v Land Rheinland-Pfalz*, [2005] ECR I-2753.

178 Council Directive 1999/31/EC of 26 April 1999 on the landfill of waste, [1999] OJ L 182/1.

TFEU, in such a way that the requirement to pursue the same objective becomes a prerequisite of more stringent protective measures.[179]

Further, next to the environmental objectives, non-environmental objectives, such as economic development and social security, are relevant for the qualification of a national measure as a more stringent protective measure under Article 193 TFEU. Article 191(3) TFEU states:

In preparing its policy on the environment, the Union shall take account of:

- available scientific and technical data,
- environmental conditions in the various regions of the Union,
- the potential benefits and costs of action or lack of action,
- *the economic and social development of the Union as a whole and the balanced development of its regions.* [author's emphasis]

As the last bullet shows, Union policy on the environment shall take account of the economic and social development of the Union as a whole. The clause in Article 191(3) TFEU refines the principle of integration and inverse integration,[180] now codified by Article 7 TFEU, stating that the Union shall ensure consistency between its policies and activities, taking all of its objectives into account and in accordance with the principle of conferral of powers. In the structure of Title XX TFEU, this clause finds its way into Article 193 TFEU. Accordingly, to qualify as a 'more stringent protective measure', a measure must accord with *all* the Union objectives of the Union measure at hand, environmental and non-environmental, in a balanced manner.

This reasoning seems to be confirmed in the *ERG II* case.[181] The *ERG II* case considers the implementation of the Environmental Liability Directive in Italy. This directive aims at establishing a framework for environmental liability based on the 'polluter pays' principle, to prevent and remedy environmental damage (Article 1). Article 7 of the Directive allows competent authorities to decide in cooperation with the relevant operators which remedial measures should be implemented. Moreover,

179 According to Hofhuis, the French, German and Italian versions suggest a closer relationship between the Union measure and the national measure than the English, Spanish (*mayor*) and Dutch (*verdergaande*) versions, Hofhuis (2006), p. 53.

180 On the principle of integration, see Jans (2010).

181 Joined cases C-379/08 and 380/08, *Raffinerie Mediterranee (ERG) SpA, Polimeri Europa SpA and Syndial SpA v Ministero dello Sviluppo economico and Others (C-379/08) and ENI SpA v Ministero Ambiente e Tutela del Territorio e del Mare and Others (C-380/08)*, [2010] ECR I-2007 (*ERG II*).

the competent authority is required in any event to invite any person on whose land remedial measures are to be carried out to submit their observations and must take them into account. In the context of the remediation of the environmental damage occurred in the Rada di Augusta, in Sicily, Italian authorities imposed reparatory measures without hearing the operators who should have undertaken these measures and the owner of the field where the reparatory measures were to be taken. Before the Court of Justice, the Italian measure was described as a more stringent measure under Article 16 of the Directive, which as stated above, is worded similarly to Article 193 TFEU. The Court of Justice stated:

'[. . .] *a Member State cannot validly rely on Article 16(1) of Directive 2004/35, that is, the pursuit of the same objective of protecting the environment as laid down in the directive (see Case C-6/03 Deponiezweckverband Eiterköpfe [2005] ECR I-2753, paragraph 41), if it maintains or adopts provisions or authorises a practice enabling the competent authority to disregard,* [. . .], *the operators' right to be heard and the obligation to invite the persons on whose land remedial measures are to be carried out to submit their observations and,* [. . .] (paragraph 65).'

In *ERG II*, the Court of Justice considered the operator's right to be heard and the right of the persons whose land was affected by remedial measures to submit their observations, as laid down in Article 7 of the Environmental Liability Directive, as a minimum level of protection guaranteed by the Environmental Liability Directive, which according to the Court of Justice cannot reasonably be called into question.[182] The rights referred to by the Court of Justice in this case are social rights contributing to the social development of Europe as a whole.[183] The explicit reference to paragraph 41 of the *Deponiezweckverband Eiterköpfe* case, in which the requirement to pursue the same objectives as the Union measure is declared, confirms that social values can contribute to meeting the criteria to qualify as a more stringent protective measure.

In the light of Articles 7 and 191(3) TFEU, a similar reasoning can be applied to economic goals. To qualify as 'a more stringent protective measure' national law must not only follow the primary environmental objectives of a Union measure, but must also be in line with any secondary, non-environmental goals it contains. This ensures that the national legislator respects the balance struck by the Union legislator between

[182] Idem, para. 66.

[183] Article 41 of the Charter of Fundamental Rights of the European Union, [2016] OJ C 202/389.

environmental, economic and social values. Sincere cooperation between the Union and the Member States is also enhanced by such an approach. To sum up, I argue that to qualify as 'a more stringent protective measure' national law must pursue the same objectives as those pursued by the Union legislator, in a balanced manner.

It goes without saying that in order to qualify as 'a more stringent protective measure', national law must not only *pursue* the same objectives, but must also be *in accordance* with the Union measure concerned. A closer look at *Deponiezweckverband Eiterköpfe* and *ERG II* cases confirms this.

In the *Deponiezweckverband Eiterköpfe* case, as regards the use of different methods to assess the amount of organic matter remaining in waste accepted in landfills and about the fact the German law also covered certain kinds of non-municipal waste while the relevant provisions of the Directive covered only municipal waste, the Court of Justice stated that these measures were compatible ('in keeping') with the Directive. Concerning the assessment of organic matter, the Court of Justice stated that these measures constituted a more stringent protective measure only after having stated that the measures were in keeping with the Directive. In regard to the covering of non-municipal waste, the Court of Justice stated that the measure concerned, which pursued the same objectives as the Directive, but covered more kinds of waste than the Directive, was compatible with the Directive and constituted a more stringent protective measure.

In *ERG-II* the Court of Justice explicitly did not consider a national measure pursuing the general objective of a Union measure but disregarding its operational framework, a 'more stringent protective measure'.[184] The measure imposed by the Italian authorities was adopted without applying the criteria for determining the 'best' recovery measure, as laid down in Annex II of the Directive, in order to speed-up the remediation action. As mentioned above, the Court of Justice responded that:

[184] Joined cases C-379/08 and 380/08, *Raffinerie Mediterranee (ERG) SpA, Polimeri Europa SpA and Syndial SpA v Ministero dello Sviluppo economico and Others (C-379/08) and ENI SpA v Ministero Ambiente e Tutela del Territorio e del Mare and Others (C-380/08)*, [2010] ECR I-2007 (*ERG II*). See also Case C-281/11, *European Commission v Republic of Poland*, ECLI:EU:C:2013:855, para. 71 in which the Court of Justice stated that the national measure concerned was a more stringent protective measure and thus could not be considered as being in contrast with the Directive at hand.

*[...] a Member State cannot validly rely on Article 16(1) of Directive 2004/35, that is, the pursuit of the same objective of protecting the environment as laid down in the directive [...] if it maintains or adopts provisions or authorises a practice enabling the competent authority to disregard, [...], the obligation to carry out a detailed examination of the potential options for environmental recovery* [as established in Annex II, LS].[185]

In this case, the Court of Justice concluded that a national measure adopted by the competent authority without following the operational framework set out in Article 7 and Annex II of the Environmental Liability Directive could lead, *contrary to the objectives laid down in the directive*, to an inappropriate assessment of the significance of the damage and/or the remedial measures which should be taken.[186] This prevented Italy from validly relying on Article 16 of the Directive, which has a similar formulation to Article 193 TFEU. I see no reason why this reasoning should not apply to Article 193 TFEU.

### *1.3.3 Establishing a Higher Goal or Stricter Means*

There is no discussion in the literature about the requirement that, in order to fall under Article 193 TFEU, a national measure must come closer than the Union in achieving the goals under Article 191 TFEU.[187] This requirement covers the following two aspects. First, it covers measures establishing a higher (more ambitious) *goal*. For example, in the *Deponiezweckverband Eiterköpfe* case, one of the German measures fixed lower thresholds for organic waste remaining in waste accepted in landfill than the Directive did (paragraph 34, last sentence). Second, it covers measures providing more stringent *means* or *instruments* than those required by the Union measure. For example, in the *Windmills* case an Italian regional measure introduced a *general* prohibition on the building of windmill parks in and near areas covered by the Natura 2000 network.[188] This measure was claimed to be more stringent than that required by Article 6(3) of the Habitats Directive. This provision only

[185] Joined cases C-379/08 and 380/08, *Raffinerie Mediterranee (ERG) SpA, Polimeri Europa SpA and Syndial SpA v Ministero dello Sviluppo economico and Others (C-379/08) and ENI SpA v Ministero Ambiente e Tutela del Territorio e del Mare and Others (C-380/08)*, [2010] ECR I-2007 (*ERG II*), para 65.

[186] Such a measure would have been accepted only if the competent authority could have demonstrated the grounds justifying there being no need for a detailed examination in the light of those criteria, or that it was not possible to carry out such an examination due, for example, to the urgency of the environmental situation.

[187] Krämer (2011), p. 115.

[188] Case C-2/10, *Azienda Agro-Zootecnica Franchini sarl and Eolica di Altamura Srl v Regione Puglia*, [2011] ECR I-6561 (*Windmills*).

prohibits projects if, after an appropriate assessment, it is shown that the project adversely affects the integrity of the site concerned. Both measures pursue the same goal, namely that of ensuring the conservation of a Natura 2000 site, but the instruments were different.[189] The Court of Justice clearly stated that the Italian measure constituted a more stringent protective measure under Article 193 TFEU (paragraph 52).

It is understood that if the field of application of a Union environmental measure partially or wholly overlaps with the field of application of another Union environmental measure, the national measure in question must go further than the aggregated level of protection required by the two Union environmental measures concerned. For example, national provisions imposing upon operators of certain industrial activities an obligation to draw up a document setting out their major accident prevention policy and produce a safety report fall under the fields of application of both the Environmental Liability Directive and the so-called 'Seveso II Directive'.[190] The Environmental Liability Directive does not oblige the Member States to impose such measures.[191] However, for those operators covered by the Seveso II Directive, the duties to have a major accident prevention policy and to produce a safety report are *not* more stringent protective measures, since such measures are required under Articles 7 and 9 of the Seveso II Directive.

### *1.3.4 'More Stringent Protective Measures' or 'More Stringent Measures'?*

While the Treaty refers to the concept of 'more stringent protective measures', secondary law usually refers to the concept of 'more stringent measures'. Yet the latter category of measures can be considered as a specification of the former. It is not a separate category of measures. Therefore, I agree with Jans & Vedder that the concept of 'more stringent protective measures' in Article 193 TFEU covers measures going further

[189] In this section, I used the terms 'instrument' and 'means' to avoid using confusion with the term 'type' used in Section 1.3.1. In the *Windmills* case we have an example of a national measure using a different instrument than the one required by the EU measure (*specific* appropriate assessment versus *generic* appropriate assessment), without breaching the requirement of being of the same type. Both instruments are a form of appropriate assessment.

[190] Council Directive 96/82/EC of 9 December 1996 on the control of major-accident hazards involving dangerous substances, [1997] OJ L 10/13.

[191] Article 5 of the Directive allows competent authorities to require operators to take measures to prevent environmental damage from occurring.

than required and not only measures going further than allowed.[192] The reason for this conclusion is the following.

Distinct from Article 193 TFEU, minimum clauses in secondary Union environmental law are mostly addressed to the Member States. These clauses usually state that Member States are *allowed* to take more stringent measures.[193] This seems to indicate that Member States have an incontestable *right* to adopt more stringent measures. This begs the question as to how these clauses relate to Article 193 TFEU. In line with the general rule that secondary Union law must be interpreted in line with primary Union law, I argue that minimum clauses in secondary Union law must be regarded as a manner by which the Union legislator fulfils its obligation under Article 193 TFEU, showing compliance with Article 4(3) TEU. Therefore, minimum clauses in Union directives and regulations can be regarded as a restatement of Article 193 TFEU and are meant to reassure the Member States that the Union legislator has not restricted the Member States' right to introduce or maintain more stringent measures. Minimum clauses in secondary law use a different wording than that used in Article 193 TFEU only because minimum clauses are addressed to the Member States, while Article 193 TFEU is addressed to the Union legislator.

It should be noted that reassuring the Member States that their right has not been eliminated by the Union legislator is not the only role that minimum clauses play. Under the principle of sincere cooperation in Article 4(3) TEU, the Union and the Member States must, in full mutual respect, assist each other in carrying out tasks which flow from the Treaties. The second sentence of Article 193 TFEU states that more stringent protective measures must be compatible with the Treaties, which requires complex analysis. Minimum clauses in secondary law can be regarded as the way by which the Union legislator assists the Member States in their task, in this case a competence protected under

[192] Jans & Vedder (2012), pp. 114 and 115, with reference to Case C-6/03, *Deponiezweckverband Eiterköpfe v Land Rheinland-Pfalz*, [2005] ECR I-2753, para 44 and Case C-100/08, *Commission of the European Communities v Kingdom of Belgium*, [2009] ECR I-140 summary publication, in particular paras. 60, 66 and 67 of the Dutch version of this judgment. To the contrary, although more implicitly, Winter (1998) and Winter (2000b), p. 666 and B.W. Wegener, Answers to the Questionnaire redacted in the context of the Avosetta meeting of February 2009 in Monção, Portugal, available at www.avosetta.org.

[193] Minimum clauses in Union environmental law are analysed further, *infra*, Chapter 3, Section 3.3.

Title XX TFEU. They increase legal certainty. This topic will be further elaborated in Chapter 3.[194]

In the following, when I refer to more stringent protective measures, I am referring to both more stringent protective measures and more stringent measures.

## 1.4 Gold-Plating: A Misleading Overarching Concept

After having analysed the various elements of, on the one hand, the concept of 'more stringent protective measures' and, on the other hand, the concept of 'gold-plating', it is possible to compare the scope of application of these two concepts. As discussed in Section 1.4.1, at first glance, these two concepts could be considered as synonyms, or, at least, it could be argued that gold-plating is an overarching concept including the concept of 'more stringent protective measures'. This is misleading and, as further explained in Chapter 2, it can jeopardise the functioning of the system of environmental protection envisaged by the Treaties.

### *1.4.1 Gold-Plating as an Overarching Concept*

Section 1.2 has indicated which measure can be considered gold-plating. On the basis of the information provided in Section 1.3, it is possible to write a similar enumeration for more stringent protective measures. Table 1.1 represents schematically the various measures considered more stringent protective measures and those considered gold-plating.

As we can see from Table 1.1, not all cases of gold-plating are more stringent protective measures. Firstly, more stringent protective measures under Article 193 TFEU do not cover cases where a Member State does not take advantage of exceptions. The general idea accepted in the literature is that using opt-out clauses results in *less* stringent protection.[195] For example, Article 8(3) of the CITES Regulation[196] states:

> Exemption from the prohibitions referred to in paragraph 1 may be granted by issuance of a certificate to that effect by a management authority of the Member State in which the specimens are located, on a case-by-case basis where the specimens [fall under one of the categories thereafter indicated, LS].

[194] On the links between minimum clauses and the review of the lawfulness of more stringent protective measures see further, *infra*, Chapter 2, Section 2.1.

[195] For example, Veltkamp (1998), p. 188 and Jans & Vedder (2012), p. 114, footnote 64. See also Misonne (2011), p. 198.

[196] Council Regulation (EC) No 338/97 of 9 December 1996 on the protection of species of wild fauna and flora by regulating trade therein, [1997] OJ L 61/1.

Table 1.1 Schematic comparison of measures covered by the concepts of gold-plating and MSPMs

| Measures covered by the two concepts | Gold-plating | MSPMs |
|---|---|---|
| *Extending the scope of application of the legal regime introduced by Union law* | Yes | Depends |
| *Substituting wider national legal terms for those used in the Union law* | Yes | Depends |
| *Interpreting concepts left vague by the Union more stringently than strictly required* | Yes | Depends |
| *Adopting means to achieve a Union goal that are more stringent than strictly necessary* | Yes | No |
| *Not taking full advantage of derogations clauses* | Yes | No |
| *Adding in some way to the substantive requirement* | Yes | Depends |
| *Implementing a provision before the date given in the directive* | Yes | Depends |
| *Retaining or introducing national standards that are higher than those required by the directive* | Yes | Yes |
| *Enforcing a level of protection more strictly than required by a Union measure explicitly regulating the enforcement regime* | Yes | Yes |

Article 8(3) is formulated as an exception with respect to Article 8(1). The relevance of this finding for the distinction between gold-plating and more stringent protective measures is visible by looking at the *Tridon* case.[197] Mr. Tridon is a trader who between November 1995 and November 1997, sold to partners or customers captive born and bred specimens of species of macaw occurring in the overseas département of Guyane (France). France, which had made use of this exception, had prosecuted Mr. Tridon for breaching Article 6(1) of the old CITES Regulation, which is worded similarly to Article 8(1) of the new CITES Regulation. After noticing that Article 8(3) of the Regulation only establishes an exception and that France had not used it, the Court of Justice did not assess the national measure in light of the free movement of goods as required by the national court. This can only be explained by concluding that the

[197] Case C-510/99, *Criminal Proceedings against Xavier Tridon*, [2001] ECR I-7777.

Court of Justice considered French law nothing more than the implementation of the Regulation, and that national law did nothing more than what was required by Union law. French law in this case established gold-plating, but not a more stringent protective measure.

Another example would be Article 8(4) of the Environmental Liability Directive allowing Member States to exempt operators from bearing the costs of preventive and reparatory measures if they duly operate their installations in accordance with the requirements of a permit.[198] The decision not to implement this exception qualifies as gold-plating, because burdens not required by Union law are imposed. However, a national measure not taking advantage of the option to exempt operators from bearing the costs of remediation measures does not qualify as 'a more stringent protective measure', because national law is *less* stringent than the required minimum level. Accordingly, Article 17.16(4) of the Dutch Environmental Management Act (EMA),[199] which states that the State can refrain from recovering the costs of a remedial action from an operator if these costs cannot be reasonably imposed upon the operator,[200] is a case of gold-plating but it is not a more stringent protective measure. Dutch law adds a reasonability test and operators cannot recover from the State the costs they incurred themselves. This increases the burdens upon business, but it does not increase the level of protection of the environment required by the Union legislator. The same applies to the measures adopted by Austria, Belgium (at federal level), Bulgaria, Germany Hungary, Ireland, Poland, Romania and Slovenia, which by 2010 had not implemented the option under Article 8(4) of the Environmental Liability Directive.[201]

Similarly, Article 7 of the Birds Directive establishes that, under certain conditions, species listed in Annex II may be hunted under national legislation. If Member States do not use this option, they do not keep burdens to a minimum. In the Netherlands, the Birds Directive allows the hunting of thirty-one species.[202] Section 3.20 of the Nature

[198] Directive 2004/35/CE of the European Parliament and of the Council of 21 April 2004 on environmental liability with regard to the prevention and remedying of environmental damage, [2004] OJ L 143/56.

[199] *Wet milieubeheer*, Stb. 1979, 442, many times amended.

[200] According to the government, this option comes close to a non-transposition of Article 8(4), see Proceedings of the Second Chamber of the States General, Kamerstukken II 2006/2007, 30 920, nr. 7, p. 8.

[201] Based on the implementation report of the Commission, COM(2010) 581 final.

[202] Annex II/1 and Annex II/2 of the Directive.

Protection Act[203] allows hunting for five species only,[204] four of which are covered by the Birds Directive. This is because the Dutch parliament considers hunting as having lower importance than nature conservation.[205] A similar approach was followed in other countries, although in a more limited form.[206] In these cases national law is a case of gold-plating, but it is not an example of more stringent protective measure.

This finding is perfectly in line with the fact that these two concepts – i.e. more stringent protective measures and gold-plating – focus on different objectives. As indicated above, the concept of 'more stringent protective measures' focuses on environmental protection, while gold-plating focuses on economic values.

Secondly, the concept of 'more stringent protective measures' under Article 193 TFEU does not always cover cases where Member States adopt stricter means to achieve a Union goal than otherwise possible. If Union environmental law leaves discretion with respect to the methods and means of achieving a Union goal, any choice by a Member State that ensures compliance with the Union goal is seen as a correct implementation of the Union measure, regardless of whether the method chosen by the Member State is stricter than would have otherwise been possible. For example, the Air Framework Directive established *emission* limit values for certain pollutants into ambient air.[207] It thus established a clear goal that the Member States had to achieve. However, the Member

[203] *Wet van 16 december 2015, houdende regels ter bescherming van de natuur*, Stb. 2016, 34.

[204] It should be noted that Dutch law allows hunting in the context of the prevention of damage (Article 9 Directive). This is regulated under Sections 3.12–3.19 of the Nature Protection Act.

[205] See the discussion that took place during the parliamentary debate of the Flora and Fauna Act (*Flora- en Faunawet*, Stb. 1998, 402), which the Nature Protection Act replaces, Proceedings of the Second Chamber of the States General, Kamerstukken II 1995/96, 23 147, nr. 7, p. 20 with further reference to Proceedings of the Second Chamber of the States General, Kamerstukken II 1993/94, 22 980, nrs. 4 and 7.

[206] For the period 1981–1991 see the implementation report of the Commission, COM(93) 592 final, pp. 58–62. For example, Belgium reported that only eight of the thirty-one species listed in Annex II of the Directive can be hunted in Flanders or Wallonia. For other periods see COM(2000) 180 final, pp. 15–17; COM(2002) 146 final, pp. 15–17; Report to the Commission on the implementation of Directive 79/409/EEC on the Conservation of Wild Birds, Part II. Summary of the national reports by the Member States, Update for 2002–2004, pp. 24–27 (Commission Report 2002–2004); and Report to the Commission on the implementation of Directive 79/409/EEC on the Conservation of Wild Birds, Part II. Summary of the national reports by the Member States, Update for 2005–2007.

[207] Council Directive 96/62/EC of 27 September 1996 on ambient air quality assessment and management, [1996] OJ L 296/55.

States were left with an almost completely free choice as to how to achieve this goal.[208] For example, until 2009,[209] the Netherlands applied the limit values directly to any decision of a competent authority affecting air quality, unless otherwise provided.[210] Limit values had to be respected by any decision affecting air quality. In such a system, if the project contributed to worsening an already bad situation, the permit had to be refused. A study performed in 2006 at the request of the Commission shows that France often adopted measures to reduce industrial and power plant emissions, Germany and Italy predominantly adopted measures aiming to reduce emissions from road traffic and Spain mostly undertook studies.[211] Studies are surely less burdensome than measures restricting road traffic or industrial activities. Accordingly, assuming that the less stringent regimes pursued in other Member States were equally applicable in the Netherlands, the Dutch approach followed until 2009 could be considered a case of gold-plating. At the same time, the Dutch regime in force until 2009 cannot be considered a more stringent protective measure.

Similarly Article 3 of the so-called Old Waste Directive required Member States to take appropriate steps to encourage the prevention, recycling and processing of waste, the extraction of raw materials and energy therefrom, and any other process for the reuse of waste.[212] It also indicated which measures were available.[213] Member States could employ studies and factual measures, such as campaigns promoting recovery, to fulfil Article 3 of the Directive. Alternatively, Member States could adopt measures regulating the production of products and their

[208] These goals are established by means of limit values inserted in so-called daughter directives; see further, infra, Chapter 2, Section 2.2.3.

[209] See Section 5.16(1)(d) EMA which provides that public authorities exercising certain listed competences can exercise such competences only if the act to be taken is indicated in the National Cooperation Programme on Air Quality, entered into force in 2009, or when they do not contrast with it (Section 5.16(1) EMA. Schippers & Besselink (2009), pp. 75 ff., par. 4). Limit values are directly applied only in the context of a series of cases exhaustively listed in Section 5.16(2) EMA.

[210] Stb. 2001, 269, for example, Sections 5 and 6 on sulphur dioxide.

[211] Nagl, Moosmann & Schneider (2006), p. 49.

[212] Council Directive 75/442/EEC of 15 July 1975 on waste, [1975] OJ L 194/39.

[213] (1) Rules concerning the use of products which might be a source of technical difficulties as regards disposal or lead to excessive costs; (2) rules encouraging the reduction in the quantities of certain waste, the treatment of waste for recycling and reuse, the recovery of raw materials and/or the production of energy from certain waste; (3) rules on the use of certain natural resources, including energy sources, in applications where they be replaced by recovered materials.

packaging to prevent waste. Member States could also take measures encouraging recovery, such as a duty to dispose of paper separately from glass. Assuming that all the above-mentioned measures could fulfil the obligation under Article 3 of the Directive, it is clear that a Member State adopting the latter two kinds of measures imposed more burdens than Member States performing studies or promotional campaigns. The Netherlands belong to the former group. Article 3 of the Old Waste Directive was transposed by means of an extended legal framework, aiming to avoid waste rather than solving the problem of waste disposal.[214] Most importantly, Dutch law allowed the government to take measures restricting the production or commercialisation of environmentally unfriendly products,[215] and to take measures restricting how waste was collected and processed, including measures establishing return systems and separate collection systems. In the 1990s, the Netherlands introduced what is now called 'extended producer responsibility' in Section 10.5a of the Environmental Management Act.[216] In summary, the Netherlands adopted an extended legal framework targeting operators in the field of waste, waste producers and product producers, established targets and made plans to achieve them. Although Union law remained mostly vague as to the measures to be taken to prevent and recover waste, it is clear that the legal framework described above should be considered as measures which do not keep burdens to a minimum. Extended producer responsibility was not mentioned in Union law until 2008, when the so-called New Waste Framework Directive recast this field of EU environmental law.[217]

The same applies to cases where national law interprets a concept, left vague in a Union environmental measure, relatively stringently. In the absence of a clarification by the Court of Justice on the meaning of the Union law, any national interpretation must be regarded as implementing Union law. However, if a Union environmental measure requires a specific instrument to be used by the Member States, but it explicitly or

[214] Proceedings of the Second Chamber of the States General, Kamerstukken II 1974/75, 13 364, nrs. 1–3, pp. 68 and 74.

[215] Indeed, the government only took a few measures on the collection of certain materials, such as glass and paper, and products, such as refrigerators, as reported by Neuerburg & Verfaille (1991), p. 353.

[216] Here reference is made to the text of the EMA as amended by Stb. 1993, 283. The EMA was renumbered shortly thereafter, Stb. 1994, 80.

[217] Directive 2008/98/EC of the European Parliament and of the Council of 19 November 2008 on waste and repealing certain Directives, [2008] OJ L 312/3.

implicitly allows the adoption at a national level of stricter instruments, national law falls within the concept of 'more stringent protective measures'. Such reasoning cannot be applied, by definition, to vague concepts in Union law. For example, Articles 23 and 24 of the so-called Air Quality Directive require the drawing up of a plan to achieve the limit values established by the Union legislator.[218] Member States are free to choose the measures to be prescribed in such plans. This means that some Member States could prescribe stricter measures than other Member States. This would be a case of gold-plating, but not one of more stringent protective measures. Things are different in the context of measures aiming at protecting sensitive population groups. Articles 23 and 24 of the Air Quality Directive state explicitly that these kind of measures are additional. A national measure implementing such options presents a case for more stringent protective measures.

It should be noted that while it is possible to establish whether a national approach is stricter than required, it is extremely difficult to establish whether a national approach is indeed more stringent than strictly necessary. National law providing for instruments that are stricter than strictly necessary, are often the consequence of clauses in Union environmental directives such as 'appropriate measures' or 'necessary measures'. These clauses are usually linked to the achievement of a goal, but leave scope for discretion as to the means that Member States employ. Vague concepts in Union law also leave space for discretion as to their interpretation. External comparison – i.e. between Member States – and internal comparison – i.e. between legal acts in the same legal field/order – can provide guidance to establish whether a Member State went further than strictly necessary. At the same time, what constitutes an 'appropriate measure' in the Netherlands may be more stringent than what constitutes an appropriate measure in Finland. Moreover, what is appropriate today and the hand of the current environmental situation might differ from what will be appropriate tomorrow. In the example made above concerning air quality law, in the absence of more precise information about the concrete circumstances in which the national measures were adopted, it is not possible to state whether the approach followed by Spain, for example, suffices to meet Union law.

[218] Directive 2008/50/EC of the European Parliament and of the Council on ambient air quality and cleaner air for Europe, [2008] OJ L 152/1.

Thirdly, the concept of 'more stringent protective measures' under Article 193 TFEU does not cover all national measures extending the scope of application of a Union measure. It depends what is meant by extending the scope of a Union measure. If it means applying the legal regime established by the Union measure to subjects or matters not covered by the Union environmental measure, then it is only possible to speak of gold-plating, because we do not have a Union measure to which the national measure can be compared. Consider, for example, the so-called IPPC Directive.[219] Its scope is to prevent and control pollution generated from a listed number of industrial activities (Article 1). If a Member State decided to apply the IPPC regime to an industrial activity not listed in Annex I to the IPPC Directive, this measure would not qualify as 'a more stringent protective measure', but only as 'gold-plating'.[220] When the EMA was passed in 1993, one of the main concerns of the Dutch legislator was to create a uniform system. The same assessment framework applied to small, medium and large establishments alike.[221] Dutch law focused on establishments and not on installations.[222] When more industrial installations belong to the same establishment, they are regulated by the same permit.[223] In 2005 the Dutch legislator saw no reason to change the existing system and recognised that in certain cases the so-called Integrated Pollution Prevention and Control regime of the IPPC Directive, which covers only certain industrial installations, would have been applied upon non-IPPC installations.[224] Accordingly, this case can be considered one of gold-plating, but not one of more stringent protective measure.

[219] Directive 2008/1/EC of the European Parliament and of the Council of 15 January 2008 concerning integrated pollution prevention and control (Codified version), [2008] OJ L 24/8.

[220] At the time of writing, the Court of Justice has not expressed its opinion on this matter.

[221] Teekens (2005), pp. 13 and 14.

[222] On the meaning of the concept of '*inrichting*' see Van der Veen (2005), p. 143 and Ba'stmeijer & De Vries (2005), p. 139. On the relationship between the concept 'installation' and the concept 'establishment' see Van 't Lam, Jurgens & Michiels (2002), in particular chapters 2 and 3.

[223] Section 1.1(1) EMA and Section 1.1(4) EMA read in conjunction with Section 8.1 EMA (today Section 2.1 GAEP).

[224] Proceedings of the Second Chamber of the States General, Kamerstukken II 2003/04, 29 711, nr. 3, p. 13 and Proceedings of the Second Chamber of the States General, Kamerstukken II 2003/04, 29 711, nr. 6, p. 4.

Similar reasoning can be applied to national measures substituting broader national terms than those used in a directive,[225] and to measures 'adding in some way' to its substantive requirements. These national measures will also not qualify as 'more stringent protective measures' if the broader national term covers cases falling outside the field regulated by the Union environmental measure concerned.

Instead, if by extending the scope, the extension of the regime applied by a Union environmental measure to a subject or matter not covered by that legal regime, but still falling within the field of application of the Union environmental measure at hand, this qualifies as 'a more stringent protective measure' and 'gold-plating'. For example, the CITES Regulation.[226] This regulation aims at protecting any species of wild fauna and flora (Article 1). However, the Regulation offers a more specific kind of protection for certain species.[227] Some species are not specifically regulated at all.[228] If a Member State decides to extend the legal regime that the Regulation establishes for Annex A to species not explicitly regulated by the Regulation, this extension will qualify as 'a more stringent protective measure'.[229] This is because the wording used to describe the scope of the Regulation is sufficiently broadly formulated to allow such an extensive interpretation.

All other measures are covered by the concept of 'more stringent protective measures' and 'gold-plating'. However, it should be remembered that national measures qualify as 'more stringent protective measures' only if they follow the same objective as the Union measure and are of the same type. Hence, if the national law maintains or introduces national standards which are higher than those required by Union law for a *different purpose* or by means of a *different legal instrument* from a directive, this qualifies as 'gold-plating' but not of 'more stringent protective measures'. As regards the requirement of following the same objective, we can build upon the previous example of the CITES

[225] For example, the proposed substitution of the Dutch term '*inrichting*' for the term '*installatie*'. Proceedings of the Second Chamber of the States General, Kamerstukken II, 2003–2004, 29 711, nr. 2, p. 2 and 3.

[226] Council Regulation (EC) No 338/97 of 9 December 1996 on the protection of species of wild fauna and flora by regulating trade therein, [1997] OJ L 61/1.

[227] See Annexes A, B, C, and D, to Regulation 338/97.

[228] Case C-219/07, *Nationale Raad van Dierenkwekers en Liefhebbers VZW and Andibel VZW v Belgische Staat* [2008] ECR I-4475. In this case, Belgian law applied a completed prohibition of any commercial use for species not listed in Regulation 338/97.

[229] Idem, para. 19.

Regulation. If national law extends the legal regime adopted by the CITES Regulation for Annex A species to all other species, national law qualifies as 'a more stringent protective measure' only if the national measure is to increase the level of protection provided for these endangered species. If the same measure had been taken for the purpose of preventing exotic species from impacting on native species, I believe that it does not qualify. This is because the national measure concerned falls outside what would be regulated by the CITES Regulation, as the regulation does not aim to protect native species from invasive aliens. In this example, national law qualifies as gold-plating because the national measure extends the field of application of the legal regime of the CITES Regulation to a different aim from that regulated by the CITES Regulation, and by doing so it increased the burdens upon industry and citizens.

As regards the condition that national law must use the same type of measure as in Union law, we can use, for example, the Air Quality Directive. This Directive aims at, inter alia, defining and establishing objectives for ambient air quality designed to avoid, prevent or reduce harmful effects on human health and the environment as a whole (Article 1). This is done by means of measures limiting the amount of pollutants in the ambient air. Article 23 of the Directive allows the Member States to take into consideration sensitive groups of the population while establishing their plans to fulfil the obligations in the Directive. The Netherlands uses this possibility, but with a 'Dutch twist'. Section 5.16 EMA allows the Government to pass an order regulating the assessment of building projects increasing the number of sensitive people exposed to air pollution in areas where limit values are potentially or actually exceeded. This happened with the Governmental Order on Sensitive Locations.[230] This order states that, for example, schools, nurseries and healthcare centres (not including hospitals) must be built at a minimum distance of 300 m from national roads and 50 m from provincial roads if they are located in areas where limit values have been (or are at risk of being) exceeded.[231] Since, as discussed further in Chapter 3, the directives do not focus on the number of people exposed to air pollution, my opinion is that this is a case of gold-plating falling outside the scope of application of the Air Quality Directive. In cases such as the one just described, national law qualifies as 'gold-plating' only, since the burdens on industry are increased.

[230] *Besluit gevoelige bestemmingen*, Stb. 2009, 14.

[231] This order only applies to sites built after 16 January 2009.

The above shows that in all cases where national law qualifies as 'a more stringent protective measure' it also qualifies as 'gold-plating'. Basically, gold-plating covers three kinds of measures:

a) Measures not keeping burdens to the minimum, such as when Member States do not take advantage of exceptions;
b) More stringent protective measures; and
c) Spillovers and 'related measures'.

My view is that it is difficult to imagine any more stringent protective measure that does not qualify as 'gold-plating'.[232] This explains why institutions at Union and national level, industry and academics use the concept of 'gold-plating' as an overarching concept. The concept contains national measures that qualify as 'gold-plating which is more stringent protective measures', on the one hand, and 'gold-plating which is not more stringent protective measures', on the other. This practice, however, does not take sufficient account of the rationale underlying the two concepts here analysed, as further discussed in the next section.

### *1.4.2 Revealing the Misleading: Gold-Plating and the Functioning of the System of Environmental Protection Envisaged by the Treaties*

A closer look at the constitutive elements of, on the one hand, the concept of 'more stringent protective measures' and, on the other hand, the concept of 'gold-plating', shows that both concepts are based on three main conditions: 1) the presence of a Union measure, 2) the correct transposition thereof, and 3) the stringency of the legal regime. However, the conditions defining the concept of 'more stringent protective measures' are formulated more restrictively. More precisely, the concept of 'more stringent protective measures' applies only to national measures falling within the scope of application of the Union measure. The concept of 'gold-plating' seems also to apply to national measures outside the scope of a Union measure – i.e. national spillovers and measures regulating matters related to the Union measure concerned. In addition, the concept of 'more stringent protective measures' requires national law to follow all the objectives of the Union measure in a balanced manner. Finally, and most importantly, the concept of 'more stringent protective measures' regards the stringency of the legal regime from the perspective of the level of environmental protection. On the other hand, the concept of gold-plating is related to the level of burdens inflicted on

[232] This would imply a stricter national environmental measure which lowered the burdens on industry. Theoretically possible, but hard to find in real life!

Table 1.2 Schematic overview of the conditions for establishing MSPMs and gold-plating

| Conditions | MSPM | Gold-plating |
|---|---|---|
| *Presence of a Union norm* | falls within the scope of application | falls within the scope; *or* extend the scope, *or* somehow linked to it |
| *Correct implementation thereof* | follows all objectives of the Union measure, in balanced manner | respects the minimum level of protection |
| *Stringency of the legal regime* | higher goals; *or* stricter means to achieve the Union's goals | more requirements, therefore higher burdens for business |

industry and citizens. Table 1.2 provides a schematic representation of this comparison.

In the light of this comparison, we can confirm what was already evident at the hand of the comparison made in Section 1.4.1, namely that more stringent protective measures and gold-plating are *not* synonymous. More importantly, the focus on burdens in the definition of gold-plating has the potential to deprive the concept of 'more stringent protective measure' of one of its constituent requirements: 'a higher level of environmental protection'. A higher level of environmental protection is a burden for business, at least in general terms.[233] Gold-plating policies and the gold-plating concept is business centric. Moreover, it mostly focuses on the costs of environmental protection for business, under estimating the potential benefits that environmental regulation can have for business. Chapter 4 will show how costs/benefits analyses used in the United Kingdom to establish whether gold-plating is justified do not take environmental benefits into sufficient account.

The use of gold-plating as an overarching concept, or even worse as synonym of more stringent protective measures, can erode the foundation of the system of environmental protection envisaged by the Treaties, namely, that environmental protection remains primarily a Member State's responsibility. As stated in the introduction to this book, shared competences in the field of environmental protection means that Member States have to protect the environment and certain measures have to be taken by the Union.[234] As regards the level of environmental

[233] This aspect is further discussed in Chapter 4.
[234] Krämer (2011), p. 440.

protection, the Court of Justice has established that since Member States may adopt stricter measures, Union environmental measures do not need to be based on the highest level of environmental protection that is technically possible.[235] As stated in the literature, this shows that the European system of environmental protection is based on the idea that Member States will adopt stricter measures.[236] The concept of gold-plating, and the business-centric approach pursued therewith, has the power to block the adoption of more stringent protective measures.

Empirical evidence from the Netherlands confirms this. Since the introduction of the Dutch policy on gold-plating in 2003,[237] Dutch law has been systematically reformed so as to remove gold-plating, especially in the fields of nature conservation and ambient air quality. For example, in the field of waste management, provisions promoting extended producer responsibility are mostly limited to fields already covered by Union measures. While the return system for tyres can be considered a more stringent protective measure,[238] the measures taken in the field of batteries,[239] electric and electronic equipment,[240] scrap vehicles,[241] packaging, paper and cardboards[242]serve to implement Union directives.[243] The Dutch government decided that, for the moment, it will not apply the provisions on extended producer responsibility to other sectors, to avoid increasing the burdens on industry.[244]

Similarly, Dutch nature conservation law was reformed in 2009 first,[245] and in 2010 later.[246] Most notably,[247] first, the legislator added

235 Case C-284/95, *Safety Hi-Tech Srl v S. & T. Srl.*, [1998] ECR I-4301, para. 49.

236 Jans, Squintani et al. (2009) p. 418.

237 Further discussed in Chapter 4.

238 Stb. 2003, 564.

239 Stb. 1995, 45.

240 Stb. 2004, 340 and Stcrt. 2004, 142.

241 Stb. 2002, 259.

242 Stb. 2005, 183.

243 Proceedings of the Second Chamber of the States General, Kamerstukken II 2007/08, 31 501, nr. 3, p.7.

244 Proceedings of the Second Chamber of the States General, Kamerstukken II 2005/06, 27 664, nr. 41, *Voortgangsrapportage Landelijk afvalbeheerplan* (LAP), pp. 46–48 as regards, for example, measures on PVC fibres and optical-fibre cables; and Proceedings of the Second Chamber of the States General, Kamerstukken II 2007/08, 31 501, nr. 3, p. 8.

245 Stb. 2009, 18.

246 Stb. 2010, 135. It should be noted that this Act regulates certain projects and it has temporary effect. However, as regards nature conservation, it applies to all projects and it has definitive effect, see Proceedings of the Second Chamber of the States General, Kamerstukken II 2009/10, 32 127, nr.3, p. 4.

247 For a systematic analysis see Squintani & Zijlmans (2013).

the adjective 'significant' to Section 19d of the Nature Conservation Act 1998. As a consequence, activities not significantly affecting the achievement of the conservation values protected in a Natura 2000 area were assessed but no longer subjected to a permit requirement.[248] Moreover, the term 'other activities' was deleted from Sections 19f–19h and 19k. Now, only projects and plans are covered by these provisions. Further, the 2010 reform changed Article 19d of the Nature Conservation Act 1998 in such a way that it does not now apply to human activities affecting other values than those prescribed by the Birds Directive and the Habitats Directive. This means, inter alia, that the protection of Article 19g of the Nature Conservation Act 1998 enshrining the precautionary principle does not cover damage to values other than those regulated under the Birds Directive and the Habitats Directive.[249] The government explained that these reforms aimed to follow the Directive more closely.[250] In general, the government stated that the reform sought to eliminate cases where Dutch law goes further than required in order to meet the concerns of industry, agriculture and other sectors of Dutch civil society.[251]

As regards air quality, the cases of gold-plating mentioned in Section 1.4.1 concerning the Netherlands were eliminated in a series of reforms adopted between 2005 and 2009.[252] In addition, the 2005 reform eliminated the standstill principle from the field of air quality law.[253] This means that in areas in which air quality is better than required under Union law, air quality can be worsened. All these measures were taken to allow for socio-economic developments while respecting Union law obligations.[254]

[248] Proceedings of the Second Chamber of the States General, Kamerstukken II 2006/07, 31 038, nr. 3, p. 14.

[249] Backes, Poortinga & Woldendorp, (2010), p. 35.

[250] Proceedings of the Second Chamber of the States General, Kamerstukken II 2006/07, 31 038, nr. 3, pp. 13–15 for the 2009 reform. Proceedings of the Second Chamber of the States General, Kamerstukken II 2009/10, 32 127, nr. 3, p. 73 for the 2010 reform.

[251] Proceedings of the Second Chamber of the States General, Kamerstukken II 2006/07, 31 038, nr. 3, p. 1.

[252] First with the Air Quality Order of 2005, Stb. 2005, 316; then with a ministerial Decree from 2007, Stcrt. 2007, 214; finally with the Air Quality Act of the same year, *Wet luchtkwaliteit* Stb 2007, 414 and the National Cooperation Programme on Air Quality.

[253] Article 2(1) Air Quality Order 2005 established that the standstill rule of Article 5.2(3) EMA did not apply to the limit values set in the order.

[254] For example, Proceedings of the Second Chamber of the States General, Kamerstukken II 2005/06, 30 489, nr. 3, p. 3.

In certain cases, these policies were applied rather dogmatically. For example, a simple reference to the existence of the Dutch policy on gold-plating was sufficient to avoid extending the field of application of the strict liability regime of the Environmental Liability Directive to operators other than those listed under Annex III to the Directive.[255]

A similar approach to gold-plating is evident in the United Kingdom. For example, as regards the implementation of the Environmental Liability Directive, the Partial Regulatory impact assessment of the government highlighted that gold-plating in the three cases mentioned above would have led to additional costs of £2.8m and with an additional benefit of more than £4.8m.[256] The government answered that costs/benefits analysis is only one ground to assess the opportunity of gold-plating and that it has a presumption against gold-plating.[257] In the end the government maintained its original approach except in a couple of cases.[258] At the same time, the government underlined how the new regulations did not amend or replace existing legislation, because the government did not want to downgrade the existing status quo.[259]

The above-mentioned examples make clear that national policies based on gold-plating restrict the practical value of Article 193 TFEU. Consequently, they have a negative impact on a system in which the Union legislator can opt to 'lower the high level of protection' at Union level in view of the possibility that Member States have to pursue a 'higher high level of protection' at national level. Moreover, as discussed in Chapter 2, stricter national standards for the protection of the environment can spur the development of Union environmental law, leading to an amelioration of the quality of European environmental law.

In conclusion, the concept of gold-plating can be considered a threat for environmental protection. Accordingly, it should be avoided.

[255] Section 17.7(a), subparagraph 2, EMA. For the parliamentary discussion surrounding this provision see, Proceedings of the Second Chamber of the States General, Kamerstukken II 2006/07, 30 920, nrs. 12, 13 and 19 and Proceedings of the Second Chamber of the States General, Kamerstukken II 2006/07, 30 920, HAN8159A08.

[256] Defra, Consultations on options for implementing the Environmental Liability Directive, Defra/WAG/DOENI, November 2006, p. 8.

[257] House of Lords, The Environmental, Food and Rural Affaires Committee, Implementation of the Environmental Liability Directive: Government Response to the Committee's Sixth Report of Session 2006–07, Fourth Special Report of Session 2006–07, p. 3.

[258] See Chapter 4, Section 4.4.

[259] Explanatory Note to the Environmental Damage (Prevention and Remediation) Regulations 2009, p. 3.

Therefore, the use made by Union institutions of this concept and the negative connotation that these institutions give to gold-plating is regrettable. A more neutral concept needs to be developed and applied. This is discussed in the next section.

## 1.5 Conclusions: From Gold-Plating to 'Green-Plating *and* Gold-Plating'

As concluded in the previous section, gold-plating is a business-centric concept. It is perfectly understandable that business uses it to lobby policymakers at Union and national levels. At the same time, the very nature of gold-plating makes it unsuitable to be used in more neutral environments, such as the academic one. Public institutions should also refrain from using such a concept, unless they are only competent for pursuing economic interests. Mostly, this is not the case; political institutions are responsible for the attainment of a variety of objectives, which must be pursued in an integrated manner. At Union level, this is clearly the case as regards the Commission, the Council and the European Parliament. They are responsible for the attainment of the objectives listed in Article 3 TEU and refined in the rest of the Treaties. Article 7 TFEU states that the Union shall ensure consistency between its policies and activities, taking *all* of its objectives into account in accordance with the principle of conferral of powers. Gold-plating takes business interest into account. It does not take environmental interests into consideration. More stringent protective measures do take into consideration environmental, economic and societal interests. Article 191(3) TFEU clearly mentions these interests which infers the meaning of the concept of 'more stringent protective measures' as discussed in Section 1.3. However, civil society and policymakers seem to consider this term incapable of representing the whole spectrum of the ongoing legislative practice at national level. Several measures affecting business at national level fall outside the scope of application of Article 193 TFEU, as shown above. If we consider the ongoing discussion on the actual meaning of Article 193 TFEU, we should be asking ourselves whether the concept of 'more stringent protective measures' should be maintained, especially in academic and institutional environments.

Accordingly, it would be beneficial if a new concept was developed. One broad enough to cover legal realities falling outside Article 193 TFEU, but capable of taking into account all public values pursued by the European Union on an equal footing. I propose here to anchor this new concept to the principle of sustainability. This principle is recognised by the European Union, as evident in Article 3(5) TEU, as being one its objectives. Economic values, environmental values and social values are equally important under the principle of sustainability. As further explained below, *green-plating* seems the term more logically linked to the concept of sustainability.

The concept of 'green-plating' could be seen as the middle way between the concepts of gold-plating and more stringent protective measures. First, green-plating is not a legal term. Accordingly, it is not limited by the legal framework developed under the Treaties for the concept of 'more stringent protective measures'. It is suitable to cover legislative practices falling outside the scope of application of Article 193 TFEU, and it can easily be adapted to new developments. Second, *green-plating* makes a direct reference to the environment. It is not business-centric. Of course, it could be argued that the colour of sustainability is not just green. However, 'polychromatic-plating' or 'purple-plating' do not sound appealing. Moreover, green is the colour associated with sustainability in those contexts in which environmental values are oppressed by economic ones. This could explain why, circa 2007, the UK government made use of this concept, without defining it, to justify gold-plating. As indicated above, during the transposition of the Energy Performance of Buildings Directive, the UK government defended a case of gold-plating by stating that climate change is important enough to justify going further than European requirements.[260] The government called this case of gold-plating '*green-plating*'.

Accordingly, the reference to the colour green in green-plating is justifiable in the field dominated by a business-centric approach. To ensure that under the concept of 'green-plating', economic and social values are equally taken into account while assessing the sustainability of going beyond Union requirements, ad hoc cost/benefits assessments must be developed, as discussed in Chapter 4. Only in those cases in which the benefits of a national measure going beyond Union requirements are higher than its costs, the national measure at hand can be defined as being a case of green-plating. When the costs of a national measure going beyond Union requirements are higher than its benefits, the concept of 'gold-plating' can be retained.[261] This means that the

[260] Thomas & Lynch-Wood (2008), p. 199 with reference to Hansard HC Deb., vol. 460 col. 646 16 May 2007 (Yvette Cooper MP, Minister for Housing and Planning).

[261] This concept is therefore similar to what in MacLeod et al. (2009), p. 18 is called 'inappropriate over-implementation'.

concept of 'green-plating' does not replace that of 'gold-plating'. In my proposal, national measure going beyond Union requirements are divided in two categories: a) cases of green-plating, i.e. cases in which benefits prevail and b) cases of gold-plating, i.e. cases in which costs prevail. Both concepts cover the same three kinds of measures:

a) Measures not keeping burdens to the minimum, such as when Member States do not take advantage of exceptions;
b) More stringent protective measures; and
c) Spillovers and 'related measures'.

In the absence of a clear assessment of the costs and benefits or of a convincing assumption that costs are higher than the benefits, I will use the concept of green-plating in order to smooth reading.

# 2 Green-Plating and Environmental Protection

## 2.1 Introductory Remarks

I concluded the previous chapter by introducing the concept of 'green-plating' and juxtaposing it with that of 'gold-plating'. In my proposal, national measures going beyond Union requirements are divided in two categories: a) cases of green-plating, i.e. cases in which benefits prevail and b) cases of gold-plating, i.e. cases in which costs prevail. The distinction between these two concepts lies in the outcome of the costs/benefits analysis. This chapter focuses on one aspect of the benefits, namely the benefits of national measures going beyond Union requirements for the high level of protection of the environment, without, however, quantifying them in exact terms. Given this limited perspective concerning costs/benefits analyses, in this chapter only the term green-plating is used, unless I refer to the no-gold-plating policies.

The minimum high level of environmental protection established by measures based on Article 192 TFEU is the starting point of any case of green-plating. Without knowing what the required minimum level is, it is not possible to state that national law goes beyond such level. The concept of high level of environmental protection has already been analysed in detail by Misonne in 2011.[1] Hence, there is no need to discuss this concept once again. The focus of this chapter as regards this concept concerns the ongoing practice of green-plating and the effects that green-plating has on the development of EU environmental law.

As regards the former aspect, it has long been held in the literature that Member States do not go beyond the required level of protection

[1] Misonne (2011).

under EU measures based on Article 192 TFEU.[2] Empirical research performed in the United Kingdom and the Netherlands on request of the national government confirmed this picture for these two Member States.[3] In this chapter, I argue that the picture presented in the literature was, at least until the development of the no-gold-plating policies in several EU Member States, not as accurate as one might think. This is because scholars looked at green-plating in broad terms, thereby missing many cases in which national requirements go or went beyond EU environmental standards. Even the empirical studies on actual cases of green-plating in the United Kingdom and the Netherlands provide a misleading picture of the ongoing practice. This is due to the fact that these studies were based on a bottom-up approach, meaning that the researchers asked industry to highlight which national measures were not required by EU law. This approach assumed a level of understanding of environmental regulation that did not resemble reality. This means that industry's failure to highlight green-plating does not mean that green-plating does not exist. Industry complained about green-plating, but it did not know what it was. A top-down systematic approach to green-plating is the only way to appreciate the extents of this phenomenon. Building upon the empirical research performed in my Ph.D. thesis defended in November 2013,[4] Section 2.2 concludes that green-plating is more systematic and widespread than argued in literature so far. Moreover, Section 2.2 provides an overview of the reasons for green-plating, going beyond what has been stated so far in the literature.[5]

The picture painted in Section 2.2 changes with the development of the no-gold-plating policies in the United Kingdom, the Netherland and other Member States and the coming of the Better Regulation Agenda, which, as discussed in Chapter 1, blame gold-plating for the perceived excess of regulatory burdens evoked by industry. It is in the last decade that the negative picture depicted in literature became reality, at least to a greater extent than it was at the time these scholars made their claims. Section 2.3

[2] Pagh (2006), Jans & Squintani et al. (2009), Jans & Vedder (2012) pp. 113–122.

[3] In particular, the Davidson Review (2006) for the UK, and the ECORYS, OpdenKamp Adviesgroep en Europa Instituut, Koppen op EG-regelgeving. Eindrapportage definitief, Rotterdam 2006; see also Europa Instituut en Asser Instituut, National Koppen op EG-regelgeving. Tweede ronde van meldingen van het bedrijfsleven over 'koppen' in de Nederlandse wet- en regelgeving, juridisch bekeken, Leiden 2007 for the Netherlands.

[4] The case studies concerned waste law, nature conservation law, air quality law, industrial emissions and environmental damage, see Squintani (2013), Chapters 4–8.

[5] Cf. Jans & Squintani et al. (2009).

shows how national no-gold-plating policies can lead to a systematic elimination of national measures going beyond Union requirements. Still, such policies do not mean that green-plating does no longer occur.

Regarding the effects that green-plating has on the development of EU environmental law, Section 2.4 concludes that green-plating facilitates the development of EU environmental law. Building upon the analysis of how EU environmental law and national law, most notably Dutch law, developed over the entire period of their existence, I provide examples of how cases of green-plating became the minimum EU requirements following a recasting or amendment of EU environmental measures. This is logical if we think that EU law does not fall from the sky, but builds upon existing experiences, as confirmed by the literature on the upload of national (environmental) law at EU level discussed in this chapter. Over time, what is green-plating today, could become the minimum EU standard tomorrow. This finding allows me to conclude that environmental protection in the European Union should be seen as a chain of national and EU measures that develops over time. Accordingly, no-gold-plating policies should not be seen as innocent expressions of national liberty. They can deprive the EU legislature of one of its driving factors, something that is hardly reconcilable with the principle of sincere cooperation under Article 4(3) TEU.

## 2.2 Green-Plating as Real-Life Phenomenon

In 2006, Pagh strongly criticised what he called *'the stricter' mantra*.[6] The idea that a minimal level of environmental protection at Union level will be integrated with stricter national standards at the national level is misleading, most notably because it seems that Member States do not maintain or introduce national standards to provide a higher level of environmental protection.[7] In 2009, building upon a first set of empirical data provided within the Avosetta Group network,[8] my co-authors and I wrote that Member States only sparingly and incidentally use their power to lay down or maintain more stringent environmental standards after European harmonisation.[9] Echoing these

[6] Pagh (2006), pp. 5–15.

[7] For example, Krämer (2011), p. 440 and Jans, Squintani et al. (2009), p. 435.

[8] This network is composed by leading environmental law scholars from many EU member States. These data are still available at the Avosetta Group website, www.avosetta.org.

[9] Jans, Squintani et al. (2009), p. 434.

publications, other scholars followed the view that green-plating is a paper chimera and not a real-life phenomenon.[10] In 2011, Krämer wrote that national law relies heavily on the European Union for environmental measures, and that in many Member States national environmental law is more or less equivalent to EU-derived environmental law.[11]

Three empirical studies, one performed in the United Kingdom, the Davidson Review, and two in the Netherlands, the ECORYS Report and the Europa Instituut en Asser Instituut Report,[12] all came to the conclusion that industry allegations of widespread green-plating practices in these two countries are misplaced. These reports moved from potential cases of green-plating indicated by industry. Only in a few cases did industry correctly point out green-plating, but these cases were considered not enough to sustain the statement that green-plating was a widespread phenomenon in either country.

In light of the literature review and the three empirical studies just presented, it is fair to state that the general impression is that green-plating is a chimera – it does not exist in real life. Yet, as written by my co-authors and I in 2009, our statement was not based on a fully developed empirical research.[13] It was based on a first set of empirical data. Moreover, the empirical reports performed in the United Kingdom and the Netherlands moved from the assumption that industry was best placed to assess green-plating. This assumption proved to be wrong, as, in many cases, industry considered the minimum EU standard to be green-plating.

During my Ph.D. on which this book is based, five different environmental fields were researched systematically for green-plating, particularly in the Netherlands. The room for green-plating was established by analysing the EU measure and the national implementing measures in their totality. Court of Justice judgments and Commission implementation reports also provided information on the existence of green-plating from an EU-wide perspective. Cases of green-plating were divided in the three categories of measures falling under the concept: a) measures not keeping burdens to the minimum, b) more stringent protective measures and c) spillovers and related measures. In each of the five

[10] Eg. Langlet & Mahmoudi (2016), p. 105; Faure and De Smedt (2013), p. 310.
[11] Krämer (2011), p. 440.
[12] ECORYS, OpdenKamp Adviesgroep en Europa Instituut, Koppen op EG-regelgeving. Eindrapportage definitief, Rotterdam 2006; see also Europa Instituut en Asser Instituut, National Koppen op EG-regelgeving. Tweede ronde van meldingen van het bedrijfsleven over 'koppen' in de Nederlandse wet- en regelgeving, juridisch bekeken, Leiden 2007.
[13] Jans and Squintani et al. (2009), p. 419.

environmental fields researched, multiple examples of each kind of green-plating occurring in a variety of Member States were retrieved. This finding allowed me to conclude that green-plating is more widespread and systematic than literature and empirical studies showed. Hence, green-plating is a real-life phenomenon, although the no-gold-plating policies developed in the second half of 2010s jeopardise its existence. The many pages consisting of the empirical studies composing my Ph.D., which is available at the repository of the University of Groningen,[14] are not reproduced in this book. Here, I limit myself to providing some examples of green-plating. These examples are divided into cases of green-plating establishing a higher goal than that required by the EU legislator (Section 2.2.1) and cases of green-plating establishing stricter means/instruments to achieve the EU goals than those required by the EU legislator (Section 2.2.2). Not all cases of green-plating presented in this section still exist today; some have been eliminated in light of the national no-gold-plating policies, as further discussed in Section 2.3.

Besides showing that green-plating is a real-life phenomenon, this section provides an overview of the reasons for maintaining or introducing national measures going beyond the EU minimum requirements (Section 2.2.3).

### *2.2.1 Establishing Higher Goals Than Required by the EU Legislator*

The most intuitive cases of green-plating concern cases in which national law pursues a higher environmental goal than the EU does. In Chapter 1, I have already mentioned at the *Deponiezweckverband Eiterköpfe* case,[15] in which a German measure fixed lower thresholds for organic waste remaining in waste accepted in landfill than the Landfill Directive did.[16] In other words, more organic waste must be recovered than required by the EU legislator. This is an example of a national measure establishing a higher target than required by the EU legislator.

The goal-oriented approach followed in the field of waste law, as in other fields, provides for a clear benchmark on which to assess the presence of this kind of green-plating. Following the 6th Environmental Action Programme[17] and the Thematic Strategy on the Prevention and

[14] Persistent link: http://hdl.handle.net/11370/59d395e2-eb3f-464e-83d8-f8c6735965ba
[15] Case C-6/03, *Deponiezweckverband Eiterköpfe v Land Rheinland-Pfalz*, [2005] ECR I-2753.
[16] Council Directive 1999/31/EC of 26 April 1999 on the landfill of waste, [1999] OJ L 182/1.
[17] Decision No 1600/2002/EC of the European Parliament and of the Council of 22 July 2002 laying down the Sixth Community Environment Action Programme, [2002] OJ L 242/1.

Recycling of Waste,[18] in December 2005 the Commission presented its proposal for a New Waste Framework Directive,[19] repealing Directive 2006/12/EC,[20] which had codified the Waste Framework Directive.[21] Included among the reasons for the recasting process was the mention of bringing the Waste Framework Directive in line with the new approaches adopted by the Thematic Strategy (such as life cycle thinking). This required the introduction of a specific objective, namely that of reducing the environmental impact from waste generation and management, taking into account the whole life cycle (Article 1),[22] the introduction of minimum standards and the use of the end-of-life criterion (mainly Article 4).[23] One of the provisions operationalising this approach is Article 11(2) stating:

In order to comply with the objectives of this Directive, and move towards a European recycling society with a high level of resource efficiency, Member States shall take the necessary measures designed to achieve the following targets:

(a) by 2020, the preparing for re-use and the recycling of waste materials such as at least paper, metal, plastic and glass from households and possibly from other origins as far as these waste streams are similar to waste from households, shall be increased *to a minimum* of overall 50% by weight;

(b) by 2020, the preparing for re-use, recycling and other material recovery, including backfilling operations using waste to substitute other materials, of non-hazardous construction and demolition waste excluding naturally occurring material defined in category 17 05 04 in the list of waste shall be increased *to a minimum* of 70% by weight [emphasis added by the author].

The use of the term 'to a minimum' in these provisions makes clear that, if a Member State aimed at more ambitious targets than those indicated in this article, it would go beyond the EU requirements. This is exactly

[18] COM(2005), 666 final.

[19] Directive 2008/98/EC of the European Parliament and of the Council of 19 November 2008 on waste and repealing certain Directives, [2008] OJ L 312/3.

[20] Directive 2006/12/EC of the European Parliament and of the Council of 5 April 2006 on waste, [2006] OJ L 114/9. This Directive replaced Directive 75/442 in 2006. However, this replacement only covered linguistic aspects. No change occurred with regard to the content.

[21] COM(2005), 667 final.

[22] Idem, p. 2.

[23] Ibidem.

what occurs in the Netherlands. As recognised by the government, the National Waste Management Plan 2009–2021 sets stricter binding standards than the Directive requires.[24] By 2015, the preparation for reuse and recycling of waste materials, including at least household paper, metal, plastic and glass, or comparable waste, should be increased to an overall 60% by weight and, by 2021, the preparation for reuse and recovery of other materials shall be increased to 95% by weight. As we can see, by setting binding targets which are more stringent than those required by the New Waste Framework Directive, the Netherlands has adopted more stringent measures. Similar findings apply to other Member States. In 2013, a broad comparative study performed for the Committee of the Regions reports that recycling targets for household waste for the regions of Scotland (UK) and Grand Besançon (F) as well as for the Greater Manchester District (UK), regional recycling targets of Flanders and Wales and a national target for Spain are more ambitious than the target of the Directive, either because they are higher or because they must be reached earlier.[25]

Higher goals can also be found in the field of air quality law. In the 1980s, Union law established immission limit values and emissions limit values.[26] However, immissions-oriented measures focused on individual pollutants and there was no harmonised assessment and management framework. In the 1990s the Air Framework Directive established such a

24 VROM, *Landelijk Afvalbeheerplan* 2009–2021 (LAP2), pp. 91 and 92.

25 Ecologic Institute (Albrecht Gradmann), Umweltbundesamt Österreich (Thomas Weissenbach (main author) and Hubert Reisinger) and RIMAS (Francesca Montevecchi), Ambitious waste targets and local and regional waste management, European Union, June 2013, p. 44 and 45. This report, performed on request of the Committee of the Region, states that for the target year 2020, the comparable target value for recycling of household waste of Wales is 64%. Flanders sets its even more ambitious recycling target of 70% even sooner for the year 2015.

26 Under EU air quality law, an emission limit value looks at what *exists* a man-driven activity. An immission limit value looks at what *enters* this environmental medium. Immissions-oriented measures were included in Council Directive 80/779/EEC of 15 July 1980 on air quality limit values and guide values for sulphur dioxide and suspended particulates, [1980] OJ L 229/30; Council Directive 82/884/EEC of 3 December 1982 on a limit value for lead in the air, [1982] OJ L 378/15; and Council Directive 85/203/EEC of 7 March 1985 on air quality standards for nitrogen dioxide, [1985] OJ L 87/1. Examples of emissions-oriented measures were Council Directive 84/360/EEC of 28 June 1984 on the combating of air pollution from industrial plants, [1984] OJ L 188/20; Council Directive 88/609/EEC of 24 November 1988 on the limitation of emissions of certain pollutants into the air from large combustion plants, [1988] OJ L 336/1 and Council Directive 89/369/EEC of 8 June 1989 on the prevention of air pollution from new municipal waste incineration plants, [1989] OJ L 163/32.

framework.[27] This Directive did not replace the existing immissions-oriented directives. It established the basis on which assessment methods and immissions limit values had to be established. The immissions limit values were then established in four daughter directives which replaced the 1980s directives.[28] During the implementation of these Directives, the Dutch legislator stated that transposing the First Daughter Directive's deadlines would have meant downgrading the existing levels of ambient air quality, which were higher than that required under the 1980s directives,[29] something that the Ministry refused to do. The Air Quality Directive does not change the limit values for the various pollutants, but it adds target and limit values for $PM_{2,5}$ (Article 15 and 16). In the context of the review of the implementation of the Air Quality Directive, the European Environment Agency commissioned an evaluation of current limit and target values as set in the Air Quality Directive. The evaluation indicates that several Member States have established stricter limit values than required.[30] As regards sulphur dioxide, Austria, the United Kingdom, Hungary, Poland and Sweden reported that they have more stringent limit values and/or that they allow fewer exceedances. Similarly, as regards nitrogen dioxide, Austria, Hungary, Poland and Sweden reported that they have more stringent limit values and/or that they allow fewer cases of exceedances. The United Kingdom (Scotland), Finland, Estonia and Austria have stricter standards for particulate matters ($PM_{10}$ and/or $PM_{2,5}$). The United Kingdom and Hungary also have stricter standards for lead and benzene.[31] As regards benzene, Poland also has a stricter limit value than required. Poland and Hungary also have stricter standards for carbon monoxide.

[27] Council Directive 96/62/EC of 27 September 1996 on ambient air quality assessment and management, [1996] OJ L 296/55.

[28] Council Directive 1999/30/EC of 22 April 1999 relating to limit values for sulphur dioxide, nitrogen dioxide and oxides of nitrogen, particulate matter and lead in ambient air, [1999] OJ L 163/41; Directive 2000/69/EC of the European Parliament and of the Council of 16 November 2000 relating to limit values for benzene and carbon monoxide in ambient air, [2000] OJ L 313/12; Directive 2002/3/EC of the European Parliament and of the Council of 12 February 2002 relating to ozone in ambient air, [2002] OJ L 67/14 and Directive 2004/107/EC of the European Parliament and of the Council of 15 December 2004 relating to arsenic, cadmium, mercury, nickel and polycyclic aromatic hydrocarbons in ambient air, [2004] OJ L 23/3.

[29] Stb. 2001, 269, explanatory memorandum, pp. 18 and 20.

[30] De Leeuw & Ruyssenaars (2011), p. 30, and Annex A.

[31] As regards the United Kingdom, the limit values for lead entered into force in 2008. The limit values for benzene are more stringent in Scotland and Northern Ireland.

In addition, several Member States have limit or target values for other pollutants.

In the field of nature conservation, it is difficult to establish whether the Member States pursue higher targets than those proposed by the Birds Directive[32] and the Habitats Directive,[33] given that the targets are not specific. Yet it is not impossible. The Birds Directive aims at preserving the status of conservation of birds and at maintaining, protecting and re-establishing their natural habitats.[34] Therefore, in addition to provisions to protect birds from direct threats – such as from being killed and captured – the Birds Directive protects birds from indirect threats, such as the destruction of their breeding sites. Article 1 of the Birds Directive states that it relates to the conservation of all species of naturally occurring birds in the wild in the European territory of the Member States to which the TEU applies. It covers the protection, management and control of these species and lays down rules for their exploitation. Further, it specifies that it also applies to the eggs, nests and habitats of birds. It has thus a broad field of application. Still, the Directive does not apply to domestic species and to exotic species. Finally, it does not apply to species occurring in the former colonies of certain Member States and birds occurring, for example, in Russia[35] but not in the Member States. Member States protecting species not covered by the Directive can be considered to pursue a higher goal than that required by the EU legislator.[36]

The Netherlands established green-plating in this regard. The Birds Act 1936, as amended in the 1970, defined protected birds as any bird occurring in the wild in Europe with the exception of the domesticated mute swan (*Cygnus olor*), domesticated species of pigeons and other species listed in Hunting Act 1954. The term 'Europe' came from the Birds Act 1912 and indicated that birds not occurring in the wild in the Netherlands were also protected as soon as they were found on Dutch

[32] Council Directive 79/409/EEC of 2 April 1979 on the conservation of wild birds, [1979] OJ L 103/1. Now recast by Directive 2009/147/EC of the European Parliament and of the Council of 30 November 2009 on the conservation of wild birds, [2010] OJ L 20/7.

[33] Council Directive 92/43/EEC of 21 May 1992 on the conservation of natural habitats and of wild fauna and flora, [1992] OJ L 206/7.

[34] Fois (2008), p. 77.

[35] For example, bird species regularly migrating between Africa and Russia, passing by the EU, is covered as it would be considered a *regularly* occurring bird.

[36] Outside of the scope of application of an EU measure, it is only possible to speak of green-plating, and not of more stringent protective measures, as discussed in Chapter 1, Section 1.4.

territory, for example by being introduced by man. This sought to avoid conflicts between Dutch law and the Paris Convention for the Protection of Birds 1902 to which, inter alia, Russia belonged.[37] The field of application of the Birds Act 1936 thus exceeded the borders of the European Union (at that time European Economic Communities). Furthermore, in 1993 the Dutch legislator changed Section 3 of the Birds Act 1936 to cover birds resulting from cross-breeding between one or more protected species listed by administrative order.[38] This amendment intended to implement the CITES Regulation,[39] and not only protected birds from being exploited but also from other human activities.[40] Therefore, in pursuing a consistent regime, Dutch law extended the field of application of the legal regime of the Birds Directive to cross-breeding of bird species, which is not covered by the Directive.

As regards habitats protection, twelve years after the Birds Directive was adopted, the Commission adopted a proposal for a directive implementing the Bern Convention.[41] The Habitats Directive establishes rules to protect conservation areas and measures to protect species in need of strict protection. The Directive pursues the creation of the so-called Natura 2000 network, which is a network of areas of special conservation within the Union territory.[42] The Habitats Directive protects species of wild flora and fauna naturally occurring on the European territory of the Member States from both direct and indirect threats (Article 1). In addition, and most importantly, the Habitats Directive differs from the Birds Directive in that the Habitats Directive protects certain habitats independently from the protection of species. It recognises their intrinsic value and protects them by requiring the Member States to designate certain areas as Special Areas of Conservation (SAC) and to avoid

[37] Proceedings of the Second Chamber of the States General, Kamerstukken II 1910/11, 249, nr. 3, p. 5.

[38] This amendment was enacted by Stb. 1993, 586, Section I, letter C. These provisions were implemented by Section 1 of Stb. 1994, 625.

[39] Council Regulation (EC) No 338/97 of 9 December 1996 on the protection of species of wild fauna and flora by regulating trade therein, [1997] OJ L 61/1.

[40] Stb. 1994, 625, explanatory memorandum, p. 12.

[41] Convention on the Conservation of European Wildlife and Natural Habitats, Bern, September 19, 1979, ETS No.104. Council Decision 82/72/EEC of 3 December 1981 concerning the conclusion of the Convention on the conservation of European wildlife and natural habitats (Bern Convention), [1982] OJ L 38/3. The Bern Convention was explicitly mentioned as one of the grounds for the proposal of the Habitats Directive, COM(88) 381 final, p. 2.

[42] Fois (2008), p. 78.

pollution and damage resulting from human activities which seriously affect their integrity (Articles 3–6).[43]

The Habitats Directive aims to contribute to ensuring biodiversity through the conservation of natural habitats and wild fauna and flora in the European territory of the Member States (Article 2(1)). Article 2(2) of the Directive specifies that measures taken pursuant to the Habitats Directive are aimed at the conservation of natural habitats *of Community interest*. As regards the meaning of Article 2(2), the Commission stated in its guidance on the protection of species under the Habitats Directive that:

> *The concept of FCS* [Favourable Conservation Status, LS] *is not limited to the Natura 2000 network or to the species protected by this network (i.e. Annex II species). It applies to the overall situation of all species* [and habitats, LS] *of Community interest (Annexes II, IV and V), which needs to be assessed and surveyed in order to judge whether it is favourable or not.*[44]

As we can see, the Commission refers only to species of Community interest.[45] There is no reason why this reasoning should not also apply to habitats. Indeed, the specification in Article 2(2) of the Directive shows that the actual goal of the Habitats Directive is that of protecting certain natural habitats. The protection of such habitats is how the Directive contributes towards ensuring biodiversity. Therefore, habitats not having a Community interest are not regulated by the Habitats Directive. A combined reading of letter b and Article 1, letter c shows that such habitats of Community interests are

> *terrestrial or aquatic areas distinguished by geographic, abiotic and biotic features, whether entirely natural or semi-natural, in danger of disappearance in their natural range or having a small natural range, following their regression or by reason of their intrinsically restricted area, or presenting outstanding examples of typical characteristics of one or more of the nine following biogeographical regions: Alpine, Atlantic, Black Sea, Boreal, Continental, Macaronesian, Mediterranean, Pannonian and Steppic. Such habitats can be listed under Annex I.*

[43] Krämer (2011), p. 190 refers to the slow implementation rate of the Member States and of the far-reaching opposition of German *Länder* to the Directive. Today, approximately 12% of the terrestrial area of the Member States is covered by this provision, mostly overlapping with the areas under the Birds Directive.

[44] Commission of the European Communities, *Guidance document on the strict protection of animal species of Community interest under the Habitats Directive 92/43/EEC*, Final version February 2007, p. 10, available at http://ec.europa.eu/environment/nature/legislation/habitatsdirective/index_en.htm#interpretation [last accessed on July 2017].

[45] The Commission bases this statement on Article 2(2) of the Directive.

Outside the field of application of the Directive, Member States can take measures protecting other habitats. In addition, the Habitats Directive aims to contribute to ensuring biodiversity through the conservation of natural habitats (Article 2(1)). This means that habitats of Community interest are protected for conservation values. Member States can also take measures to protect habitats of Community interest for other reasons than nature conservation, such as for natural beauty.

In the United Kingdom and, at least until 2016, in the Netherlands, national law protected other nature reserve sites than those covered by the Natura 2000 Network. In the United Kingdom, national law regulates the so-called Sites of Special Scientific Interest (SSSIs) – or in Northern Ireland as Areas of Special Scientific Interest (ASSIs) - and Marine Nature Reserves (MNRs).[46] In the Netherlands, habitats not having a Community interest were protected by law until 2016. Further, until 2010, habitats of Community interest were protected for other purposes than nature conservation. Under the Nature Conservation Act 1967, nature reserves protected the ecological and cultural values of the designated area (Sections 1 and 12).[47] Ecological values include the conservation values protected by the Birds Directive and the Habitats Directive, but also the protection of conservation values not falling under these two Directives – at least not explicitly. The relevance of national values leads to the protection of habitats lacking a Community interest.[48] In addition, habitats of Community interest were also protected by national values that are not regulated by Union law.[49] When the proposal for the Nature Conservation Act 1998 was sent to the parliament in 1993, the legislator maintained the approach followed under the Nature Conservation Act 1967. Under the Nature Conservation Act 1998, nature reserves protected sites with cultural and ecological value, regardless of whether they were covered by Union law. In the context of a debate on the precautionary principle, the Dutch legislator explained the reasons

[46] Sections 28 to 33 of Part 2 of the Wildlife and Countryside Act detail the law regarding SSSIs. Sections 34 to 53 deal with other protected areas within Great Britain. For an overview of the sites see the government page at: http://jncc.defra.gov.uk/page-4

[47] The Dutch terms are *natuurwetenschappelijke waarden* and *natuurschoon*.

[48] It should be noted that in certain circumstances, protecting national habitats lacking a Community interest could be necessary to implement the obligations arising out Article 4(1) of the Bern Convention. This is not gold-plating. At the time of writing, the government intends to eliminate the regime of protection for nature reserves lacking a Community interest; Brief of the State Secretary H. Bleker of 14 September 2011, '*Aanpak Natura 2000*', reference number 230499, p. 10.

[49] Backes & Van den Broek (2005), p. 478; and Woldendorp (2006), p. 83.

behind this decision. According to him, once the Habitats Directive criteria were translated into Dutch law, they had to apply to all protected areas regardless of whether they implement the Directive: it was important to apply the same legal regime to all sites.[50]

### *2.2.2 Establishing Stricter Means than Required by the EU Legislator*

From a quantitative perspective the most common form of green-plating takes the form of national measures establishing stricter means/instruments to achieve an EU goal than required by a measure based on Article 192 TFUE. This is logical considering that each EU measure usually has only one article setting out the goals of the measure, while it has many provisions concerning the means for achieving such goals. There are simply more provisions in respect of which Member States can adopt green-plating. During my Ph.D. research, I was able to retrieve and analyse cases of green-plating pertaining to the means to achieve an EU goal in all fields of environmental law, especially as regards a) measures not keeping burdens to the minimum and b) more stringent protective measures. As regards spillovers and related measures, green-plating takes the form of measures establishing a higher goal than that required by the EU legislator. This is because this kind of green-plating falls outside the scope of application of the EU measure concerned. Hence, by definition, national law goes beyond the EU goal. I have not retrieved examples of spillovers and related measures aiming at achieving an EU goal as such.

#### a) Measures Not Keeping Burdens to the Minimum

As regards measures not keeping burdens to the minimum, in the field of waste law, Article 10 of the Waste Framework Directive covered installations or undertakings that recover waste. In both cases an exception could be granted under certain conditions (Article 11). Establishments or undertakings exempted from the permit requirements needed to be registered. In 1995–1997 the Flemish region of Belgium, Denmark, Germany, France, the Netherlands, Austria, Finland and Sweden did not exempt establishments and undertakings from any permit requirement.[51] As for the Netherlands, when waste law was integrated into the Environmental Management Act, permit requirements were

[50] Proceedings of the Second Chamber of the States General, Kamerstukken II 1996/97, 23 580, nr. 11, p. 11.

[51] COM(1999) 752 final, p. 17.

regulated in Chapter 8 of this Act, which applied to industrial establishments in general.[52] The general rule was that any establishment had to be subjected to a permit to be established, changed and exploited, unless an order stated otherwise (Article 8.1). Establishments for the recovery of waste were explicitly mentioned as establishments for which a permit was required.[53] Waste producers discarding their own waste at the place of production were also not exempted from the permit requirement.[54]

In the field of nature conservation, in the Commission's report on the period 1981–1991, the Commission noted that no Member State allowed the exploitation of all the species listed under Annex III/2 to the Directive.[55] For example, Greece, France and Spain reported that for the period 1981–1991, they did not allow the exploitation of any of the species listed under Annex III/2 to the Directive. As regards hunting, the Commission's report for the period 1981–1991 also shows that several Member States allowed hunting for fewer species than those listed in the Directive.[56] Similar findings can be made from the Commission's reports for other periods, albeit some changes were made as to which species can be exploited and/or hunted.[57] In the Netherlands, hunting is still banned, unless it serves nature conservation goals.[58] Section 3.20 of the Nature Protection Act allows hunting for only five species, three of which were covered by the Birds Directive. In the past, the government recognised that such a shortlist represents stricter standards.[59]

52 It should be noted that the EMA did not integrate all existing systems, Gilhuis (1993), p. 87.

53 Category 28 under Annex I of Stb. 1993, 50.

54 The content of the permit could be influenced by whether an establishment discarded waste coming from inside the establishment concerned or from outside.

55 COM(93) 592 final, p. 50.

56 Idem, pp. 58–62. For example, Belgium reported that only eight of the thirty-one species listed in Annex II of the Directive can be hunted in Flanders or Wallonia.

57 COM(2000) 180 final, pp. 15–17; COM(2002) 146 final, pp. 15–17; Report to the Commission on the implementation of Directive 79/409/EEC on the Conservation of Wild Birds, Part II. Summary of the national reports by the Member States, Update for 2002–2004, pp. 24–27 (Commission Report 2002–2004); and Report to the Commission on the implementation of Directive 79/409/EEC on the Conservation of Wild Birds, Part II. Summary of the national reports by the Member States, Update for 2005–2007.

58 Dutch law allows hunting in the context of the prevention of damage. This is regulated under Sections 3.12 till 3.19 of the Nature Protection Act, implementing Article 9 of the Directive.

59 Proceedings of the Second Chamber of the States General, Kamerstukken II 1995/96, 23 147, nr. 7, pp. 23 and 24.

Under air quality law, Articles 3(4) and 5(4) of the First Daughter Directive indicated that Union ambient air quality law also covers emissions of sulphur dioxide and particulate matters from natural sources. The approach of the First Daughter Directive was clarified and extended to all pollutants by the Air Quality Directive (Article 20). Similarly, Article 21 permits the subtraction of contributions from winter sanding or salting of roads.[60] If Member States refrain from using such options, they are not keeping burdens to a minimum. Under the Air Framework Directive and its First Daughter Directive, the Netherlands did not fully exempt contributions from natural sources. At the national level, Section 1 of the Air Protection Act defined 'polluting substances' as substances present in the air and capable of damaging or negatively affecting human health or capable of damaging plants, animals or goods.[61] The Dutch legislator did not mention the difference between pollution from natural sources and that from anthropogenic sources. In the order on nitrogen dioxide,[62] pollution from natural sources was explicitly covered.[63] This approach was maintained in the transposition of the Air Framework Directive. In general, the Dutch legislator considered the existing definitions as assuring the correct implementation of the Directive.[64] Accordingly, the term 'pollutant' was not translated into national law, suggesting that pollution from natural sources was still covered. From 2005, Union law and Dutch law have been progressively converging.[65] Under the Air Framework Directive, the Netherlands has not yet used the power to exempt contributions from winter sanding or salting. The government stated that it intends to implement this opt-out only if necessary.[66]

[60] This option originates in a request from Finland during the negotiations of the First Daughter Directive, European Union, the Council, Interinstitutional file 97/0266, document number 5719/01/REV1, page 6, note 12.

[61] Stb. 1986, 78.

[62] Stb. 1987, 33.

[63] Stb. 1987, 33, explanatory memorandum, p. 6, where the government indicates that natural concentrations of nitrogen dioxide are low.

[64] Proceedings of the Second Chamber of the States General, Kamerstukken II 1997/98 25 686, nr. 3, especially p. 2 where the aspects needing transposition are also indicated.

[65] First with Section 5(1) of the Air Quality Order 2005, then with the Air Quality Act 2007. Finally, Section 5.19(4) EMA sates that contribution from natural sources are subtracted if the limit values are not respected.

[66] Proceedings of the Second Chamber of the States General, Kamerstukken II 2007/08, 31 589, nr. 3, p. 35.

As regards emissions from industrial installations covered by the Industrial Emissions Directive,[67] several Member States, such as Austria, Belgium (except Wallonia), Germany and Italy, indicated that they do not fully use the opt-out clause in Article 9(3) of the Directive, allowing the Member States to exempt installations covered by the Union Emissions Trading Scheme from requirements on energy efficiency.[68] By not making use of this exception ground, these Member States did not keep burdens to the minimum. Besides, in the context of permit provisions regulating conditions other than normal operating conditions, which include accidents or incidents, Article 9(6), last sentence, of the IPPC Directive[69] allowed the Member States to authorise derogations from BAT for six months if a rehabilitation plan approved by a competent authority ensured that emissions limit values would be met and the project would lead to a reduction in pollution.[70] The Netherlands did not implement this exception.[71]

In the field of the Environmental Liability Directive,[72] Article 8(4) of the Directive allows relieving operators from bearing the costs incurred to remedy environmental damage. In 2010 the Commission published

67 Directive 2010/75/EU of the European Parliament and of the Council of 24 November 2010 on industrial emissions (integrated pollution prevention and control), [2010] OJ L334/17.

68 Vito Report (2011), p. 35 and Vito Report (2011), Annex A, p. 14, 40, 140 and 334. This report was commission by the Commission concerning the implementation of Directive 2008/1/EC. VITO, Analysis of the reports submitted by the Member States on the implementation of Directive 2008/1/EC, Directive 2000/76/EC, Directive 1999/13/EC and further development of the web platform to publish the information. Report on subtask 3.2: Analysis report of Member States implementation of IPPC and WI Directives. Part I: Member States Reports on their implementation of Directive 2008/1/EC concerning integrated pollution prevention and control for the period 2006–2008 – Final Report, March 2011 (hereafter: 'Vito Report' [2011]).

69 Council Directive 96/61/EC of 24 September 1996 concerning integrated pollution prevention and control, [1996] OJ L 257/26. Codified by Directive 2008/1/EC of the European Parliament and of the Council of 15 January 2008 concerning integrated pollution prevention and control (Codified version), [2008] OJ L 24/8.

70 Jongma (2002), p. 84.

71 Neither Title 8 nor 17 of the Environmental Management Act mentions this possibility. See also Proceedings of the Second Chamber of the States General, Kamerstukken II 2003/04, 29 711, nr. 3, p. 46, where the transposition table shows the omission sign '(. . .)' where Article 9(6), second sentence, of the IPPC Directive should have been. See also Jongma (2002), p. 209.

72 Directive 2004/35/CE of the European Parliament and of the Council of 21 April 2004 on environmental liability with regard to the prevention and remedying of environmental damage, [2004] OJ L 143/56.

the first report on the implementation of the Environmental Liability Directive.[73] This report indicates that several Member States do not keep burdens to a minimum. As regards the permit and state-of-the-art defences, Austria, Belgium (at federal level), Bulgaria, Germany, Hungary, Ireland, Poland, Romania and Slovenia do not use them. The Netherlands subjects them to a reasonability test. Denmark, Finland and Lithuania allow the permit defence but not the state-of-the-art defence, while France allows the state-of-the-art defence but not the permit defence. According to the report, Sweden takes the middle ground and admits the permit and state-of-the-art defences as mitigating factors in the decision process. Besides, Article 3(1) of the Environmental Liability Directive applies a system of strict liability to activities listed under Annex III. Annex III allows the exemption from the application of Article 3(1) of the Directive for waste management operations that spread sewage sludge from urban waste water treatment plants for agricultural purposes. The Commission's report indicates that only some Member States use this opt-out clause.[74] Also, the Netherlands does not implement this option. Title 17.2 of the Environmental Management Act applies to activities mentioned in Annex III to the Directive, without exempting these kind of activities.

### b) More Stringent Protective Measures

As regards more stringent protective measures within the meaning of Article 193 TFEU, a picture similar to that painted for measures not keeping burdens to the minimum emerges. In each field of environmental law covered in my Ph.D., multiple examples of green-plating could be retrieved.

In the field of waste management, for the period 2001–2003 some Member States, such as Austria and Belgium, indicated that they had developed producer-related obligations regarding the keeping of information as allowed, thus not required, by Article 14 of the Waste Framework Directive.[75] In 2009, the number of Member States covering producers of waste increased substantially. Only three Member States reported that they did not require keeping a register of certain waste

[73] COM(2010) 581 final.

[74] The Member States that used this option are: Bulgaria, France, Latvia, Malta, Portugal, Romania, Slovakia, Slovenia and the United Kingdom.

[75] SEC(2006) 972, p. 20.

producers.[76] In the Netherlands, another example of more stringent protective measures stems from the fact that the legal regime applicable to industrial waste and collected domestic waste has been equated to that applicable to dangerous waste, which is more stringent than the general regime.[77]

Under nature conservation law, the Commission's report for the period 1981–1991 indicates that several Member States allowed the exploitation of fewer species than those listed under Annex III/1 to the Directive.[78] Moreover, the Commission's report for the period 1996–1998 indicates that Finland prohibited the use of devices producing noise to kill or attract birds.[79] Similarly, the Commission's report for the period 2002–2004 notes that the United Kingdom also took more stringent protective measures than those required under Article 8 of the Directive.[80] In particular, England, Scotland and Wales introduced a total ban on the use of lead shot in wetlands. In the context of the regulation of means for killing and capturing birds, the Netherlands goes beyond the minimum requirements, given that it uses a positive list rather than a negative list for cases falling under Article 7 of the Birds Directive. Section 3.21 of the Nature Protection Act prohibits using any other method or means than those listed in that provision.

Concerning air quality law, Article 6 of the Air Framework Directive allowed the Member States to use modelling and objective estimation techniques *in addition* to measurement techniques. Article 6(2–4) of the Air Quality Directive still allows the application of modelling techniques *in addition* to measurement techniques. In the early 1990s, the Dutch legislator had already indicated the importance of integrating measurement techniques.[81] In the Air Quality Order 2001, the legislator explicitly stated that the Netherlands would introduce all the assessment stations required by the First Daughter Directive as though measurements were

[76] Institute for European Environmental Policy, A Report on the implementation of Directive 75/442/EEC on waste, May 2009, pp. 26–28. The quality of the information provided by the Member States was poor, making this data less reliable.

[77] Title 10.6 of the Environmental Management Act.

[78] COM(93) 592 final, p. 50.

[79] COM(2002) 146 final, p. 20.

[80] Commission Report 2002–2004, p. 30. That the United Kingdom was working on measures limiting the use of these means had already been in reported in the Commission report for 1996–1998.

[81] Proceedings of the Second Chamber of the States General, Kamerstukken II 1988/89, 21 163, nr. 3, pp. 52 and 53.

the only assessment technique to be applied.[82] In addition, the legislator stated that the Netherlands would also use modelling and calculations to offer a complete and precise picture of air quality in the country and mitigate for the shortcomings of measurement techniques.[83] As regards modelling, case law shows that the Netherlands applies the so-called street-level and point-by-point assessment method.[84] Like the Netherlands, Denmark, Sweden and the United Kingdom assess air quality at street level, while Germany, Greece and Portugal do not.[85] Modelling, in addition to measurements, allows for a more precise assessment of air quality and hence for a better implementation of the Directive's goals. This can thus be considered a case of more stringent protective measures.

With regard to emissions from installations covered by the IPPC Directive, seventeen Member States indicated that they subject permits for IPPC installations to a maximum time limit, something which the old IPPC Directive did not require.[86] For example, Malta has a time limit of a maximum of five years, Spain a maximum of eight years and Belgium (Flanders) a maximum of twenty years.[87] In addition, the report commissioned by the Commission under the old IPPC Directive provides some indication of the legal value that BREF (best available techniques REFerence) documents have in the various Member States.[88] The binding force of BREF documents under the old Directive is a question open for discussion. Officially, they do not have legal value.[89] They are not even mentioned in the Directive. However, the Commission created them from Article 16 of the Directive, establishing the Commission's reporting duties.[90] According to Annex IV, information published by the Commission pursuant to Article 16(2) or by international organisations have to be taken into consideration, bearing in mind the likely costs and benefits, among another eleven factors.[91] In 2005, Lee stated that BREF

[82] Stb. 2001, 269, explanatory memorandum, pp. 33–36.
[83] Ibidem. On the assessment methods see Van den Houd (2004).
[84] With regard to the point-by-point assessment method, see Van Rij & Annema (2010), pp. 209–210, with reference to ABRvS 21 May 2008, 200706306/1.
[85] Proceedings of the Second Chamber of the States General, Kamerstukken II 2005/06, 30 489, nr. 3, p. 11 with reference to Germany, Greece and Portugal.
[86] Vito Report (2011).
[87] Idem, p. 38.
[88] The methodology applied in the report allows only indicative findings, Idem, p. 106.
[89] COM(2003), 354 final, p. 16. Lee (2005), p. 168.
[90] Lee (2005), p. 168.
[91] Van't Lam & Uylenburg (2005), pp. 56–57 underlines the vagueness of the clause 'take into consideration'.

documents carry considerable scientific, *if not legal*, authority.[92] Other academics, however, underlined a series of limitations which prevent BREF documents from having legal value.[93] The Court of Justice also seems to deny the legal value of BREF documents.[94] In the Netherlands things were different. The Dutch government and Council of State agree that only in specific circumstances is it possible to deviate from a BAT indicated in a BREF document.[95] In 2011, almost all IPPC installations complied with the emissions limit values based on BREF documents.[96] Two case studies performed under the Vito report published in 2011 showed that the Netherlands is the only Member State in which all selected installations have emissions limit values within the range offered by the BREF documents applicable to the selected installations.[97]

In the context of the Environmental Liability Directive, the first report on the implementation of the Directive published in 2010 indicates that fourteen Member States extend the scope of 'damage to protected species and habitats' to habitat or species not listed in Annex I to the Birds Directive and Annexes I, II and IV to the Habitats Directive, which the Member States designate for equivalent purposes as those laid down in these two Directives.[98] Under Article 2(1)(c) of the Environmental Liability Directive, this is just an option. In addition, eight Member States have introduced a system of mandatory financial security at national level, entering into force at various dates up to 2014.[99] Under

[92] Lee (2005), p. 168.

[93] Kat (2005), p. 56; Robesin (2008), p. 57; Pallemaerts (1996), pp. 175–176.

[94] Case C-473/07, *Association nationale pour la protection des eaux et rivières-TOS en Association OABA tegen Ministère de l'Ecologie, du Développement et de l'Aménagement durables*, [2009] ECR I-319, para 30.

[95] Stb. 2005, 527, explanatory memorandum, p. 10; ABRvS of 24 January 2007, n. 200602467/1 and ABRvS of 19 July 2006, n. 200509633/1. Cf. Bröring (2007), pp. 22–24.

[96] Sira Consulting, *Administratieve en bestuurlijke lasten Richtlijn Industriële Emissies – Onderzoek naar het Effect van de Richtlijn Industriële Emissies op de administratieve en bestuurlijke lasten*, June 2011, p. 17 (English summary) (hereafter: Sira Report [2011]), p. 35.

[97] Vito Report (2011), p. 147.

[98] COM(2010) 581 final. These Member States are: Austria, Belgium, Cyprus, the Czech Republic, Estonia, Greece, Hungary, Latvia, Lithuania, Poland, Portugal, Spain, Sweden and the United Kingdom.

[99] These Member States are: Bulgaria, Portugal, Spain, Greece, Hungary, Slovakia, the Czech Republic and Romania. These systems are subject to risk assessment of relevant sectors and operators, and dependent on various national implementing provisions providing for issues such as ceilings, exemptions, etc.

the Directive there is no obligation in this sense.[100] Moreover, Belgium, Denmark, Finland, Greece, Hungary, Latvia, Lithuania and Sweden include activities not mentioned in Annex III to the Directive in the scope of strict liability.

### *2.2.3 Reasons for Green-Plating*

In 'Gold Plating' of European Environmental Measures (*Journal for European Environmental and Planning Law*, 2009), my co-authors and I provided an overview of some of the reasons used by the Member States to justify going beyond EU requirements.[101] Three main categories were indicated: a) Environmental reasons, including the wish not to downgrade pre-existing standards, and cases of successful lobby during the implementation process; b) Unintended gold-plating, referring to cases in which the national legislator unknowingly or without any purpose went beyond EU requirements and c) Unavoidable gold-plating, referring to cases in which gold-plating was dictated by the need of internal coherence of the national legal order. These categories are retained here, but they are further refined. Further, a new category, d) Economic consideration, is added. This addition shows that the enumeration of categories mentioned in this section is not meant to be exhaustive. New categories can be added based on new empirical insight.

#### a) Environmental Protection

A reason expected to be used to justify green-plating is the need for environmental protection. Legal practice confirms this assumption. For example, the New Waste Framework Directive regulates the so-called extended producer responsibility (Article 8). In addition to establishing a general option, Article 8 of the Directive provides specific examples of how the extended producer responsibility could be pursued. The Directive describes these specific measures as options and not as obligations. Member States using these options would be establishing more stringent measures. The Netherlands used these options. The Netherlands had already introduced extended producer responsibility in the 1990s.[102]

[100] Article 14 of the Environmental Liability Directive requires the Member States to encourage the development of financial security instruments and markets through the appropriate economic and financial operators, including financial mechanisms in case of insolvency, with the aim of enabling operators to use financial guarantees to cover their responsibilities under the Directive.

[101] Jans and Squintani et al. (2009).

[102] TK 1991/92, 21 246, nr. 5, pp. 7 and 8, which introduced Article 10.5a in the EMA.

Despite the presence of the Dutch policy on gold-plating, the act transposing the New Waste Framework Directive did not only maintain the provisions on extended producer responsibility.[103] Some provisions regulating the extended producer responsibility have been strengthened. For example, Section 10.15 of the Environmental Management Act now allows measures to be adopted during the development of products. Previously, it allowed measures to be adopted from the moment products were manufactured. Moreover, previously Section 10.15 could have been used only to prevent waste from occurring. Now, it can be used to encourage recovery and reuse.[104] The government explained that such measures have been taken to fully implement the principle of extended producer responsibility.[105]

Similarly, in 1987 when Directive 82/884/EEC on lead was transposed into the Dutch legal order,[106] the limit value for lead was more stringent than required.[107] The legislator explained that a stricter limit value was necessary because the health of children is affected more than that of adults. The Directive did not take the health of children sufficiently into consideration, according to the Netherlands.[108]

The *Balsamo* case shows that an Italian local authority, the municipality of Cinesello Balsamo, prohibited the supply of non-biodegradable plastic bags to consumers.[109] Later, the Italian legislator introduced a similar prohibition at the national level.[110] Both bans aim at reducing the impact that plastic bags have on the environment when they are abandoned.

[103] Stb. 2011, 103 and Stb. 2011, 104.

[104] Since 2012, Sections 10.15–10.18 EMA have been replaced by Section 9.5.2 EMA without changing their content. Stb. 2011, 269. Proceedings of the Second Chamber of the States General, Kamerstukken II 2007/08, 31 501, p. 14. This act introduced a new Title 9.5 regulating general provisions regarding substances, preparations and products.

[105] Proceedings of the Second Chamber of the States General, Kamerstukken II 2009/10, 32 392, nr. 3, pp. 20 and 21.

[106] Council Directive 82/884/EEC of 3 December 1982 on a limit value for lead in the air, [1982] OJ L 378/15.

[107] Stb. 1987, 34. Instead of a maximum of 2 microgram/m$^3$ as yearly average (Article 2(2) Directive), Article 3 of the order sets a maximum of 0.5 microgram/m$^3$.

[108] Stb. 1987, 34, explanatory memorandum, p. 13. The legislator based this statement on several studies performed around the world until that time and in particular on the WHO's Guideline of 1987, World Health Organization, *Air Quality Guidelines for Europe. WHO Regional Publications, European Series No. 23* (1987) Copenhagen.

[109] Case C-380/87, *Enichem Base and Others v Comune di Cinisello Balsamo*, [1989] ECR 2491.

[110] Law of 26 December 2006, n. 296 which, with regard to plastic bags, introduced a ban as of 1 January 2011.

The pre-existence of a national high level of protection of the environment influences choices on green-plating. The desire to avoid downgrading the existing level of protection plays a role in practice. For example, as stated above, the Netherlands used the legal regime of the Habitats Directive to cover values other than those required by the Directive. The government explicitly stated that national values have the same rank as those deriving from the Directive.[111] It can be argued that the Dutch government tried to avoid downgrading the level of protection of the old natural reserves.[112] This is today no longer the case, as further discussed in the next section. Similarly, in Belgium the wish to avoid downgrading convinced the Flemish government to maintain its regulation on soil sanitation, despite this being more stringent than required by the Environmental Liability Directive.[113]

Sometimes, downgrading was avoided between the moment of transposition and the moment of entering into force of the Union requirement. For example, this was the case for the transposition of certain aspects of the Air Framework Directive and its First Daughter Directive into the Dutch legal order. When these directives were adopted, the Netherlands already had limit values in line with some of those prescribed by the directives. The government stated that transposing the deadlines indicated by the directives would have downgraded the existing level of ambient air quality. It can be argued that downgrading the level of protection for only a few years would have been unreasonable, although, in general, legally acceptable from a Union law perspective.[114]

### b) Unintentional Green-Plating

There are cases where the national legislator does not seem to realise that it is maintaining or introducing green-plating. These cases of green-plating seems to derive from at least two different sources. First of all, legal practice in the Netherlands shows that when an EU measure is not clear about its meaning, Member States might interpret the EU measure differently than actually meant, potentially leading to green-plating. For

[111] Proceedings of the Second Chamber of the States General, Kamerstukken II 2001/02, 28 171, nr. 6, p. 6.

[112] Ibidem.

[113] Jans and Squintani et al. (2009), pp. 424 and 425.

[114] Naturally, national law must not endanger the achievement of future Union objectives, Case C-129/96, *Inter-Environnement Wallonie ASBL v Région wallonne,* [1997] ECR I-7411, para. 45.

example, the Air Framework Directive and its First Daughter Directive were unclear with respect to the places where limit values for the protection of human health had to be assessed.[115] It was discussed whether the Directives required the assessment of air quality on the whole territory or only as regards locations in which the public might be exposed to air pollution.[116] Dutch law decided to follow a criterion focusing on the quality of ambient air rather than following a criterion based on the exposure of human beings.[117] Limit values had to be respected in the whole of the country irrespective of whether human health was at risk.[118] This was confirmed by the case law of the Dutch Council of State and led to several decisions being annulled.[119] Only after the clarification brought on this matter by the Air Quality Directive, the Dutch government decided to amend its national law and follow the exposure criterion.[120] The Netherlands was certain that it had interpreted the provisions appropriately. When implementing the Air Framework Directive and its First Daughter Directive, the Dutch legislator never realised that he potentially went beyond EU requirements.

Similarly, when the Dutch legislator implemented the IPPC Directive, it did not consider the binding force attributed to BREF documents as being a case of green-plating. As discussed above, under the IPPC Directive the legal value of these documents was debated.[121] At the time of the implementation, the Netherlands already had a practice by which courts did not traditionally allow decisions of competent authorities to establish a lower level of protection than that based on a technical

[115] Article 6(1) Air Framework Directive required the assessment of the ambient air quality throughout the territory of the Member States. At the same time, Annex VI(I) (b) First Daughter Directive stated that the limit values for for the protection of ecosystems or vegetation do not need to be assessed in the whole of the territory of a Member State, but only in a part thereof.

[116] Backes & Van Nieuwerburg (2005); Backes (2006c), pp. 14–17. See also TK 2004/05 29 667, nr. 12 and TK 2005/06 30 489, nr. 3, p. 11.

[117] Stb. 2001, 269, explanatory memorandum, pp. 17 and 32.

[118] Backes (2006c), p. 11.

[119] Schippers & Besselink (2005), pp. 110 ff., par. 7, with reference to ABRvS of 15 September 2004, n. 200401178/1; ABRvS of 17 November 2004, n. 20030738/1; ABRvS of 1 December 2005, n. 200400084/1, ABRvS of 26 January 2005, n. 200400465/1; ABRvS of 16 February 2005, n. 200308882/1; ABRvS of 13 April 2005, n. 200407748/1; ABRvS of 20 April 2005, n. 200406300/1; ABRvS of 21 April 2005, n. 200501512/1; ABRvS of 22 June 2005, n. 200406192/1 and ABRvS of 22 June 2005, n. 200409619/1.

[120] Article 2(3) and Articles 65 and 22 Stcrt. 2007, 220 as amended by Stcrt. 2008, 245 (2040).

[121] Chapter 2, section 2.2, above.

document.[122] This could explain why the Netherlands interpreted the Directive as requiring taking BREF documents as basis for the granting of permits.[123] National law was not seen as being more stringent than required on this point.

A second kind of inadvertent green-plating concerns Union provisions which are rather clear, but that have been transposed in a way that green-plating still occurs. This can be the case when the national legislator re-elaborates the text of the EU measure at hand.[124] For example, Article 8(4) of the Environmental Liability Directive permits relieving operators from bearing the costs incurred to remedy environmental damage. Besides restricting the applicability of these provisions in light of a reasonability test, as discussed above, the Dutch legislator addressed Section 17.16(4) of the Environmental Management Act to the public authority. In contrast, the addressee of Article 8(4) of the Directive is the operator. This suggests that while under the Directive an operator could recover from the State the costs it incurred itself,[125] under Section 17.16 the operator cannot recover such costs. The Dutch Council of State noted the anomaly of the difference between the text of the Dutch provision and the text of the Directive as regards the addressee of Article 17.16 of the Environmental Management Act.[126] The government disagreed with Council of State's opinion and it did not change the formulation.[127] The Dutch government does not seem to have realised that through re-elaboration, stricter standards were introduced.

[122] Bröring (1993), p. 357. More recently, Leemans (2007), pp. 50–52 with reference to case law: ABRvS of 8 February 2006, n. 200508181/1; ABRvS of 29 November 2006, n. 200604103/1, ABRvS of 21 February 2007, n. 200606952/1; and ABRvS of 29 November 2006, n. 200600905/1.

[123] Stb. 2005, 527, explanatory memorandum, p. 10; ABRvS of 24 January 2007, n. 200602467/1 and ABRvS of 19 July 2006, n. 200509633/1. Cf. Bröring (2007), pp. 22–24.

[124] On re-elaboration and gold-plating see, Anker et al. (2015).

[125] See by analogy Article 8(3), last sentence, Directive 2004/35/EC stating: '[. . .] *Member States shall take the appropriate measures to enable the operator to recover the costs incurred.*' Cf. Betlem (2005), pp. 171 ff.; Betlem argues that Article 8(3) of the Environmental Liability Directive only covers cases where a public authority acted. This is not found in the Directive. Article 8(1) also covers cases where operators take measures themselves. In addition, the last sentence of Article 8(3) is only fully meaningful if it is applied to cases where operators took measures themselves.

[126] Proceedings of the Second Chamber of the States General, Kamerstukken II 2006/07, 30 920, nr. 4, p. 6.

[127] Idem, p. 7 and Proceedings of the Second Chamber of the States General, Kamerstukken II 2006/2007, 30 920, nr. 7, p. 8.

Also the use of copy-and-paste (also called copy-out principle),[128] including in what could be considered its most extreme form, i.e. dynamic reference,[129] can lead to inadvertent green-plating.[130] This is because by means of copy-and-paste, exception clauses are not exploited. Such clauses need an ad hoc transposition. I have already mentioned above that the Netherlands transposed Annex III to the Directive by means of a dynamic reference. This legislative technique did not allow activating the exception in Annex III concerning certain operators. This means that operations that spread sewage sludge from urban waste water treatment plants for agricultural purposes in the Netherlands do not benefit from the exemption under Article 3(1) of the Environmental Liability Directive. Also in this case, the Dutch legislator did not seem to be aware of the fact that the transposing act went beyond the EU standards.

### c) Unavoidable Green-Plating

Environmental protection is not the only reason driving green-plating. Legal practice reveals examples of stricter national standards adopted to protect legal certainty, including the need to protect the internal coherence of the national legal order. For example, I indicated above that the Netherlands uses modelling and calculation techniques *in addition* to measurement to assess ambient air quality. The Dutch legislator stated that the Netherlands would also use modelling and calculations to offer a complete and precise picture of air quality in the country and mitigate for the shortcomings of measurement techniques.[131] As we can see, the Dutch government aims to provide an evaluation of ambient air quality that is as precise as possible. This should prevent disputes over the assessment method and the quality of data. Other cases of national measures going beyond EU requirements aim at simplifying the enforcement of certain provisions. This was the reason justifying extending the scope of application of the protection regime stemming from the Birds Directive to hybrids in the Netherlands.[132] The government justified

[128] Anker et al (2015), pp. 17–44.

[129] Dynamic reference means that national law refers to the provisions of a Directive as they evolve over time. This is part of the so-called referencing principle, Ibidem.

[130] On copy-and-paste and gold-plating, Ibidem.

[131] Stb. 2001, 269, explanatory memorandum, pp. 33–36. On the assessment methods see Van den Houd (2004).

[132] In 1993 the Dutch legislator changed Section 3 BA-36 to cover birds resulting from cross-breeding between one or more protected species listed by administrative order.

covering hybrids by the fact that, although cross-breeds do not usually occur in nature and are mostly the consequence of a breeding process, it is difficult to distinguish between hybrids and non-hybrids.[133] This approach was intended to avoid disputes over whether a bird occurs naturally on Dutch territory.

With respect to cases of green-plating resulting from the desire to protect the internal coherence of the national legal order, we have to consider that the transposition of Union law does not occur in a vacuum.[134] National law often predates Union law, though, sometimes, national law has a more general character. For example, measures of access to justice in environmental matters are a species of the broader genus of access to justice in administrative matters. The adoption of a specific regime only applicable to measures transposing Union law on access to justice in environmental matters could lead to fragmentation of the national rules on access to justice in administrative matters. To avoid fragmentation, national legislators may decide to maintain or introduce green-plating.

Legal practice shows at least two different approaches to ensuring the internal coherence of the national legal order. Firstly, fragmentation can be avoided by means of spillovers, through which a Member State extends a regime originating in Union law to the rest of a certain sector. The application of the legal regime of the Habitats Directive to cover values other than those protected by the Directive, discussed above,[135] represents an example of this kind of green-plating. A similar example was given as regards the transposition of the Environmental Liability Directive to the United Kingdom. The United Kingdom used the option allowing the application of the regime of the Directive to national nature reserves. Green-plating was justified inter alia because having two

This amendment was enacted by Stb. 1993, 586, Section I, letter C. These provisions were implemented by Section 1 of Stb. 1994, 625. Later Section 1 of the Fauna and Flora Act replaced this regime. It indicates that the concept 'species' includes sub-species, geographical population variations and hybrids. As we can see, the field of application of the Flora and Fauna Act covers all sorts of species of flora and fauna present in nature, including hybrids. At the same time, the Fauna and Flora Act imposes a specific protection regime only for certain species. The other species are protected by means of a general duty of care.

133 Stb. 1994, 625, explanatory memorandum, p. 12. See also Proceedings of the Second Chamber of the States General, Kamerstukken II 1991/92, 22 201, nr. 5, p. 23.

134 Jans and Squintani et al. (2009), p. 426.

135 Chapter 2, section 2.2.1, above.

systems of liability for protected sites would have been inefficient and it would have led to uncertainty for operators.[136]

Another way to avoid fragmentation is to extend a rule already present in national law to the provisions transposing Union law. In 2001, for example, the Dutch transposition of the permit and state-of-the-art defences under the Environmental Liability Directives was modelled on the rules of general Dutch administrative law. Article 8(4) of the Environmental Liability Directive permits relieving operators from bearing the costs incurred to remedy environmental damage. The transposition of this provision was highly debated in the Dutch parliament. Part of the conservative faction in the Dutch parliament wanted a strict implementation of the permit and state-of-the-art defences.[137] The PvdA, the Dutch Labour Party, instead pushed to refrain from transposing these defences. The government successfully proposed a third option. Section 17.16(4) of the Environmental Management Act adds a reasonability test:[138] the State can refrain from recovering the costs of a remedial action from an operator if these costs cannot be *reasonably* imposed upon the operator. To justify this choice, the government referred to general administrative law.[139] The government made clear reference to the defences foreseen for cases where a public authority takes action in place of the infringer in order to restore legality (Section 5:25 of the Dutch General Administrative Law Act [GALA]).[140] Section 5.25 GALA states that the infringer is a debtor for the costs related to the enforcement of an administrative coercion sanction, except if he can prove that these costs cannot be reasonably attributed to him, entirely or partially.

A similar justification pattern was employed by the Dutch legislator to justify the duty to keep information in the context of waste management. Article 35(2) of the New Waste Framework Directive requires establishments or undertakings covered by a permit or registration regime to keep a chronological record of, inter alia, the quantity, nature

[136] Jans and Squintani et al. (2009), p. 426.
[137] Proceedings of the Second Chamber of the States General, Kamerstukken II 2006/07, 30 920, nr. 8 (so-called Amendment Madlener).
[138] Winter et al. (2008), pp. 178 and 179 state that Dutch law goes beyond merely meeting the minimum required by the Directive.
[139] Proceedings of the Second Chamber of the States General, Kamerstukken II 2006/07, 30 920, nr. 7, p. 8. Under civil law, the fulfilment of the requirements of a permit does not exclude liability; see Bergkamp (2005a), p. 392.
[140] In the Dutch legal order, this public authority power is seen as an administrative sanction called administrative coercion (*bestuursdwang*). On this sanction see Damen et al. (2009), pp. 653 ff.

and origin of the waste, and they have to make that information available, on request, to the competent authorities. For hazardous waste, the records must be preserved for at least three years. Member States can require the producers of non-hazardous waste to comply with paragraphs 1 and 2. The Netherlands uses this option, at least to some extent. With respect to the possibility of applying a registration duty upon waste producers, Article 10.38 of the Environmental Management Act requires any person discarding industrial waste or hazardous waste, including the producer of the waste, to keep a record of certain information concerning the waste. Information must be kept for at least five years. As we can see, the Netherlands uses the option indicated in the Directive. Members of Parliament pointed this out to the government,[141] which replied that the requirement may go further than what is required by the Directive, but it is in line with similar duties in other fields of Dutch administrative law.[142]

Another form of unavoidable green-plating stems from the need to fully comply with international obligations, other than those deriving from the European Union. For example, the use of a positive rather than a negative list of animal hunting means and methods in the Netherlands serves to fulfil obligations deriving from the Benelux Agreements of 1970 and 1984.[143] In 1977, the Agreement was enlarged also to cover the regulation of certain methods of hunting.[144] Under Decisions M(83) 27,[145] M(96) 8[146] and M(98) 4,[147] implementing the provisions of the Agreement, hunting is allowed only by listed means and methods. In other words, Benelux countries must establish a *positive* list of hunting means and methods. A connection with the need to fulfil international obligations was also present in the context of ambient air quality. The

141 Proceedings of the Second Chamber of the States General, Kamerstukken II 2009/10, 32 392, nr. 6, p. 5.

142 Proceedings of the Second Chamber of the States General, Kamerstukken II 2009/10, 32 392, nr. 7, p. 2, with reference to provisions such as Article 5.8 of the Environmental Permits Order, *Besluit omgevingsrecht* Stb. 2010, 143, as amended by Article II, letter J, punt 11 Stb. 2010, 781.

143 Article 3.21 of the Nature Protection Act. See also Title 3.3 of the Nature Protection Order, *Besluit natuurbescherming* Stb. 2016, 383. For the Benelux Agreement see 847 UNTS 255.

144 1317 UNTS 320.

145 Trb. 1997, 252.

146 Ibidem.

147 Trb. 2002, 11.

Dutch government used an international obligation to justify establishing more assessment stations for lead than required by Union law.[148]

### d) Economic Considerations

Despite the generalised idea that stricter environmental standards are negative for economic development, green-plating can also be justified in light of economic considerations. Indeed, legal practice shows different justifications linked to economic considerations to maintain or introduce green-plating. For example, green-plating was justified in the Netherlands by the need of establishing and preserving a level playing field on the national market. This rationale was used by the Dutch legislator to justify the application of best available techniques (BAT) specified in BREF documents to non-IPPC installations. Another example of an economic justification for green-plating is that of lowering administrative burdens. This was the case as regards the proposed Dutch transposition of Article 7 of the Industrial Emissions Directive, on accidents and incidents, and Article 8 of the same Directive, on non-compliance. These cases and other ones are fully analysed in Chapter 4, Section 4.2.2.

## 2.3 National No-Gold-Plating Policies' Influence on Green-Plating

In Chapter 1, I discussed the development of no-gold-plating policies in several Member States. There, I concluded that the most advanced policies exist in the United Kingdom and the Netherlands. The comparison performed in Chapter 1 about these two no-gold-plating policies revealed several similarities, but also some differences. Most notably, the United Kingdom applies cost/benefit analyses to assess the possibility of green-plating, while the Netherlands does not do so. Moreover, the Netherlands seems to have a slightly more stringent formulation of its policy, at least under the third phase of development of such a policy under which any case of green-plating should have been avoided or eliminated in all cases, than the United Kingdom does. In the Netherlands the room for allowing green-plating seems, on paper, more restricted than in the United Kingdom. In this section, I show how the Dutch policy has been applied in practice so far.

The influence of such policy can be seen in basically all fields of environmental law. Since 2005, Dutch environmental law has been

[148] Stcrt. 2001, nr. 135, explanatory memorandum, p. 4.

systematically reformed so as to remove green-plating. Yet differences emerge among the various fields of environmental law taken into consideration in my Ph.D. Probably in response to the many articles published in specialised and popular papers, the Dutch no-gold-plating policy has been applied quite strictly in the field of nature conservation, in which today the implementation is almost one-on-one. This result was reached by a series of reforms.[149] For example, initially, the specific prohibitions in the Flora and Fauna Act diverged from the Birds Directive in many ways. Section 9 of the Flora and Fauna Act prohibited deliberate and non-deliberate actions and it prohibited injuring or tracking down birds. Section 10 prohibited disturbing birds, regardless of whether this affected the conservation status of the species. Section 11 prohibited disturbing nests, holes, resting places, places of residence and places of reproduction, even when the disturbance was not intentional. Section 12 prohibited searching for the eggs of protected birds. Finally, Section 13 prohibited keeping bird nests. A quick comparison with Article 5 of the Birds Directive shows that Sections 9–13 of the Flora and Fauna Act were stricter than required by the Directive. After several stakeholders started complaining that the law was too stringent, the government stated that it was possible to reduce the impact of the prohibitions that do not originate in the Birds Directive and the Habitats Directive by extending the power to derogate from the various prohibitions.[150] In 2004, the government enlarged the grounds for establishing exceptions and granting exemptions.[151] For example, activities disturbing birds could have been exempted from Article 10 of the Flora and Fauna Act if the disturbance did not significantly affect the species concerned.[152] The Nature Protection Act 2016 eliminates all these cases of stricter national standards.[153]

A similar pattern can be recognised in the context of habitats protection. When we compare the Nature Conservation Act 1998 as amended in 2005 with the Habitats Directive, we notice some differences. First, Dutch law applied the legal framework of Article 6(3) of the Habitats Directive to all activities and not only to projects and plans. In addition, Dutch law applied *regardless* of whether a project or activity significantly

[149] Squintani and Zijlmans (2013).
[150] Stb. 2004. 501, explanatory memorandum, pp. 15 and 16.
[151] Stb. 2000, 525, later amended by Stb. 2004, 501 and Stb. 2007, 253.
[152] Stb. 2000, 525, as amended by Stb. 2004, 501.
[153] Wet van 16 december 2015, houdende regels ter bescherming van de natuur (Wet natuurbescherming), Stb. 2016, 34, Section 3.1.

disturbed the species present in the protected area. Besides, the concept of 'conservation value' used in Sections 19d-19j of the Nature Conservation Act 1998 included cultural and ecological characteristics of the protected area that are not covered by the Directives. Further, national nature reserves, which were areas not falling under the legal regimes of the Directives, were still legally protected.[154] When the legal regime of the Nature Conservation Act 1998 as reformed in 2005 provoked criticism from civil society,[155] the government responded to these complaints by means of a reform in 2009.[156] This reform redressed the cases of green-plating mentioned above. First, it added the adjective 'significant' to Section 19d of the Nature Conservation Act 1998. As a consequence, activities not significantly affecting the achievement of the conservation values protected in a Natura 2000 area were assessed but no longer subjected to a permit requirement.[157] Moreover, the term 'other activities' was deleted from Sections 19f–19h and 19k. Hence, only projects and plans were covered by these provisions. In both cases, the government explained that these reforms aimed to follow the Directive more closely.[158] In general, the government stated that the reform sought to eliminate cases where Dutch law went further than required in order to meet the concerns of industry, agriculture and other sectors of Dutch civil society.[159] In 2010, a further reform was passed to fight the economic crisis.[160] This reform changed Article 19d of the Nature Conservation Act 1998 in such a way that it did not now apply anymore to human activities affecting other values than those prescribed by the Birds Directive and the Habitats Directive. This means, inter alia, that the protection of Article 19g of the Nature Conservation Act 1998 enshrining the precautionary principle did not cover damage to other values than those regulated under the Birds Directive and the

[154] Squintani and Zijlmans (2013).
[155] Proceedings of the Second Chamber of the States General, Kamerstukken II 2006/07, 31 038, nr. 3, p. 1.
[156] Stb. 2009, 18.
[157] Proceedings of the Second Chamber of the States General, Kamerstukken II 2006/07, 31 038, nr. 3, p. 14.
[158] Idem, pp. 13–15.
[159] Idem, p. 1.
[160] Stb. 2010, 135. It should be noted that this Act regulates certain projects and it has temporary effect. However, as regards nature conservation, it applies to all projects and it has definitive effect, see Proceedings of the Second Chamber of the States General, Kamerstukken II 2009/10, 32 127, nr.3, p. 4.

Habitats Directive.[161] Consequently, one of the instances of green-plating indicated above was removed. The government explained that this deletion was performed because the Habitats Directive does not require its regime to be applied to values other than those covered by the Directive.[162] Further, it was explicitly indicated that the existence of this case of green-plating caused practical problems. The government concluded that although these values were still important, the regime established for nature reserves lacking a Community interest was sufficient to guarantee their protection.[163] In 2017, even this legal regime was eliminated by the Nature Protection Act.[164]

The application of the Dutch no-gold-plating policy seems to occur in a rather dogmatic manner. In none of the cases in which stricter national standards were eliminated in the field of nature conservation were costs/benefits analyses performed. Also in the field covered by the Environmental Liability Directive, as regards the possibility to extend the field of application of the strict liability regime of the Environmental Liability Directive to other operators than those listed under Annex III to the Directive, Section 17.7 of the Environmental Management Act transposes Article 3 of the Environmental Liability Directive by means of a dynamic reference to the Directive. Strict liability is applied to the activities listed in Annex III to the Directive. Besides, Section 17.7(a), subparagraph 2, of the Environmental Management Act permits orders specifying other operators subject to other strict liability regimes. This provision was at the heart of parliamentary debate for almost a year. The original government proposal did not include such a provision because of the policy restricting gold-plating.[165] The government even rejected the opinion of the Council of State that other activities should also be covered.[166] However, a member of the Dutch Labour Party proposed adding this provision also to cover the activities listed in the Industrial Activities

[161] Backes, Poortinga & Woldendorp, (2010), p. 35.

[162] Proceedings of the Second Chamber of the States General, Kamerstukken II 2009/10, 32 127, nr. 3, p. 73.

[163] Idem, p. 74.

[164] Stb. 2016, 34. Article 2.11 of the Act makes it possible to designate and protect national nature reserves, but this possibility has not been used yet.

[165] Proceedings of the Second Chamber of the States General, Kamerstukken II 2006/07, 30 920, nr. 2, proposed Article 17.7 and Proceedings of the Second Chamber of the States General, Kamerstukken II 2006/07, 30 92,0 nr. 3, p. 4.

[166] Proceedings of the Second Chamber of the States General, Kamerstukken II 2006/07, 30 920, nr. 4, pp. 5 and 7. The Council of State did not provide many arguments to support its position.

Order.[167] The amendment, which implied an extension of the field of application of Title 17.2 of the Environmental Management Act, aimed at fulfilling the polluter pays principle. According to the Dutch Labour Party, limiting the strict liability regime to Annex III activities was unjustifiable since, in the past, other activities proved capable of causing environmental damage.[168] Initially, the government followed the position of the Labour Party. In addition to environmental concerns, the government argued for the insertion of this provision on grounds of equality.[169] However, following criticism within the Dutch Senate,[170] the government proposed the compromise that can be seen in Section 17.7(a), subparagraph 2, of the Environmental Management Act.[171] Activities other than those listed under Annex III to the Directive can be covered by the liability regime of Title 17.2 of the Environmental Management Act if this is established in a governmental order. In other words, Article 17.7 only offers the option of extending the field of application of Title 17.2 of the Environmental Management Act, but it does not actually require its extension.[172] Such an order has not been adopted yet. As we can see, despite the advice of the Dutch Council of State and the explicit request stemming from the lower chamber of the Dutch parliament, stricter standards were avoided by means of simple reference to the Dutch no-gold-plating policy made by a member of the Dutch Senate.

The above does not mean that green-plating does not exist in the Netherlands. Actually, even in the third phase of development of the Dutch no-gold-plating policy, under which any case of green-plating should have been avoided or eliminated in all cases, new cases of national measures going beyond EU requirements were introduced. For example, in Section 2.2.3 I mentioned that during the transposition of the New

[167] Proceedings of the Second Chamber of the States General, Kamerstukken II 2006/07, 30 920, nr. 12. The amendment used the formula 'to be indicated by governmental order'. Approximately 218,000 activities were regulated at that time under the Industrial Activities Order. There are approximately 2,500 IPPC installations.

[168] Proceedings of the Second Chamber of the States General, Kamerstukken II 2006/07, 30 920, nr. 13, p. 1.

[169] Minister Cramer used the expression 'sauce for the goose is sauce for the gander', TK 2006/07, 30 920, HAN8159A08.

[170] Proceedings of the First Chamber of the States General, Kamerstukken I 2007/08, 30920, B, pp. 2 and 3.

[171] The government was anxious to avoid time consuming discussions, TK 2006/07, 30 920, HAN8159A08.

[172] Proceedings of the Second Chamber of the States General, Kamerstukken II 2006/07, 30 920, nr. 19.

Waste Framework Directive, the field of application of the provisions on waste prevention and recovery was extended. This strengthening occurred exactly during the third phase of development of the Dutch no-gold-plating policy. Similarly, the enlargement of the responsibility of operators of IPPC installations in case of accidents or incidents, discussed above, was proposed under the third phase of development of the Dutch no-gold-plating policy. It seems that environmental concerns, legal certainty, economic considerations and inadvertent decisions with unforeseen consequences can all lead to green-plating, despite the presence of the Dutch policies constraining it.

## 2.4 Green-Plating and the Development of EU Environmental Law

Clauses in secondary law based on Article 192 TFEU showing the room for green-plating do not fall from the sky. They derive from the compromises reached between EU institutions and Member States during the decision-making process. In this section, I first provide an account of the tendencies towards environmental protection in the three main EU institutions involved in the legislative process (Section 2.4.1). This includes an analysis of how national law is uploaded into EU environmental law. Then, I show how green-plating contributed to the development of the Industrial Emission Directive, the Waste Framework Directive and the Air Quality Directive (Section 2.4.2).

### *2.4.1 Green and Non-Green Actors and the Upload of Green National Standards*

Political scientists have been analysing the positions taken by the Union institutions towards environmental protection for years. The *Commission* has a specific role: that of principal initiator of Union environmental provisions. As stated by Lenschow, the Commission balances its role as 'motor of integration' with the need to be responsive to the requests of the Member States.[173] In the 1970s and 1980s, a balance was achieved by using policy programmes which went further than the status quo in the Member States to gain a supranational role in proposing legislation. On the other hand, the Commission also took on board the requests of *green* Member States that wished to raise their national standards to the

[173] Lenschow (2010), p. 313.

supranational level to avoid competitive disadvantages.[174] The Commission itself is sensitive to frontrunners in environmental matters, to avoid distortion of the European internal market.[175] For example, Lee notes that Directive 94/62/EC on packaging waste was the Union's response to national schemes, in particular those in Germany and France.[176]

The latter aspect is strengthened by the fact that the Commission has a limited staff which relies on the expertise of national experts working for the environmental ministries in the various Member States to develop its proposals.[177] From 1993, the Commission considered the Member States as partners in the environmental policymaking scene.[178] Today, the Commission's tendency to design environmental policy jointly with the Member States seems to be reinforced by the need to ensure its smooth implementation.[179]

The *European Parliament* has had a positive attitude towards environmental protection since the 1970s. Traditionally, it is described as the greenest institution.[180] However, as indicated by Lenschow, it is not clear whether the acquisition of a co-legislative power has affected the 'pro-environment' attitude of the European Parliament.[181] Legislative competence means accountability and this could lead to milder positions on environmental protection.[182] Furthermore, the working relationships with the other institutions, and the political representation of the European Green Party, which in 2004 dropped to 5% after the enlargements of the Union, can moderate the European Parliament's positions towards environmental protection.[183] In addition, the personality of the chairman of the Committee on the Environment, Public Health and Food Safety (ENVI) and intra-committee discussions can influence the

[174] Ibidem.

[175] Börzel (2002), p. 200.

[176] Lee (2005), pp. 215 and 216.

[177] Lenschow (2010), p. 313.

[178] Ibidem with reference to Commission, Towards Sustainability: A European Community Programme of Policy and Action in Relation to the Environment and Sustainable Development, Office for Official Publications of the European Communities, 1993, pp. 113–116.

[179] Lenschow (2010), p. 313.

[180] Idem, p. 315.

[181] Idem, p. 316.

[182] Ibidem with reference to Holzinger, K., *Politik des kleinsten gemeinsamen Nenners? Umweltpolitische Entscheidungsprozesse in der EG am Beispiel des Katalysatorautos*, Edition Sigma, 1994.

[183] Rasmussen (2007) as interpreted by Lenschow (2010), p. 316.

positions expressed by ENVI and thus moderate the attitude of the European Parliament as a whole.[184]

As distinct from the European Parliament, the *Council* has never been considered a 'green institution'. Although it is considered as a Union institution, its composition clearly indicates that it is made up of national actors, namely a representative from each Member State at ministerial level, authorised to commit the government of that Member State.[185] Representatives of national governments put forward national interests, making the Council a forum for negotiation.[186] As indicated in 2002 by Börzel, some Member States act as *pace-setters* in the environmental field within the Council.[187] Pace-setters are Member States actively pushing – or 'uploading' – their *green* national policies at the Union level.[188] For example, Andersen & Liefferink note that Denmark uploaded its national plan for aquatic environment into the urban and waste water and nitrate directives.[189] Similarly, Axelrod & Vig point out that the Netherlands uploaded its standards for small car and truck emissions.[190] It should be noted that Member States wishing to upload their environmental policies also try to influence the Commission's initial proposal.[191] For example, Emmott reports that the United Kingdom seconded an official from the Department of the Environment to DG XI of the Commission to 'kick-start' the drafting of the IPPC Directive.[192]

A particular kind of pace-setter is called a *forerunner*. Forerunners undertake unilateral actions without waiting for European cooperation. A particular kind of forerunner is the so-called *pusher-by-example*, such

[184] Lenschow (2010), pp. 316–317. Especially in the period 2004–2009, ENVI seemed to have distanced itself from its previously strong proactive role.

[185] Article 16 TEU. A representative of the Commission also participates.

[186] Takács (2009), p. 74.

[187] Börzel (2002), pp. 193–214.

[188] Idem, p. 197 indicates that, in the pre-2004 enlargement phase, this group included Austria, Denmark, Finland, Germany, the Netherlands and Sweden. Jordan (2001) explained that, since the 1990s, the United Kingdom has also been pushing environmental legislation, albeit on a case-by-case basis. Lieferrink & Andersen (1998a), p. 71 note that Denmark, Germany and the Netherlands were renowned as the 'green troika'. In 2010 Lenschow (2010), p. 314 still describes countries such as Germany, the Netherlands and Denmark as leaders in the context of environmental protection within the Council.

[189] Börzel (2002), p. 199 and Andersen and Liefferink (1997), p. 14.

[190] Börzel (2002), p. 199 and Axelrod & Vig (1998).

[191] Sbragia (2000), p. 298.

[192] Emmott (1999), p. 28.

as Sweden, which not only takes unilateral actions before the Union, but also lobbies the Union to take the same measures.[193] Distinct from forerunners, the so-called *pushers* only argue for higher environmental standards at Union level, while applying the minimum level at their own national level and waiting for Union action.[194] For example, Articles 5(4) and 6(3) of the Environmental Liability Directive state that competent authorities *may* take preventive and reparatory measures themselves, if an operator fails to comply with its obligations, cannot be identified or is not required to bear the costs under the Directive, a so-called subsidiary State liability. The provisions on subsidiary State liability were compulsory in the original Commission proposal.[195] In the Council, Belgium, Greece, *the Netherlands* and Spain argued for a system obliging the competent authority to take measures itself or to ensure that such measures were taken, limiting the Member States' freedom to choose between two obligations.[196] However, the United Kingdom, France, Italy, Portugal and Germany preferred a voluntary system.[197] The Rapporteur for the European Parliament explicitly stated that a voluntary subsidiary State responsibility could have endangered the effectiveness of the Environmental Liability Directive.[198] Nonetheless, the European Parliament did not uphold the Rapporteur's recommendation on this point and hence accepted the position of the Council. In conclusion, in order to lower the burdens on the Member States,[199] the subsidiary State liability is only optional. This option has not been implemented by the Dutch legislator. The government stated that it decided not to use the option provided by the Directive to avoid imposing excessive economic burdens on competent authorities.[200] Authorities have to fulfil other public functions in addition to that of protecting the environment.

193 Liefferink & Andersen (1998a) and (1998b); see also Andersen & Liefferink (1997).

194 Liefferink & Andersen (1998a) and (1998b) referring to Germany and the Netherlands.

195 COM(2002) 17 final, proposed Articles 4(4) and 5(2).

196 Council of the European Union, Institutional File 2002/0021 (COD), nr. 7771/02, p. 10, footnote 38 and p. 11, footnote 39 and nr. 9600/02, pp. 7–10.

197 Council of the European Union, Institutional File 2002/0021 (COD), nr. 14289/02, note 54.

198 European Parliament A5–0461/2003 Recommendation for Second Reading, Amendment 11 juncto 28. See also Krämer (2005a), p. 132.

199 COM(2002) 17 final, p. 29. Krämer (2005b), p. 83 notes that Member States considered an obligatory 'safety net' too burdensome.

200 Proceedings of the Second Chamber of the States General, Kamerstukken II 2006/07, 30 920, nr. 3, p. 19.

The pro-environment attitude of pace-setters is opposed by so-called *foot-draggers*.[201] Foot-draggers are those Member States that try to block or delay Union policies from entering into force or obtain compensation for their implementation. For example, Börzel notes that southern Member States opposed the Large Combustion (Plants) Directive and gained the option of not applying certain aspects of it.[202]

Finally, some Member States act as *fence-sitters*. They build tactical coalitions with pace-setters or foot-draggers on a case-by-case basis. This group was, at least in 2002, formed by Belgium, France, Ireland, Italy, Luxembourg and, to certain extent, the United Kingdom.[203] Their attitude is explained in terms of economic incentives – only in certain cases will their national industries benefit from strong European environmental standards – and an inability to systematically upload their points of view.[204] Clashes between pace-setters and foot-draggers can lead to compromises which, in turn, can lead to space for green-plating.

### *2.4.2 The Recast Process as Means for Green-Plating to Shape the Development of EU Environmental Law*

Many EU measures based on Article 192 TFEU have been recast, replaced or amended over time. In some fields, such as air quality law and waste management, amendments and renegotiation rounds have occurred more than once. At any such moment, Member States have another chance to upload their national standards. This means that what was green-plating can become the minimum EU high level of protection later. A close look at the development of waste management law, air quality law and the regulation of industrial emissions shows how cases of green-plating under the original directives were transformed in the minimum EU high level of protection by the recasting, replacing or amending of directives.

For example, in the 1980s, the Dutch government established stricter limit values for lead than those required under Directive 82/884/EEC

[201] In 2002 Börzel listed Portugal, Greece and Spain as foot-draggers to which, for a certain period, she added Ireland, Italy and the United Kingdom. Lenschow (2010), p. 314 points out that the central and eastern European countries which accessed in 2004 and 2007 do not seem to form a systematic anti-environment block. However, there are cases where they fought together to gain benefits in exchange for passing environmental legislation.

[202] Börzel (2002), p. 205.

[203] Idem, p. 206.

[204] Idem, p. 207.

on lead.[205] When it was transposed into the Dutch legal order, the limit value for lead was more stringent than required. The legislator explained that a stricter limit value was necessary because the health of children is affected more than that of adults and the Directive did not take the health of children sufficiently into consideration.[206] With the First Daughter Directive, the minimum EU high level of protection became the same as the Dutch standard.[207]

Similarly, in the context of waste management, Dutch law in the 1990s introduced a unified system requiring the best available techniques from all installations, including waste management installations. The most important characteristic of the permit regime regulated under Chapter 8 of the Environmental Management Act previously and the General Act on Environmental Permits today is that establishments disposing of or recovering waste must employ the best available techniques.[208] Only with the introduction of the IPPC Directive first, and the Industrial Emissions Directive later, did the application of the best available techniques to installations for waste disposal under the Waste Framework Directive become the minimum EU high level of protection.[209] Today the New Waste Framework Directive clearly mandates the taking into

[205] Council Directive 82/884/EEC of 3 December 1982 on a limit value for lead in the air, [1982] OJ L 378/15. For the Dutch implementing act, Stb. 1987, 34. Instead of a maximum of 2 microgram/m$^3$ as yearly average (Article 2(2) Directive), Article 3 of the order sets a maximum of 0.5 microgram/m$^3$.

[206] Stb. 1987, 34, explanatory memorandum, p. 13. The legislator based this statement on several studies performed around the world until that time and in particular on the WHO's Guideline of 1987, World Health Organization, *Air Quality Guidelines for Europe. WHO Regional Publications, European Series No. 23* (1987) Copenhagen.

[207] Article 6 of and Annex IV to Council Directive 1999/30/EC of 22 April 1999 relating to limit values for sulphur dioxide, nitrogen dioxide and oxides of nitrogen, particulate matter and lead in ambient air, [1999] OJ L 163/41.

[208] Section 8.13 of the Environmental Management Act, today Section 2.14(1)(c) of the General Act on Environmental Permits.

[209] Council Directive 96/61/EC of 24 September 1996 concerning integrated pollution prevention and control, [1996] OJ L 257/26, later codified by Directive 2008/1/EC of the European Parliament and of the Council of 15 January 2008 concerning integrated pollution prevention and control (Codified version), [2008] OJ L 24/8, and now recast by Directive 2010/75/EU of the European Parliament and of the Council of 24 November 2010 on industrial emissions (integrated pollution prevention and control), [2010] OJ L334/17. The Industrial Emissions Directive has extended this duty to a greater number of installations for the disposal or recovery of waste, Annex I, paragraph 5 of the Industrial Emissions Directive. However, even the Industrial Emissions Directive does not cover all installations for the disposal or recovery of waste covered by Dutch law. Dutch law still goes further than required.

account of best available techniques for waste management installations covered by the permit regime of the New Waste Framework Directive.[210]

This example is strictly linked to the manner in which the legal value of BREF documents has developed over time. As discussed above,[211] the Netherlands recognised binding force to best available techniques indicated under BREF documents since the very beginning, despite the fact that under the IPPC Directive, their binding force was denied even by the Court of Justice.[212] Today, the Industrial Emissions Directive clearly establishes that best available techniques, indicated under the executive part of BREF documents, as soon as they are published in a Commission decision,[213] constitute the minimum EU high level of protection.

It would be counter-intuitive to consider these examples just coincidences. As showed in the previous section, over time Member States have continuously tried to upload their national standards into EU environmental law either directly, during the negotiations taking place within the Council, or indirectly by means of lobby towards the Commission. Even when the strengthening of EU environmental standards followed a request of the EU Parliament, such as in the case of the introduction of binding targets for the recovery of certain streams of waste from households,[214] it cannot be discounted that existing cases of green-plating did play a role, at least in the form of a source of inspiration. Therefore, considering national measures as a mere source of administrative burdens means misconceiving reality.[215]

Actually, negative experiences with green-plating can serve to reduce regulatory burdens coming from unclear Union provisions. I mentioned above that the uncertainty existing under the Air Framework Directive and its First Daughter Directive as regards where to assess air quality. The

[210] Article 27 of the New Waste Framework Directive.

[211] Chapter 2, Section 2.2.2.

[212] Case C-473/07, *Association nationale pour la protection des eaux et rivières-TOS en Association OABA tegen Ministère de l'Ecologie, du Développement et de l'Aménagement durables*, [2009] ECR I-319.

[213] Article 13(5) in conjunction with Articles 14(3) and 15(3) of the Industrial Emissions Directive.

[214] European Parliament legislative resolution on the proposal for a directive of the European Parliament and of the Council on waste (COM(2005) 0667 – C6–0009/2006 – 2005/0281(COD) ), Codecision procedure: first reading, Article 8, and the indirect reference to the position of the European Parliament in second reading, available in COM(2008) 559 final. For the rejection of such binding targets in the past, Van Calster (2000), p. 170, and Amended Commission proposal, OJ 1989 C 326/6.

[215] Similarly, Anker et al. (2015).

Netherlands interpreted and thus implemented the Directive in such a manner that the regulatory regime became too cumbersome for Dutch society. Reforms at national level seemed impossible under the regime of the Air Framework Directive, due to negative opinions of both the Council of State and the European Commission.[216] Changes had to take place at EU level first. Today, Annex III to the Air Quality Directive clarifies that compliance with the limit values shall not be assessed at locations in which, basically speaking, human beings are not exposed to air pollution. Such a clarification followed the advice of an expert group, the so-called CAFE group, working on the review of the First Daughter Directive.[217] Moreover, within the Council, the Netherlands, along with other delegations including Germany, France and the United Kingdom, pushed for linking the assessment of the limit values to the concept of exposure.[218] As we can see, the negative experience gained by the Netherlands under the Air Framework Directive due to the unclear formulation of the provisions of the Directive played a role in the reshaping of EU air quality law.

The examples discussed in this section clearly show the manner in which the system of environmental protection envisaged under the Treaties works. When Member States retain the main responsibility for environmental protection and make use of the power to adopt green-plating, national experiences are built, which can then be uploaded at EU level during (re)negotiation procedures so as to set a minimum standard for the whole Union or to correct imbalances in existing EU systems. Green-plating thus plays a central role in the development of EU environmental law, something which policies on gold-plating, and to a certain extent also scholarly writing, tend to forget.

## 2.5 Conclusions: Environmental Protection in the European Union as a Chain Made of Union and National Standards, Including Green-Plating

In this chapter, I showed that green-plating is not a chimera. Actually, I would be surprised to read that, as regards a specific EU environmental

[216] Proceedings of the Second Chamber of the States General, Kamerstukken II 1991/92, 22486, 3, p. 2. Proceedings of the Second Chamber of the States General, Kamerstukken II 2004/05 29 667, nr. 12 and Proceedings of the Second Chamber of the States General, Kamerstukken II 2005/06 30 489, nr. 3, p. 11.

[217] CAFE working group on implementation, recommendation on the review of Council Directive 1999/30/EC, June 2004, p. 8.

[218] Council of the European Union, Interinstitutional File 2005/0183, doc. numb. 8494/06.

measure based on Article 192 TFEU, no Member State adopted a single provision going further than required. Green-plating is a real-life phenomenon which, at least until the 2010s, occurred much more systematically and widely than at times argued in the literature. This phenomenon impacts the development of EU environmental law. It served, and can still serve, as a stepping stone for increasing the minimum EU high level of protection of the environment, through the recasting, replacement or amendment of EU measures based on Article 192 TFEU. Accordingly, I argue that environmental protection in the European Union should be seen as a chain made of Union and national standards, including stricter standards, which integrate with one another over time. The refinement of the EU high level of protection does not only benefit the environment, but it can also serve to identify and eliminate the negative effects that unclear EU provisions can have on society.

This means that, as anticipated in Chapter 1, the demonisation of green-plating taking place at national and EU level is completely misplaced. I do not argue here that stricter national standards never affect economic development, an argument further discussed in Chapter 4. My point is that green-plating also has positive features and it plays a central role, under the system envisaged by the Treaties, for the protection of the environment. I therefore agree with those authors that concluded that a 'no-gold-plating' principle makes little sense as a dominating transposition principle in environmental legislation,[219] and that the decision not to adopt national environmental legislation going beyond the relevant EU measure frustrates the functioning of Article 5 TEU and of Article 193 TFEU.[220] I agree also with those authors that consider that 'the absence of gold-plating can reverse the whole system of environmental protection under [the Treaties]'.[221] In particular, national policies on green-plating can deprive the European Union of a source of development of its legislation in the field of the environment.

It should be clear that I am not arguing that green-plating must be pursued. Green-plating is not an obligation. Besides, the presence of no-gold-plating policies are not a negative development per se. There can be cases of stricter national standards with little added value from the perspective of environmental protection, but clear negative effects for economic development. No-gold-plating policies can improve the quality

[219] Anker et al. (2015).
[220] Krämer (2011), p. 440.
[221] Jans, Squintani et al. (2009), p. 435.

of the debate on green-plating and help revert those cases in which the costs of stricter standards are higher than the benefits. It is the blind application of a policy to avoid green-plating, such as it seems to have occurred in certain cases in the Netherlands, which should be deplored. By assuming that green-plating is bad, the discussion on stricter standards is polarised in the Netherlands. As a result, green-plating was in many cases rejected, without an objective evaluation of its costs and benefits. This deprives Union institutions of a source of information that facilitates the development of Union environmental measures.

In contrast, an application of no-gold-plating policies based on transparent cost/benefit analyses, such as in the United Kingdom at least to a certain extent,[222] does not prevent useful data from emerging. This proceduralisation of the decision about whether to maintain or introduce green-plating surely represents a better manner to sincerely cooperate with Union institutions than the one seen in the Netherlands.[223] Accordingly, in Chapter 4, I will further discuss how costs/benefits analysis should take form in the context of the discussion on green-plating. In the conclusions to this book, I will analyse the role that law can play in the context of this proceduralisation.

[222] Chapter 1, Section 1.2.1. See also Chapter 4, Section 4.4, in which I also show the shortcomings of such instruments.

[223] This reasoning can be placed within the realm of the so-called proceduralisation doctrine, see in particular Lee (2005), pp. 163–180.

# 3 Green-Plating and Legal Certainty

## 3.1 Introductory Remarks

I concluded the previous chapter by stating that environmental protection in the European Union should be seen as a chain made of Union and national standards, including stricter standards, which integrate with one another over time. The refinement of the EU high level of protection of the environment does not only benefit the environment, but it can also serve to identify and eliminate the negative effects that unclear EU provisions can have on society. This last sentence implies that there is a link between green-plating and legal certainty. Chapter 2 focused on the link between green-plating and legal certainty from two perspectives. First, legal certainty can be used to justify maintaining or introducing green-plating.[1] Second, green-plating can serve to improve the clarity of EU provisions.[2]

In this chapter, the linkage between green-plating and legal certainty is looked at from the perspective of the principle of sincere cooperation under Article 4(3) TEU. More precisely, I focus on the relationship between green-plating and legal certainty from the perspective of the duty of the EU legislator and judiciary to respect the Member States, established under the first sentence of Article 4(3) TEU. As introduced in Chapter 1,[3] Article 193 TFEU is addressed to the EU legislator. The EU legislator shall refrain from restricting the adoption of more stringent protective measures. Minimum clauses in secondary law are a means by which the EU legislator fulfils this obligation. In light of the first sentence of Article 4(3) TEU, the EU legislative and judiciary powers shall

[1] Chapter 2, Section 2.2.3.
[2] Chapter, 2, Section 2.4.2.
[3] Chapter 1, Section 1.3.

ensure, among others, legal certainty about the possibility of introducing or maintaining national measures going beyond EU requirements. This is especially important as regards the review of the legality of more stringent protective measures. Under the second sentence of Article 193 TFEU, Member States must comply with the Treaties when establishing more stringent protective measures. This is not an easy task, as discussed below. The EU legislature and the EU judiciary must endeavour to provide as much clarity as possible as regards what national measures can qualify as more stringent protective measures and whether they will withstand the legality review performed by the Court of Justice. Only then can the EU argue to cooperate with true sincerity with the Member States.

This chapter argues that minimum clauses can provide guidance to the Member States as regards both issues. Yet, for this to be the case in practice, legislative and judicial practice must be more streamlined. In order to sustain this argument, Section 3.2 provides an analysis of the manner in which the Court of Justice reviews the legality of green-plating. This analysis shows the randomness of the Court of Justice's jurisprudence on this point. This means that Member States can hardly predict whether their stricter standards will withstand judicial scrutiny by the Court of Justice. Further, Section 3.3 provides an overview of the various clauses used by the EU legislature indicating the room for green-plating. Also in this case, no clear *modus operandi* can be established. Accordingly, I postulate that the EU legislature and judiciary do not do their best to enhance legal certainty regarding green-plating.

Empirical data show that such uncertainty can affect the adoption of green-plating. At times, Member States refrain from establishing standards going beyond EU requirements, not because they do not want to, but because they are afraid that the Court of Justice will consider their standards to be in breach of the Treaties. In light of the importance of green-plating for the development of EU environmental law, as concluded in Chapter 2, such a finding is not only at odds with the principle of sincere cooperation. It is also in tension with the high level of protection principle under Article 191 TFEU.

In order to improve the ongoing practice, Section 3.4 juxtaposes the various kinds of minimum clauses in EU environmental law with the various elements of the legality review performed by the Court of Justice. This exercise allows me to build a model by which legislative practice is linked to that of the judiciary. Under this model, the level of clarity by which clauses in secondary law indicate the room for green-plating is linked to the stringency of the legality review performed by the Court of Justice. If applied consistently, the model developed in this chapter into legislative and judicial practice contributes to the fulfilment by the EU legislative and judiciary powers of their obligation to cooperate sincerely with the Member States, fostering in turn the functioning of the EU system on environmental protection.

## 3.2 The Court of Justice's Legality Review of Green-Plating

The second sentence of Article 193 TFEU states that 'more stringent protective measures must be *compatible* with the Treaties'. Besides, Article 193 TFEU concludes by requiring that the Commission shall be notified of 'more stringent protective measures'. These two clauses concern the legality of green-plating in the form of more stringent protective measures. The requirement of being compatible with the Treaties, however, applies as regards all measures falling within the scope of EU law. Besides, certain national measures, regardless of whether they are more stringent protective measures or cases of spillovers and related measures, must be notified to the Commission before they can enter into force. Accordingly, in this section the various categories of cases of green-plating are dealt with in a unitary manner. What is stated as regards measures falling under Article 193 TFEU can be applied mutatis mutandis to cases of green-plating falling outside such a provision. First, in Section 3.2.1, the theory concerning the review of legality of green-plating is exposed. Section 3.2.2 focuses on the manner in which the proportionality principle is applied in practice. Three categories of green-plating are analysed under this section: a) positive lists, i.e. national requirements restricting human activities not explicitly mentioned in a document adopted under public law; b) national bans and c) other kinds of national measures. By looking at the first two categories of measures separately, some trends can be recognised. Yet, these trends are full of contradictions and questions left open. Besides, when all these trends are taken into consideration together, it becomes clear that Member States are left without clear guidance on how the Court of Justice reviews the legality of green-plating.

A better picture appears in Section 3.2.4, analysing the case law of the Court of Justice concerning the notification requirement. As a general rule, this requirement indeed does not have the force of invalidating a case of green-plating that has not been notified to the Commission. On the contrary, cases of green-plating in the form of technical standards fall under the notification duty established by Directive 2015/1535/EU.[4] Failure to notify the Commission of the national measure leads to its inapplicability.

Despite better predictability concerning the manner in which the Court of Justice reviews the notification duty, the overall picture remains negative. In Section 3.2.3, I show that this lack of clear guidance limits green-plating. In light of the role played by green-plating under the system of environmental protection envisaged by the Treaties, discussed in Chapter 2, it can hardly be argued that the fuzzy manner in which the proportionality principle is applied offers a proper basis for fostering the application of the principle of a high level of environmental protection and, more generally, of the principle of sincere cooperation under Article 4(3) TEU.

### *3.2.1 The Review of Legality of Green-Plating: Theory Overview*

The clause 'more stringent protective measures must be compatible with the Treaties' has been extensively analysed in the literature. As argued by Krämer, 'compatible with the Treaties' means that more stringent protective measures must be compatible with any provision in the Treaties, in particular those on the free movement of goods or on undistorted competition.[5] Until recently, it remained unclear whether the term 'Treaties' also covered secondary law. Some German academics argued that the term 'Treaties' in Article 193 TFEU excludes secondary and tertiary Union legislation.[6] Other academics challenged this.[7] The Court of Justice expressed its opinion about this matter in the *Windmills* case[8] presented earlier.[9] In this case the Court of Justice reviewed the legality of an Italian more stringent protective measure – compared to the measures in the Birds Directive and the Habitats Directive – in the light

[4] Directive 2015/1535/EU of the European Parliament and of the Council of 9 September 2015 laying down a procedure for the provision of information in the field of technical regulations and of rules on Information Society services, [2015] OJ L241/1.

[5] Krämer (2011), p. 115. For example, Case C-510/99, *Criminal Proceedings against Xavier Tridon*, [2001] ECR I-7777, para. 46.

[6] Epiney (2005), p. 126 with further references.

[7] For example, Krämer (2011), p. 116, Pagh (1996), p. 242.

[8] Case C-2/10, *Azienda Agro-Zootecnica Franchini sarl and Eolica di Altamura Srl v Regione Puglia*, [2011] ECR I-6561 (Windmills).

[9] Chapter 1, Section 1.3.3.

of Directives 2001/77/EC and 2009/28/EC.[10] This demonstrates that the 'compatible with the Treaties' clause also covers Union secondary law. Ultimately, as Krämer argues, secondary law is based on the Treaties.[11] This is no different for national measures falling outside the scope of application of Union law or implementing Union obligations.

In addition to the Treaties and secondary law, cases of green-plating must comply with general principles of EU law. The Court of Justice stated in *Deponiezweckverband Eiterköpfe* that the Union proportionality principle is not applicable to reviewing the legality of more stringent protective measures, inasmuch as other provisions of the Treaty (e.g. Articles 34–36 TFEU) are not involved.[12] De Cecco rightly argues that in essence, more stringent protective measures, even when they partially serve to implement Union obligations, are national measures falling under the sovereignty of the Member States.[13] With respect to Article 6(3) TEU and the protection of fundamental rights, a similar conclusion can be drawn: European Fundamental Rights are not applicable for reviewing the legality of more stringent protective measures, inasmuch as other provisions of the Treaties are not involved. Until recently, the same could be said of the Charter of Fundamental Rights of the European Union. More stringent protective measures cannot be regarded as 'implementing Union law' within the meaning of Article 51 of the Charter. With the *Akerberg* case, however, it has become unclear whether the broad interpretation given by the Court of Justice to Article 51 of the Charter also covers more stringent protective measures.[14] On the other hand, cases of green-plating taking the form of measures *implementing* options left open in Union obligations can clearly

[10] Directive 2001/77/EC of the European Parliament and of the Council of 27 September 2001 on the promotion of electricity produced from renewable energy sources in the internal electricity market, [2001] OJ L 283/33; and Directive 2009/28/EC of the European Parliament and of the Council of 23 April 2009 on the promotion of the use of energy from renewable sources, [2009] OJ L 140/16.

[11] Krämer (2011), p. 116.

[12] Case C-6/03, *Deponiezweckverband Eiterköpfe v Land Rheinland-Pfalz*, [2005] ECR I-2753.

[13] De Cecco (2006), pp. 25 and 26. See Sections 3.2.2 and 3.2.3 above. See Case C-6/03, *Deponiezweckverband Eiterköpfe v Land Rheinland-Pfalz*, [2005] ECR I-2753, para. 61, last sentence.

[14] Case C-617/10 *Aklagaren v Hans Akerberg Fransson*, ECLI:EU:C:2013:105 (*Akerberg*), paras. 17–21. According to AG Sharpston, national law falls within the scope of Union law when, inter alia, it implements Union law, regardless of the margin of discretion enjoyed by the Member States and of whether national law goes further than what is required by Union law, Opinion of AG Sharpston in Case C-427/06, *Birgit Bartsch v Bosch und Siemens Hausgeräte (BSH)*, [2008] ECR I-7245 (*Bartsch*), para. 62 with reference to case law.

be reviewed in light of the general principles of Union law, the European Fundamental Rights and the EU Charter.[15] For example, in the *Zuckerfabrik Franken* case, after mentioning the duty of the Member States to take all necessary measures to ensure the fulfilment of the Union's objectives,[16] and having noted that Member States had discretion with respect to how to go about achieving the Union's goal, the Court of Justice reviewed the national implementing measures in the light of the Union principle of legal certainty and of the Union principle of proportionality (paragraphs 19–29). In the *Marthe Klensch and Others* case, the Court of Justice stated that when Union measures allow Member States to choose between various options for implementation, Member States have to comply with the Union principle of equality and Article 40(3) EEC (currently, 40(2) TFEU).[17] Such a principle restricted Luxembourg in its choice of implementation options to those indicated by the Union measure concerned.[18] As regards environmental protection, in the *Standley* case, the Court of Justice concluded that the provisions of the so-called Nitrates Directive[19] left sufficient flexibility to the Member States to observe the Union principle of proportionality while adopting measures implementing the Union obligations arising from the Directive.[20]

Naturally, general principles of Union law and European Fundamental Rights are relevant to reviewing the legality of 'more stringent protective measures' and other kinds of green-plating when, in the words of *Deponiezweckverband Eiterköpfe*, 'other provisions' of the Treaty (and secondary Union law, I would like to add) are 'involved'. For instance, when

[15] See Article 263, second paragraph, TFEU and Article 51 of the Charter. For literature, see, for example Jans & Vedder (2012), p. 31 and Lenaerts & Van Nuffel (2011), p. 852, both with references to case law.

[16] Case C-77/81, *Zuckerfabrik Franken GmbH v Federal Republic of Germany* [1982] ECR 681, para. 18.

[17] Joined cases C-201 and 202/85, *Marthe Klensch and others v Secrétaire d'État à l'Agriculture et à la Viticultur*, [1986] ECR 3477, paras. 8–12.

[18] Council Regulation (EEC) no 857/84 of 31 March 1984 adopting general rules for the application of the levy referred to in article 5c of Regulation (EEC ) no 804/68 in the milk and milk products sector, OJ 1984, l 90, p. 13. Article 2(1) of this Regulation stated: 'The reference quantity referred to in article 5c (1) of the abovementioned regulation shall be equal to the quantity of milk or milk equivalent delivered by the producer during the 1981 calendar year (formula A), or to the quantity of milk or milk equivalent purchased by a purchaser during the 1981 calendar year (formula B), plus 1%'.

[19] Council Directive 91/676/EEC of 12 December 1991 concerning the protection of waters against pollution caused by nitrates from agricultural sources [1991] OJ L375/1.

[20] Case C-293/97, *The Queen v Secretary of State for the Environment and Ministry of Agriculture, Fisheries and Food, ex parte H.A. Standley and Others and D.G.D. Metson and Others*, [1999] ECR I2603 (*Standley*), para. 50.

national measures are in conflict with the rules on the free movement of goods, the proportionality principle is relevant for assessing any justification of the national measure.[21] Here a distinction must be made between a) the *scope* of the review performed under the proportionality principle and b) its *intensity*.

## a) The Scope of the Proportionality Principle in the Context of Green-Plating

Although the language used by the Court of Justice in its case law is sometimes confusing,[22] it is generally accepted that, under the proportionality test, national law must be suitable, necessary and not excessively burdensome (the so-called proportionality *sensu stricto*).[23] The suitability test requires that national law must be capable of achieving the goals it pursued.[24] The necessity test evaluates whether national law could achieve its goals by means of measures with less impact on Union law.[25] Finally, proportionality *sensu stricto* means that even if national law is suitable and necessary, it still cannot be too burdensome upon the values affected.

In view of the ruling of the Court in Justice in *Deponiezweckverband Eiterköpfe*, it has been argued in the literature that the proportionality principle *sensu stricto* is not applicable in the context of 'more stringent protective measures'.[26] However, in a more recent case the Court of Justice did refer to the proportionality principle *sensu stricto* when reviewing a more stringent protective measure.[27] In the *Windmills* case, reviewing the legality of Italian legislation, it stated that:[28]

> [. . .] the principle of proportionality referred to in Article 13 of Directive 2009/28, which is one of the general principles of European Union law, requires that measures adopted by Member States in this field do not exceed the limits of what is appropriate and necessary in order to attain the objectives legitimately

[21] Wiers (2002), p. 72, with reference to the review of national measures affecting the achievement of Union's goals in general.

[22] Wiers (2002), p. 74, with an overview of the various expressions and reference to case law.

[23] For example, Emiliou (1996), p. 134, Barnard (2007), p. 81 and Wiers (2002), p.73.

[24] Mortelmans (2008), p. 650.

[25] Emiliou (1996), pp. 29–32.

[26] Jans (2007), pp. 712–713.

[27] In Case C-6/03, *Deponiezweckverband Eiterköpfe v Land Rheinland-Pfalz*, [2005] ECR I-2753, para. 62, the Court of Justice did not mention this aspect of the proportionality test.

[28] Case C-2/10, *Azienda Agro-Zootecnica Franchini sarl and Eolica di Altamura Srl v Regione Puglia*, [2011] ECR I-6561 (Windmills), para. 73.

pursued by the legislation in question; when there is a choice between several appropriate measures recourse must be had to the least onerous, and the disadvantages caused must not be disproportionate to the aims pursued.

The last part of this passage clearly refers to proportionality *sensu stricto*. It should be noted that, in this case, the Union proportionality principle was referred to in Article 13 of Directive 2009/28/EC. Future case law will have to clarify whether the Court of Justice will apply the same reasoning to cases where a Union directive or regulation does not contain an explicit reference to the proportionality principle. Based on a rather old case, it can be sustained that in the context of a review based on primary EU law, the Court of Justice does not seem to exclude a review based on the proportionality *sensu stricto* test.[29]

### b) The Intensity of the Proportionality Review in the Context of Green-Plating

In the literature, it has been argued that more stringent (protective) measures should be subjected to a stricter proportionality test than that applied to other kinds of national measures affecting Union law. According to Jans, more stringent (protective) measures should be subjected to a proportionality test similar to that applied under Article 114(4–6) TFEU.[30] In his opinion, Member States have to demonstrate why the protection offered by the directive at hand does not offer a solution in the specific case. Jans bases his reasoning on the fact that any Union minimum standard must ensure the achievement of a 'high level of protection'; otherwise, the directive itself would not fulfil the suitability test and thus be disproportional. However, if the high level of protection offered by a directive is an adequate level of protection, then the national level of protection cannot be necessary.[31] In other words, Jans seems to test more stringent (protective) measures on the basis of the same necessity test as for the Union provisions concerned. In fact, he seems to test both measures with regard to the same 'high level of protection'.

I argue that two situations must be distinguished. In chapter 2,[32] I indicated that green-plating can take the form of measures pursuing

[29] Case 302/86, *Commission of the European Communities v Kingdom of Denmark*, [1988] ECR 4607.
[30] Jans (2007). Jans refers to exceptional situation justifying the need of higher protection.
[31] Jans (2007), p. 715.
[32] Chapter 2, Sections 2.1 and 2.2.

a higher goal than that pursued by the EU legislator, or of measures establishing a stricter means to achieve the EU goal.

If a national legislator pursues a *higher goal* than that pursued by the EU legislator, green-plating cannot be subjected to the same necessity test applied to the Union measure concerned. If the same necessity test applied, it would be extremely difficult to justify the necessity of maintaining or introducing green-plating. Article 193 TFEU would be deprived of most of its meaning. It should be noticed that in *Deponiezweckverband Eiterköpfe* the Court of Justice stated that in a more stringent (protective) measure, the level of protection is a matter falling under the competence of the Member States.[33] Accordingly, this case indicates that there is 'a high level of protection' (Union standard) and 'a higher level of protection' (national standard). I see no legal ground for which, after that Union law has allowed the Member States to introduce a higher level of protection, the Court of Justice should review the national standard on the basis of the 'lower' Union high level of protection.[34] In other words, the Union high level of protection and the national higher level of protection should be reviewed by *two* different necessity tests.

This reasoning seems to find confirmation in the *Tridon* case.[35] In this case the Court of Justice was called upon to review the compatibility of a case of green-plating from France with the free movement of goods. French law extended the legal regime applied under the CITES Regulation[36] to Annex A species (threatened or rare species)[37] also to Annex B species (species which are not threatened but which might be endangered by too intense trade).[38] At the hearing, the Commission submitted that the absolute prohibition of trade in specimens of species in Annex B to the CITES Regulation, particularly with respect to captive born and bred specimens, went beyond what was necessary to ensure the effective protection of those species.[39] The Commission submitted that the protection of the species in question could have been accomplished

[33] Case C-6/03, *Deponiezweckverband Eiterköpfe v Land Rheinland-Pfalz*, [2005] ECR I-2753, para 61.

[34] To a similar extent De Cecco (2006), pp. 25 and 26.

[35] Case C-510/99, *Criminal Proceedings against Xavier Tridon*, [2001] ECR I-7777.

[36] Council Regulation (EC) No 338/97 of 9 December 1996 on the protection of species of wild fauna and flora by regulating trade therein, [1997] OJ L 61/1.

[37] For this species, the Regulation aims at avoiding further degradation of the status of conservation and at its improvement.

[38] For these species, the Regulation aims at avoiding degradation of the status of conservation.

[39] Case C-510/99, *Criminal Proceedings against Xavier Tridon*, [2001] ECR I-7777, para. 57.

by measures less stringent than an absolute prohibition of trade, such as marking of birds by means of rings or microchip transponders, or blood analyses to establish the ancestry of the animal, as provided for by Regulation (EC) No 939/97.[40] The Court of Justice replied that the presence of a less stringent regime at Union level does not in itself justify the conclusion that the national measure concerned is disproportionate.[41] A more stringent (protective) measure can be regarded as disproportionate to the aim pursued only if it appears that the aim may be achieved just as effectively by measures less restrictive of intra-Community trade. As we can see, two different tests were applied.

Differently, if green-plating takes the form of stricter means to achieve the EU goal, the Court of Justice should subject the national measure to the same necessity test of the Union measure. This is because the goal of the Union measure and of the national measure is the same. In such circumstances, I agree with Jans that it is difficult to find a justification for adopting a means that is stricter than the Union one for achieving the same Union goal, given that the Union means is supposed to be adequate and necessary. However, also in this case, I do not see grounds for stating that green-plating should be subjected to the same requirements applicable in the context of Article 114(4–6) TFEU. If the Treaty makers wanted this to be the case, they would have regulated this explicitly.

In conclusion, despite the slight uncertainty as regards the content and intensity of the proportionality test, as well as the scope of application of the Charter indicated in the previous sub-heading, this section shows that the theory concerning the review of green-plating is rather crystallised. The next section shows that certain aspects of judicial practice are not as crystallised as the theory.

### 3.2.2 *How the Proportionality Test Is Applied in Practice as Regards Green-Plating*

Although the EU proportionality principle is not applicable in reviewing the legality of green-plating as such, it does play a role if, once again in the words of *Deponiezweckverband Eiterköpfe*, 'other provisions of the Treaty are involved'. When 'other provisions' are involved, the following question is relevant: Can Member States predict how the Court of Justice

[40] Commission Regulation (EC) No 939/97 laying down detailed rules concerning the implementation of Council Regulation (EC) No 338/97 on the protection of species of wild fauna and flora by regulating trade therein, OJ 1997 L 140/9.

[41] Case C-510/99, *Criminal Proceedings against Xavier Tridon*, [2001] ECR I-7777, para. 59.

will review green-plating? The analysis below of the case law of the Court of Justice on this issue shows that only in some well-defined circumstances Member States can predict the manner in which the Court of Justice reviews in light of the proportionality principle. Indeed, when Member States use so-called positive lists, i.e. the prohibition of all products that are not inserted on a list established under public law, to protect human health or biodiversity, the Court of Justice applies the so-called proceduralisation of the proportionality principle. This scenario is presented first, in (a) below. In all other cases, the analysis of the case law of the Court of Justice does not show a clear *modus operandi*. National bans are usually reviewed in a rather stringent manner, but there are cases in which the review by the Court of Justice has been quite lenient, see (b) below. As regards other kinds of green-plating, each case is assessed in a manner which is peculiar to that case, see (c) below.

### a) The Proceduralisation of the Proportionality Test in the Context of Positive Lists

In certain cases, the Court of Justice proceduralised the proportionality principle, meaning that national law was expected to establish a procedure to consider the economic interests affected by the national measure. This is a practice which is not new in the case law of the Court of Justice dealing with the free movement of goods.[42] Such an approach is used when national measures allow the commercialisation of only those products which are listed in a document having binding force under public law. In the *Commission v Belgium* case[43] and in the *Nationale Raad van Dierenkwekers en Liefhebbers*, both dealing with nature conservation, we can see two examples of this approach applied to green-plating.[44] The former being only available in French and Dutch while being essentially a copy of the latter, I will focus first on the *Nationale Raad van*

[42] On the proceduralisation of the proportionality principle see Barnard (2007), pp. 85 and 86. For cases following this approach see, for example, Case C-344/90, *Commission of the European Communities v French Republic*, [1992] ECR I-4719, paras. 8 and 16, and Case C-24/00, *Commission of the European Communities v French Republic*, [2004] ECR I-1277, para. 25 and Joined Cases C-154/04 and C-155/04, *The Queen, on the Application of Alliance for Natural Health and Nutri-Link Ltd v Secretary of State for Health (C-154/04) and The Queen, on the Application of National Association of Health Stores and Health Food Manufacturers Ltd v Secretary of State for Health and National Assembly for Wales (C-155/04)*, [2005] ECR I-6451, para. 70.

[43] Case C-100/08, *Commission of the European Communities v Kingdom of Belgium*, [2009] ECR I-140 summary publication, para. 104 of the Dutch version.

[44] Case C-219/07, *Nationale Raad van Dierenkwekers en Liefhebbers VZW and Andibel VZW v Belgische Staat*, [2008] ECR I-4475, paras. 33–38.

*Dierenkwekers en Liefhebbers* case. This case concerns a Belgian measure which, among other things, makes the holding of mammals subject to the prior inclusion of their species in a positive list and which also applies to specimens of species which are legally held in other Member States. In the context of the review in light of the principle of proportionality, the Court of Justice stated:

33 However, the Court has consistently held that legislation, such as that referred to in the main proceedings, which makes the holding of mammals subject to the prior inclusion of the species to which they belong in a positive list and which also applies to specimens of species which are legally held in other Member States is in compliance with Community law only if a number of conditions are satisfied (see, by analogy, inter alia, Case C-344/90 *Commission v France* [1992] ECR I-4719, paragraphs 8 and 16, and Case C-24/00 *Commission v France*, paragraph 25).

34 First, the drawing up of such a list and the subsequent amendments to it must be based on objective and non-discriminatory criteria (see, to that effect, inter alia, Case C-192/01 *Commission v Denmark* [2003] ECR I-9693, paragraph 53).

35 Secondly, that legislation must make provision for a procedure enabling interested parties to have new species of mammals included in the national list of authorised species. The procedure must be one which is readily accessible, which presupposes that it is expressly provided for in a measure of general application, and can be completed within a reasonable time, and, if it leads to a refusal to include a species – it being obligatory to state the reasons for that refusal – the refusal decision must be open to challenge before the courts (see, by analogy, Case C-344/90 *Commission v France*, paragraph 9, and Case C-24/00 *Commission v France*, paragraphs 26 and 37).

36 Lastly, an application to obtain the inclusion of a species of mammal in that national list may be refused by the competent administrative authorities only if the holding of specimens of that species poses a genuine risk to the protection of or compliance with the interests and requirements mentioned in paragraphs 27 to 29 of this judgment (see, by analogy, inter alia, Case C-344/90 *Commission v France*, paragraph 10, and Case C-24/00 *Commission v France*, paragraph 27).

37 In any event, an application to have a species included in the list of species of mammal which may be held may be refused by the competent authorities only on the basis of a full assessment of the risk posed to the protection of the interests and requirements mentioned in paragraphs 27 to 29 of this judgment by the holding of specimens of the species in question, established on the basis of the most reliable scientific data available and the most recent results of international research (see, by analogy, inter alia, *Alliance for Natural Health and Others*, paragraph 73).

38 Where it proves impossible to determine with certainty the existence or extent of the risk envisaged because of the insufficiency, inconclusiveness or

imprecision of the results of the studies conducted, but the likelihood of real harm to human or animal health or to the environment persists should the risk materialise, the precautionary principle justifies the adoption of restrictive measures.

As we can see, the Court of Justice makes use of a three-step approach, each step incorporating its own requirements. First, the positive list must have been drawn up by following objective considerations which do not discriminate. Second, there must be a procedure, provided for in a general binding rule, to ask for an amendment of the positive list. The procedure for asking for such amendments must be open to interested parties and must not take too long to be completed. Further, decisions not to amend the positive list must be duly motivated and challengeable in a court of law. Third, the decision not to amend the positive list must be based on a genuine risk that the goals pursued by the national legislator, which must be established on the basis of the most reliable scientific data available and the most recent results of international research taking into account the precautionary principle, will not be achieved.

The Court of Justice's claim that its proceduralised approach to the review of positive lists under the principle of proportionality is consistent is quite accurate. Still, one aspect of the positive list assessed in the *Commission v Belgium* case was not reviewed in the light of this approach, but, as further discussed in the next section, by means of a different approach.[45] For the rest, the consistency in the application of the proceduralisation of the proportionality test approach seems to be confirmed by the fact that it is not used in the case of negative lists, such as that adopted under French law in the *Tridon* case.[46] This case concerns a decree of the French government, adopted in application, inter alia, of Article L.211–1 of the Code Rural. This provision prohibits for the wild species it lists, which include certain species of macaw, the destruction or removal of eggs or nests, the destruction, mutilation, capture or removal or the preservation by taxidermy of birds or, whether they are living or dead, the transport, door-to-door sale, use, offering for sale, sale or purchase thereof. Mr. Tridon was accused in the main proceedings of having transferred for consideration captive born and bred specimens of species of macaw whose use for commercial purposes is prohibited

[45] Case C-100/08, *Commission of the European Communities v Kingdom of Belgium*, [2009] ECR I-140 summary publication, in particular paras. 112 and 113.

[46] Case C-510/99, *Criminal Proceedings against Xavier Tridon*, [2001] ECR I-7777.

throughout national territory by the French government decree. By allowing the commercialisation of all wild species not listed under the decree, national law made use of a negative list. In assessing the proportionality of the national measure, which went further than required under EU law on the protection of birds, the Court of Justice did not make use of the proceduralisation of the proportionality test approach. It made use of a more casuistic *modus operandi* further discussed below.

### b) The Proportionality of Green-Plating in the Form of National Bans

Except for the cases in which national law makes use of positive lists, the approach of the Court of Justice to the review in light of the proportionality principle changes on a case-by-case basis. This is true also for cases in which national law establishes a national or local ban.

Sometimes, the suitability test and the necessity test are not applied, because the effects of the national measure on the allegedly breached provision of EU law were too limited. This occurred in the *Windmills* case.[47] This case concerns a local measure prohibiting the location of new wind turbines not intended for self-consumption on sites forming part of the Natura 2000 network, with the possibility of exemption for wind turbines intended for self-consumption with a capacity not exceeding 20 kW. An undertaking confronted with this prohibition brought the matter to court. The national court decided to ask the Court of Justice for a preliminary ruling on, among other things, the compatibility of the national measure with Article 6(3) of the Habitats Directive. Before the Court, the undertaking that wanted to build a windmill farm argued that the national more stringent protective measure was in breach of Article 194 TFEU, regulating the European Union policy on energy. The Court of Justice replied:

> 56 Suffice it to observe in that connection that Article 194(1) TFEU states that European Union policy on energy must have regard for the need to preserve and improve the environment.
>
> 57 Moreover, a measure such as that at issue in the main proceedings, which prohibits only the location of new wind turbines not intended for self-consumption on sites forming part of the Natura 2000 network, with the possibility of exemption for wind turbines intended for self-consumption with a

[47] Case C-2/10, *Azienda Agro-Zootecnica Franchini sarl and Eolica di Altamura Srl v Regione Puglia*, [2011] ECR I-6561.

capacity not exceeding 20 kW, is not, in view of its limited scope, liable to jeopardise the European Union objective of developing new and renewable forms of energy.

As indicated in paragraph 57, the Court of Justice did not proceed with reviewing the compatibility of the national measure with the suitability and necessity tests. The Court of Justice does not seem to doubt that the national measure has an effect on the achievement of the policy goals pursued by the European Union under Article 194 TFEU. Still the Court of Justice considered the scope of the national measure to be limited. Thanks to its limited scope, the national measure did not jeopardise the achievement of the European Union objective of developing new and renewable forms of energy. Hence, the national measure affected the goals pursued under Article 194 TFEU, but did not jeopardise it. There seems to be a kind of *de minimis* rule, or to use a more traditional term in the context of the free movement law, *remoteness* test,[48] as regards the negative effects that a more stringent protective measure has on the Treaties. The existence of a *de minimis* rule or remoteness test should be reassuring for the Member States. Thanks to such a *de minimis* rule or remoteness test, national law going beyond EU requirements does not need to be reviewed by the Court of Justice. Unfortunately, it is unclear when the *de minimis* rule or remoteness test applies and when the national legislator can be certain that its national measure falls under this test. Would the national measure at hand in the *Windmills* case have trespassed the *de minimis* rule or remoteness test if, for example, it had not allowed for the possibility of exemption for wind turbines intended for self-consumption with a capacity not exceeding 20 kW? What about if only 10 kW for self-consumption were eligible for the exemption? Or did the fact that the national measure only applied to windmills built in or nearby Natura 2000 locations mean that the national measure was so limited in scope that the achievement of the European Union objective of developing new and renewable forms of energy was not jeopardised? If this is the reason, would it apply also to a national measure covering the whole territory of a Member State? It can be assumed that it was a combination of the fact that this case concerned a local measure, having a limited geographical scope and allowing for exemptions that triggered the *de minimis/remoteness* test. We do not know. This is exactly the problem with this judgment. The Court of Justice is

[48] For a recent discussion on the exactness of this terminology see Gormley (2015), pp. 925–939.

silent on the exact reason for which it concluded that no further assessment was necessary. In light of this finding, I am of the opinion that this judgment does not provide enough information to clarify to the Member States when their more stringent protective measures can be considered to be exempted from review by the Court of Justice. It is impossible to predict when a *de minimis* rule or remoteness test will be respected. The *Windmills* case can hardly serve as a precedent on this issue.

In other cases, the national measure failed the proportionality test because it treated different objects or persons alike, or similar objects or persons differently. This means that the equality principle can be applied as a part of the proportionality principle. This has been the case, for example, in an infringement procedure against Belgium, *Commission v Belgium*, based on a breach of the free movement of goods.[49] Belgian law was more stringent than the Birds Directive and the CITES Regulation on a series of aspects concerning the protection of birds. As regards the absolute prohibition of being in possession of birds, and their derivates, which are not listed in a specific list set up by the Flemish Government, the Court of Justice concluded:[50]

> 111 Ladite interdiction absolue de détenir les espèces en question, qui constitue manifestement un obstacle considérable à l'utilisation et au commerce desdites espèces par les marchands d'oiseaux établis en Région flamande, ne saurait être regardée comme nécessaire pour atteindre l'objectif de lutte contre la fraude de grande envergure invoqué par le Royaume de Belgique.
>
> 112 En effet, dans la mesure où le Royaume de Belgique soutient pour sa part que le marquage au moyen d'une bague fermée anodisée est de nature à assurer la protection des oiseaux contre ladite fraude, cet État membre n'a pas démontré en quoi une interdiction absolue de détention par les marchands d'oiseaux, édictée par ailleurs à l'article 7 bis, cinquième alinéa, de l'arrêté royal de 1981 et qui touche indistinctement tous les spécimens d'oiseaux non mentionnés à l'annexe I de cet arrêté, serait proportionnée à l'objectif allégué de lutte contre la fraude.
>
> 113 Ladite interdiction, en privant les marchands d'oiseaux de la faculté d'obtenir des dérogations, apparaît comme étant d'autant plus disproportionnée qu'elle constitue une entrave au commerce de l'ensemble de ces marchands, partant, même ceux qui ne participent pas à la fraude internationale alléguée par le

[49] Case C-100/08, *Commission of the European Communities v Kingdom of Belgium*, [2009] ECR I-140 summary publication, in particular paras 112 and 113. In this case aspects of the national measure have been reviewed by the Court of Justice. The majority of the more stringent protective measures were reviewed in light of the proceduralisation of the proportionality test approach discussed above.

[50] Only the French and Dutch versions of this judgment are available.

Royaume de Belgique, alors pourtant que cet État membre n'a pas démontré que ces derniers seraient l'exception et que, par ailleurs, la détention et le commerce desdits spécimens par les particuliers ne sont pas prohibés.

As written in paragraph 112 of this judgment, the national measure was disproportionate because it limited the free movement of goods not only for those traders taking part in the fraud, but also for those traders who did not take part in it. This reasoning means that two different situations were treated similarly, hence breaching the principle of equality. In addition, the national measure was disproportionate because it did not apply to private persons who are not traders, meaning the general public. In other words, by treating traders not taking part in the fraud differently from the general public, national law treated differently two situations which are similar, thus breaching the principle of equality. As such, the linkage between the principle of equality and that of proportionality is not illogical. By treating differently two groups of persons which are similar from the perspective of the goal pursued by the measure at hand, the ability of such a regulatory measure to achieve its goal can be jeopardised. Accordingly, by breaching the equality principle, the national measure would also fail the suitability test under the proportionality principle. Besides, if the regulatory measure under scrutiny does not distinguish between two groups of persons, which are different from one another, from the perspective of the goal pursued by the regulatory measure at hand, such a measure would go beyond what is necessary to achieve its goal. Accordingly, by breaching the principle of equality, the national measure would also fail the necessity test under the principle of proportionality.

While the theoretical linkage between these two principles is logical, the manner in which the Court of Justice applied it in the *Commission v Belgium* case can be questioned. First, treating the general public differently from traders specialising in the trading of birds and their derivates does not appear to be in breach of the principle of equality. The volume of birds and their derivates dealt with by specialised traders can be expected to be significantly higher than that dealt with by a member of the general public. Accordingly, it is unclear why the Court of Justice considered that between these two groups of persons there were no objective considerations which allowed speaking of differentiation rather than discrimination.[51] Furthermore, as regards the fact that the

[51] On the relevance of this difference in the case law of the Court of Justice related to environmental protection see Case C-213/96, *Outokumpu Oy*, [1998] ECR I-1777.

national measure treated specialist traders taking part in the fraud and specialist traders not taking part in the fraud by means of the same regime, the principle of equality was breached specifically because the Flemish government did not prove that specialist traders not taking part to the fraud are an exception to the general practice. The Flemish government spoke of widespread (*grande envergure*) fraud as regards the trading in birds and their specimens by which birds born in the wild were illegally captured and then traded as if they were born in captivity, hence falling outside the scope of protection offered by EU law on the protection of birds.[52] Neither the Commission, nor the Court of Justice, at least till paragraph 113, questioned the existence of such widespread fraud. Paragraph 113 does not specify what the Court of Justice meant when it stated that the Flemish government has not proven that specialist traders not taking part in the fraud are an exception. If the fraud is as widespread as argued by the Flemish government, how can the group of specialised traders not taking part in the fraud not be an exception? Further, what percentage of traders qualifies as exceptional? Is it 1%, 5% 10%, or 30%? And how do you prove it? I do not argue that the Belgian measure at hand in the main proceedings should have been considered in compliance with the principle of proportionality. My point is that the manner in which the Court of Justice made use of the principle of equality in the context of the proportionality principle in this case does not foster legal certainty. It actually raises more questions than it answers. Luckily, this judgment is only published in French and in Dutch.

Sometimes, the Court of Justice requires Member States to prove that less stringent means were not sufficient to achieve the goal pursued. This means that Member States have to prove that they comply with the necessity test. The most stringent form of application of this approach can be seen in the second infringement procedure against Austria concerning the ban of transporting goods via lorry on a part of the Austrian highway network connecting Germany and Italy,[53] also known as the *Inntalautobahn No. 2* case.[54] Given that limit values established under the Air Framework Directive[55] had been exceeded more times than allowed

[52] Case C-100/08, *Commission of the European Communities v Kingdom of Belgium*, [2009] ECR I-140 summary publication, paras. 49, 90 and 109.

[53] Case C-28/09, *European Commission v Republic of Austria*, [2011] ECR I-13525.

[54] Enchelmaier (2013), pp. 183–202.

[55] Council Directive 96/62/EC of 27 September 1996 on ambient air quality assessment and management, [1996] OJ L 296/55.

by the Directive, Austria introduced a sectoral traffic prohibition for lorries of over 7.5 tonnes. This was the second attempt by Austria to pass such a restriction; at the beginning of 2000s, a similar attempt failed to pass the proportionality test because Austria did not provide a study on the necessity of the traffic restriction.[56] Following the performance of such a study, the traffic restriction was proposed once again in a reinforced manner. Indeed, the *Inntalautobahn No. 2* case concerns a measure that is more radical than that at issue in the *Inntalautobahn No. 1* case. The lorries concerned by the implementation of the prohibition in the *Inntalautobahn No. 2* case were not only those on the 'north–south axis' (the Italy–Brenner–Innsbruck–Langkampfen–Germany link) and the 'north-west axis' (the Vorarlberg–Eastern Europe link), but also those on the 'south-west axis' (the Italy–Innsbruck–Vorarlberg/Lake Constance region link). According to estimates, when the first stage of the sectoral traffic prohibition was implemented on 2 May 2008, 35,000 lorry journeys a year were affected. With the implementation of the second stage on 1 January 2009, the measure was to affect 200,000 journeys a year, representing 7.3% of total journeys by lorry on the A12 motorway. The effects of the measure extended to about 300 km of the Austrian network of fast highways. The Commission considered the Austrian ban a measure more stringent than otherwise required under the Air Framework Directive. Such a measure was in breach of the Treaty provisions on the free movement of goods. The Court of Justice concluded:

139 Next, as regards the question whether the restriction of the free movement of goods goes beyond what is necessary to attain that objective, the Commission submits that measures such as an extension of the traffic prohibition for lorries in certain Euro classes to lorries in other classes or the replacement of the variable speed limit by a permanent 100 km/h speed limit, although liable to affect the free movement of goods, would have enabled the objective sought to be attained while restricting the exercise of that freedom to a lesser extent.

140 As the Court stated in Case C-320/03 *Commission v Austria*, paragraph 87, before adopting a measure so radical as a total traffic ban on a section of motorway constituting a vital route of communication between certain Member States, the Austrian authorities were under a duty to examine carefully the possibility of using measures less restrictive of freedom of movement, and

[56] Case C-320/03, *Commission of the European Communities v Republic of Austria*, [2005] ECR I-9871 (Inntalautobahn No. 1).

discount them only if their inappropriateness to the objective pursued was clearly established.

141 With respect, first, to the possibility of extending the traffic prohibition for lorries in certain Euro classes to lorries in other classes, it must be recalled that the limit for emissions of oxides of nitrogen was fixed at 5 g/kWh for lorries in class Euro III and that class Euro IV reduced this to 3.5 g/kWh.

142 The Republic of Austria takes the view, however, that lorries corresponding to class Euro IV often emit more nitrogen dioxide than those corresponding to standard Euro III. For that reason, it considers that, before extending the traffic prohibition for lorries to lorries in class Euro III, a more thorough study should be made of the impact of nitrogen dioxide emissions on the environment.

143 In view of the fact that each successive Euro class undeniably includes a substantial reduction of emissions of oxides of nitrogen, it has not been shown that extending the traffic prohibition for lorries in certain Euro classes to lorries in other classes would not have been able to contribute to the objective sought as effectively as the implementation of the sectoral traffic prohibition.

144 With respect, secondly, to the Commission's suggestion of replacing the variable speed limit by a permanent 100 km/h speed limit, the Republic of Austria submits, relying on the data in the Ökoscience report, that that replacement would lead only to an additional annual reduction of 1.1% of nitrogen dioxide emissions in the zone concerned, whereas a reduction of those emissions by 1.5% is claimed for the sectoral traffic prohibition.

145 It must be observed that the information in the Ökoscience report relates inter alia to the speeds at which road users actually drove in that zone from November 2007 to October 2008. A significant part of that information thus relates to the situation of the Republic of Austria as it appeared at the end of the period prescribed in the reasoned opinion, which was 8 June 2008. That information may be taken into account in the assessment of the merits of the present action.

146 According to that report, at the time when a speed limit of 130 km/h applied at Vomp, the average speed of passenger vehicles was approximately 116 km/h, while during the investigation period in which a permanent speed limit of 100 km/h was introduced their average speed was 103 km/h. The introduction of the permanent speed limit thus brought about a reduction of only 13 km/h compared to the periods in which the speed limit was 130 km/h.

147 While the effect of a speed limit on the speed actually practised by road users may indeed be influenced by the way in which they accept the limit, the fact remains that it is for the Member State concerned to ensure that such a measure is actually complied with, by adopting compulsory measures with penalties if need be. The Republic of Austria cannot thus rely on the average speed measured in the zone concerned, 103 km/h, to assess the effect of implementing a permanent speed limit of 100 km/h.

148 Consequently, it appears that replacing the variable speed limit by a permanent speed limit of 100 km/h offers a potential for reducing nitrogen dioxide emissions which was not sufficiently taken into account by the Republic of Austria. Moreover, as may be seen from paragraph 67 above, the existence of that potential is corroborated by the IFEU report.

149 In addition, it must be noted that the restrictive effect on the free movement of goods of replacing the variable speed limit by a permanent speed limit of 100 km/h is less than that of implementing the sectoral traffic prohibition. That replacement would not affect the movement of lorries whose maximum authorised speed is in any case limited.

150 In those circumstances, it must be concluded, having regard to the criteria set out in paragraph 140 above, that it has not been shown that the two principal alternative measures put forward by the Commission as measures less restrictive of the free movement of goods are not appropriate. Without it being necessary to examine the other measures suggested by the Commission, the present application must therefore be allowed.

Besides the length of the Court of Justice's analysis of the necessity of the national measure, it is striking that at paragraph 147 the Court of Justice went so far in its review as to question the methodology applied by the study commissioned by the Austrian Government. Such a review is not in contrast with the general approach of the Court of Justice to justifications based on mandatory requirements.[57] Although Member States do not have to prove that no other conceivable measure could enable that objective to be attained under the same conditions,[58] Member States must base their assessments on appropriate evidence or analysis.[59] In its case law, the Court of Justice shows that, if the Commission does not confine itself to contesting such evidence and

[57] Enchelmaier (2013), pp. 199 and 200.

[58] E.g. Case C-333/14, *Scotch Whisky Association and Others v The Lord Advocate and the Advocate General for Scotland*, ECLI:EU:C:2015:845, para. 55; Case C-400/08, *European Commission v Kingdom of Spain*, [2011] ECR I-1915, paras. 75, 123; C-250/07, *Commission of the European Communities v Hellenic Republic*, [2009] ECR I-4369, paras. 17, 34; C-518/06, *Commission of the European Communities v Italian Republic*, [2009] ECR I-3491, para 84; Case C-110/05, *Commission of the European Communities v Italian Republic*, [2009] ECR I-519, para 66; Case C-158/94, *Commission of the European Communities v Italian Republic*, [1997] ECR I-5789, para 54.

[59] E.g. Case C-254/05, *Commission of the European Communities v Kingdom of Belgium*, [2007] ECR I-4269, para 36; C-185/04, *Ulf Öberg v Försäkringskassan, länskontoret Stockholm*, [2006] ECR I-1453, para 22; C-137/04, *Amy Rockler v Försäkringskassan*, [2006] ECR I-1441, para 25; C-8/02, *Ludwig Leichtle v Bundesanstalt für Arbeit*, [2004] ECR I-2641, para 45; C-42/02, *Diana Elisabeth Lindman*, [2003] ECR I-13519, para 25; Case C-320/03, *Commission of the European Communities v Republic of Austria*, [2005] ECR I-9871 (Inntalautobahn No. 1).

analysis on legal issues,[60] the Court of Justice is willing to review the merits of the evidence. In this case, the Commission has presented a report disputing the findings of the Austrian Government's study. However, a close reading of the case and the information reported on both studies shows that the Court of Justice made selective use of the data in order to uphold the Commission's claim that the Austrian measure did not fulfil the necessity test.[61] The reader will excuse me for entering the realm of mathematics to sustain this point.

According to the Commission, the so-called IFEU report showed that a permanent speed limit of 100 km/h would have been more effective than the traffic ban.[62] Yet this study was based on a theoretical reduction of average speed from 130 to 100 km/h, thus a reduction of 30 km/h, corresponding to a reduction of emission by 1.8%. This reduction would have been 0.3% points higher than that achieved by the traffic ban introduced by Austria, which aimed at a 1.5% reduction. The Austrian government study had reviewed the speed limitation option as well, but it actually showed by means of empirical data that the average speed reduction was only of 13 km/h. Indeed, the average speed under the 130 km/h limit was 116 km/h, while under the 100 km/h limit the average speed was 103 km/h, corresponding to a reduction of emission of 1.1%.[63] This would have meant a reduction which was 0.4% points lower than that envisaged by the traffic ban. Even accepting the Court of Justice's argument made at paragraph 147 that, by strictly enforcing the 100 km/h limit, Austria could achieve a reduction of 16 km/h, the reduction of emissions achievable by the 100 km/h speed limit would have been significantly lower than that indicated by the IFEU report, even lower than that pursued by the traffic ban, if my understanding of the numbers is not mistaken.[64] The expression *iudex non calculat* underlines that lawyers should refrain from entering mathematical discussions. Yet

[60] For cases in which the Court of Justice did not assess the merits of the evidences and analyses, Enchelmaier (2013), p. 200 with reference to Case C-157/94, *Commission of the European Communities v Kingdom of the Netherlands*, [1997] ECR I-5699, para 63; Case C-158/94, *Commission of the European Communities v Italian Republic*, [1997] ECR I-5789, para 59.

[61] A negative note as regards the *modus operandi* of the Court of Justice in this regard has also be moved by Enchelmaier (2013), pp. 199–202, albeit on (partially) different grounds.

[62] Case C-28/09, *European Commission v Republic of Austria*, [2011] ECR I-13525, para 67.

[63] Idem, para 68.

[64] According to the formula 30:1.8=16:x, a 16km/h reduction would lead to a 0.96% emissions reduction, hence 0.54% points less than envisaged by the Austrian government and 0.84% points less than estimated on the basis of the IFEU report.

it is highly unprobable that an additional average reduction of 3 km/h would lead to a reduction of emissions that is 0.3% points higher than the one pursued by means of the proposed traffic ban.

In light of this analysis, I am of the opinion that the Court of Justice's approach to the necessity test in this case is biased due to a general idea that the Austrian measure greatly affected the transport of goods in one of the major road routes of Europe. Accordingly, what is the value the Court of Justice's approach in this case for predicting the outcome future cases? If the validity of Member States' studies can be so lightly discredited by the Court of Justice, how can they be certain that their cases of green-plating will withstand a review in light of the proportionality principle?

Probably the only lesson to be learned is that national bans are not welcomed by the Court of Justice. Case law in the field of species conservation shows that national bans are in principle rejected by the Court of Justice on grounds related to the necessity test. This was, for example, the case in the infringement procedure against Germany, known as the *Crayfish* case.[65] Under German law applicable at the time of the proceedings, the import of all species of live crayfish was subject to the grant of a licence. Under national law regulating the granting of the licence, a licence might be granted only for the purposes of research or teaching. The importation of live crayfish for commercial purposes, in particular for restocking private pools or for consumption was, thus, prohibited. Yet there was the possibility to apply for derogation. The German provisions went beyond EU law on the protection of species. In reviewing the German measure, the Court of Justice stated:

24 As far as the prevention of the risks of crayfish plague and of faunal distortion is concerned, the Commission submits that this objective could have been achieved by measures having less restrictive effects on intra-Community trade.

25 For example, instead of simply prohibiting imports of all species of live freshwater crayfish, the Federal Republic of Germany could have confined itself to making consignments of crayfish from other Member States or already in free circulation in the Community subject to health checks and only carrying out checks by sample if such consignments were accompanied by a health certificate issued by the competent authorities of the dispatching Member State certifying that the product in question presented no risk to health, or instead confined itself

[65] Case C-131/93, *Commission of the European Communities v Federal Republic of Germany*, [1994] ECR I-3303; see also Case C-100/08, *Commission of the European Communities v Kingdom of Belgium*, [2009] ECR I-140 summary publication, para. 104 of the Dutch version.

to regulating the marketing of crayfish in its territory, in particular by subjecting to authorisation only the restocking of national waters with species likely to be carrying the disease and restricting release of animals into the wild and restocking in areas in which native species are to be found.

26 However, the Federal Government has not convincingly shown that such measures, involving less serious restrictions for intra-Community trade, were incapable of effectively protecting the interests pleaded.

27 Moreover, the conditions which importers are required to observe under the authorisation system applied by the German authorities so as to mitigate the harshness of the import ban laid down by the Federal legislation, which require the traders concerned to comply with all health measures, to use imported crayfish in a way which prevents them from being released into the environment and to ensure that the water in which they are kept is disinfected, show that the defendant Government itself considers that those means, less restrictive of intra-Community trade than a total import ban, are sufficient for achieving the objective of protecting native crayfish against crayfish plague and faunal distortion.

28 It follows that the Commission's complaint is well founded.

As we can see from the cited paragraphs, the Court of Justice required Germany to prove that the less stringent means suggested by the Commission, or those used by Germany itself as a means of exception, were not appropriate to achieve the goal pursued by Germany by means of a total ban. In paragraph 27, the Court of Justice seems to require Germany to transform the derogation regime into the general rule.

If such a *modus operandi* of the Court of Justice towards national bans is applied consistently, no such ban could withstand the legality review of the Court. This is not the case. There are cases in which the Court of Justice assessed the national law banning a certain human activity by providing guidance suggesting to the national court that the proportionality test is respected. This was the case in the *Windmills* judgment.[66] As indicated above,[67] this judgment concerns a local measure prohibiting the building of windmill farms in or nearby Natura 2000 sites. The second part of the preliminary question referred by the national court concerned the compatibility of such a ban with Directive 2001/77/EC on the promotion of electricity produced from renewable energy sources in the internal electricity market and Directive 2009/28/EC on the

[66] Case C-2/10, *Azienda Agro-Zootecnica Franchini sarl and Eolica di Altamura Srl v Regione Puglia*, [2011] ECR I-6561 (Windmills).

[67] Chapter 1, Section 1.3.3 and Chapter 2, Section 2.1.

promotion of the use of energy from renewable sources.[68] The way in which the Court of Justice reviewed the national measure in light of these two directives should be looked at separately.

As regards Directive 2001/77, Article 6(1) thereof requires Member States to evaluate the legislative and regulatory framework with regard to administrative procedures, in particular authorisation procedures, which are applicable to production plants for electricity produced from renewable energy sources. The objectives of that evaluation procedure are to streamline and reduce administrative barriers and to ensure that the rules applicable to that type of production plant are objective, transparent and non-discriminatory. The Court of Justice only answered the questions concerning the objectiveness and transparency of the procedure. According to the Court of Justice:

63 In that connection, it should be pointed out, first, that a total ban on the construction of new wind turbines in areas forming part of the Natura 2000 network, deriving from a legislative provision, is not contrary to the objectives of streamlining and reducing administrative barriers and, in principle, constitutes a sufficiently transparent and objective procedure.

This paragraph shows that the Court of Justice considers a total ban to be a streamlined procedure. Apparently, the absence of a procedure is a streamlined procedure. The Court of Justice seems also to consider a total ban a transparent and objective procedure. Yet the Court of Justice is not fully sure. The expression 'in principle' suggests that there could be cases in which a total ban is not a transparent and objective procedure. Accepting that a total ban is a procedure, it is hard to see how a total ban could fail to be a *transparent* procedure. Accordingly, the formula 'in principle' refers to the possibility that a total ban is not an *objective* procedure. However, the Court of Justice did not assess the objectiveness criterion of its own; rather, it dealt with the objectiveness criterion only in conjunction in the last requirement mentioned under Article 6(1) of the Directive, i.e. that national procedures are non-discriminatory. The Court of Justice stated:

64 Next, as to whether the measure is discriminatory, it should be recalled that the prohibition of discrimination laid down in Article 6(1) of Directive 2001/77 is

[68] Respectively, Directive 2001/77/EC of the European Parliament and of the Council of 27 September 2001 on the promotion of electricity produced from renewable energy sources in the internal electricity market, [2001] OJ L 283/3, and Directive 2009/28 /EC of the European Parliament and of the Council of 23 April 2009 on the promotion of the use of energy from renewable sources and amending and subsequently repealing Directives 2001/77/EC and 2003/30/EC, [2009] OJ L 140/16.

simply a specific expression of the principle of equality, which is one of the fundamental principles of European Union law and requires that comparable situations must not be treated differently and that different situations must not be treated in the same way unless such treatment is objectively justified (see, inter alia, Case C-280/93 *Germany v Council* [1994] ECR I-4973, paragraph 67; Case C-303/05 *Advocaten voor de Wereld* [2007] ECR I-3633, paragraph 56; and Case C-127/07 *Arcelor Atlantique et Lorraine and Others* [2008] ECR I-9895, paragraph 23).

65 In the present case, it is for the referring court to determine whether the difference in treatment between the projects for the construction of wind turbines and projects relating to other industrial activities proposed for sites forming part of the Natura 2000 network may be justified on the basis of objective differences between those two kinds of project.

66 In that context, the referring court must have regard to the particular features of wind turbines, taking account in particular of the dangers which they may represent for birds, such as the risk of collision, disturbances and displacement, barrier effects forcing birds to change direction and habitat loss or degradation.

As we can see, the Court of Justice did not provide a definitive answer. It simply repeated the requirements under the principle of equality and then asked the national court to assess whether the national measure treated the building of windmills differently from other kinds of industrial plants for the production of electricity coming from renewable energy sources, and whether such a discrimination could be justified by objective criteria. As regards this last aspect of the assessment, the Court of Justice instructed the national court to take into account the specific features of wind turbines and their negative effects on birds. In light of the tone used by the Court of Justice in listing the negative effects of wind turbines on birds, and the fact that none of the other possible power plants affects birds in the same way as wind turbines do, the Court of Justice seems to steer the analysis of the national court towards the conclusion that the national measure is not discriminatory.

As regards the review in light of Directive 2009/28/EC, Article 13(1) thereof provides that 'Member States shall ensure that any national rules concerning the authorisation, certification and licensing procedures that are applied to plants and associated transmission and distribution network infrastructures for the production of electricity, heating or cooling from renewable energy sources [. . .] are proportionate and necessary'. In particular, Member States are required to take appropriate steps to ensure that those rules are 'objective, transparent, proportionate, do not discriminate between applicants and take fully into account the particularities of individual renewable energy technologies'. The Court of Justice stated:

73 In this regard, the principle of proportionality referred to in Article 13 of Directive 2009/28, which is one of the general principles of European Union law, requires that measures adopted by Member States in this field do not exceed the limits of what is appropriate and necessary in order to attain the objectives legitimately pursued by the legislation in question; when there is a choice between several appropriate measures recourse must be had to the least onerous, and the disadvantages caused must not be disproportionate to the aims pursued (see, inter alia, Case C-331/88 *Fedesa and Others* [1990] ECR I-4023, paragraph 13, and Joined Cases C-133/93, C-300/93 and C-362/93 *Crispoltoni and Others* [1994] ECR I-4863, paragraph 41).

74 It is for the referring court to determine whether the national measure at issue is proportionate. That court must take account in particular of the fact that the legislation at issue in the main proceedings is confined to wind power plants and does not extend to other forms of renewable energy production, such as photovoltaic plants. Moreover, the prohibition applies solely to new wind turbines for commercial purposes, as wind power plants intended for self-consumption and having a capacity not exceeding 20 kW are excluded from the scope of that prohibition.

As we can see, once again, the Court of Justice does not answer the question in a definitive manner, but it simply repeats the requirements under the proportionality principle. It then instructs the national court to apply the test. As regards the requirements for the proportionality principle, it is striking that the Court of Justice referred to the three limbs of the proportionality test as defined in *Fedesa*. Indeed, the Court of Justice explicitly refers to the suitability test, the necessity test and the proportionality *sensu stricto* test. As stated above, it is argued in the literature that this last test should not be applied by the Court of Justice in the context of more stringent protective measures.[69] It could be that in this case the Court of Justice evaluated the review of the national measure in light of an EU secondary measure. After having followed a democratically legitimated legislative process, such a measure provides a balance between environmental protection, energy security and economic considerations. This could be the reason for which the Court of Justice felt confident in evoking a test that could allow the judiciary to sit on the chair of the legislative power. The fact that the national measure did not aim to achieve a national goal strengthens such a consideration.

[69] Jans (2007), pp. 712–713.

Indeed, the total ban aimed to achieve the goals of the Habitats Directive. The national measure simply establishes a means/instrument to achieve the EU goal that is more stringent than the one previewed by the EU legislator. Given that the goal pursued by the national measure had been established by the EU legislature, it is easier to argue that the proportionality *sensu stricto* test does not place the judiciary in the position to trespass the boundaries established by the *trias politica* principle.

Another unclear aspect of the Court of Justice's reply to the preliminary question posed by the Italian court concerns the fact that the Court of Justice referred the matter back to the national court. It is the national court that has to apply the proportionality principle. At first glance, such an approach could be seen as welcome from the perspective of the judicial subsidiary theory.[70] Yet it is unclear why the matter was referred back to the national court as regards the proportionality test under Directive 2009/28/EC, while it was dealt by the Court of Justice itself as regards Article 194 TFEU and, albeit only partially, Directive 2001/77/EC. The manner in which, at paragraph 74, the Court of Justice stresses the peculiar features of the national measure suggests that the Court of Justice had already reached a conclusion on this matter. It should be noted that paragraph 74 refers to the very same features used by the Court of Justice at paragraph 57 to come to the conclusion that the total ban did not breach Article 194 TFEU. If the national measure was not capable of jeopardising the European Union objective of developing new and renewable forms of energy under Article 194 TFEU, how can it jeopardise the goal of promoting energy from renewable sources pursued by Directive 2009/28/EC? Why did the *de minimis/remoteness* approach discussed above not apply here? Further, why was the Court of Justice of the opinion that it had enough information to provide a definitive answer as regards the compatibility of the national measure with the European Union objective of developing new and renewable forms of energy under Article 194 TFEU, while it did not have enough information to state the same about the objective of promoting energy from renewable sources under the Directive? Are these two objectives so different as to justify such different approaches in answering the preliminary questions? Similarly, why was the Court of Justice of the opinion that it had enough information to conclude that the national measure at hand in the main proceeding fulfilled, at least in principle, the requirement of

[70] On judicial subsidiarity see Bogojevic (2015), pp. 5–25. More vaguely on this concept, Krämer (1996b), p. 17; and Tridimas (2011), p. 740.

offering an objective procedure under Article 6 of Directive 2001/77/EC, while it does not have enough information to establish whether the national measure establishes a proportionate and necessary procedure under Directive 2009/28/EC? What is the difference between the requirement of 'objective procedure' and that of 'proportionate and necessary procedure' under the two directives?

When the judgments of the Court of Justice discussed in this section, concerning national measures banning certain human activities, are compared, it becomes clear that it is impossible to predict how the Court of Justice will apply the necessity test. The three cases analysed above highlight the presence of at least four different approaches: i) a *de minimis/remoteness*-test based approach,[71] ii) an equality test–based approach,[72] iii) a strict necessity test–based approach[73] and iv) a judicial subsidiarity–based approach.[74] Taking all the above into consideration, national legislators and courts will not be able to find much guidance in the case law of the Court of Justice about the manner in which this court assesses national bans.

### c) The Proportionality Review of Green-Plating Other Than Positive Lists and National Bans

When the case law dealing with positive lists, in which a proceduralisation-based approach was followed is taken into consideration next to the judgments of the Court of Justice concerning national measures banning certain human activities, at least five different approaches to legality review can be established. If an even broader approach to the review of green-plating is taken, by looking at all different kinds of green-plating, at least two other approaches can be identified, thus bringing the total of approaches to at least seven.

First, there are cases in which the proportionality principle is applied in a rather theoretical and marginal manner, i.e. without the need of

[71] Case C-2/10, *Azienda Agro-Zootecnica Franchini sarl and Eolica di Altamura Srl v Regione Puglia*, [2011] ECR I-6561 (Windmills), case as regards compatibility with Article 194 TFEU (paras 56 and 57).

[72] Case C-100/08, *Commission of the European Communities v Kingdom of Belgium*, [2009] ECR I-140 summary publication; and Case C-2/10, *Azienda Agro-Zootecnica Franchini sarl and Eolica di Altamura Srl v Regione Puglia*, [2011] ECR I-6561 (Windmills), as regards compatibility with Directive 2001/77/EC (paras 64–66).

[73] Case C-28/09, *European Commission v Republic of Austria*, [2011] ECR I-13525; and Case C-131/93, *Commission of the European Communities v Federal Republic of Germany*, [1994] ECR I-3303 (*Crayfish*).

[74] Idem, as regards the compatibility with Directive 2009/28/EC.

presenting scientific studies as it was the case in the *Inntalautobahn No. 2* case. For example, this soft necessity test–based approach was followed in the *Aher-Waggon* case.[75] This case concerns a German measure that made aircraft registration in Germany conditional upon compliance with noise limits not required by EU law. As regards the proportionality of the measure, the Court of Justice stated:

20 It is also settled case-law that national legislation which restricts or is liable to restrict intra-Community trade must be proportionate to the objectives pursued and that those objectives must not be attainable by measures which are less restrictive of such trade (Joined Cases C-34/95, C-35/95 and C-36/95 *KO v De Agostini and TV-Shop* [1997] ECR I-3843, paragraph 45, and Case C-189/95 *Franzén* [1997] ECR I-5909, paragraph 75).

21 As regards the imposition of stricter standards than those laid down in the Directive, suffice it to state that, as the German Government has explained, limiting noise emissions from aircraft is the most effective and convenient means of combating the noise pollution which they generate. Without extremely costly investment, it is generally difficult to reduce noise emissions appreciably by carrying out works in the vicinity of airports.

22 Furthermore, the restriction, through stricter rules governing noise emissions from aircraft, on the possibility of registering an aircraft in Germany applies to all aircraft, new or used, irrespective of their origin, and does not prevent aircraft registered in another Member State from being used in Germany.

23 As regards, more particularly, the exemption from those stricter standards for aircraft registered in the Member State in question before the Directive was implemented, those aircraft must, as the German Government has explained, also comply with the stricter noise standards when they undergo technical modification, even if it has no bearing on noise emissions, or when they are temporarily withdrawn from service. Furthermore, their number can be determined by the German authorities.

24 The national authorities were thus entitled to consider that the number of aircraft not meeting the stricter noise standards was necessarily going to fall and, therefore, that the overall level of noise pollution could not fail to diminish gradually. Furthermore, the effectiveness of that policy of progressively eliminating from the national fleet aircraft not meeting the stricter noise standards would be undermined if their number could be increased, to an extent not foreseeable by the national authorities, by aircraft from other Member States.

25 Legislation of the kind at issue in the main proceedings therefore does not appear to be disproportionate.

[75] Case C-389/96, *Aher-Waggon GmbH v Bundesrepublik Deutschland*, [1998] ECR I-4473.

As it appears from the cited paragraphs, no specific study was required. A rather theoretical and light approach to the necessity test sufficed in paragraph 21. Besides, as regards the discriminatory nature of the national measure, which shows that once again the equality principle was applied as a part of the proportionality principle, the Court of Justice failed to appreciate that, as indicated by Jacobs, aircraft previously registered in another Member State could not be registered in Germany even though aircraft of the same construction which had already obtained German registration before the German measure was adopted could retain that registration.[76] Indeed, at paragraphs 22 and 23 the Court of Justice applied the equality principle in a rather simplified manner, which did not take into consideration the real meaning of the national measure at hand for the registration of foreign aircraft marketed before the entry into force of the contested measure.

Second, there are cases in which the national measure is considered in conformity or in breach of the Treaties without even applying a proportionality review; therefore this category could be called silent proportionality test–based approach. A case in which the national measure was considered in keeping with the Treaties without applying the proportionality test can be seen in *PrussenElektra*.[77] This case concerns a German measure under which network operators in Germany had to purchase electricity produced from renewable sources within their area of supply at fixed minimum prices. The Court of Justice did not only consider that the national measure was not discriminatory, it also refrained from assessing the proportionality of the contested measure, despite the fact that the private parties in the main proceedings, the Commission and the Advocate General all had contested the compatibility of the national measure with this principle.[78]

As regards a case in which a national measure was considered in breach of the Treaties without applying the proportionality test, reference can be made to Case C-64/09, *Commission v France*,[79] concerning the review of an allegedly more stringent protective measure under the

[76] Jacobs (2006), p. 190.

[77] Case C-379/98, *PreussenElektra AG v Schhleswag AG, in the presence of Windpark Reußenköge III GmbH and Land Schleswig-Holstein*, [2001] ECR I-2099.

[78] This can be evinced from the Opinion of AG Jacobs, in this case, paras. 192, 200, 210, 235, and 236.

[79] Case C-64/09, *European Commission v French Republic*, [2010] ECR I-03283.

so-called End-of-Life Vehicles Directive.[80] French law allowed the removal of a scrap vehicle from the register of car owners only if a certificate proving that the vehicles had been factually destroyed was provided by an official shredder. The directive only required a certificate to prove that the vehicle had been given to an official shredder. French law was hence stricter than required by EU law. Given that only French shredders provided a certificate that a scrap vehicle had been factually destroyed, the French measure limited the free movement of goods, according to the Commission. The Court of Justice stated:

35 In the first place, recital 1 in the preamble to Directive 2000/53 states that the directive seeks to minimise the impact of end-of-life vehicles on the environment, but does not provide for complete harmonisation and thus does not prevent Member States from adopting more stringent protective measures (see, inter alia, Case C-6/03 *Deponiezweckverband Eiterköpfe* [2005] ECR I-2753, paragraph 27). Such measures must, however, be compatible with the provisions of the EC Treaty and, inter alia, must not frustrate the achievement of the objective pursued in the second instance by that directive, namely to ensure the smooth functioning of the internal market and to avoid distortions of competition in the Union.

36 In that regard, the Court finds, as has been pointed out by the Commission, that Article 5(3) of Directive 2000/53 provides a precise description of the procedure to be followed for cancelling the registration of an end-of-life vehicle, in order to ensure, as stated by recital 2 in the preamble to the directive, coherence between national approaches. In the context of that procedure, a very specific function is given to a key document entitled ‘certificate of destruction’.

37 That function of the document may not be altered. Even if it were to be conceded that the French system affords better traceability of end-of-life vehicles, it is clear that that system was giving the ‘certificate of destruction’ a function different from that laid down in Article 5(3) of Directive 2000/53. Such an alteration of the function of that certificate is liable to jeopardise the coherence between the national approaches referred to in the preceding paragraph and, consequently, the functioning of the internal market.

38 Likewise, the issue of a document entitled ‘receipt of acceptance for destruction’ which, in the French Republic’s submission, fulfils the function of the ‘certificate of destruction’ provided for in Article 5(3) of Directive 2000/53 is liable to give rise to confusion capable of undermining the achievement of the objective pursued by that provision.

39 It follows from the foregoing that the third plea is also well founded.

[80] Directive 2000/53/EC of the European Parliament and of the Council of 18 September 2000 on end-of-life vehicles, [2000] OJ L 269/34.

As we can see from the cited paragraphs, the Court of Justice linked the second sentence of Article 193 TFEU to the secondary objectives of the Directive, i.e. the smooth functioning of the internal market. Once the Court of Justice concluded that the national measure was liable to jeopardise the achievement of such objective, it concluded that the plea of the Commission was well founded. No justification was taken into account, despite the fact that France had explicitly relied on environmental considerations.

### 3.2.3 *Fuzzy Proportionality as a Barrier to Green-Plating*

The analysis performed above confirms that the Court of Justice's review of green-plating is rather random. The following seven approaches were recognised, based on case law analysis:

i) a *de minimis/remoteness* test–based approach;[81]
ii) an equality test–based approach;[82]
iii) a strict necessity test–based approach;[83]
iv) a proceduralisation–based approach;[84]
v) a judicial subsidiarity–based approach;[85]
vi) a soft necessity test–based approach;[86] and
vii) a silent proportionality test–based approach.[87]

It should be noted that this is an open list. No clear *modus operandi* could be recognised as regards the application of most of these approaches. This finding is in line with those of De Búrca, who reviewed how the

[81] Case C-2/10, *Azienda Agro-Zootecnica Franchini sarl and Eolica di Altamura Srl v Regione Puglia*, [2011] ECR I-6561 (*Windmills*), case as regards compatibility with Article 194 TFEU (paras 56 and 57).

[82] Case C-100/08, *Commission of the European Communities v Kingdom of Belgium*, [2009] ECR I-140 summary publication; and Case C-2/10, *Azienda Agro-Zootecnica Franchini sarl and Eolica di Altamura Srl v Regione Puglia*, [2011] ECR I-6561 (*Windmills*), as regards compatibility with Directive 2001/77/EC (paras 64–66).

[83] Case C-28/09, *European Commission v Republic of Austria*, [2011] ECR I-13525; and Case C-131/93, *Commission of the European Communities v Federal Republic of Germany*, [1994] ECR I-3303 (*Crayfish*).

[84] Case C-100/08, *Commission of the European Communities v Kingdom of Belgium*, [2009] ECR I-140 summary publication, para. 104 of the Dutch version. Similarly, Case C-219/07, *Nationale Raad van Dierenkwekers en Liefhebbers VZW and Andibel VZW v Belgische Staat*, [2008] ECR I-4475, paras. 33–38.

[85] Idem, as regards the compatibility with Directive 2009/28/EC.

[86] Case C-389/96, *Aher-Waggon GmbH v Bundesrepublik Deutschland*, [1998] ECR I-4473.

[87] Case C-379/98, *PreussenElektra AG v Schleswag AG, in the presence of Windpark Reußenköge III GmbH and Land Schleswig-Holstein*, [2001] ECR I-2099; Case C-64/09, *European Commission v French Republic*, [2010] ECR I-03283.

Court of Justice applies the proportionality test in general.[88] Generally speaking, the more the national measure affects a fundamental freedom, the more strictly the Court of Justice applies the proportionality test. I do not disagree with Jacobs that the Court of Justice has been quite lenient towards environmental protection in the context of the legality review performed in light of the free movement of goods.[89] Yet, as highlighted by Jacobs himself, this leniency has been mostly focused on accepting the environment as a ground for applying the *Cassis-de-Dijon* line of justifications, at times bypassing the limitation concerning discriminatory measures.[90] Jacobs did not refer to the manner in which the proportionality test was applied. The review of positive lists for protecting biodiversity or national bans for various environmental purposes and other kinds of green-plating shows the lack of a clear *modus operandi* of the Court of Justice, with judgments that can be considered particularly stringent and others being particularly lenient. I could not find a trend that Member States can use to predict the approach to, and therefore the outcome of, the legality review performed by the Court of Justice.

Such a lack of legal certainty does affect Member States' choice to adopt green-plating. In the fields of nature conservation and waste management, there are cases in which the Netherlands had doubts about the possibility that certain stricter measures would have withstood a legality review in light of the provisions on the free movement of goods. For example, in the context of nature conservation the Netherlands prevented a provision prohibiting the import of non-endangered exotic species from entering into force.[91] To prevent species becoming endangered,[92] Section 13(1)(b) of the Flora and Fauna Act provision prohibited the exploitation of non-endangered exotic species listed by order. During the parliamentary debate, some members of the Dutch parliament referred to Article 193 TFEU (then Article 130t EEC) to support the adoption of this provision. They added that such a prohibition would have been compatible with Article 36 TFEU (then Article 36 EEC). After an initial positive attitude toward the adoption of this provision, the

88 De Búrca (2000), pp. 97–99.

89 Jacobs (2006).

90 See also Gormley (2015).

91 Before the reform occurred with the Nature Protection Act 2016, such a possibility was regulated under Section 13(1)(b) of the Flora and Fauna Act.

92 Proceedings of the Second Chamber of the States General, Kamerstukken II 1997/98, 23 147, nr. 74 later slightly changed, see Proceedings of the Second Chamber of the States General, Kamerstukken II 1997/98, 23 147, nr. 106.

government stated that the import and export of goods is a matter that cannot be easily regulated unilaterally; international collaboration is required to avoid conflict within Europe and with the World Trade Organisation (WTO).[93] Ultimately, the government and parliament agreed to suspend the entry into force of Section 13(1)(b) of the Flora and Fauna Act. Following the remarks made by the Commission, stating that the implementation of Section 13(1)(b) of the Flora and Fauna Act would represent an unjustifiable violation of current Article 34 TFEU,[94] the government blocked the entry into force of this section.

As regards waste management, Article 3 of the Old Waste Directive, requiring the Member States to encourage waste prevention, recycling and reuse, was transposed in the Netherlands by means of an extended legal framework, aiming to avoid waste rather than solving the problem of waste disposal.[95] Most importantly, Chapter 5 of the Waste Act[96] allowed the government to take measures restricting the production or commercialisation of environmentally unfriendly products,[97] and to take measures restricting how waste was collected and processed, including measures establishing return systems and separate collection systems. Notwithstanding the good intentions of the Dutch legislator, the prevention of waste remained a problem.[98] Chapter 5 of the Waste Act remained mostly unapplied, at least until 1991.[99] Experts used the words 'symbolic value' and 'disappointing results' when referring to the provisions on waste prevention in the Waste Act.[100] Indeed, the government only took a few measures on the collection of certain materials,

93 Proceedings of the Second Chamber of the States General, Kamerstukken II 1997, Handelingen, 9–613.

94 Proceedings of the Second Chamber of the States General, Kamerstukken II 2000/01, 23 147, nr. 127, p. 2.

95 Proceedings of the Second Chamber of the States General, Kamerstukken II 1974/75, 13 364, nrs. 1–3, pp. 68 and 74.

96 Afwalstoffenwet, Stb. 1977, 455.

97 Environmentally-unfriendly goods are goods which, after having been used, due to their nature, composition, weight or volume, are not suitable for recovery. The Minister explained that Articles 27 and 28 aimed, in the first instance, at regulating and reducing the commercialisation of certain goods on the Dutch market. Measures limiting the production of these goods would have been taken in the context of international agreements, Proceedings of the Second Chamber of the States General, Kamerstukken II 1974/75, 13 364, nrs. 1–3, p. 89.

98 Addink (1991a), p. 11.

99 Neuerburg & Verfaille (1991), p. 353.

100 Groen (1988), p. 245 and Henselmans (1988), p. 215 with reference to: CRMH, *Advies eigener beweging over afvalpreventie (beperking van het ontstaan van afval en de bevordering van het hergebruik)*, Rijswijk, June 1987.

such as glass and paper, and products, such as refrigerators.[101] One of the reasons impeding the application of Chapter 5 of the Waste Act was the fear of affecting the functioning of the internal market.[102]

I would be surprised if similar considerations did not block green-plating in other Member States as well. The unpredictability of the legality review performed by the Court of Justice is a rather well-known phenomenon. In light of the findings presented in Chapter 2, namely that green-plating fosters the development of the high level of protection of the environment under Article 191 TFEU, the fuzzy approach to the proportionality test described in this section is deplorable. It surely does not represent a laudable example of how to cooperate sincerely with the Member States. They are indeed left with little guidance on how to shape the content of national measures so as to maximise the possibility of complying with the Treaties. Section 4 provides a model to improve predictability as regards the *modus operandi* of the Court of Justice. This model links the review of legality with the manner in which the EU legislator has regulated the room for green-plating in measures based on Article 192 TFEU. In order to properly develop this model, Section 3 provides an analysis of the manner in which the room for green-plating can be identified. First, however, to complete the analysis of how the Court of Justice reviews the legality of green-plating, the role played by the notification duty in this regard remains to be seen.

### 3.2.4 *Notification as a Tool for the Review of the Legality of Gold-Plating?*

Article 193 TFEU concludes by requiring that the Commission shall be notified of 'more stringent protective measures'. Notwithstanding its mandatory formulation, the actual relevance of this obligation is questionable. First, little information is available on its use.[103] In 2012, I made multiple requests to the Commission for access to information under Regulation (EC) 1049/2001.[104] These requests aimed to establish whether the Commission had information about the use of more stringent protective measures in the context of several directives. In most cases, the Commission answered that the information was not available

[101] Neuerburg & Verfaille (1991), p. 353.
[102] Ibidem.
[103] Jans, Squintani et al. (2009), p. 434.
[104] Regulation (EC) 1049/2001 May 2001 regarding public access to European Parliament, Council and Commission documents, [2001] OJ L 145/43.

to it.[105] In those cases where the Commission did have information, I asked whether such information derived from notifications under Article 193 TFEU and its predecessors, from notification obligations in secondary Union environmental law, or from other sources. The Commission answered that such information was not acquired from notifications made under Article 193 TFEU. The information derived, in particular, from other sources, such as national reports produced in the context of the preparation of implementation reports.

This is probably the consequence of the fact that, according to the case law of the Court of Justice, the notification requirement of Article 193 TFEU is fulfilled if a Member State notifies its more stringent protective measures along with the notification of the measures implementing the Union act.[106] No *special* '193 notification' is required. Moreover, in the *Windmills* case,[107] the Court of Justice ruled that even if a Member State failed to notify the Commission of 'a more stringent protective measure', this does not affect the legality of that measure.[108] In sum, a violation of the notification duty under Article 193 TFEU does not affect the legality of more stringent protective measures.

It goes without saying that if more stringent protective measures take the form of so-called technical standards in the context of current Directive 2015/1535/EU[109] they are subject to the notification requirements of that Directive as well. According to this Directive, the Commission must be notified before national measures introducing technical standards for products or Information Society Services are adopted, if

105 In the context of nature conservation see letter of I. Codescu of 22 June 2012, reference number ENV.A.1./MV/ts/Ares(2012) 756413 (the last six numbers were written by hand). In the context of waste management, air quality and industrial emissions, see email of G. Gerzsenyi of 20 March 2012, no reference number.

106 Case C-194/01, *Commission of the European Communities v Republic of Austria*, [2004] ECR I-4979, para. 73, referring to the duty to notify other dangerous substances than those listed under the EU-LHW, enshrined in Directive 91/689/EEC.

107 Case C-2/10, *Azienda Agro-Zootecnica Franchini sarl and Eolica di Altamura Srl v Regione Puglia*, [2011] ECR I-6561 (*Windmills*).

108 See also Case C-129/16, *Túrkevei Tejtermelő Kft. v Országos Környezetvédelmi és Természetvédelmi Főfelügyelőség*, ECLI:EU:C:2017:547. See also Dougan (2000), p. 880 with further reference to case law.

109 Directive 2015/1535/EU of the European Parliament and of the Council of 9 September 2015 laying down a procedure for the provision of information in the field of technical regulations and of rules on Information Society services, [2015] OJ L241/1; previously, Directive 98/34/EC of the European Parliament and of the Council of 22 June 1998 laying down a procedure for the provision of information in the field of technical standards and regulation OJ 1998 L 204/37.

they do not serve to implement Union obligations.[110] Under Directive 2015/1535/EU, there is a standstill clause in place, meaning that national law cannot be adopted as long as the Commission has not given its approval, which may be silent.[111] If this standstill obligation is violated, national law cannot be applied. The same conclusion holds for national measures that are technical standards that fall outside the scope of application of Union environmental measures, including cases of spill-overs and 'related measures'. On the contrary, national measures implementing Union obligations, including cases of green-plating, are not subject to the standstill obligation under the Directive. Article 5(1) of the Directive states:

> Member States shall communicate to the Commission any draft technical regulation, *except where it merely transposes the full text* of an international or European standard, in which case information regarding the relevant standard shall suffice [author emphasis].

As we can see, when technical standards serve to transpose the full text of a European standard, Member States do not need to notify the Commission of the draft technical regulation. They only have to communicate information about the relevant European standard.

## 3.3 Clauses Indicating the Room for Green-Plating

As already stated, the EU legislator's duty to cooperate sincerely with the Member States means, among other things, that the EU legislator must guide the Member States towards the room left for green-plating in Union law. In this section, I describe first the two categories of clauses used by the Union legislator to indicate this room, namely: a) minimum clauses and b) options. Both categories are further subdivided as described in Section 3.3.1. Next, in Section 3.3.2 I analyse the kind of information that Member States can derive from these various kinds of clauses about the opportunity for green-plating. As explained in this section, the various clauses provide different levels of clarity as regards, first, what kind of measure a Member State can take under Article 193 TFEU and, second, what level of protection

[110] Technical measures also covers requirements adopted in the light of the environment and affecting the life cycle of a product after it has been placed on the market (Article 1(4) Directive).

[111] The Commission has three months to express disapproval. For an example of the application of this Directive, see Case C-433/05, *Criminal Proceedings against Lars Sandström*, [2010] ECR I-2885.

is allowed. In Section 3.4, I argue that such guidance should influence the manner in which green-plating is reviewed.

### 3.3.1 *Legislative Techniques to Show the Room for Green-Plating*

There are two main legislative techniques used by the EU legislator to show the Member States the room for green-plating. First, the Union legislator shows the opportunity for green-plating by means of minimum clauses. In the literature,[112] two kinds of minimum clauses are distinguished: a) explicit minimum clauses and b) implicit minimum clauses. Second, the Union legislator indicates the room for green-plating by means of options. The main difference between these two kinds of legislative techniques is that the latter is, generally speaking, more specific than the former. Indeed 'options' usually refers to a given measure that can be adopted or non-adopted by the Member States in the implementation phase.

It is unclear whether the EU legislator is aware of such techniques. By looking at the implementation reports of the Commission, it is possible to see that this institution keeps track of the use that Member States make of options. Similarly, the implementations reports provide information about the presence of national targets that are stricter than those established by the EU legislator. In Chapter 2, I made specific reference to the Commission's reports showing that Member States had adopted stricter targets for waste recovery and air pollution than those required under relevant EU law. Instead, few references can be found to the presence of national measures establishing stricter means than those required by the EU legislator to achieve an EU goal. Despite the attention given by the Commission to what Member States do when implementing options and minimum clauses related to the *height* of the level of protection of the environment, I have not retrieved documents showing that the three EU institutions mainly involved in the legislative process are aware of the difference between minimum clauses and options as regards the manner in which they indicate the room for green-plating. This difference is further explained below.

#### a) Minimum Clauses

Minimum clauses usually state that Member States are *allowed* to take more stringent measures. As discussed in Chapter 1,[113] they reassure the

[112] See Hofhuis (2006), pp. 71–83, with further references.
[113] Chapter 1, Section 1.3.4.

Member States that EU measures based on Article 192 TFEU comply with Article 193 TFEU. A distinction exists between explicit minimum clauses and implicit minimum clauses.

Explicit minimum clauses are clauses literally stating that Member States are allowed to maintain or introduce more stringent protective measures.[114] At times, explicit minimum clauses are formulated in relation to the content of the EU measure based on Article 192 TFEU as a *whole*. For example, Article 16(1) of the Environmental Liability Directive states: 'This Directive shall not prevent Member States from maintaining or adopting more stringent provisions in relation to the prevention and remedying of environmental damage, [. . .].'[115] Similarly, Article 14 of the Birds Directive states: 'Member States may introduce stricter protective measures than those provided for under this Directive.' Article 15 of the old CITES (Convention on International Trade in Endangered Species of Wild Fauna and Flora) Regulation followed a similar wording. Interestingly, when the old CITES Regulation was renewed, Article 15 was not repeated. Still, Recital 3 of the CITES Regulation states: 'Whereas the provisions of this regulation do not prejudice any stricter measure which may be taken of maintained by the Member States, in compliance with the Treaty, in particular with regards to the holding of species covered by this regulation.'

In some cases, explicit minimum clauses are not related to the whole of the content of the EU measure based on Article 192 TFEU at hand. They relate only to a specific part thereof. For example, Article 7(2) of the Air Quality Directive states: 'In each zone or agglomeration where fixed measurements are the sole source of information for assessing air quality, the number of sampling points for each relevant pollutant shall not be less than the minimum number of sampling points specified in Section A of Annex V.' As we can see, this provision clearly states that Section A of Annex V pursues only minimum harmonisation, and thus that the Member States are allowed to have more sampling points. Similar formulations can be seen for example in Article 7(3) of the Noise Directive,[116] which allows the Member States to maintain or introduce more stringent requirements for strategic noise maps than those

[114] See Sevenster (1992), pp. 68–69 for an enumeration of old directives and regulations falling within this category.

[115] See also Recital 29 of the Directive.

[116] Directive 2002/49/EC of the European Parliament and of the Council of 25 June 2002 relating to the assessment and management of environmental noise, [2002] OJ L 189/12.

indicated in Annex IV to that Directive. Similarly, Article 8(4) of the same Directive allows the Member States to maintain or introduce more stringent requirements for action plans than those indicated in Annex V.

Implicit minimum clauses are, instead, clauses that by mean of their content and purposes lead to minimum harmonisation.[117] Usually these provisions are recognisable by the use of terms such as 'not later than', 'at least' or 'not more than'. For example, Article 7(2) of Directive 2003/4/EC states: 'The information to be made available and disseminated shall be updated as appropriate and shall include at least: [. . .].'[118] An enumeration of information followed this sentence. The dictum 'at least' makes clear that the Directive only requires a minimum amount of information to be made available and disseminated. Member States may decide to make available and disseminate other information than those listed under Article 7(2) of the Directive. A formulation similar to that of Article 7(2) of Directive 2003/4/EC can be seen in Article 16(1) of the CITES Regulation, which states: 'Member States shall take appropriate measures to ensure the imposition of sanctions for at least the following infringements of this Regulation: [. . .]'. An enumeration of infringements follows this sentence. Once again, the dictum 'at least' allows the Member States to introduce sanctions for other infringements than those indicated under Article 16(1).

### b) Opt-In and Opt-Out Clauses

In addition to minimum clauses, Union environmental measures often include *opt-in* and *opt-out* clauses addressed to the Member States. By making use or non-use of such clauses, Member States go beyond EU requirements.[119] Usually, these clauses allow for specific measures to be adopted ('*opt-in* clauses') or not to be adopted ('*op-out* clauses'). For example, Article 15(2) of the New Waste Framework Directive (Directive 2008/98/EC) represents an example of an *opt-in* clause.[120] It states: 'Member States may decide that the costs of waste management are to be borne partly or wholly by the producer of the product from which the

[117] See Sevenster (1992), pp. 68–70 for several examples of such clauses.

[118] Directive 2003/4/EC of the European Parliament and of the Council of 28 January 2003 on public access to environmental information and repealing Council Directive 90/313/EEC, [2003] OJ L 41/26.

[119] As regards the linkage between opt-out clauses and green-plating see Veltkamp (1998), p. 188 and Jans & Vedder (2012), p. 114, footnote 64. See also Misonne (2011), p. 198.

[120] Directive 2008/98/EC of the European Parliament and of the Council of 19 November 2008 on waste and repealing certain Directives, [2008] OJ L 312/3.

waste came and that the distributors of such product may share these costs.' Accordingly, Member States may hold more subjects liable than required by Union law. Although no reference is made to the level of environmental protection provided, it can be assumed that enlarging the pool of liable subjects to include the producers and distributors of the products from which the waste came encourages these subjects to produce and distribute products with a lower waste impact.

Instead, Article 8(4) of the Environmental Liability Directive provides an opt-out clause. It states:[121]

> The Member States may allow the operator not to bear the cost of remedial actions taken pursuant to this Directive where he demonstrates that he was not at fault or negligent and that the environmental damage was caused by: (a) an emission or event expressly authorised by, and fully in accordance with the conditions of, an authorisation conferred by or given under applicable national laws and regulations which implement those legislative measures adopted by the Community specified in Annex III, as applied at the date of the emission or event; (b) an emission or activity or any manner of using a product in the course of an activity which the operator demonstrates was not considered likely to cause environmental damage according to the state of scientific and technical knowledge at the time when the emission was released or the activity took place.

If a Member State does not use this option, the regime in Article 8(1) applies. In other words, the operator bears the costs, leading to a higher level of internalisation of environmental costs and, arguably, a higher level of environmental protection.

It is also possible that secondary Union environmental measures contain provisions permitting a choice between two or more different legal instruments or regimes. We could call these kinds of clauses '*A-or-B* clauses', in which Member States must choose between A or B. The decision to use option A rather than option B, or vice versa, can influence the level of environmental protection at national level. For example, Article 16(1) of the IPPC Directive stated:

> Member States shall ensure that, in accordance with the relevant national legal system, members of the public concerned have access to a review procedure before a court of law or another independent and impartial body established by law to challenge the substantive or procedural legality of decisions, acts or omissions subject to the public participation provisions of this Directive when:

[121] Directive 2004/35/EC of the European Parliament and of the Council of 21 April 2004 on environmental liability with regard to the prevention and remedying of environmental damage, [2004] OJ L 143/56.

(a) they have a sufficient interest; or (b) they maintain the impairment of a right, where administrative procedural law of a Member State requires this as a precondition.

If a Member State does not implement the option offering the lowest high level of environmental protection among those offered by the EU measure at hand, it does not keep burdens to the minimum.

### *3.3.2 Information Carried by Minimum Clauses and Options*

The various legislative techniques described in the previous section provide the Member States with information about the room for green-plating. Three kinds of information are distinguished in this section: a) information about the *existence* of the room for green-plating, b) information about the *kind* of measure that is allowed and c) information about the *height* of the level of protection of the environment that can be pursued. All minimum clauses and options provide information about the existence of the opportunity for green-plating. Only certain clauses provide information about the kind of measure that is allowed and the height of the level of protection that can be pursued. In most of the cases only information about what kind of measure is allowed is provided. In certain cases, not even this information is provided. In total, clauses indicating the room for green-plating can be divided in three categories:

a) clauses only showing the existence of the room for green-plating;
b) clauses showing the existence of the room for green-plating and the kind of measure that can be adopted; and
c) clauses showing the existence of the room for green-plating, the kind of measure that is allowed and the height of the level of protection that can be pursued.

It should be noted that my analysis of EU secondary law concerning the use of these different legislative techniques has not revealed any pattern in the manner in which the EU legislature operates. No clear *modus operandi* emerged in this context. As stated above, the EU legislature does not seem to make conscious use of these different legislative techniques.

#### a) Clauses Only Showing the Existence of the Room for Green-Plating

In the previous section, I showed that, at times, explicit minimum clauses are formulated in relation to the content of the EU measure based on Article 192 TFEU *as a whole*. Article 16(1) of the Environmental

Liability Directive and Article 14 of the Birds Directive were used as examples of this legislative technique. These two clauses essentially state that green-plating under these two Directives is allowed. The only information with which the Member States are provided concerns the existence of the opportunity for green-plating. Faced with these kinds of clauses, Member States do not know what kind of measure is allowed and what height of the level of protection can be pursued. These two kinds of information can only be retrieved by interpreting the other provisions of these two Directives in light of such minimum clauses. Yet, Article 14 of the Birds Directive, for example, does not state that Member States can pursue a level of conservation which is 'outstanding', rather than the required 'favourable' level. Similarly, Article 14 of the Birds Directive does not state that a certain bird not listed under Annex I to the Directive can be protected by means of the same regulatory framework as that applied for birds that are listed on Annex I to the Directive. Such a finding is typical for explicit minimum clauses that are formulated in relation to the content of the EU measure based on Article 192 TFEU as a whole. All other clauses provide extra information.

### b) Clauses Showing the Existence of the Room for Green-Plating and the Kind of Measure That Could Be Adopted

In Section 3.3.1, I showed that certain explicit minimum clauses are linked to a specific provision of an EU measure. For example, I mentioned that Article 7(2) of the Air Quality Directive uses an explicit minimum clause to show that Member States could establish more sampling stations than those required under one of the Annexes to the Directive. A closer look at Article 16 of the Environmental Liability Directive shows that, after saying that green-plating is allowed under that directive, it adds: "[...] including the identification of additional activities to be subject to the prevention and remediation requirements of this Directive and the identification of additional responsible parties." Both articles provide more than just the information about the existence of the room for green-plating. They also show what kind of measure can be adopted. Article 16 of the Environmental Liability Directive shows that Member States can identify additional activities to be subject to the prevention and remediation requirements of this Directive. This clause, however, does not state how many more activities can be covered. Similarly, Article 7(2) of the Air Quality Directive does not provide information about the quality of the air that can be pursued. Hence, both clauses are silent about the height of the level of protection that can be pursued. This is a typical feature of this kind of clause.

Implicit minimum clauses follow this same finding. Implicit minimum clauses are always linked to a specific provision in an EU measure. In Section 3.3.1, I referred to Article 7(2) of Directive 2003/4/EC and Article 16(1) of the CITES Regulation as examples of this kind of clauses. Both of these provisions provide information about the existence of the room for green-plating. Additionally, they indicate what kind of measure is allowed. Under Article 7(2) of Directive 2003/4/EC extra information can be made available or disseminated. Under Article 16(1) of the CITES Regulation, extra sanctions can be established. None of these provisions indicates the height of the level of protection that can be pursued. The amount of extra information or extra sanctions that Member States can adopt based on these clauses is undetermined. Even when implicit minimum clauses are linked to limit values, they only indicate the kind of measure that is allowed, and not the height of the level of protection that can be pursued. For example, the hour limit value for sulphur dioxide established under Annex XI to the Air Quality Directive is set at 350 μg/m3, and is *not* to be exceeded *more than* 24 times per calendar year. Based on this information, Member States know that they can set stricter limit values. Yet the Directive does not say how much more stringent the national limit value might be.

The above findings can apply also as regards opt-in clauses. Opt-in clauses can indeed omit information about the height of the level of protection that can be pursued at the national level. For example, in Section 3.3.1, I referred to Article 15(2) of the New Waste Framework Directive stating that Member States may decide that the costs of waste management are to be borne partly or wholly by the producer of the product from which the waste came and that the distributors of such a product may share these costs. This provision includes two options. Both options show the kind of measure that can be established. Under the first option Member States may hold financially liable, in full or in part, the producer of the product from which the waste came. Under the second option, Member States may choose that the distributors of such products shall share these costs. The latter option is silent as regards the share that can be attributed to the distributors. Similarly, the first option does not define the concept of 'partly borne'; the height of the level of protection of the measure is left to the Member States. In contrast, the first option provides information about the height of the level of protection when it states that the costs can be 'fully borne' by the producer of the product from which the waste came. As we can see, certain opt-in clauses can be formulated in such a manner that the height of the level of protection that can be pursued is additionally indicated to the Member States. This category of measures is further discussed in the next section.

Similarly to opt-in clauses, A-or-B clauses do not always provide information about the height of the level of protection that can be pursued. This depends on the manner in which such clauses are formulated. For example, in Section 3.3.1 I referred to the A-or-B clause in Article 16(1) of the IPPC Directive. Under this option, Member States can choose between a locus standi based on sufficient interests or impairment of rights. Member States know what kind of measure is allowed. Yet the meaning of 'sufficient interest' or 'impairment of a right' is not further defined, thus, Member States can decide the height of the level of protection under both options.

### c) Clauses Showing the Existence of the Room for Green-Plating, the Kind of Measure That Is Allowed and the Height of the Level of Protection That Could Be Pursued.

As anticipated in the previous section, opt-in clauses and A-or-B clauses can, at times, provide all three kinds of information concerning green-plating. They can indicate the presence of the room for green-plating, they can indicate what kind of measures is allowed, and they can indicate the height of the level of protection that can be pursued. For example, the option to hold the producer of the product from which the waste came fully liable for the costs of processing the waste shows that not only the kind of measure is known to the Member States under this provision. The Member States also know how far they can go with the height of the level of protection: they can hold the producer of the product from which the waste came *fully* liable.

This is also a characteristic typical of opt-out options. In Section 3.3.1, I referred to Article 8(4) of the Environmental Liability Directive to provide an example of opt-out option. Under this option, Member States know that they do not have to go beyond the EU requirements under that provision of the Directive. The default rule under the Directive, namely the rule that applies if the opt-out clause is not transposed, not only shows the kind of measure that is allowed, but also the height of the level of protection that can be pursued.

## 3.4 Lighting the Path: A Model to Spur Legal Certainty as Regards the Legality Review of Green-Plating

In Section 3.2, I concluded that there are different approaches to the review of the legality of green-plating. Some approaches imply a stricter legality review than others. There is indeed no doubt that a strict necessity–based approach, such as that seen in the *Inntalautobahn No. 2* Case, is more stringent that the soft necessity test–based approach seen in the *Aher-Waggon* Case. In Section 3.3, I showed that there are different approaches to guide the Member States as regards the room for green-plating. Some clauses provide more information than others and therefore they ensure more clarity about what Member States can do. Opt-out clauses indeed offer much more clarity than general minimum clauses. I argue that by relying on the principles of sincere cooperation and legal certainty, it is possible to link the manner in which the EU legislature indicates the room for green-plating with the manner in which the EU judiciary reviews the legality of green-plating. This approach is inspired by the principle of legitimate expectations,[122] which was officially recognised as being a principle of EU law as early as the 1970s.[123] Yet I do not argue that the legislative technique adopted by the EU legislator gives the Member States the right not to be contested in their national choices concerning green-plating. The requirements developed by the Court of Justice in the context of this principle are too stringent to support such a claim.[124] The point is that, by linking the decision-making phase with the legal review phase, more legal certainty and a higher level of sincere cooperation can be achieved than under current practice.

As a matter of logic, opt-out clauses are the clearest instrument to indicate space for green-plating. Such clauses clearly indicate which measures the Member States do *not* have to take to pursue a higher level

[122] On this principle see, Tridimas (2006), pp. 242, and 286–289, Groussot (2005), pp. 15 and 16, and Usher (1988), p. 52.

[123] Case 2/75, *Einfuhr- und Vorratsstelle für Getreide und Futtermittel v C. Mackprang*, [1975] ECR 607, para 4; Opinion of AG Warner in Case 2/75, *Einfuhr- und Vorratsstelle für Getreide und Futtermittel v C. Mackprang*, [1975] ECR 607, p 622–623. Before this case was this principle was called 'protection of (legitimate) confidence' Case 1/73 Westzucker GmbH v Einfuhr- und Vorratsstelle für Zu cker [1973] ECR 723, ECLI:EU:C:1973:78 paras 6 and 10; Case 81/72 Commission v Council [1973] ECR 575, ECLI:EU:C:1973:60 paras 10 and 13; Opinion of EG in Case 169/73 Compagnie Continentale France v Council of the European Communities [1975] ECR 117, ECLI:EU:C:1974:135. I am thankful to Daniel Overgaauw for this suggestion.

[124] Case T-20/91, *Helmut Holtbecker v Commission of the European Communities*, [1992] ECR II-2599, para 53.

of protection than that strictly required by Union law. As regards the legality of national measures not using opt-out clauses, there is almost no doubt that such national measures comply with Union law since the Union legislator itself proposes these measures. Accordingly, they should benefit from the least stringent forms of legality review among those indicated in Section 3.2, namely the *de minimis/remoteness*–based approach, the soft necessity test–based approach, or even the silent proportionality–based approach.[125]

General minimum clauses, such as those worded similarly to Article 193 TFEU, are instead clauses that allow for the most uncertainty. General minimum clauses do not provide information about what kind of measures can be taken and about what level of protection can be pursued. Such clauses only provide information about the existence of the possibility to adopt stricter measures. In such circumstances, no presumption of legality can apply. In case the national measure pursues a stricter means than required by the EU legislator to achieve the EU goal, the most stringent of the approaches to legality review among those seen in Section 3.2 should be applied, namely the strict necessity test–based approach or even the silent proportionality–based approach.[126] The review should also include the proportionality *sensu stricto* as the EU goal is pursued. Instead, if based on a general minimum clause, the national measure pursues a higher goal than the one pursued by the EU legislator, one of the intermediary forms of proportionality could be followed, such as the proceduralisation–based approach or the judicial subsidiarity–based approach.

Opt-in clauses and minimum clauses linked to specific provisions, such as Article 4(6) of the Air Framework Directive, which allowed the adoption of stricter limit values, are somewhere in the middle. The level of clarity offered by the latter clauses depends on how they are formulated. In most cases, these kinds of clauses provide information about what kind of measure can be established, but they do not provide information about the height of the level of protection that is compatible with Union law. If an opt-in or minimum clause is clearly formulated, and a Member State follows such indications accurately, there should be a presumption that national law is compatible with Union law, at least

[125] In this context, reference is made to the silent proportionality–based approach leading to the acceptance of the national measure.

[126] In this context, reference is made to the silent proportionality–based approach leading to the rejection of the national measure.

as regards the instrument used. This would mean that the necessity test does not need to be performed in an intensive manner. When opt-in minimum clauses, next to indicating the competence to green-plating, and the kind of measure that can be adopted in this regard also indicate the height of the level of protection that can be pursued, then the same legal regime should apply as to opt-out clauses.

These considerations lead to the following scheme (Table 3.1), which, if applied consistently, will increase legal certainty and the level of sincere cooperation between the EU institutions and the Member States.

## 3.5 Conclusions: From Unclarity to Clarity as Regards Green-Plating

In this chapter, I showed that the manner in which the legality of green-plating is reviewed by the Court of Justice is unclear. At least seven different approaches applied by the Court of Justice could be retrieved in this regard. It is therefore difficult to predict how the Court of Justice will review green-plating, and hence whether the national measure will be approved by the EU judiciary. Such a lack of clarity has a real impact on Member States' decision to introduce or maintain green-plating. Having seen in Chapter 2 the importance that green-plating has for the functioning of the system envisaged under the Treaties to protect the environment, the existence of a lack of clarity as regards the legality review of green-plating should not be praised or ignored. Further, this chapter also showed that there is no clear *modus operandi* as regards the manner in which the EU legislature guides the Member States in the context of their power to maintain or introduce green-plating. Two different main legislative techniques employed by the EU legislator to indicate the room for green-plating, i.e. minimum clauses and options, were described as regards which information they actually provide. In most of the cases, no information is provided as regards the height of the level of protection of the environment that Member States may pursue. Only opt-out clauses and certain opt-in clauses provide such information. More often only the kind of measure that can be adopted is indicated. This is especially the case for specific minimum clauses, i.e. clauses linked to a specific provision and certain opt-in clauses. At times, general minimum clauses, i.e. clauses which are not linked to a specific provision and are worded in general terms, only provide information about the existence of the room for green-plating.

Table 3.1 The relationship between minimum clauses and legal certainty

| Kind of clause | Level of clarity about green-plating | Level of stringency of legality review | Approaches to proportionality |
|---|---|---|---|
| Opt-out clauses | HIGH: *known competence, known kind of measures, and known height of level of protection* | LOW | *de minimis/remoteness*-based approach, the soft necessity test based–approach, or even the silent proportionality based–approach |
| Opt-in clauses | MEDIUM-HIGH: *known competence, known kind of measures and (possibly) known height of the level of protection* | MEDIUM-LOW | proceduralisation–based approach or the judicial subsidiarity–based approach – in case of high level of clarity see approaches to opt-out clauses |
| Specific minimum clauses | MEDIUM: *known competence, and known kind of measures* | MEDIUM | Proceduralisation–based approach or the judicial subsidiarity–based approach. |
| General minimum clauses | LOW: *known competence* | HIGH-MEDIUM depending on whether a stricter means or a higher goal is pursued | in case of a higher means: strict necessity test–based approach or even the silent proportionality–based approach, including the proportionality *sensu stricto* test – in case of a higher goal: proceduralisation–based approach or the judicial subsidiarity–based approach |

Inspired by the principle of legitimate expectations, in Section 3.4 I proposed to link the various legislative techniques employed to guide the Member States vis-a-vis green-plating and the legality review of green-plating performed by the Court of Justice. In essence, the more guidance the EU legislature provides, the less stringent the legality review by the Court of Justice should be, at least in those cases in which Member States correctly apply the indications provided by the EU legislator. In this manner, clarity and sincere cooperation between the EU institutions and the Member States can be enhanced. In turn, such improvements meliorate the conditions for the proper functioning of the EU system of environmental protection.

# 4 Green-Plating and Economic Development

## 4.1 Introductory Remarks

The previous chapter showed first the link between green-plating and legal certainty. Moreover, it proposed a model to improve clarity about the room for national standards going beyond EU requirements. Legal certainty is not only important for the achievement of the environmental goals of the EU and national legislators, it is also important for economic development.[1] Clarity about standards and their possible development facilitates the gathering of information, influencing the decisions of public and private parties to make economic investments. There is, therefore, a link between green-plating and economic development. The importance of this linkage is also evident in the definitions of gold-plating available at national and EU level. In Chapter 1, I indeed concluded that these definitions are business centric. National policies on gold-plating focus on the alleged negative impact that stricter national standards can have on economic development, in general, and specifically on the competitiveness of national industry on the internal market.

As the claims on the negative effects of green-plating are usually not further refined by those promoting a halt to this phenomenon, this chapter offers first an empirical overview of what specific economic reasons have been brought forward by national legislators in relation to green-plating. Section 4.2 also shows that there are cases in which economic reasons actually justified adopting or maintaining green-plating.

1 On the linkage between legal certainty and economic theory, Tangea, Portuese and Gough (2014), pp. 1–26. More indirectly, Hinton (1997), pp. 1–28.

The presence of cases in which green-plating has been justified in light of economic considerations shows that the statement that green-plating is bad for economy should be further investigated. To this end, Section 4.3 discusses the so-called Porter Hypothesis, as it holds that environmental regulation can be positive for the competitiveness of national industry. Finally, Section 4.4 analyses how national legislators assess the costs and benefits of green-plating. To this extent, use is made of empirical material coming from the United Kingdom, in the form of statutory instruments implementing EU environmental directives in which green-plating is analysed in ad hoc costs/benefits models.

The picture arising from such research is that the cost/benefit models employed so far rely on a methodology that is short-term and short-view–biased and does not take sufficient account of the reach of literature and scientific insight on the relationship between environmental regulation and economic development.

## 4.2 Economic Considerations Justifying the Absence or Presence of Green-Plating

### *4.2.1 Economic Considerations Justifying the Absence of Green-Plating*

Because national policies on gold-plating are business centric, it is only logical that the main reason for reverting existing cases of green-plating and avoiding introducing new such cases is usually linked to economic considerations. Four kinds of economic considerations can be distinguished based on Member States' practice. Despite being clearly linked with one another, these four kinds of economic considerations can be framed in two main categories. First, there are those cases focusing on *lowering regulatory burdens*, seen as a goal in itself. Within this category, we can further distinguish between cases in which green-plating was avoided to keep burdens for *industry* to a minimum and cases in which green-plating was avoided to keep burdens for *public administrations* to a minimum.

For example, Article 9(2) of the Old Waste Framework Directive states that permits may be granted for a fixed period.[2] Article 23(2) of the New Waste Framework Directive maintains this option.[3] Arguably, Member

[2] Council Directive 75/442/EEC of 15 July 1975 on waste, [1975] OJ L 194/47, as amended by Council Directive 91/156/EEC of 18 March 1991 amending Directive 75/442/EEC on waste, [1991] OJ L 78/32.

[3] Directive 2008/98/EC of the European Parliament and of the Council of 19 November 2008 on waste and repealing certain Directives, [2008] OJ L 312/3.

States employing this option establish more stringent measures. Dutch law did this until 2010. In the Netherlands, prior to the implementation of the Old Waste Framework Directive, permits were already being granted for a fixed period under the Dutch Waste Act. According to Section 41(2) of the Dutch Waste Act,[4] permits had to be granted for a fixed time not exceeding ten years. This allowed a complete re-examination of all of the grounds for the permit when the undertakings requested renewal.[5] More precisely, Section 41 of the Dutch Waste Act allowed provinces to link the expiration date of permits to the date of expiration of a provincial waste plan, which had to be redrafted every ten years. In addition to facilitating the application of the provincial waste plan, this provision also ensured that establishments kept up with new environmental standards and technological developments.[6] In the 1990s, this case of green-plating was partially maintained. Section 8.17 of the Environmental Management Act established that permits for establishments disposing of waste from outside the establishment, or disposing of dangerous waste or landfill waste, had a maximum validity of ten years. This rule, which aimed at keeping permits current with the developments that have occurred in waste management,[7] did not apply to establishments disposing of waste from inside the establishment. For these establishments, the general rule is that permits apply indefinitely unless the permit states otherwise.[8] As can be seen, except for this latter kind of installation, the Dutch legislator employed the option provided for by Article 9(2) of the Old Waste Framework Directive. This can be connected to the desire to facilitate the application of provincial plans and with the aim of protecting the environment. After the entering into force of the Dutch policy on gold-plating, this case of green-plating was revised. In 2010, the General Act on Environmental Permits established that permits for establishments disposing of waste have an indefinite duration.[9] According to the government, environmental protection is guaranteed by the duty to update permits if new techniques become

[4] *Afvalstoffenwet*, Stb. 1977, 455.

[5] Proceedings of the Second Chamber of the States General, Kamerstukken II 1976/77, 13 364, nr. 10, p. 10.

[6] Ibidem.

[7] Proceedings of the Second Chamber of the States General, Kamerstukken II 1988/89, 21 087, nr. 3, p. 80.

[8] Section 8.16 of the Environmental Management Act.

[9] Section 2.23 of the General Act on Environmental Permits and Section 5.4 BOR.

available.[10] The main reason provided by the government to justify removing green-plating was the need to reduce administrative burdens.[11] This change derived from the wishes expressed by stakeholders during the evaluation of the First National Waste Management Plan (*Landelijk Afvalbeheerplan*).[12]

Similarly, when the United Kingdom transposed the Environmental Liability Directive,[13] it looked at the burdens associated with the introduction of cases of green-plating about, among others, the exclusion of the permits and state-of-the-art defences previewed under Article 8(4) of the Directive. Apart from cases in which genetically modified organisms (GMOs) cause environmental damage in Wales, the burdens on business caused by the non-implementation of this option were estimated to be higher than the benefits.[14] Accordingly, minimum implementation was pursued as regards this aspect of the Directive under The Environmental Damage (Prevention and Remediation) Regulations 2009.[15]

In other cases, the desire to keep burdens to a minimum focuses on the burdens of *public administrations*. For example, Articles 5(4) and 6(3) of the Environmental Liability Directive permits the adoption of measures in cases of so-called orphan damage, environmental damage for which an operator can neither adopt measures nor be identified.[16] Articles 5(4) and 6(3) state that competent authorities *may* take preventive and reparatory measures themselves, if an operator fails to comply with its obligations, cannot be identified, or is not required to bear the costs under the Environmental Liability Directive – the so-called subsidiary State liability. In the proposed version of the Directive, Articles 4(4) and 5(2) included an obligation rather than an option in this regard. Not all parties agreed to the proposal.[17] It was in the spirit of reaching a compromise with the

[10] Proceedings of the Second Chamber of the States General, Kamerstukken II, 2008/09, 31 953, nr. 24, p. 39 and VROM, *Landelijk Afvalbeheerplan* 2009–2021 (LAP2), p. 110.

[11] Stb. 2010, 143, explanatory memorandum, p. 72 and VROM, Landelijk Afvalbeheerplan 2009–2021 (LAP2), p. 110.

[12] Ibidem.

[13] Directive 2004/35/CE of the European Parliament and of the Council of 21 April 2004 on environmental liability with regard to the prevention and remedying of environmental damage, [2004] OJ L 143/56.

[14] Defra & WAG, Impact Assessment of the Environmental Damage Regulations (England) and the Environmental Damage Regulations (Wales) 2008, p. 1.

[15] Statutory Instruments 2009, No. 153.

[16] On 'orphan damage', see in particular, Wennerås (2005), pp. 147–148 and Krämer (2005a), p. 132.

[17] COM(2002) 17 final.

Member States that disagreed with this proposal that the obligation was changed into an option in the final version.[18] Despite the fact that the Netherlands was in favour of an obligation on this issue,[19] when it had to transpose the Directive it decided not to make use of the options allowed by these provisions. The Dutch legislator decided that Article 5(4), second sentence, and Article 6(3), second sentence, of the Environmental Liability Directive did not need transposition.[20] The government explained this decision by referring to the wish to avoid imposing excessive economic burdens on competent authorities.[21] Authorities have to fulfil other public functions in addition to that of protecting the environment. A system of compulsory liability would limit public authorities' freedom in setting priorities.

In addition to the desire to lower economic burdens, Member States justify not maintaining or introducing green-plating by referring to the wish to pursue *economic development*, in general, and in particular their desire to *preserve or increase the competitiveness* of national industry in the European internal market. Remaining within the context of the Environmental Liability Directive, the Netherlands made use of the latter ground to justify avoiding extending the strict liability regime of the Directive to operators other than those covered by it. The Environmental Liability Directive distinguishes between activities listed under Annex III and other operational activities. Annex III activities, due to their intrinsically more dangerous nature, are subjected to a strict liability regime under Article 3(1). Under Article 16 of the Directive, Member States are allowed to take more stringent protective measures. This includes extending the list of operators covered by the strict liability regime required by the Directive. The Dutch legislator does not use this option, at least for

[18] COM(2002) 17 final, p. 29. Krämer (2005b), p. 83 notes that Member States considered an obligatory 'safety net' too burdensome. Indeed, the United Kingdom, France, Italy, Portugal and Germany preferred a voluntary system, Council of the European Union, Institutional File 2002/0021 (COD), nr. 14289/02, note 54.

[19] Council of the European Union, Institutional File 2002/0021 (COD), nr. 7771/02, p. 10, footnote 38 and p. 11, footnote 39 and nr. 9600/02, pp. 7–10.

[20] Proceedings of the Second Chamber of the States General, Kamerstukken II, 2006/07 30 920, nr. 3, p. 27. The government recognises that this obligation could arise on the basis of the other provisions, such as Article 6 of the Habitats Directive. However, if Article 6 of the Habitats Directive requires States to take measures, this cannot be green-plating because, as explained in Chapter 1, national law is doing nothing more than fulfilling Union obligations.

[21] Proceedings of the Second Chamber of the States General, Kamerstukken II 2006/07, 30 920, nr. 3, p. 19.

the moment. Section 17.7 of the Environmental Management Act transposes Article 3 of the Environmental Liability Directive by means of a dynamic reference to the Directive. Strict liability is applied to the activities listed in Annex III to the Directive. The use of a dynamic reference ensures that the strict liability of the Directive does not apply to operators other than those listed in Annex III. At the same time, Section 17.7(a), subparagraph 2, of the Environmental Management Act allows the Dutch government to pass an order specifying other operators subject to strict liability regimes. As discussed in Chapter 2, Section 2.3, this provision was at the heart of parliamentary debate for almost a year. To end the parliamentary debate, government proposed the compromise that can be seen in Section 17.7(a), subparagraph 2, of the Environmental Management Act.[22] Activities other than those listed under Annex III of the Directive can be covered by the liability regime of Title 17.2 of the Environmental Management Act if this is established in a government order. In other words, Article 17.7 only offers the option of extending the field of application of Title 17.2 of the Environmental Management Act, but it does not actually require its extension.[23] Such an order has not been adopted yet.

References to the former ground, i.e. that green-plating is detrimental for economic development, have been used in the Netherlands mostly in the fields of ambient air quality and nature conservation. For example, in the context of ambient air quality, the Air Framework Directive employed goal-oriented obligations.[24] Member States had to respect emissions limit values, but were free to choose the means for achieving these goals (Articles 7(1) and 9). Only in two cases did the Directive prescribe that Member States had to establish a plan or programme indicating how to meet the obligations stemming from the Directive (Article 8(1 and 3) and Article 7(3)). Annex IV to the Air Framework Directive lists the minimum information to be provided in a plan. However, as clarified by the Court of Justice, it is up to the Member States to give concrete form to the content of plans and programmes.[25] This

[22] The government was anxious to avoid time consuming discussions, Proceedings of the Second Chamber of the States General, Kamerstukken II 2006/07, 30 920, HAN8159A08.

[23] Proceedings of the Second Chamber of the States General, Kamerstukken II 2006/07, 30 920, nr. 19.

[24] Council Directive 96/62/EC of 27 September 1996 on ambient air quality assessment and management, [1996] OJ L 296/55.

[25] Case C-237/07, *Dieter Janecek v Freistaat Bayern*, [2008] ECR I-236. Jans (2008b), pp. 514–515. The Court of Justice has clarified that the plan and programmes in Article 7(3) must form

clarification is particularly important under the Air Quality Directive, since Chapter IV (Articles 23–25) of the Air Quality Directive requires Member States to make plans any time a limit value is actually or potentially exceeded.[26] Under the Air Framework Directive, it is possible to argue that applying the emissions limit values of the daughter directives directly to public authority decisions affecting ambient air quality is a more burdensome way to achieve the goals of the Air Framework Directive than if a plan-based approach were followed.[27] Generally, plans allow more flexibility in the application of the emissions limit values. Therefore, a Member State that applies the emissions limit values directly to public authority decisions, such as the Netherlands, does not keep burdens to a minimum.

When, in the 1980s, the EU directives on air pollution[28] were transposed into the Dutch Air Protection Act, the limit values had to be applied by all competent authorities taking decisions affecting air quality.[29] For example, permits for industrial installations were directly assessed in light of the limit values, even when such installations only marginally contributed to air pollution.[30] Notwithstanding the fact that in the late 1980s the Dutch legislator had indicated its intention to move towards a plan-based approach,[31] in the 1990s, it continued to apply limit values directly to any decision of a competent authority affecting

a set of measures aiming at solving a concrete and specific situation; Case C-320/03, *Commission of the European Communities v Republic of Austria*, [2005] ECR I-9871 (Inntalautobahn No. 1).

[26] On this topic see, Squintani & Van Rijswick (2016).

[27] On the plan-based approach see Squintani & Van Rijswick (2016).

[28] Council Directive 80/779/EEC of 15 July 1980 on air quality limit values and guide values for sulphur dioxide and suspended particulates, [1980] OJ L 229/30; Council Directive 82/884/EEC of 3 December 1982 on a limit value for lead in the air, [1982] OJ L 378/15; and Council Directive 85/203/EEC of 7 March 1985 on air quality standards for nitrogen dioxide, [1985] OJ L 87/1. Examples of emissions-oriented measures were Council Directive 84/360/EEC of 28 June 1984 on the combating of air pollution from industrial plants, [1984] OJ L 188/20; Council Directive 88/609/EEC of 24 November 1988 on the limitation of emissions of certain pollutants into the air from large combustion plants, [1988] OJ L 336/1 and Council Directive 89/369/EEC of 8 June 1989 on the prevention of air pollution from new municipal waste incineration plants, [1989] OJ L 163/32.

[29] For example, Article 2 on sulphur dioxide in Stb. 1986, 78.

[30] Proceedings of the Second Chamber of the States General, Kamerstukken II1988/89 21 163, nr. 3, p. 49.

[31] Proceedings of the Second Chamber of the States General, Kamerstukken II1988/89 21 163, nr. 3, pp. 49–51. This approach is in line with the structure of the Environmental Management Act in which Chapter 5 follows Chapter 4 regulating plans and programmes, Tonnaer (1994), pp. 521 and 522.

air quality,[32] unless expressly not applied.[33] The 1998 transposition of the Air Framework Directive did not change this legal framework.[34] The Air Quality Order 2001 established that competent authorities should apply the limit values, unless otherwise provided.[35] The Air Quality Order 2001 clarified that limit values had to be respected by any decision affecting air quality.[36] In areas where limit values were exceeded, plans or projects could be allowed only if the competent authority ensured that such plans or projects ensured the best amelioration of air quality reasonably achievable.[37] As stated by Backes, a simple amelioration was not enough.[38] A comparative study performed by Backes highlighted that the Netherlands was one of the few Member States assessing planning decisions directly on limit values, including future limit values, and that, with the exception of Sweden, other Member States directly applied the limit values only for decisions having significant effect on air quality.[39] It is difficult to state whether the Netherlands went beyond the requirements of the Directive. However, the government and academics recognised this to be the case, at least to a certain extent.[40] I could not find a clear explanation for this potential case of green-plating. It seems that the Dutch legislator did not consider its original transposition as being more stringent than otherwise required.

Since 2005, the Dutch system has undergone a series of reforms to lower burdens.[41] First, Section 7(3) of the Air Quality Order 2005 allowed derogation from applying the limit values if the activity improved, or at least did not worsen, air quality directly or *overall* (Dutch law refers to

[32] Stb. 1993, 42, amending, *inter alia*, Stb. 1986, 78, Stb. 1987, 33 and Stb. 1987, 34.

[33] Stb. 1993, 42, Sections XXIII (B–C), XXIV (B–C) and XXV (B–C).

[34] However, it refined some elements. Article 5.2a was added to the Environmental Management Act. This provision required that the order establishing limit values transposing those in the Air Framework Directive had to establish rules concerning plans, programmes and action programmes.

[35] Stb. 2001, 269, for example, Sections 5 and 6 on sulphur dioxide.

[36] Stb. 2001, 269, explanatory memorandum, pp. 23–25. An indicative list was added to this effect.

[37] ABRvS of 15 September 2004, n. 200401178/1, ECLI:NL:GHSGR:2004:BM1321.

[38] Backes (2006b), pp.88 ff., par. 3.2.

[39] Backes (2006c), pp. 11–13. This study focused only on certain Member States.

[40] Proceedings of the Second Chamber of the States General, Kamerstukken II 2005/06 30 489, nr. 3, pp. 37 and 38. Backes (2006b), pp. 88 ff, par 2.2.

[41] A first element of the Dutch legislator's reform efforts had already been enacted in 2004 with the establishment of the national plan on air quality, VROM, *Nationaal Luchtkwaliteitsplan 2004. Beleidsplan van het ministerie van VROM*, Ministerie van VROM, The Hague.

*per saldo*, which has been translated as *per balance* in academic writing).[42] *Per balance* in this context means that a plan or project will be considered to have a positive effect even when it worsens air quality at a given location, as long as it improves air quality over a broader area.[43] Second, in 2007, the Air Quality Act amended the Environmental Management Act so that decisions have to be assessed in the light of a five-year plan indicating how limit values will be achieved, namely the National Cooperation Programme on Air Quality.[44] Section 5.16(1)(d) of the Environmental Management Act provides that public authorities exercising certain listed competences can exercise such competences only if the act to be taken is either indicated in, or not contrary to, the National Cooperation Programme on Air Quality.[45] Limit values are directly applied only in the context of a series of cases listed in Section 5.16(2) of the Environmental Management Act. This list is exhaustive,[46] as confirmed by case law.[47] Under Section 5.16 of the Environmental Management Act, no assessment needs to take place if decisions do not worsen air quality or have a marginal effect on air quality (in Dutch the so-called NIBM rule).[48] The NIBM rule follows the example of other Member States[49] and specifies a 3% parameter as the threshold below which decisions are not affected by limit values.[50] In addition, even if the assessment takes place, the *per balance* approach and the adoption of additional measures still permits the adoption of a decision affecting air quality.

In 2009 the National Cooperation Programme on Air Quality came into force. Between 2009 and 2015, the Netherlands has been following a

[42] See for example, Boeve & Van den Broek (2012), p. 78.

[43] Stb. 2005, 316, explanatory memorandum, p. 19, offering the example of a ring road around a city. Such a ring worsens air quality around the ring but improves air quality in the city area. This rule is further regulated in Stcrt. 2007, 214.

[44] The limit values and the other air quality standards are now listed in Annex II to the Environmental Management Act. At a local level, Section 5.9 establishes that municipalities should make plans to achieve the limit values, and their margin of tolerance.

[45] Section 5.16(1) of the Environmental Management Act. Schippers & Besselink (2009), pp. 75 ff., par. 4.

[46] Proceedings of the Second Chamber of the States General, Kamerstukken II 2005/06, 30 489, nr. 3, pp. 36 and 75; Proceedings of the Second Chamber of the States General, Kamerstukken II 2005/06, 30 489, nr. 8, pp. 15 and 16.

[47] ABRvS of 15 July 2009, n. 200806111/1/H3, ECLI:NL:RVS:2009:BJ2650, and ABRvS of 12 August 2009, r. 200809302/1/H3, ECLI:NL:RVS:2009:BJ5109.

[48] Proceedings of the Second Chamber of the States General, Kamerstukken II 2005/06, 30 489, nr. 3, p. 4.

[49] Idem, p. 29 with reference to Germany.

[50] Stb. 2007, 440 and Stcrt. 2007, 218.

plan-based approach. All these measures were taken to allow socio-economic developments as already indicated in 2005/2006.[51]

### 4.2.2 Economic Considerations Justifying the Presence of Green-Plating

The previous section shows what can be rightly considered the general approach as regards green-plating in several EU countries. Green-plating is limited to boost economic development. Yet there are cases in which adopting green-plating was explicitly linked to economic considerations. Empirical evidence brings four different kinds of economic justifications to the surface. This is an open enumeration.

First, green-plating can be pursued when it leads to *societal economic net benefits*. This was the case in the United Kingdom in the context of the transposition of the Environmental Liability Directive. In the United Kingdom, the transposition of this Directive aimed at a one-on-one implementation. Still, green-plating occurred as regards certain points.[52] In particular, the United Kingdom decided to apply the regime of the Directive to nature reserve areas other than those covered by the Directive. The Directive applies only to Natura 2000 sites; the United Kingdom also applies the regime of the Directive to Sites of Special Scientific Interest (SSSIs). The justification provided by the government for this case of green-plating was that, based on the impact assessment, the costs of avoiding green-plating were higher than those brought by green-plating. Indeed, when looking at the costs of this case of green-plating, the government focused on the costs of remediating damage or choosing to take anticipatory measures, and the costs of enforcement. It estimated that the total costs (present value) of minimal transposition (i.e. without extending to SSSIs) would have been few million pounds lower than when green-plating took place.[53] On the other hand, it estimated the benefit of this case of green-plating by looking at additional remediation of rivers, habitats and species and land contamination with benefits to society (80% of the estimate), and reduced damage and risks to the environment (20%). The government estimated that the total benefits (present value) of minimal transposition would have been lower than when green-plating was pursued.[54] When looking at the net benefit of

[51] Proceedings of the Second Chamber of the States General, Kamerstukken II, 2005/06, 30 489, nr. 3, p. 3.

[52] Jans & Squintani et al. (2009).

[53] This estimation also took into account not extending the permit defense to damage caused by GMOs in Wales.

[54] This estimation also took into account not extending the permit defense to damage caused by GMOs in Wales.

extending the regime of the Directive to SSSIs, the government concluded that these were higher than pursuing one-on-one transposition.

Secondly, there are cases in which green-plating is pursued, as it *improves the level playing field at national level.* This economic ground to justify green-plating was first highlighted during the transposition of BREF documents under the IPPC Directive,[55] now replaced by the Industrial Emissions Directive,[56] in the Netherlands. Article 1 of the IPPC Directive clearly stated that the Directive applied to the industrial activities listed in Annex I thereto. Article 2 of the Industrial Emissions Directive uses a similar formulation. Outside the scope of application of the directives, Member States are not precluded from passing national legislation regulating non-IPPC installations by means of an integrated approach based on Best Available Techniques (BAT). The Netherlands uses this possibility. When the Dutch Environmental Management Act was passed in 1993, one of the main concerns of the Dutch legislator was to create a uniform system. The same assessment framework applied to small, medium and large establishments alike.[57] Dutch law focused on establishments and not on installations.[58] When more industrial installations belong to the same establishment, they are regulated by the same permit.[59] In 2005, the Dutch legislator saw no reason to change the existing system and recognised that in certain cases the IPPC regime of the Directive would have been applied upon non-IPPC installations.[60] According to the Dutch government, such an enlargement of the field of application of the IPPC regime did not increase the regulatory burdens

55 Council Directive 96/61/EC of 24 September 1996 concerning integrated pollution prevention and control, [1996] OJ L 257/26. Codified by Directive 2008/1/EC of the European Parliament and of the Council of 15 January 2008 concerning integrated pollution prevention and control (Codified version), [2008] OJ L 24/8.

56 Directive 2010/75/EU of the European Parliament and of the Council of 24 November 2010 on industrial emissions (integrated pollution prevention and control), [2010] OJ L334/17.

57 Teekens (2005), pp. 13 and 14.

58 On the meaning of the concept of '*inrichting*' see Van der Veen (2005), p. 143 and Bastmeijer & De Vries (2005), p. 139. On the relationship between the concepts of 'installation' and 'establishment' see Van't Lam, Jurgens & Michiels (2002), in particular chapters 2 and 3.

59 Sections 1.1(1) and 1.1(4) of the Environmental Management Act, read in conjunction with Section 8.1 of the Environmental Management Act (today Section 2.1 of the General Act on Environmental Permits).

60 Proceedings of the Second Chamber of the States General, Kamerstukken II 2003/04, 29 711, nr. 3, p. 13 and TK 2003/04, 29 711, nr. 6, p. 4.

of non-IPPC installations, since the existing status quo was maintained.[61] In 2005, however, the Dutch legislator introduced the concept 'IPPC installation'.[62] This allows differentiating between establishments including IPPC installations and establishments without IPPC installations. Indeed, BREF documents are usually analysed by a group of experts who elaborates a note (a so-called BREFs Dutch Note) intending to further explain a BREF document to Dutch industry and authorities. In this phase the industry representatives are audited and it is decided whether a BREF document is applicable to establishments without an IPPC installation.[63] BREF documents are applied to establishments without an IPPC installation if a level playing field within the Netherlands is needed, if the BREF document concerned is an acceptable specification of an existing Dutch guideline, or if the application of the BREF document concerned does not lead to extra administrative and management burdens.[64] After such an evaluation, BREF documents and the BREFs Dutch Note are consolidated in a so-called Dutch Emissions Directive and in the so-called LBOW recommendations (until 2004, Recommendation of the Dutch Commission for an Integrated Water Management).[65]

Thirdly, green-plating can be economically sound if it reduces *administrative burdens*. This has been the case as regards the Dutch transposition of the provisions on accidents and incidents under the Industrial Emissions Directive. Following the example given by the Environmental Liability Directive, Article 7 of the Industrial Emissions Directive states that national law must require operators to take action in the event of any incident or accident significantly affecting the environment. Operators must inform the competent authority, take measures to limit the environmental consequences and to prevent further possible incidents or accidents. Competent authorities may require operators to take complementary measures. Article 7 only covers incidents or accidents having significant consequences for the environment. Under Article 193 TFEU,

[61] Proceedings of the Second Chamber of the States General, Kamerstukken II 2003/04, 29 711, nr. 6, p. 4.

[62] On this insertion, see Proceedings of the Second Chamber of the States General, Kamerstukken II 2004/05, 29 711, nr. 6, pp. 5 and 6.

[63] Taal (2005), pp. 70–71. Stb. 2005, 527, explanatory memorandum, p. 8.

[64] Stb. 2005, 527, explanatory memorandum, p. 9.

[65] Taal (2005), p. 71. On the incorporation of BREF documents, see also Proceedings of the Second Chamber of the States General, Kamerstukken II 2003/04, 29 711, nr. 3, pp. 9 and 10.

Member States are not prevented from also applying the legal regime of Article 7 of the Directive to incidents or accidents lacking significant consequences. The Netherlands uses this option. Title 17.1 of the Dutch Environmental Management Act regulates incidents in industrial establishments. It applies to any industrial establishments and it requires measures to be adopted regardless of whether the consequences for the environment are significant.[66] In the legislative proposal for the transposition of the Industrial Emissions Directive, the government proposed transposing Articles 7 and 8 of the Industrial Emissions Directive conjunctively.[67] In contrast to Article 7, but similar to the legislative practice followed under Article 17.1 of the Dutch Environmental Management Act, the application of Article 8, which regulates cases of non-compliance, is not conditional upon exceeding a threshold.[68] As noted by the Council of State, the conjunctive transposition of Articles 7 and 8 of the Directive implies the extension of the legal regime of Article 7 of the Directive to incidents or accidents *not* having significant consequences.[69] Given that the government maintained the proposed approach in the final version of the transposition act, the government cannot speak of a one-on-one implementation.[70] Although Article 17.2(4) of the Dutch Environmental Management Act allows competent authorities to exempt operators from the notification duty, this case of green-plating still occurs. On the one hand, Article 17.2(4) of the Dutch Environmental Management Act does not allow exempting operators from taking measures. On the other hand, competent authorities have to insert provisions into permits to exploit the option provided under Article 17(4). As regards the reasons for this case of green-plating, the government provided three. Among them, the government stated that transposition by means of two separate legal regimes would run counter to the reform of Title 17.1 of the Dutch Environmental Management Act introduced in 2011.[71] This reform aimed at lowering administrative burdens by introducing the possibility to replace the duty to notify each

[66] Section 17.1 of the Environmental Management Act.

[67] Proceedings of the Second Chamber of the States General, Kamerstukken II 2011/12, 33 197, nr. 2, Article III.

[68] Article 8(1) of the Directive states: '*Member States shall take the necessary measures to ensure that the permit conditions are complied with.*'

[69] Proceedings of the Second Chamber of the States General, Kamerstukken II 2011/12, 33 197, nr. 4, pp. 3 and 4.

[70] Stb. 2013, 159, Article III.

[71] Stb. 2011, 452.

individual incident or accident with a duty to report periodically on the incidents or accidents not having significant consequences for the environment.[72] I understand from this reasoning that this case of green-plating is justified by economic considerations.

Finally, green-plating can be used to gain a competitive advantage on the internal market. My empirical study concerning green-plating in the Netherlands in the field of waste law shows an indirect link between existing cases of green-plating and the aspiration of Dutch industry to become the raw-material centre for Europe.[73] I did not retrieve documents in which the Dutch government justifies existing cases of green-plating in light of this wish. Yet, government officials stressed how Dutch expertise in the treatment of waste can be used to strengthen the economic position of the Netherlands on the internal market for waste.[74] As further discussed in Section 3 below, Dutch expertise is based, inter alia, on green-plating.

The above presented cases suggest that the relationship between green-plating, on the one hand, and economy on the other, cannot be considered to be bad at all times. Environmental standards, including green-plating, could even be considered to be beneficial for economy. This is exactly what the Porter Hypothesis, discussed in the next section, sustains.

## 4.3 Economic Benefits of Environmental Regulation: The Porter Hypothesis

As shown above, and as discussed in the literature, environmental standards, in particular green-plating, are often seen as sources of additional costs which drive up prices and thus lead to smaller market shares, relocation and/or cessation of production.[75] This is the main assumption driving the Dutch and UK policies, as seen in Chapter 1. The examples discussed in the previous section suggest that there could be cases where stricter environmental standards could be beneficial for the national

[72] Proceedings of the Second Chamber of the States General, Kamerstukken II 2009/10, 32 445, nr. 3, p. 3. This reform did not apply to accident or incidents with significant effects on the environment. Such a limitation was in line with Article 14 of the IPPC Directive.

[73] Dutch Waste Management Association, *Annual Review 2010*, p. 1.

[74] Dutch Waste Management Association, Netherlands imports more waste, Waste Forum, September 2011, p. 2.

[75] Jenkins (1998), pp. 3 with further references. MacLeod et al. (2009), pp. 16–19.

economy. This possibility was formulated by the American economist Porter, who in 1991 stated that:

*Strict[er] environmental regulations do not inevitably hinder competitive advantage against foreign rivals.*[76]

Later, Porter refined what became known as 'the Porter hypothesis' as follows:

*Properly designed environmental regulation can trigger innovation that may partially or more than fully offset the costs of complying with them.*[77]

The Porter hypothesis, which focuses on substantive environmental provisions, rests on the idea that pollution is a form of economic waste, and involves unnecessary and incomplete utilisation of resources.[78] Therefore, pollution/waste reduction could improve the way firms use resources and thus lead to cost savings. Additionally, firms may also find ways to convert waste into saleable products and so increase revenues.[79] Stringent environmental regulation can also lead to a 'first move advantage' in the development and exploitation of new environmental techniques, technologies and applications.[80] In other words, *efficient* stricter environmental regulation can lead to win-win situations.[81]

The validity of such a hypothesis has long been discussed in the literature. While it has never been properly falsified,[82] especially because every case where competitiveness was hindered could be blamed on inefficient regulation,[83] it has also never been generally accepted.[84] For example, in 2008 Lanoie, Patry & Lajeunesse concluded a study on the total factor productivity of the Quebec manufacturing sector suggesting

[76] Porter (1991), p. 96. Comparative added by me to adapt the formula to the European Union context. For a recent overview of the theoretical framework of the Porter's Hypothesis see Wagner (2003).

[77] Porter & Van der Linde (1995a), p. 98. It should be noted that this hypothesis focuses on regulatory burdens and not specifically on administrative burdens. Moreover, this hypothesis refers to improvements in the performance of the firms affected by regulation and not to the overall benefits for a country. Therefore, the Porter Hypothesis is less broad than the costs/benefits analysis performed by the UK government.

[78] Porter & Van der Linde (1995b), p. 122.

[79] Porter & Van der Linde (1995b), p. 125.

[80] MacLeod et al. (2009), p. 20.

[81] Wagner (2003), in particular pp. 20 and 21.

[82] MacLeod et al. (2009), pp. 20 and 22, with references and assessment of empirical studies.

[83] Wagner (2003), p. 12, note 3, and 34.

[84] Lanoie, Patry & Lajeunesse (2008), pp. 121–122, with reference to the empirical studies performed to verify the Porter Hypothesis.

that, in the long run, stricter environmental regulation can lead to competitive advantages. However, they also stated that this does not appear true for highly polluting industries in highly competitive markets.[85] In 2009, Heyes underlined how competitive advantages linked to stricter environmental regulation are stronger for big firms, especially when they have a controlling position on the market.[86] He also underlined how stricter environmental regulation could lead to predatory behaviours or other anti-competition practices. In 2006, Oosterhuis showed examples in which command-and-control regulation to spur substitution of hazardous chemical substances led to comparative economic advantages on the EU internal market.[87]

In 2013, I performed a study in which I looked at the relationship between economic development and green-plating in one of the fields which Porter indicated as prone to showing evidence of the validity of his hypothesis, waste management.[88] In that study, I highlighted the development of green-plating in the Netherlands under the Waste (Framework) Directive between 1975 and 2013. The findings were juxtaposed with economic data concerning the development of Dutch industry in this sector, the manner in which Dutch government and the Dutch Waste Management Association look at these data, as well as to the stringency of the regulatory framework. Highlights from the analysis of the development of green-plating in this sector are reported in Section 4.3.1. Its relevance for the economic development of the Dutch waste industry is presented in Section 4.3.2 and discussed in Section 4.3.3.

### 4.3.1 *Green-Plating in Dutch Waste Management*[89]

Until the 1970s, dumping practices were a reality in the Netherlands.[90] To bring these practices to an end the Waste Act was passed in 1977.[91] The Waste Act focused on an environmentally sound disposal of waste and on waste recovery.[92] Over time, the legal framework on waste

85 Lanoie, Patry & Lajeunesse (2008), especially p. 128.
86 Heyes (2009).
87 Oosterhuis (2006). See also Ekins & Venn (2009), pp. 215–217.
88 Squintani (2013b).
89 This section is based on Squintani (2013b).
90 Proceedings of the Second Chamber of the States General, Kamerstukken II 1974/75, 13 364, no. 3, p. 34.
91 *Afvalstoffenwet*, Stb. 1977, 455.
92 Proceedings of the Second Chamber of the States General, Kamerstukken II 1976/77, 13 364, no. 5, p. 11 on the two pillars of the Waste Act.

management has been strengthened. Most notably, in the 1990s, when waste management was integrated with other sector-specific acts into the Environmental Management Act,[93] the functioning of the instruments introduced with the Waste Act was reinforced, and priority was given to waste prevention.[94]

The New Waste Framework Directive was transposed in 2011 by means of an amendment to the Environmental Management Act.[95] From the point of view of green-plating, this Act is particularly interesting because it was prepared in accordance with Guideline 331 of the Dutch Lawmaking Guidelines.[96] Accordingly, a legislative proposal should not contain any rules beyond those necessary for the transposition of the Directive, other than for technical reasons.[97] Furthermore, the Dutch government stated that, although more stringent protective measures are allowed under the Directive, measures that could affect the level playing field among Member States should be avoided.[98] Clearly, this statement can be linked to the Dutch policy on gold-plating presented in Chapter 1.[99] However, the government also indicated that the transposition of this Directive had to take into consideration the existing status quo, which, as further discussed below, went further than required by Union law.[100] As can be seen, the Dutch government seemed ready to maintain green-plating, albeit implicitly.[101]

For example, Article 9 of the Old Waste Framework Directive applied the permit requirement to establishments or undertakings disposing of their waste at the place of production. In addition, Article 10 covered

93 Environmental Management Act (*Wet milieubeheer*), Stb. 1979, 442, as amended.

94 Proceedings of the Second Chamber of the States General, Kamerstukken II 1988/89, 21 246, no. 3, p. 8.

95 Stb. 2011, 103 and Stb. 2011, 104.

96 Prime Minister's Circular of 18 November 1992, last amended by Prime Minister's Order, Minister of the Interior, 1 April 2011, nr. 310225, houdende vaststelling van de negende wijziging van de Aanwijzingen voor de regelgeving, Stcrt. 2001, nr. 6602.

97 Proceedings of the Second Chamber of the States General, Kamerstukken II 2009/10, 32 392, no. 3, p. 2.

98 Proceedings of the Second Chamber of the States General, Kamerstukken II 2009/10, 32 392, no. 7, p. 4.

99 Chapter 1, Section 1.2.2.

100 Proceedings of the Second Chamber of the States General, Kamerstukken II 2009/10, 32 392, no. 3, p. 14.

101 I will only focus on the provisions of Directive 2008/98/EC which have replaced the provisions of the Directive 2006/12/EC. Due to the general nature of these provisions, there is a greater chance that a discussion on the application of Dutch policy on gold-plating took place within the parliament.

installations or undertakings that recover waste. In both cases, an exception could be granted under certain conditions (Article 11). Today, the New Waste Framework Directive maintains this approach (Articles 23–26). Member States that do not exempt operators from the permit requirement do not keep burdens to a minimum. Dutch law does not keep burdens to a minimum. In the 1990s, permit requirements were regulated in Chapter 8 of the Environmental Management Act, which applied to industrial establishments in general. The general rule was that any establishment had to be subjected to a permit to be established, changed and exploited, unless an order stated otherwise (Article 8.1). Establishments for the recovery of waste were explicitly mentioned as establishments for which a permit was required.[102] Waste producers discarding their own waste at the place of production were also not exempted from the permit requirement.[103] In 2009, two years before the transposition of the New Waste Framework Directive, the General Act on Environmental Permits replaced the provisions of Chapter 8 of the Environmental Management Act. Under the new Act, only establishments with an IPPC installation or establishments listed in a specific order are subject to a permit requirement.[104] With regard to the management facilities of waste, Annex I sub C to the Environmental Permits Order states that establishments for the disposal or recovery of waste must have a permit, unless they fall under one of the thirty-three categories explicitly mentioned therein (Section 2.1(2)) and Category 28.10 in Annex I, sub C.[105] The 2011 transposition act did not touch upon this system.[106] As can be seen, the Netherlands partly enforced the opt-out clause available under the New Waste Framework Directive in 2009. The use of this clause was part of a more general reform of the Dutch permitting system that aimed at lowering administrative burdens.[107] This was done in accordance with the Dutch policy on gold-plating. However, it should be noted that only certain activities are exempted under the General Act on

[102] Category 28 under Annex I to Stb. 1993, 50.

[103] The content of the permit could be influenced by whether an establishment discarded waste coming from inside the establishment concerned or from outside.

[104] Stb. 2008, 496, *Wet algemene bepalingen omgevingsrecht.*

[105] Stb. 2010, 143, *Besluit omgevingsrecht* (BOR) as amended by, in particular, Article II, letter J, point 11 of Stb. 2010, 781. Activities involving non-separate collection were not exempted, nor were activities with mixed waste. New categories were exempted with Article II, letter G, point 13 of Stb. 2012, 558 amending Category 28.10 in Annex I, sub C to the BOR.

[106] Proceedings of the Second Chamber of the States General, Kamerstukken II 2009/10, 32 392, no. 3, p. 13.

[107] Stb. 2010, 781, explanatory memorandum, p. 30.

Environmental Permits and the Environmental Permits Order system. In particular, the reform covered installations for the recovery of homogenous flows of 'material unpackaged goods' (*vaste bulkgoederen*).[108] For example, activities for the recovery of ink cartridges for printers are covered by this reform. Activities were selected using generally applicable criteria, such as the homogeneity of the activities covered, and three specific waste-related criteria: a) activities must focus on the recovery of waste, in particular the recovery of raw materials; b) activities can be easily controlled without the need for complex analysis or studies[109] and c) activities facilitate extended producer responsibility systems.[110] The transposition of Article 24 of the New Waste Framework Directive represents a perfect example of the 'no-gold-plating, unless' regime which characterised the Dutch policy on gold-plating until the 2010 coalition agreement. Certain kinds of human activities concerning waste can, due to their very nature, be regulated by means of an ex post control mechanism, i.e. inspections. Others require complex assessments. Accordingly, they should be subjected to an ex ante control mechanism as well, i.e. the permit. More generally, environmental concerns only partially seem to have driven the decision to use the opt-out clause in Article 24 of the New Waste Framework Directive. Instead, they justify the green-plating.

Another case of green-plating occurs in the field of the targets for reuse or recycling. Article 11 of the New Waste Framework Directive establishes explicit *minimum* targets for the preparing for reuse and the recycling of at least paper, metal, plastic and glass from households (increase of an overall 50% by weight by 2020) and of non-hazardous construction and demolition waste (increase of an overall 70% by weight by 2020). The clause 'to a minimum of' used in these provisions specifies that Member States can establish stricter targets. The Netherlands uses this option. As recognised by the Dutch government, the National Waste Management Plan 2009–2021 sets stricter binding standards than the Directive requires.[111] The amount of waste being recycled in the Netherlands has increased steadily,[112] and by 2015, the preparation for reuse

[108] Idem, p. 36.
[109] Ibidem.
[110] Idem, p. 37.
[111] VROM, *Landelijk Afvalbeheerplan 2009–2021* (LAP2), pp. 91 and 92.
[112] *CBS, PBL, Wageningen UR (2010), Afvalproductie en wijze van verwerking, 1985–2008 (indicator 0204, version 09, 22 September 2010).* www.compendiumvoordeleefomgeving.nl. CBS, The Hague; Planbureau voor de Leefomgeving, The Hague/Bilthoven and Wageningen UR, Wageningen. See also Dutch Waste Management Association, Annual Review 2010, Afvalforum, p. 6.

and recycling of waste materials including at least household paper, metal, plastic and glass, or comparable waste, should be increased to an overall 60% by weight. In addition, by 2021, the preparation for reuse and recovery of other materials shall be increased to 95% in weight. As can be seen, by setting binding targets that are more stringent than those required by the New Waste Framework Directive, the Netherlands has adopted more stringent measures. Curiously, the government gave no attention to this fact during the transposition of the New Waste Framework Directive.[113] The Dutch policy on green-plating did not apply.

Further, in line with the principle that the polluter should pay, Article 14 of the New Waste Framework Directive states that the costs of waste management shall be borne by the original waste producer or by the current or previous waste holders. In addition, the Member States *may* decide that the costs of waste management are to be borne partly or wholly by the producer of the product from which the waste came, and that the distributors of such products may share these costs. As can be seen, Article 14 provides an option with respect to the liability for the costs of waste management of the producers of the product from which the waste came. Member States using this option may be establishing more stringent measures. The Netherlands uses this option. From 1993, Dutch law has had two instruments that follow the principle of extended producer responsibility. Section 15.32 of the Environmental Management Act introduced the possibility of establishing a return deposit and a return premium. In addition, Title 15.10 of the Environmental Management Act allows the introduction of a system of so-called Waste Management Contributions, if an industrial association so requires. Waste Management Contributions are based on private funds that cover the cost for establishing the infrastructure required to recover products. Title 15.10 of the Environmental Management Act allows such contributions to be made compulsory for all producers or importers of the goods concerned on the Dutch market.[114] According to the Dutch government, the system described above increases waste prevention and recycling.[115]

[113] In particular, Proceedings of the Second Chamber of the States General, Kamerstukken II 2009/10, 32 392, no. 3, pp. 6 and 7 and Proceedings of the Second Chamber of the States General, Kamerstukken II 2009/10, 32 392, no. 7.

[114] Such a measure serves to ensure the functioning of the infrastructures, which are developed by industry itself, Proceedings of the Second Chamber of the States General, Kamerstukken II 1992/93, 23 256, no. 3.

[115] Proceedings of the Second Chamber of the States General, Kamerstukken II 1993/94, 23 256, no. 5, pp. 2 and 3.

Therefore, this case of green-plating seems to be linked to environmental concerns. The government also stated that Union law leaves space for such rules.[116] This suggests that the Dutch legislator was aware of exceeding the minimum requirements imposed by the Directive.

In 2011, the government indicated its intention to redress this case of green-plating, albeit partially. In the legislative proposal for the transposition of the New Waste Framework Directive, a provision allowed the recovery of only *a part* of the costs from the producers of the products from which the waste came.[117] This change was in line with the minimum requirements established by the Directive. However, several members of Parliament questioned the meaning and the effects of the change. Some of them feared that the polluter pays principle and the principle of extended producer responsibility would have been negatively affected, along with legal certainty.[118] Others wanted the government to go even further. The People's Party for Freedom and Democracy called for the abolition of all provisions following extended producer responsibility.[119] The government replied that legal certainty should be guaranteed and therefore that it would have refrained from downgrading the status quo.[120] Unfortunately, due to an error of correlation with a parallel legislative proposal,[121] the current Section 9.5.2(3), letter b, of the Environmental Management Act allows the recovery of only a part of the costs from the producers of the products from which the waste came.[122] However, the parliamentary history of Section 10.17 of the Environmental Management Act casts doubt on the validity of Section 9.5.2(3), letter b, of the Environmental Management Act. The Dutch legislator did not want to downgrade the status quo. The transposition of Article 14 of the New Waste Framework Directive shows that legal certainty is considered a sufficient reason to justify green-plating. Interestingly, the claim of legal certainty made by certain exponents of

[116] Proceedings of the Second Chamber of the States General, Kamerstukken II 1992/93, 23 256, no. 3, p. 7.

[117] Proceedings of the Second Chamber of the States General, Kamerstukken II 2009/10, 32 392, no. 2.

[118] Proceedings of the Second Chamber of the States General, Kamerstukken II 2009/10, 32 392, no. 6, pp. 5–8.

[119] Idem, p. 4.

[120] Proceedings of the Second Chamber of the States General, Kamerstukken II 2009/10, 32 392, no. 7, p. 10.

[121] Proceedings of the Second Chamber of the States General, Kamerstukken II 2007/08, 31 501, no. 2 adopted with Stb. 2011, 269.

[122] Section V, letter B1, Stb. 2011, 103 and Section I, letter D, Stb. 2011, 269.

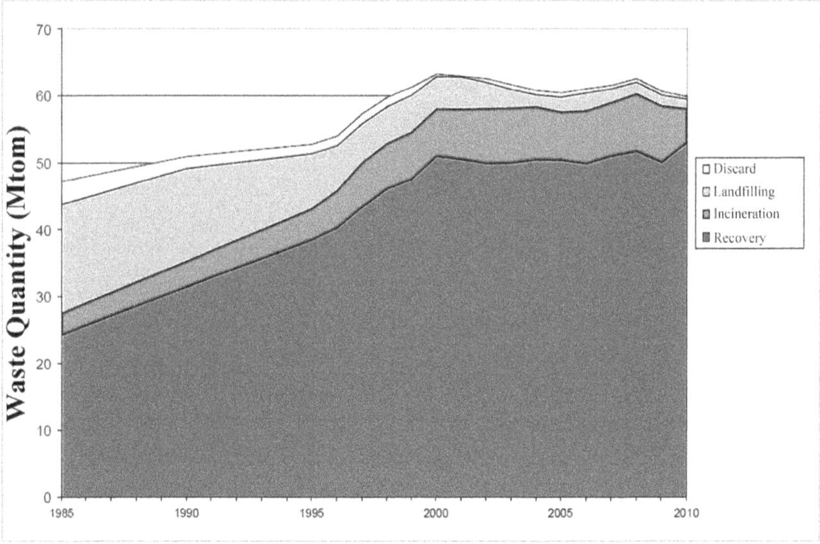


Figure 4.1 Waste trends in the Netherlands 1985–2010[123]

Parliament did not rely on studies or empirical data. It was formulated on an abstract level. The decision to maintain green-plating was not supported by a substantiated cost/benefit analysis. Only due to a mistake was this case of green-plating partially redressed.

### *4.3.2 Green-Plating in Dutch Waste Management and the Development of Dutch Waste Industry*

The effects of the Dutch regulatory framework for waste management, including the cases of green-plating described above, seem to have beneficial effects. Figure 4.1 shows that the amount of waste recovered in the Netherlands has been increasing steadily.

Both in 2010 and in 2014, the Dutch Ministry responsible for environmental protection underlined that environmental protection in the field of waste management does not seem to affect the economic growth of the sector.[124] If we compare the figures concerning the turnover of Dutch waste management industry in 2010/2011 with those concerning

[123] Adapted from Figure 2.1 in *Landelijk Afvalbeheerplan 2009–2021 - Naar een materiaalketenbeleid*, 3 December 2014, p. 20.

[124] VROM, *Landelijk Afvalbeheerplan 2009–2021 - Naar een materiaalketenbeleid*, 16 February 2010, pp. 24 and 25 and IenM, *Landelijk Afvalbeheerplan 2009–2021 - Naar een materiaalketenbeleid*, 3 December 2014, pp. 19 and 20.

2012/2013, we can see an increase from 5.7 billion euros per year to 7 billion euros per year.[125] Actually, the decrease in the amount of waste being landfilled, which can be partially linked to the increased amount of waste being recovered, could explain why the Netherlands could become a raw-material centre for Europe.[126] The Dutch Waste Management Association, in close dialogue with the political worlds, highlights the potentials of good functioning waste management policy, which, as seen in the previous section, includes green-plating, for the economic growth of the sector in two different manners.

First, waste management services can be exported to fulfil the needs of other Member States. For example, in September 2011, the Netherlands started disposing of 248,000 tons of waste from Naples, for 12 million euros. The importance of this economic opportunity and its linkage to the quality of waste management systems in the Netherlands is well represented by the following quotes from a Dutch Waste Management Association publication on waste imports published in 2011:[127]

*The signposts at the border are going to change for good. With its considerable expertise in recycling waste streams, the Netherlands is promoting itself as a materials roundabout. Moreover, most Dutch waste-to-energy plants now have recovery (R1) status. Facilities that meet the European standards for high thermal efficiency are permitted to import combustible waste for treatment. According to statistics provided by NL Agency, more waste will be imported this year, especially from Germany and the UK in particular. Over the first five months of this year imports amounted to about 20,000 tonnes per month. This is 240,000 tonnes on an annual basis, compared with 144,000 tonnes in 2010. In May alone, import permits were issued for almost 500,000 tonnes of waste, bringing the total for this year to almost a million tonnes.*

. . .

*Hester Klein Lankhorst, head of the waste and material chains department at the Ministry of Infrastructure and the Environment, is delighted by the waste imports. 'It is a laudable development. It is much better for Dutch companies to incinerate waste with energy recovery than for it to end up in a landfill elsewhere in Europe. It is consistent with the philosophy of treating waste as a source of materials and energy. I repeatedly remind my British colleagues of the possibilities for exporting waste to the Netherlands, most recently at a meeting in Brussels.' Klein Lankhorst says the ministry is very keen to create a 'materials roundabout' in the Netherlands.*

125 Dutch Waste Management Association, Annual Review 2011, Afvalforum, May 2012, p.17 and Dutch Waste Management Association, Afval in Cijfers, May 2015, available at www.verenigingafvalbedrijven.nl/publicaties/poster-afval-in-cijfers.html (accessed June 2017).

126 Dutch Waste Management Association, Annual Review 2010, Afvalforum, p. 1.

127 Dutch Waste Management Association, Netherlands imports more waste, Afvalforum, September 2011, p. 2.

The closing sentence in the second quote links waste imports with the second source for potential economic growth. Indeed, with the concept of a '*materials roundabout*' Dutch politicians and waste operators also mean the recovery of valuable raw materials.[128] Predicting a growing scarcity of raw materials for the production of consumer goods, Dutch politicians and waste management operators invest in waste recovery to transform the Netherlands into a raw-material centre for Europe.[129] This also has implications for the labour market, which is predicted to benefit from such developments.[130]

### *4.3.3 Green-Plating in Dutch Waste Management and the Development of Dutch Waste Industry: A Verification of the Porter Hypothesis?*

It is for colleagues from the economic sciences to establish whether the manner in which the Dutch government regulates waste management represents a confirmation of the validity of the Porter hypothesis. From a legal perspective, it is possible to state that green-plating occurred in the past and still occurs today in the Netherlands in the context of waste management, as shown in Section 4.3.1, above. Equally certain is that the turnover of Dutch waste management industry is growing. The Netherlands is exporting waste management services and fostering its position on the internal market for the recovery of valuable raw materials. It can be concluded that environmental protection and economic growth are both fostered, as predicted by specific studies on this topic,[131] and actually they seem to be mutually reinforcing.

Dutch industry and government seems to be aware of the competitive advantages that the relatively favourable status of waste management in the Netherlands comports in the context of an internal market for circular economy. The attention for circular economy, which at EU level made its official entry in 2014/2015,[132] started in the Netherlands in 2010/2011,[133] and took concrete form in Dutch government plan

[128] Dutch Waste Management Association, *Grondstoffenschaarste scherp op het netvlies*, Afvalforum, May 2012, p. 5 with references to both governmental and parliamentary sources. See also the estimations in Ton Bastein et al., Kansen voor de circulaire economie in Nederland, TNO-rapport, 11 juni 2013, TNO 2013 R10864.

[129] Dutch Waste Management Association, *Annual Review 2010*, p. 1.

[130] Bastein (2013).

[131] Ibidem.

[132] European Commission, Towards a circular economy: A zero waste programme for Europe, COM (2014) 398 final.

[133] The Dutch policy on circular economy was influenced by the European Policy on Resource efficiency, in particular the European Commission, Roadmap to a Resource

presented in 2016.[134] References to the role that Dutch successes in the context of domestic waste management could play in the context of an international circular economy are visible in documents from the Dutch government and industry concerning circular economy.[135] Such documents do not speak of green-plating in this regard. Yet as demonstrated in Section 4.3.1 above, green-plating plays a crucial role in the achievement of the high level of waste recovery, higher than required under EU law, forming part of the Dutch successes in the context of domestic waste management. Unconsciously, the Dutch government and industry seems to accept that green-plating is good for the competitiveness of the Dutch economy in the field of waste management.

This result was not achieved in the short term. As shown in Section 4.3.1, some cases of green-plating were implemented many years before their effects seemingly started to benefit Dutch economy in the field of waste management. This consideration suggests the need for long-term thinking when considering the costs/benefits of green-plating.[136] Time is indeed an essential component for the success or failure of innovation dynamics and eco-innovation.[137] Yet long-term thinking is something that, as highlighted in the literature,[138] and confirmed in the next section, regulatory impact assessments rarely do.

## 4.4 Green-Plating in Regulatory Impact Assessments

No-gold-plating policies have been developed by several Member States, as discussed in Chapter 1.[139] As written by my co-authors and me in

Efficient Europe, COM (2011) 571 final, see Proceedings of the Second Chamber of the States General, Kamerstukken II 2012/2013, 33 043, nr. 15, p. 1.

[134] Proceedings of the Second Chamber of the States General, Kamerstukken II 2015/16, 32 852 and 33 043, Nr. 33, and the Annex to the document, Ministerie van Infrastructuur en Milieu en het ministerie van Economische Zaken, mede namens het ministerie van Buitenlandse Zaken en het ministerie van Binnenlandse Zaken en Koninkrijksrelaties, *Nederland circulair in 2050*, September 2016, available at www.rijksoverheid.nl/circulaire-economie (accessed July 2017).

[135] Eg. Dutch Waste Management Association, *Grondstoffenschaarste scherp op het netvlies*, Afvalforum, May 2012; Bastein et al. (2013); Proceedings of the Second Chamber of the States General, Kamerstukken II 2012/13, 33 043, nr. 15.
Proceedings of the Second Chamber of the States General, Kamerstukken II 2015/16, 32 852 and 33 043, Nr. 33.

[136] Ekins & Venn (2009), p. 198, based on two Dutch studies: TME, *Technische vooruitgang en milieukosten, aanzet tot methodiekontwikkeling*, The Hague: TME; and RIVM, *Techno 2000; Modelling van de doling van eenheidskosten van technologieën in de tijd*, Reportnummer 773008009, April. Bilthoven: RIVM.

[137] Ekins & Venn (2009), p. 197 with further references.

[138] Ekins & MacLeod (2009), pp. 233 and 234. See also Oosterhuis et al. (2006).

[139] Chapter 1, Section 1.2.

2015, some Member States are increasingly professionalising the transposition process, which can be shown by initiatives at national level in terms of transposition principles and practices.[140] Regulatory impact assessments can be used as instruments in this regard,[141] an activity that is also stimulated by the Commission.[142] With regulatory impact assessments is commonly understood the official appraisal made or coordinated by government officials of the effects of specific policy instruments on several public policy areas such as competitiveness, administrative burdens, health and environment.[143] Yet the manner in which such assessments are performed varies from country to country.[144] This occurs also as regards those countries with an explicit gold-plating policy. In the Netherlands, the discussion on the costs/benefits of green-plating is much more loosely formulated and based on rhetoric rather than concrete data. In the Netherlands the so-called BNC-fiches[145] do not provide detailed information.[146] Rather, they mainly provide qualitative assessments, based on general assumptions.[147] Additional Impact Assessments are sometimes carried out in different phases of the formal transposition process, but only on an ad hoc basis.[148] A much more detailed approach is followed in the United Kingdom.[149] The UK Regulatory Impact Assessment Toolkit identifies the need to ensure early

[140] Anker et al. (2015), p. 42.
[141] Idem, p. 39.
[142] European Commission, 'Smart Regulation in the European Union, COM (2010) 543 final.
[143] Hertin et al. (2009b), p. 413.
[144] See e.g. Jacob et al. (2008). See also Farmer, Ten Brink & Kettunen (2006), p. 395 and Hertin et al. (2009).
[145] BNC stands for *Beoordeling Nieuwe Commissievoorstellen* (in English: Assessment of New Commission's Proposals). These documents are prepared by the Workgroup for the Assessment of New Commission Proposals. They provide a short summary of the Commission's proposal, an assessment of the impact of the Commission's Proposal on the NL, the EU information about the legal basis, the principles of subsidiarity and proportionality, and the point of view of the Dutch government.
[146] See also Hertin, Jacob and Volkery (2008).
[147] Anker et al. (2015), p. 39.
[148] As regards the Industrial Emissions Directive (n. 356) the Dutch government commissioned a series of impact assessments to an external consultant, see Sira Consulting, *Administratieve en bestuurlijke lasten Richtlijn Industriële Emissies Eerste tranche: Politiek Akkoord – Onderzoek naar de administratieve en bestuurlijke lasteneffecten van het Politiek Akkoord voor de Richtlijn Industriële Emissies* (February 2010); Sira Consulting, *Administratieve en bestuurlijke lasten Richtlijn Industriële Emissies – Onderzoek naar het Effect van de Richtlijn Industriële Emissies op de administratieve en bestuurlijke lasten* (June 2011) 17 (English summary).
[149] See also Hertin, Jacob and Volkery (2008).

engagement and analysis before any EU proposal is adopted, as well as continued elaboration during the negotiation and transposition phases.[150] Of course, the exactness of the data in regulatory impact assessments should not be overestimated.[151] Such studies are indeed based on assumptions, and assumptions can be wrong or even misleading. Moreover, as written in 2015 with my co-authors, the UK regulatory impact assessments appear to have a fairly narrow focus on regulatory burdens on businesses, the public sector and consumers.[152] This section, accordingly, does not look at whether the regulatory impact assessments performed in the United Kingdom as regards the costs/benefits of green-plating are correct or not. I only look at 'how' the costs/benefits of green-plating are assessed.

A close look at the regulatory impact assessments performed in the United Kingdom in relation to statutory instruments transposing environmental directives shows that such documents take account of certain potential cases of green-plating. This is mostly the case for explicit minimum clauses or opt-in and opt-out clauses in EU environmental law.[153] Still, it is remarkable that not all possible options are discussed. I could not trace a pattern in the selection of which potential case of green-plating to discuss. There seems to be a political bias concerning the content of such regulatory impact assessments.[154] When options are discussed, costs and benefits are calculated for those options that the Government considers leading to changes in the status quo. If the status quo is maintained, costs/benefits are not assessed.

An analysis of regulatory impact assessments for the transposition of the Air Quality Directive, the Environmental Liability Directive and the Waste Directive is used here to provide insight into the manner in which the costs and benefits of green-plating are assessed in the United Kingdom. Attention is mainly given to the regulatory impact assessments of the British Government, given its leading role in the development of the UK policy on gold-plating. Welsh, Scottish and Northern Ireland governments' regulatory impact assessments are considered when they are necessary for providing

[150] HM Government, IA Toolkit. How to do an Impact Assessment (Department for Business, Innovation and Skills August 2011), more times updated.

[151] Ekins & MacLeod (2009), show that UK regulatory impact assessments tend to overestimate costs. See also MacLeod et al. (2009), p. 24–29.

[152] Anker et al. (2015), p. 39. See also Nao (2006) and Hertin et al. (2009b).

[153] About legislative techniques to show the room for green-plating see Chapter 3, Section 3.3.

[154] Hertin et al. (2009a) and Hertin et al. (2009b).

a complete picture of the ongoing practice, keeping in mind that it is not the purpose of this section to provide an exhaustive picture of such practice.

For example, the 2010 Regulatory Impact Assessment attached to the statutory instrument transposing the Air Quality Directive,[155] discussed the cost/benefit of (not) taking advantage of the opt-out clause in Article 20 of the Directive. This provision states:

*Member States shall transmit to the Commission, for a given year, lists of zones and agglomerations where exceedances of limit values for a given pollutant are attributable to natural sources. Member States shall provide information on concentrations and sources and the evidence demonstrating that the exceedances are attributable to natural sources.*

If they succeed, Article 20(2) continues: 'that exceedance shall not be considered as an exceedance for the purposes of this Directive.' Despite the prescriptive tone of this provision, the preamble introducing it shows that Member States have the possibility and not the obligation to implement this provision. At the request of the Member States,[156] Recital 15 states:

Contributions from natural sources can be assessed but cannot be controlled. Therefore, where natural contributions to pollutants in ambient air can be determined with sufficient certainty, and where exceedances are due in whole or in part to these natural contributions, these *may*, under the conditions laid down in this Directive, be subtracted when assessing compliance with air quality limit values [author emphasis].

The use of the auxiliary verb 'may' suggests that this provision does not impose an obligation. Similarly, Article 21 Air Quality Directive allows the subtraction of the effects of winter-sanding or salting of roads.[157] Member States could decide not to take advantage of these options. In both cases, they would be refraining from exploiting all options to keep burdens to a minimum.

The United Kingdom did not discuss the possibility to exploit Article 21, and focused on Article 20.[158] In assessing the costs and benefits

[155] Department for Environment, Food and Rural Affairs, Transposition of the Air Quality Directive (2008/50/EC), 2010 version 2, attached to The Air Quality Standards Regulations 2010, SI 2010 No. 1001.

[156] The Council of the European Union, Interinstitutional file 2005/0183(COD), document number 10453/06, ADD 1, p. 18.

[157] This possibility derives from a request from Finland during the negotiations of the First Daughter Directive, European Union, the Council, Interinstitutional file 97/0266, document number 5719/01/REV1, page 6, note 12.

[158] Department for Environment, Food and Rural Affairs, Transposition of the Air Quality Directive (2008/50/EC), 2010 version 2.

associated to the (non) transposition of this option, the following sources of costs were taken into account. As regards the costs for making use of this option, the government looked at the health costs associated with *not* delivering additional improvement in air quality. These were estimated, after a long series of disclaimers, to be £684m. The benefits of using this option took into account the saving in mitigation costs including technology costs, resources costs and cleaning costs. These benefits were estimated to be £1559m. In short, polluting was estimated to be cheaper than non-polluting. In light of the abundant net benefits of making use of the option in Article 20 of the Directive, the UK Government decided to exploit the option. Besides the disputable accuracy of the analysis, and the possible ethical reservations concerning the algebraic manner in which human life was treated, it strikes me that this regulatory impact assessment did not take any account of potential costs coming from not exploiting the technological investments which would have been necessary to meet the stricter environmental standards associated with the non-implementation of Article 20 of the Directive. Technological investments, and developments to meet environmental standards have no potential economic benefit under this regulatory impact assessment. This seems to be in contrast with the conclusions reached in the previous section.

A more nuanced conclusion can be reached by looking at the 2008 Regulatory Impact Assessment concerning the transposition of the Environmental Liability Directive.[159] This document considered, in particular, options concerning extending the scope of application of the Directive to nature reserves other than those covered by the Natura 2000 Network and the availability of the permit and state-of-art defences.

As regards the first option, the Directive also introduces opt-in clauses clearly indicating room for specific kinds of more stringent measures. Indeed, the Directive clearly states that Member States may extend the definition of protected species and natural habitats to any habitat or species not listed in the Birds and Habitats Directives, which the Member State designates for equivalent purposes to those laid down in these two Directives (Article 2(1)).[160] The Directive's legal regime is then also

[159] Department for Environment, Food and Rural Affairs & WAG, Impact Assessment of the Environmental Damage Regulations (England) and the Environmental Damage Regulations (Wales) 2008, December 2008.

[160] On the optional nature of this clause, see also Lee (2005), p. 205.

applied to these sites. The original Commission proposal included habitats and species not covered by the Birds and Habitats Directives, for which areas of protection or conservation have been designated pursuant to the relevant national legislation on nature conservation.[161] This provision aimed to allow the use of common criteria, and a uniform application in Europe of the 'environmental damage' concept, while retaining consideration of the fact that the aforementioned Directives allow for certain derogations about the level of protection offered to the environment.[162] In the Council, France and the United Kingdom were explicitly against the reference to areas and species protected under national law.[163] Other Member States feared a lack of harmonisation as a result of the applicability of national law.[164] At the same time, Sweden and Spain seemed to wish also to cover national nature reserves.[165] The final version leaves this aspect to the discretion of the Member States.

As regards the second option discussed in the 2008 Regulatory Impact Assessment, the Directive allows Member States to opt-out of the operators' obligation to bear the costs of preventive and reparatory measures. Article 8(4) states:

*The Member States may allow the operator not to bear the cost of remedial actions taken pursuant to this Directive where he demonstrates that he was not at fault or negligent and that the environmental damage was caused by: (a) an emission or event expressly authorised by, and fully in accordance with the conditions of, an authorisation conferred by or given under applicable national laws and regulations which implement those legislative measures adopted by the Community specified in Annex III, as applied at the date of the emission or event; (b) an emission or activity or any manner of using a product in the course of an activity which the operator demonstrates was not considered likely to cause environmental damage according to the state of scientific and technical knowledge at the time when the emission was released or the activity took place.*

The two clauses above are called 'permit defence' and 'state-of-the-art defence', respectively. Originally, the Commission proposed to make these defences compulsory for the Member States, and they restricted

161 COM (2002), 17 final, Proposed Article 2(2).

162 COM (2002), 17 final, p. 18.

163 Council of the European Union, Institutional File 2002/0021 (COD), nr. 5581/03, note 11.

164 Those Member States were Germany, Denmark, France and Finland, see Council of the European Union, Institutional File 2002/0021 (COD), nr. 7771/02, note 7.

165 Council of the European Union, Institutional File 2002/0021 (COD), nr. 5581/03, note 11 where is reported that these two Member States requested the deletion of 'where a Member States so decides'.

the field of application of the Directive as a whole.[166] Hence, they exempted the operators from the obligation to take measures and from the obligation to bear the costs of such measures altogether. A majority in the Council suggested the deletion of the permit defence and expressed reservations about the state-of-the-art defence.[167] Following a proposal of the Greek presidency, Member States agreed to insert an option for the introduction of these two defences at the national level, which, however, is limited to the obligation to bear the costs of preventive and reparatory measures.[168] It is clear that if a Member State does not take full advantage of the opportunity to reduce burdens upon operators, green-plating occurs.

When calculating the costs and benefits of the possibility of applying the regime of the Directive to national nature reserve sites and of not applying the permit and state-of-the-art defences to GMO cases in Wales, the Government looked first at the costs and benefits of a transposition which does not go beyond the EU minimum, i.e. without extending to SSSIs and retaining permit and state-of-the-art defences for GMOs in Wales. As to the costs, the government looked at costs deriving from remedial or anticipatory actions and those related to enforcement actions. It estimated these costs to be £92m. As for the benefits, it looked at additional remediation of rivers, habitats and species and land contamination with benefits to society (80% of the estimate). It also looked at the benefits related to reduced damage and risks to the environment (20%). The total benefits of minimal transposition were hence estimated at £116m. Then the Government indicated that had both options been used, the costs would have been £2m higher, and the benefits £5m lower. It concluded that the net benefits would have been £3m. The government continued to explain the relationship between these benefits and business. The following quote from the 2008 Regulatory Impact Assessment is pivotal for understanding the manner in which government looks at the relationship between green-plating and economic development:

*47 A large proportion of the costs identified in this assessment will in turn be revenue for the environmental industry. Where companies choose to undertake increased risk assessment and reduction or where they are required to undertake increased remedial measures, a*

166 COM (2002) 17 final.

167 Council of the European Union, Interinstitutional File 2002/0021 (COD), document number 7771/02 note 32.

168 Council of the European Union, Interinstitutional File 2002/0021 (COD), document number 5581/03 note 64.

*high proportion of the cost will relate to staff time but they may need to buy software or equipment or may seek professional help. To the extent that companies take out insurance products there will also be increased revenue to the insurance industry.*

*48 There is unlikely to be a net gain to the economy associated with these new revenue streams as they would displace expenditure elsewhere in the economy. These expenditures are transfer payments from one sector to another. If there are external benefits in terms of technological development, then these could be considered as economic benefits of the Regulations but to the extent that this effect exists it is not quantified in this assessment.*

This quote shows two things. First, it shows that the government is aware that the costs associated with environmental protection encountered by a part of industry are intrinsically linked to the revenues of another part of industry. The net benefits of this relationship are not really analysed and are dealt with by means of an assumption: '*There is unlikely to be a net gain*'. Second, the government is aware that environmental regulation can lead to technological development and therefore to extra benefits. These extra benefits have been called 'external benefits'.[169] Despite recognising their potential existence, the government dismisses them by stating that they are difficult to quantify. In the end, they are not taken into consideration. Once again, we have a stark contrast with what emerged from the analysis performed in Section 4.3 of this chapter.

A comparison between the British government and the Welsh government approach to the assessment of the costs and benefits related to the transposition of the Waste Directive shows how important it is to estimate all benefits deriving from green-plating.

In 2010, the British Government presented the 2010 Regulatory Impact Assessment concerning the transposition of the Waste Directive.[170] In this document, the British Government assessed the costs and benefits of (not) transposing several provisions of the Waste Directive, including Article 11 of the Directive, as well as clauses allowing the establishment of more stringent protective measures. The third sentence of Article 11(1) states that, where necessary to ensure that waste undergoes recovery operations, in accordance with the hierarchy of waste under Article 4 and in respect of human health and the environment

[169] This concept is therefore linked to those of 'innovation dynamics' and 'eco-innovation' discussed in Section 4.3.3 of this chapter.

[170] Department for Environment, Food and Rural Affairs, Impact Assessment of the Transposition of the Revised Waste Framework Directive (Directive 2008/98/EC), 2010 Defra 1012.

as provided in Article 13, Member States must establish separate collections for at least the following materials by 2015: paper, metal, plastic and glass. This obligation is subject to the technical, environmental and economic practicability of such systems. As indicated by the clauses 'at least' and 'by 2015', Member States can establish separate collection systems earlier than required and for more materials than those indicated in Article 11(1), therefore establishing room for more stringent measures.[171]

Finally, thanks to its acquired co-legislative power, the European Parliament could reinsert quantitative targets for reduction,[172] which were rejected during the Waste Framework Directive negotiations.[173] Current Article 11(2) states:

*In order to comply with the objectives of this Directive, and move towards a European recycling society with a high level of resource efficiency, Member States shall take the necessary measures designed to achieve the following targets: (a) by 2020, the preparing for re-use and the recycling of waste materials such as at least paper, metal, plastic and glass from households and possibly from other origins as far as these waste streams are similar to waste from households, shall be increased to a minimum of overall 50% by weight; (b) by 2020, the preparing for re-use, recycling and other material recovery, including backfilling operations using waste to substitute other materials, of non-hazardous construction and demolition waste excluding naturally occurring material defined in category 17 05 04 in the list of waste shall be increased to a minimum of 70% by weight.*

The use of the term 'to a minimum' in these provisions makes clear that, if a Member State aimed for more ambitious targets than those indicated in this article, it would establish more stringent measures.

171 It could be argued that such measures would not be more stringent because they are required by the second sentence of Article 11(1), which states: 'Member States shall take measures to promote high quality recycling and, to this end, shall set up separate collection of waste where technically, environmentally and economically practicable and appropriate to meet the necessary quality standards for the relevant recycling sectors.' However, this provision subjects the establishment of separate collection systems to an appropriateness assessment by the Member States that lowers the binding nature of such requirements. Accordingly, the third sentence of Article 11(1) indicates what the minimum level of protection is.

172 European Parliament legislative resolution on the proposal for a directive of the European Parliament and of the Council on waste (COM (2005) 667 – C6–0009/2006 – 2005/0281(COD) ), Co-decision procedure: first reading, Article 8, and the indirect reference to the position of the European Parliament in second reading, available in COM (2008) 559 final.

173 Van Calster (2000), p. 170, and Amended Commission Proposal, [1989] OJ C 326/6.

When we look at how the British government assessed the costs and benefits associated with the (non) transposition of the options in Article 11 of the Waste Directive, it can be noticed that only the option in section 2 played a role in the regulatory impact assessment. The British government assessed whether adding an extra separate collection service for mixed plastic, i.e. plastic other than plastic bottles composed of rigid plastic and plastic films, by 2015. In assessing the costs of such measures, the government took account of many factors, including contract costs, vehicle efficiencies, mix of housing stock, and infrastructure and gate fees for recyclables. Three types of separate collection systems, i.e. co-mingled collection,[174] two-stream collection,[175] and (weekly or fortnightly) kerbside sort collection,[176] were also taken into account. Based on these parameters, the government estimated costs to be between £26.3m and £80.6m per year.[177] As for the benefits, despite recognising that there could be benefits in introducing an extra stream of separate collection for mixed plastic, the government underlined that extra information was necessary to quantify these benefits.[178] The Government added that these benefits can be assumed to be lower than the costs, and therefore decided not to introduce a requirement on separate collection of mixed plastic.

A different approach, with a diametrically opposed outcome to the one just presented, can be found in the context of the Welsh transposition of the targets for the preparing for reuse and the recycling of waste materials under Article 11(2) of the Waste Directive. While the British government did not look at the option of setting a target going beyond the Directive, the Welsh government commissioned a separate study on this issue.[179] Following the outcomes of this study, Wales introduced a statutory target of 64% by 2020, which is higher than the minimum target indicated under the Directive.[180] Among the reasons given by the Welsh government to justify introducing this example of green-plating, we can see reference to the reduction of greenhouse gas emissions, the reduction of Wales's ecological footprint, the saving of valuable and increasingly scarce resources

[174] In which all recyclables are collected together and separated out for recycling later.
[175] In which recyclables are separated into two broad streams by the householder, and fully separated for recycling later.
[176] In which recyclables are separated by collection operatives before transportation.
[177] Department for Environment, Food and Rural Affairs, Impact Assessment of the Transposition of the Revised Waste Framework Directive (Directive 2008/98/EC), 2010 Defra 1012, p. 23.
[178] Ibidem.
[179] Scoping New Municipal Waste Targets for Wales, Eunomia, 2007; Wales Targets Impact Assessment, Eunomia, 2010.
[180] Waste (Wales) Measure 2010, 2010 nawm 8, section 3.

and the reduction of the costs for the management of waste from the perspective of local authorities (and, hence, taxpayers) through avoiding the rising costs for treatment/disposal of waste.[181] While the former two reasons are based on environmental protection, the latter two grounds are based on economic benefits. The Welsh government based the cost/benefit analysis on two studies from an external consultant firm.[182] A quote from the explanatory memorandum to the Waste (Wales) Measure 2010 reveals the importance of taking into account economic benefits of green-plating. At paragraph 8.2.9, the Welsh government states:

> *The report concluded that the cost of recycling at both a 40% rate (the current recycling rate) and a 50% rate (close to the 52% rate at which recycling will peak and plateau under current interventions) is higher than at a 70% rate. By 2024/25, the 40% recycling cost will be over £92m per annum whereas the cost of recycling at a 70% rate will be approximately £89m. Working towards and achieving a 70% rate by 2024/25, from a 2009/2010 baseline, will result in £78m savings compared with recycling at the current rate of 40%, and £59m savings compared with recycling at a rate of 50%. There are a number of reasons for this. Waste which is recycled will provide additional income which would not be the case if waste was landfilled or incinerated. Furthermore, financial savings can be made by local authorities if waste is recycled rather than landfilled as they will not have to make landfill tax payments and gate fees.*

The quoted passage shows clear parallels with the discussion points highlighted in Section 4.3 of this chapter as regards Dutch waste management. The Welsh government concludes that green-plating in the field of waste management will lead to lower costs than polluting. This estimate takes into consideration the added value of new business opportunities made available by environmental regulation. The Welsh government quantified what the UK Government had called 'external benefits' in the context of the regulatory impact assessment of the Environmental Liability Directive. The ability to estimate 'external benefits' plays a pivotal role in the decision-making process.

## 4.5 Conclusions: Green-Plating as a Motor for Economic Development

The study of national policies on gold-plating shows that policies are based on the assumption that green-plating negatively affects economic

[181] Department for Environment, Sustainability and Housing of the Welsh Assembly Government, Explanatory Memorandum to the Waste (Wales) Measure 2010, p. 50.

[182] Eunomia, Scoping New Municipal Waste Targets for Wales, 2007; and Eunomia, Wales Targets Impact Assessment, 2010.

development. Despite this assumption, we have seen examples in which green-plating seems to encourage economic development, at least potentially. In Section 4.3 of this chapter, I referred to the so-called Porter Hypothesis, which states that strict environmental regulation can result in competitive advantage for national industry. As indicated during the case study on waste management in the Netherlands, the steady increase of waste being prevented and recovered (above Union requirements) does not seem to have led to economic stagnation. In fact, there are indications suggesting that green-plating in the context of waste prevention and recovery contributes to the Dutch export of services in the field of waste management and circular economy. This suggests that green-plating has positively influenced the growth of the Dutch economy in this field. In addition, the case study of industrial emissions showed that the Dutch economy could benefit from green-plating. Dutch industry already complied with the stricter requirements of the Industrial Emissions Directive thanks to green-plating under the IPPC Directive. Dutch industry could benefit from the fact that industry in other Member States will have to make investments to meet the new standards, while Dutch industry does not. Oosterhuis's study from 2006 provided a similar conclusion after comparing the effects of environmental regulation in Sweden, Denmark and Germany in the context of the substitution of hazardous chemicals. Without pretending to validate the Porter Hypothesis, I postulate that it is time to perform in-depth, widespread studies of the consequences that green-plating has on economic development in Europe.

Cost/benefit analyses performed in the United Kingdom as regards green-plating in environmental matters show that although there is awareness about the potential benefits of stricter environmental regulation on economic growth, the long-term benefits associated with the creation of new market opportunities are rarely properly taken into consideration. As a result, regulatory impact assessments do not offer a proper basis to assess the effects of green-plating on national economies. This finding is in line with the picture available in law and economic literature,[183] which was also presented during the proceedings of this chapter.

In Chapter 2, it was argued that green-plating can play an important role in the development of EU environmental law. National policies dogmatically refuting going beyond EU minimum environmental

[183] In particular Ekins & MacLeod (2009), who at page 240 indicate another eight shortcomings of regulatory impact assessments.

standards deprive the EU legislator of important information for developing EU environmental law. National policies restricting green-plating based on costs/benefits analyses can provide guidance to the EU legislator. For this to be the case, however, the actual manner in which costs/benefits analyses estimates the effects of stricter environmental regulation on national economy must be fundamentally improved. Refusing to assess the (long-term) economic benefits of green-plating because they are difficult to assess, as the United Kingdom did in the context of the transposition of the Air Quality Directive, cannot be accepted as justification. The approach followed by Wales as regards the transposition of the New Waste Framework Directive shows that when 'external benefits' are taken into account, it is possible to conclude that green-plating favours economic development. This approach deserves more attention in academic writings. The Welsh government seems to have been able to take into account the (long-term) economic benefits of stricter environmental regulation. If the exactness of this approach were confirmed, it would provide a suitable basis to bring forward the discussion on the balance that needs to be struck between economic development and environmental protection. In turn, it would provide a basis for helping to develop EU environmental law. It is, hence, important to discuss whether EU law can stimulate an approach to green-plating that is based on costs/benefits analyses that take into consideration the long-term effects of going beyond EU standards. This discussion forms the basis of the conclusions to this book.

# Conclusions

## *Proceduralising Member States' Choice Regarding Green-Plating*

### Conclusions

The four chapters that make up this book show a common denominator, the lack of a proper understanding of the green-plating phenomenon. In Chapter 1, a clear political aversion for green-plating was shown. In Chapter 4, it has been shown that the main argument to adverse green-plating, i.e. its negative repercussion on economic development, is questionable from a substantive perspective. Moreover, it has been shown that real cost/benefit analysis to underpin the rejection of green-plating do not exist. Even in the United Kingdom, in which regulatory impact assessments evaluate the consequences of potential cases of green-plating, the government's reliance on assumptions and selective reading of data deprives these studies of the level of quality necessary to justify a political preference against green-plating. Fear of the unknown indeed cannot justify a political choice that, as shown in Chapter 2, affects the working of an instrument furthering the functioning of the high level of protection principle. Moreover, as it has been shown in Chapter 4, it cannot even be excluded that green-plating can stimulate economic development. The low political understanding of the green-plating phenomenon could thus be counterproductive. Still, not all blame should be placed on the Member States. Chapter 3 highlighted that EU institutions do not provide clear guidance regarding the room for green-plating. Such lack of clarity can surely be seen as a contributing factor to the low level of understanding of the green-plating phenomenon among Member States and (at least part of) civil society.

This statement hints to the existence of a linkage between the decision-making phase at EU level and that at national level in the context of green-plating. The question addressed here is whether EU law can use this linkage in order to halt the ongoing political bias against green-plating. This question has two dimensions. First, whether a duty exists as regards Member States' choice to adopt green-plating. If answered in the affirmative, the second question is what the content of such an obligation is.

As regards the first question, as stated in 2012 in the context of a publication focusing on Member States' obligations in the context of ecological corridors under the Habitats Directive,[1] the answer is affirmative under specific circumstances. This example focused on the establishment of the EU regulatory framework on areas of conjunction between Natura 2000 sites. The Commission's proposal for the Habitats Directive required the Member States to avoid pollution in areas outside special area of conservations.[2] Furthermore, it required the Member States to ensure the protection of distinct features of the landscape that are of outstanding importance to wildlife. Member States could derogate from this obligation, if they took counterbalancing measures ensuring that systems connecting special protected areas (alias ecological corridors) were maintained. Within the Council, the Netherlands and Germany even proposed adding a sentence stating that linking areas have particular importance.[3] Five months later, a provision, inserted in Article 3 of the proposal, imposed the obligation to maintain and, where appropriate, develop ecological corridors between special protected areas.[4] Many delegations maintained reservations, though.[5] In the end, the explicit reference to ecological corridors was not inserted in the Directive. Instead, preference was given to the concept 'features of the landscape', which clearly offers more flexibility to the Member States, than that of ecological corridors.[6] Moreover, Article 3(3) of the Directive subjects the protection of features of the landscape to a necessity and appropriateness test, with the latter clearly providing Member States with considerable discretion about the adoption of whichever feature of the landscape, hence also ecological corridors. This finding can only be overruled if

[1] Squintani (2012).
[2] COM(88) 381 final, proposed Article 8.
[3] European Communities, the Council, 13 November 1989, Doc. Num. 9862/89, Annex, p. 19.
[4] European Communities, the Council, 8 April 1991, Doc. Num. 5572/91, Annex, p. 12.
[5] Idem, where certain delegations stated that they could accept proposed Article 8 if it did not impose a formal obligation.
[6] The only definition provided for the term 'features of the landscape' is in Article 10 of the Directive.

the development of ecological corridors is necessary for the protection of a Natura 2000 site itself, hence by linking the development of ecological corridors to Article 6 of the Habitats Directive.[7]

The lack of an obligation for the development of ecological corridors outside the realm of Article 6 of the Habitats Directive does not mean that Member States' choice on whether or not to introduce green-plating in this field is free of any kind of legal constraint from an EU law perspective. It should be noted that the establishment of the Habitats Directive represents the moment in which the legal relationship between the Union and the Member States concerning the conservation of certain habitats and species was established. The Treaties regulate the establishment and execution of this legal relationship by means of, in particular, the principles of subsidiarity, proportionality and sincere cooperation.[8]

In the example of the regulation of ecological corridors, the Union restricted its powers to the benefit of the Member States, during the negotiation rounds within the Council. Albeit implicitly, this was the result of two factors. First, Member States considered themselves as better placed to choose the measures to be taken in a concrete case (subsidiarity).[9] Second, Member States feared that, in certain cases, the development of ecological corridors would have been too burdensome in relation to the objectives of the Habitats Directive (proportionality).[10] In these circumstances, it is possible to argue that, in the light of the principle of sincere cooperation, Member States are not completely free as regards whether to develop ecological corridors or not. Indeed, how could the Member States argue to sincerely cooperate with the Union when, during the decision-making phase at Union level, they claim that they are better placed to take certain measures and to assess whether a measure is appropriate, if then at national level they do nothing?

[7] Squintani (2012), Schoukens (2017), p. 51.

[8] Article 4(3) TEU and Article 5(3 and 4) TEU. On these principles, see e.g. Lenaerts & Van Nuffel (2011), pp. 131–147 with references to literature and case law.

[9] Several Member States had reservations with regard to the explicit reference to ecological corridors. At the end, the Habitats Directive refers to measures concerning features of the landscape, which is a concept allowing the Member States to choose between various instruments.

[10] Some Member States, such as Spain and Greece, asked to transform the proposed obligation into a competence. This suggests that they feared too much interference in their national competences. In particular, the reference to the appropriateness criterion in Article 3 suggests that Member States feared the imposition of overly high burdens with regard to measures taken outside a Natura 2000 site.

Accordingly, I submit that the invocation of Article 5(3 and 4) TEU by the Member States during the law-making phase at Union level has an implication for Member States' freedom of choice during the implementation phase at national level, which is trigged by Article 4(3) TEU. The consequence of the linkage between Article 5(3 and 4) TEU and Article 4(3) TEU in the example here discussed is that Member States must make a choice about whether to develop ecological corridors. Of course, this reasoning does not only apply in the context of the Habitats Directive. It applies in all cases in which the invocation of the principles of proportionality and subsidiarity during the decision-making phase at EU level leads to room for green-plating, instead of EU obligations, at national level.

The linkage between the decision-making phase at EU level and that at national level in the context of green-plating can thus be used to limit Member States discretionary power about whether to adopt green-plating or not, a least to a certain extent.

This conclusion should not come as a shock. As stated by Dworkin: 'Discretion, like the hole in the doughnut, does not exist except as an area left open by a surrounding belt of restrictions'.[11] This finding implies that if a competent authority is competent to do something, then it has to perform an assessment of the values involved in a concrete case in order to establish whether the competence should be used or not. This is a rule of law existing at national level in order to restrict the freedom that law gives to the executive power. For example, such a rule can be found in the Netherlands in the doctrine of good administration (in Dutch: *behoorlijk bestuur*).[12] In Italy, this rule belongs the doctrine of discretion (in Italian: *discrezionalità*),[13] and in Germany to that of misuse of discretionary power (in German: *Ermessensmissbrauch*).[14] In France, it is covered by the doctrine of discretionary power (in French: *pourvoir discrétionnaire*).[15] Finally, in Britain, this rule belongs to the doctrine of discretionary powers that may be reviewed in the light of whether the exercise of the power has been subjected to an assessment, and of

[11] Dwarkin (1977), p. 31.
[12] Damen et al (2009), pp. 307 ff.
[13] Perfetti et al (2007), pp. 299–301.
[14] In particular the aspect of *Willkürverbot*, see Bok (1992), pp. 147–149, with reference to case law.
[15] See Guadement (2001), pp. 579–586, in particular p. 582, with further reference to literature.

whether all relevant considerations have been taken into account.[16] Given its general recognition, this rule can be read within the letter of Article 4(3) TEU via the road of *ius commune* and by way of general principles of law.[17] It can hence be applied to the freedom that Member States, in particular the executive power,[18] have as regards green-plating.

Turning to the second question, i.e. what the content of such an obligation is, it should be noted that the existence of a duty to consider the green-plating option does not mean that Member States have to adopt green-plating. Member States are free to attach the weight that they prefer to the values involved in the assessment. They are thus free not to pursue green-plating. Indeed, the existence of an obligation in this regard would deprive the principles of subsidiarity and proportionality of much of their meaning. Moreover, the existence of a duty to adopt green-plating would be in contrast with the very meaning of this term, as defined in Chapter 1. Indeed, green-plating starts when EU substantive obligations end, or are absent.

My argument is that the linkage between Article 5(3 and 4) TEU and Article 4(3) TEU could be given form by a duty to evaluate the circumstances applicable to a concrete situation. Such an evaluation should be done in a transparent manner in order to provide information to the Union.[19] Indeed, the principle of transparency and the duty to justify a decision are two important rules of law that are capable of becoming general principles of Union law.[20] Besides, as stated in the conclusions of Chapter 4, this should occur by means of ad hoc costs/benefits analyses taking into account the potential long-term benefits of green-plating. This means that the linkage between Article 5(3 and 4) TEU and Article 4(3) TEU could be used to establish a *procedural* duty concerning green-plating. The use of ad hoc costs/benefits analyses including long-term assessment of the potential benefits of green-plating would allow

[16] See e.g. Leyland & Anthony (2008), pp. 215–218 with further references.

[17] For a similar use of national law by the CJEU see, in particular, Joined Cases C-7/56 and C-3/57 to C-7/57, Dinecke Algera, Giacomo Cicconardi, Simone Couturaud, Ignazio Genuardi, Félicie Steichen v Common Assembly of the European Coal and Steel Community, ECR English Special Edition, p. 39. See Reichel (2008), p. 245.

[18] At national level, a distinction exists between legislative discretion and administrative discretion. The legislative power usually enjoys a greater amount of freedom than the executive, see Schwarze (2006), p. 298.

[19] This seems to occur in the United Kingdom, see, for example, DEFRA/WAG/DOENI, *Consultation on options for implementing the Environmental Liability Directive*, November 2006, p. 8.

[20] Prechal & De Leeuw (2008), pp. 223–225 and 238.

for moving away from the dogmatic, or in any case politically biased, approach to green-plating taking place in countries such as the Netherlands and the United Kingdom. In turn, it would provide a basis for helping to develop EU environmental law. Would this not be a nice way to give concrete form to the principle of sincere cooperation in the field of green-plating? I would very much say so.

# Bibliography

AA.VV. (2005)
EU Environmental Policy Handbook, European Environmental Bureau, 2005.
AA.VV. (2007)
EU Environmental Guide, Amcham EU, 2007.
ADDINK (1983)
G.H. Addink, Het vergunningenstelsel in de Afvalstoffenwet: een voorbeeld van een overcomplexe bevoegdheid, *Milieu & Recht*, 4, 1983, pp. 97–105.
ADDINK (1991a)
G.H. Addink, Biedt het wetvoorstel afvalstoffen adequate oplossingen voor de belangrijkste knelpunten van het Nederlandse afvalstoffenbeleid?, in Jans & Van Acht (eds.), *Afvalstoffenrecht*, Tjeenk Willink, 1991, pp. 11–26.
ADDINK (1991b)
G.H. Addink, Afvalstoffenwetgeving, in Brussaard A.O (eds.), *Milieu & Recht*, 2$^{de}$ drukt, Tjeenk Willink, 1991, pp. 212–259.
ADDINK (1993)
G.H. Addink, Het normerend karakter van de nieuwe afvalstoffenregelgeving, *Milieu & Recht*, 12, 1993, pp. 677–687.
ADDINK (1996)
G.H. Addink, Afvalstoffen, in Brussard e.o., (eds.), *Milieurecht*, 4$^{de}$ druk, Tjeenk Willink, 1996, pp. 159–189.
ADDINK (2004a)
G.H. Addink, Afvalstoffenrechtspraak in vogelvlucht, *Milieu & Recht*, 8, 2004, pp. 470–482.
ADDINK (2004b)
G.H. Addink, Annotatie HvJ EG C-194/01, *Milieu & Recht*, 7, nr. 63, 2004, pp. 437–446.
ADDINK (2006)
G.H. Addink, Afvalstoffen, in W. Backes, P.C. Gilhuis, N.S.J. Koeman (eds.), *Milieurecht*, 6$^{de}$ druk, Kluwer, 2006, pp. 181–222.
ADINOLFI (2004)

A. Adinolfi, Nuove procedure per l'attuazione delle direttive comunitarie nelle materie di competenza regionale: verso le leggi comunitarie regionali?, *Rivista di Diritto Internazionale*, 2004, pp. 759 ff.

ADRIAANSE ET AL. (2008)

P.C, Adriaanse, T. Barkhuysen, W. Den Ouden & Y.E. Schuurmans, Effective Implementation of European Community Law, A Facilitating Role of National General Administrative Law, *Transylvanian Review of Administrative Sciences* 22E, 2008, pp. 5–33.

ALKEMA (2005)

E.A. Alkema, Noot HR 2 november 2004, nr. 00156/04 E, NJ (2005), 80.

AMBLER, CHITTENDEN & OBODOVSKI (2004)

T. Ambler, F. Chittenden & M. Obodovski, How Much Regulation Is Establishing Gold Plating? A Study of UK Elaboration of EU Directives, (London, British Chambers of Commerce, 2004).

ANDERSON & LIEFFERINK (eds.) (1997)

M.S. Anderson & D. Liefferink, *European Environmental Policy: The Pioneers*, Manchester University Press, 1997.

ANKER ET AL. (2015)

H.T. Anker, K. de Graaf, R. Purdy & L. Squintani, Coping with EU Environmental Legislation – Transposition Principles and Practices, *Journal of Environmental Law* 27 (1) 2015, 17–44.

ARENDSEN (2008)

R. Arendsen, *Geen bericht, goed bericht*, (dissertation) Vossiuspers UvA, Amsterdam University Press, 2008.

ARENTZ & WOLDENDORP (2005)

B. Arentz & H.E. Woldendorp, Soortenbescherming Flora-en faunawet: complexiteit naar climax, *Milieu & Recht*, 2005, pp. 202–211.

ATTHOFF & WALLGREN (2012)

K. Atthoff & M. Wallgren, Clarifying Gold-Plating – Better Implementation of EU Legislation, Board of Swedish Industry and Commerce for Better Regulation, 2012.

AXELROD & VIG (1998)

R.S. Axelrod & N.J. Vig, The European Union as an Environmental Governance System, in Vig & Axelrod (eds.), *The Global Environment*. Institutions, Law and Policy, CQ Press, 1998, pp. 72–97.

BÄCKER (2008)

R.J.G. Backer, De Wet Luchtkwaliteit: nieuwe ronde, nieuwe kansen?, *Milieu & Recht*, nr. 7, 2005, pp. 421–427.

BACKES (1993)

Ch.W. Backes, Het wetsvoorstel voor een Flora- en faunawet: integratie or opeenhoping van regelgeving?, in Ch.W. Backes & A.J.C. Koopmans, *Flora- en faunawet*, Tjeenk Willing, 1993, pp. 3–17.

BACKES (1995)

Ch.W. Backes Implementatie van Habitatrichtlijn in het Nederlandse (natuurbeschermingd) recht, *Milieu & Recht*, nr. 11, 1995, pp. 216–221.

BACKES (1997)
Ch.W. Backes, Afvalverwerking – zeker een Europees(rechtelijk) probleem, in Dresden e.o., *Afval: provinciaal, landelijk of Europees probleem?*, Tjeenk Willink, 1997, pp. 44–52.
BACKES (1999)
Ch.W. Backes, Introduction, in Backes Ch. & Betlem G. (eds.), *Integrated Pollution Prevention and Control*, Kluwer Law International, 1999, pp. 1–7.
BACKES (2000)
Ch.W. Backes, *Handhaving van de Vogel- en Habitatrichtlijnen, in Koopmans en Verscheuren, Handhaving van Europees milieurecht*, Boom juridische uitgevers, 2000, pp. 77–106.
BACKES (2002)
Ch.W. Backes, Geen grenzen aan het afvalstoffenbegrip?, in Dresden & Uylenburg (eds.), *Afvalstoffen: Actuele thema's rond afval en stoffen*, Kluwer, 2002, pp. 7–24.
BACKES (2005a)
Ch.W. Backes, Samenhang in het Europees milieurecht? – De relatie tussen de Richtlijn milieuaansprakelijkheid, de Vogel- en Habitatrichtlijn en de Kaderrichtlijn Water, *Tijdschrift voor Milieuschade en Aansprakelijkheidsrecht*, vol. 5, 2005, pp. 167–170.
BACKES (2005b)
Ch.W. Backes, Transformatie van Richtlijn 1999/30/EG in het recht van enkele EG-landen en –regio's en toepassing van de grenswaarden voor NO2 en PM10 in de praktijk, Centrum voor Omgevingsrecht en Beleid/ NILOS, Universiteit Utrecht, 2005.
BACKES (2006a)
Ch.W. Backes, Natuurbeschermingsrecht, Hoofdstuk 15, in ChW. Backes, P.C. Gilhuis & N.S.J. Koeman, (eds.), *Milieurecht*, 6th edition, Kluwer, 2006, pp. 482–510.
BACKES (2006b)
Ch.W. Backes, Het dossier luchtkwaliteit: anders verder!, *Tijdschrift Bouwrecht*, nr. 2, 2006, pp. 88 ff.
BACKES (2006c)
Ch.W. Backes, *Internationale vergelijking implementatie EU-richtlijnen luchtkwaliteit*, Centrum voor Omgevingsrecht en Beleid/NILOS, Universiteit Utrecht, 2006.
BACKES ET AL. (2002)
Ch.W. Backes, C.J. Bastmeijer, A.A., R.A.J. van Gestel & J.M. Verschuuren, *Codificatie van milieurechtelijke beginselen in de Wet milieubeheer*, Boom Juridische Uitgevers, 2002.
BACKES & KOOPMANS (1993)
Ch.W. Backes & A.J.C. Koopmans, Discussie, in Backes & Koopmans, *Flora- en faunawet*, Tjeenk Willing, 1993, pp. 35–47.
BACKES & VAN NIEUWERBURGH (2005)
Ch.W. Backes & T. van Nieuwerburg, Transformatie van Richtlijn 1999/30/EG in het recht van enkele EG-landen en –regio's en toepassing van de

grenswaarden voor $NO_2$ en $PM_{10}$ in de praktijk / The transposition of Directive 1999/30/EG in the national law of several EC countries and regions and application of the limit values for $NO_2$ and $PM_{10}$ in practice, Centrum voor Omgevingsrecht en Beleid/NILOS, Universiteit Utrecht, 2005.

BACKES, FRERIKS & ROBBE (2009)

Ch.W. Backes, A.A. Freriks & J. Robbe, *Hoofdlijnen natuurbeschermingsrecht*, Sdu Uitgevers, 2009.

BACKES, GILHUIS & KOEMAN (2006)

Ch.W. Backes, P.C. Gilhuis & N.S.J. Koeman (eds.), *Milieurecht*, Kluwer, 2006.

BACKES & VAN DEN BROEK (2005)

Ch.W. Backes & J.H.G. van den Broek, Gebiedsbescherming eindelijk geboden, *Milieu & Recht*, nr. 8, 2005 pp. 474–481.

BACKES, VAN NIEUWERBURG & KOELEMEIJER (2005)

C.W. Backes, T. Van Nieuwerburg, R.B.A. Koelemeijer, Transformation of the First Daughter Directive on Air Quality in Several EU Member States and Its Application in Practice, *European Environmental Law Review* 14 2005, pp. 157–164.

BACKES, PONTEN & NEUMAN (2000)

Ch.W. Backes, J.A.W.M. Ponten, & F. Neumann, *Gemeenten en de Vogel- en Habitatrichtlijn*, VMR 2000–2004.

BACKES, POORTINGA & WOLDENDORP (2010)

Ch.W. Backes, M.A. Poortinga & H.E. Woldendorp, 'Natuurbescherming in de natuurwet: Kop eraf?', in: Natuur(lijk) met recht beschermd: Naar een effectieve en hanteerbare natuurbescherming, Vereniging voor milieurecht 2010–2012, pp.19–57.

BAKKER & VAN WIJMEN (1988)

E.H. Bakker & P.C.E. van Wijmen, De natuursbeschermingswet, Vereniging voor milieurecht 1988, nr. 4, 1989.

BALDOCK (1987),

D. Baldock, *The Organisation of Nature Conservation in Selected EC Countries*, Institute for European Environmental Policy, London, 1987.

BARENTS (1999)

R. Barents, Harmonisatie binnen het Europese materiële recht, *RegelMaat*, 1999 pp. 66–72.

BARNARD (2007)

C. Barnard, *The Substantive Law of the EU, the Four Freedoms*, 2nd edition, Oxford University Press, 2007.

BASTEIN ET AL. (2013)

T. Bastein et al., Kansen voor de circulaire economie in Nederland, TNO-rapport, 11 juni 2013, TNO 2013 R10864.

BASTMEIJER (2009)

C.J. Bastmeijer, Natuurbeschermingsrecht in crisistijd: 'opzij, opzij, opzij … maak plaats, maak plats, maak plats … wij hebben ongelofelijke haast', *Milieu & Recht*, afl. 10, 2009, pp. 628–633.

BASTMEIJER & DE VRIES (2005)
C.J. Bastmeijer & J. de Vries, Implementatie van de EG milieuaansprakelijkheidsrichtlijn in Nederland, *Tijdschrift voor Milieuschade en Aansprakelijkheidsrecht*, vol. 4, 2005, pp. 135–140.
BASTMEIJER & WILLEMS (2010),
C.J. Bastmeijer & K. Willems, 'Robuust, verboden en... beschermd'. Past een klimaatbestendig natuurbeleid met aandacht voor 'wilde natuur'-beleving in het juridische Natura 2000-jasje?, in Ch.W. Backes, *Natuur(lijk) met recht beschermd: Naar een effectieve en hanteerbare natuurbescherming*, Vereniging voor Milieurecht Bju 2010–2012, pp. 85–116.
BATES (1996)
T.St.J.N. Bates, United Kingdom Implementation of EU Directives, *Statute Law Review* 17(1) 1996, pp. 27–49.
BAUW (1991)
R. Bauw, Verslag van de forumdiscussie tijdens de ochtendzitting, in Jans & Van Acht (eds.), *Afvalstoffenrecht*, Tjeenk Willink, 1991, pp. 43–46.
BAUW (2004)
E. Bauw, Richtlijn 2004/35/EG: vernieuwend, maar ook uitvoerbaar?, *Nederlandse Tijdschrift voor Europees Recht*, nr. 12, 2004, pp. 344–347.
BEIJEN (2007)
B.A. Beijen, Ploeteren met de Vogel- en Habitatrichtlijn, in A. Blomberg & T. de Gier (eds.), *Van Utrecht via Brussel naar Maastricht*, Kluwer, 2007, pp. 1–13.
BEIJEN (2010)
B.A. Beijen, *De kwaliteit van milieurichltijnen*, Boom Juridische Uitgevers, 2010.
BEKKERS ET AL. (1995)
V. Bekkers, J. Bonnes, A. De Moor-van Vugt, P. Schoneveld & W. Voermans, The Case of the Netherlands, in S.A. Pappas (ed.), *National Administrative Procedures for the Preparation and Implementation of Community Decisions*, European Institute of Public Administration, 1995, pp. 573–636.
BELLIS (2003)
R. Bellis, Implementation of EU Legislation: An Independent Study for the Foreign & Commonwealth Office, London, Foreign & Commonwealth Office, 2003.
BELOW (2009)
N. Below, elni forum 2009, The EU Directive on Industrial Emission and Its Implementation in National Key Issues and Practical Experiences 14th May 2009 in Brussels, Belgium, *Environmental Law Network International Review*, (2) (2009), pp. 93–94.
BERGKAMP (2002)
L. Bergkamp, The Proposed Environmental Liability Directive, *European Environmental Law Review*, 11, 2002, pp. 327–341.
BERGKAMP (2005a)
L. Bergkamp, Implementation of the Environmental Liability Directive in EU Member States, in ERA, 2005, pp. 389–400.

BERGKAMP (2005b)
L. Bergkamp, The European Environmental Liability Directive and Its Effects on Industry and the Economy, in R. Mellenberg & R, Uylenburg (eds.), *Aansprakelijkheid voor schade aan de natuur*, Europa Law Publishing, 2005, pp. 95– 132.
BERGKAMP (2006)
L. Bergkamp, The Proposed Waste Framework Directive and Liability for Soil and Groundwater Contamination, *Tijdschrift voor Milieuschade en Aansprakelijkheidsrecht*, 3, 2006, pp. 89–93.
BERNARD (1996)
N. Bernard, The Future of European Economic Law in the Light of the Principle of Subsidiarity, *Common Market Law Review*, 33, 1996, pp. 633–666.
BERR (1995)
C.J. Berr, Chronique de jurisprudence du Tribunal et de la Cour de justice des Communautés européennes. Libre circulation des marchandises, *Journal du droit international*, No. 2, 1995, pp. 460–461.
BESSELINK, ET AL. (2002)
I.F.M. Besselink, H.R.B.M. Kummeling, R. de Lange, P. Mendelts & S. Prechal, *De Nederlandse Grondwet en de Europese Unie*, Europa Law Publishing, 2002.
BETLEM (2005)
G. Betlem, De rol en betekenis van 'exploitant-aansprakelijkheid', *Tijdschrift voor Milieuschade en Aansprakelijkheidsrecht*, 5, 2005, pp. 171–176.
BIEZEVELD (1993)
G.A. Biezeveld, De Wet milieubeheer: een impuls voor handhaving, *Milieu & Recht* nr. 2, 1993, pp. 110–117.
BIJKERK (1997)
Y.G.C.M. Bijkerk, Is afval een provincial problem?, in Dresden e.o., *Afval: provinciaal, landelijk of Europees probleem?*, Tjeenk Willink, 1997, pp. 13–43.
BINSBERGEN (1994)
A. Binsbergen, Vogelwet 1936 herzien, *Het Vogeljaar*, nr. 4, 1994, pp. 164–165.
BINSBERGEN (1996)
A. Binsbergen, Vogelwet en Vogelrichtlijn, *Het Vogeljaar*, nr. 6, 1996, pp. 277–278.
BLEEKER (2009)
A. Bleeker, Does the Polluter Pay?, *European Energy and Environmental Law Review* 18, 2009, pp. 289–306.
BOCKEN (2006)
H. Bocken, Financial Guarantees in the Environmental Liability Directive: Next Time Better, *European Environmental Law Review*, 15, 2006, pp. 13–32.
BOEVE & Van den Broek (2012),
M.N. Boeve & G.M. van den Broek, The Programmatic Approach; a Flexible and Complex Tool to Achieve Environmental Quality Standards, *Utrecht Law Review*, 8(3) 2012, pp. 74–85.
BOEVE, GROOTHUIJSE & VAN 'T LAM (2009)
M.N. Boeve, F.A.G. Groothuijse & V.M.Y. van 't Lam, *Omgevingsrecht*, Europa Law Publishing, 2009.

BOEVE, PEETERS & POORTINGA (2010)
M.N. Boeve M. Peeters & M. Poortinga, Een nieuwe regeling voor de ambtshalve wijziging van de milieuvergunning in her licht van her richtlijnvoorstel industriële emissies, *Milieu & Recht*, nr. 2, 2010, pp. 77–84.
BOGOJEVIC (2016)
S. Bogojevic, Judicial Protection of Individual Applicants Revisited: Access to Justice through the Prism of Judicial Subsidiarity, in *Yearbook of European Law*, 34, 2015, pp. 5–25.
BOGOJEVIC (2016)
S. Bogojevic, Climate Change Law and Policy in the European Union, in Cinnamon P. Carlarne, K. R. Gray, & R. Tarasofsky, *The Oxford Handbook of International Climate Change Law*, Oxford University Press, 2016, pp. 670–687.
BOHNE & DIETZE (2004)
E. Bohne & E. Dietze, Pollution Prevention and Control in Europe Revisited, *European Environmental Law Review*, 7, 2004, pp. 198–217.
BOHNE (2006)
E. Bohne, The Quest for Environmental Regulatory Integration in the European Union. *Integrated Pollution Prevention and Control, Environmental Impact Assessment and Major Accident Prevention*, Kluwer Law International, 2006.
BOHNE (2008)
E. Bohne, The implementation of the IPPC Directive from a Comparative Perspective and Lessons for Its Recast (Part I), *Journal for European Environmental & Planning Law*, vol. 5 (1), 2008, pp. 1–33.
BOHNE (2008-bis)
E. Bohne, The Implementation of the IPPC Directive from a Comparative Perspective and Lessons for Its Recast (Part II), *Journal for European Environmental & Planning Law*, 5(3–4), 2008, pp. 319–338.
BOK (1992)
A.J. Bok, Rechtsbescherming in Franrijk en Duitsland 2nd edition, Wolters Kluwer, 1992.
BONGAERTS (1993)
J.C. Bongaerts, The Packaging Ordinance in Germany and Its Implementation First Experiences, in Wiggers-Rust e.o. (eds.), *Waste Prevention in the EEC*, Tjeenk Willink, 1993, pp. 81–92.
BOON, BROUWER & SCHILDER (2005)
B. Brouwer, *S. Regelgeving in Nederland*, Kluwer, 2005.
BORGERS (2005)
H.C. Borgers, Het Besluit luchtkwaliteit; de recente jurisprudentie in vogelvlucht, *Milieu & Recht*, nr. 6, 2005, pp. 342–350.
BORGERS (2007)
H.C. Borgers, De beste beschikbare technieken voor het bepalen van de beste beschikbare technieken, in N. Teesing (ed.), *Nederlandse milieurichtlijnen en beste beschikbare technieken, Verslag van de 95ᵃ ledenvergadering van de*

*Vereniging voor Milieurecht op 28 maart 2007*, Boom Juridisch Uitgevers, 2007, pp. 27–45.
BÖRZEL (2002)
T. Börzel, Pace-Setting, Foot-Dragging, and Fence-Sitting: Member State Responses to Europeanization, in *Journal of Common Market Studies*, 40(2), 2002, pp. 193–214.
BOSMA (2009),
W.J. Bosma, De wet 'Wijziging van de Wet milieubeheer (implementatie en derogatie luchtkwaliteitseisen)', *Tijdschrift Bouwrecht*, nr. 8, 2009, pp. 641 ff.
BOWMAN, DAVIES & REDGWELL (2010)
M. Bowman, P. Davies & C. Redgwell, *Lyster's International Wildlife Law*, 2nd edition, Cambridge, 2010.
BRANS (2001)
E.H.P. Brans, *Liability for Damage to Public Natural Resources*, Ph.D. Thesis, 2001.
BRANS (2003)
E.H.P. Brans, EC Proposal for an Environmental Liability Directive: Standing and Assessment of Damages, in *Griffin's View on International and Comparative Law*, 4(1), 2003, pp. 67–87.
BRANS (2004)
E.H.P. Brans, Richtlijn 2004/35/EG betreffende milieuaansprakelijkheid met betrekking tot het voorkomen en herstellen van milieuschade, in *TMA* 2004, num. 4, pp. 149–150.
BRANS (2005a)
E.H.P. Brans, De EU Richtlijn Milieuaansprakelijkheid, in Mellenberg R. & Uylenburg R. (eds.), *Aansprakelijkheid voor schade aan de natuur*, Europa Law Publishing, 2005, pp. 33–56.
BRANS (2005b)
E.H.P. Brans, De EU-Richtlijn Milieuaansoprakelijkheid, in *Bouwrecht*, 2005/1, pp. 14–28.
BRINKHORST (1992)
L.J. Brinkhorst, *Subsidiariteit en Milieu in de Europees Gemeenschap*. Doos van Pandora of Panacee, Rijks Universiteit Leiden, 1992.
BROEKMEYER ET AL. (2010)
M.E.A. Broekmeyer, I.M.A. Heitkönig, A.E.M. Ninaber & M. van Veen, Natuurbescherming in Nederland: een ecologische benadering, in: Natuur(lijk) met recht beschermd: Naar een effectieve en hanteerbare natuurbescherming, Vereniging voor milieurecht, 2010–12, pp. 61–84.
BRÖRING (1993)
H.E. Bröring, *Richtlijnen*, Kluwer, 1993.
BRÖRING (2007)
H.E. Bröring, Richtlijnen, beleidsregels, BREFs: mooi, mooier, mooist?, in N. Teesing (ed.), *Nederlandse milieurichtlijnen en beste beschikbare technieken, Verslag van de 95ª ledenvergadering van de Vereniging voor Milieurecht op 28 maart 2007*, Boom Juridisch Uitgevers, 2007, pp. 11–26.

BRUS (2003)
M. Brus, Case C-510/99, Procureur de la République v. Vavier Tridon, Judgment of the Court (Sixth Chamber) of 23 October 2001, in *Common Market Law Review*, 40, 2003, pp. 169–178.
BRUSSARD (1991)
W. Brussard, Natuurbeschermingsrecht, Hoofdstuk 3in Brussard W., Drupsteen Th.G., Gilhuis P.C. & Koeman N.S.J. (eds.), Milieurecht, 2nd edition, Tjeenk Willink, 1991, pp. 338–386.
BRUSSARD (1996)
W. Brussard, Natuurbeschermingsrecht, Hoofdstuk 15 in Brussard W., Drupsteen Th.G., Gilhuis P.C. & Koeman N.S.J. (eds.), *Milieurecht*, 4th edition, Tjeenk Wilink, 1996, pp. 409–442.
BURMEISTER & STAEBE (2009)
F. Burmeister & E. Staebe, Grenzen des sog. Gold Plating bei der Umsetzung europäischer Richtlijnien in nationales Recht, in Europarecht, 2009, pp. 444–457.
CALLIESS (1997)
C. Calliess, Towards a European Environmental Constitutional Law, in *European Environmental Law Review*, 1997, vol. 6, pp. 113–120.
CANNIZARO (2005)
E. Cannizaro, La riforma della Legge La Pergola e la competenza di Stato e Regioni nei processi di formazione ed attuazione di norme dell'Unione Europea, in *Rivista di Diritto Internazionale*, 2005, pp. 153 ff.
CANNIZARO (2012)
E. Cannizzaro, the Neo-Monism of the European Legal Order, in E. Cannizzaro, P. Palchieri & R.A. Wessel, *International Law as Law of the European Union*, Martinus Nijhof Publishers, 2012, pp. 35–58.
CASOLARI (2012)
F. Casolari, Giving Indirect Effect to International Law within the EU Legal Order: The Doctrine of Consistent Interpretation, in E. Cannizzaro, P. Palchieri & R.A. Wessel, *International Law as Law of the European Union*, Martinus Nijhof Publishers, 2012, pp. 395–415.
CASTELIJN ET AL. (1998)
A. Castelijn, P.O. de Jong, J. de Ridder, A.J. Schilstra & C. Lambers, Meer dan de som der delen?: Een onderzoek naar de aard van de afwegingen bij de opstelling van milieuvergunningen, ECW-achtergrondstudie nr. 34, Den Haag 1998.
CEA (2008)
CEA, *The Environmental Liability Directive, Enhancing Sustainable Insurance Solutions*, CEA, 2008.
CHALMERS (1995)
Chalmers D., Community Policy on Waste Management – Managing Environmental Decline Gently, in Barav A. & Wyatt D.A., *Yearbook of European Law*, 1994, vol. 14, Clarendon Press, 1995, pp. 257–312.

CLOSE (1978)
G. Close, Harmonisation of Laws: Use or Abuse of the Powers under the EEC Treaty, in *European Law Review*, 1978, pp. 461–481.
CONTALDI (2005)
G. Contaldi, La disciplina della partecipazione Italiana ai processi normative europei alla luce della riforma della legge La Pergola, in Il Diritto dell'Unione Europea, 2005, pp. 515 ff.
CORONER (2006)
F. Coroner, Environmental Liability Directive: How Well Are Member States Handling Transposition?, in *Environmental Liability*, 2006, pp. 226–229.
CROWHURST (2006)
G. Crowhurst, The Environmental Liability Directive: A UK Perspective, in *European Environmental Law Review*, 2006, vol. 15, pp. 266–276.
D'OLIVEIRA (1988)
U.J. d' Oliveira, Single European Act (SEA) and Environmental Policy – Some Questions, in Schwarze J. & Schermers H.G. (eds.), *Structure and Dimension of European Community Policy – Structure et dimensions des politiques communautaires*. Nomos Verlagsgesellschaft, 1988, pp. 123–125.
DAMEN ET AL. (2009)
L.J.A. Damen et al., *Bestuursrecht, Deel 1*, Boom Juridische Uitgevers, 2009.
DANIELE (2007)
L. Daniele, Diritto dell'Unione Europea, Giuffré, seconda edizione, 2007.
DAVIDSON (2006)
N. Davidson, *Davidson Review: Implementation of EU Legislation* (London, Better Regulation Executive, 2006)
DAVIES (2004)
P.G.G. Davis, *European Union Environmental Law: An Introduction to Key Selected Issues*, Ashgate Publishing, 2004.
DASHWOOD (2004)
A. Dashwood, The Relationship between the Member States and the European Union/European Community, in *Common Market Law Review* 2004, 41, pp. 355–381.
DE BRUYCKER & MORRENS (1993),
P. De Bruycker & P. Morrens, The concept of waste in EEC, in Wiggers-Rust e.o. (eds.), *Waste Prevention in the EEC*, Tjeenk Willink, 1993, pp. 3–14.
DE BÚRCA (1994)
G. de Búrca, The Principle of Proportionality and Its Application in EC Law, in *Yearbook of European Law*, Oxford University Press, 1994, pp. 105–150.
DE BÚRCA (1998)
G. de Búrca, The Principle of Subsidiarity and the Court of Justice as an Institutional Actor, in *Journal of Common Market Studies*, 1998, vol. 36, pp. 217–235.
DE BÚRCA (2000)
G. de Búrca, Proportionality and Subsidiarity as General Principles of Law, in U. Bernitz & J. Nergelius (eds.), *General Principles of European Community Law*, Kluwer Law International, 2000, pp. 95–112.

DE CECCO (2006)
De Cecco F., Room to Move? Minimum Harmonisation and Fundamental Rights, in *Common Market Law Review*, 43, 2006, pp. 9–30.
DE GIER & ROBBE (2007)
T. de Gier, & J. Robbe, Integratie of Segregatie?, in A. Blomberg & T. de Gier (eds.), *Van Utrecht via Brussel naar Maastricht*, Kluwer, 2007, pp. 101–119.
DE GROOT & PRINCEN (2004)
T.C. de Groot & S.B.M. Princen, Weg van Europa? Het Nederlandse openbaar bestuur in de Europese Unie, in *Bestuurskunde*, 2004, nr. 6, pp. 250 ff.
DE HOOP (2004)
M. de Hoop, Luchtkwaliteit en wegaanpassingen in het kader van de Spoedwet wegverbreiding, in Ramnewash-Oemrawsigh S.T. (ed.), *Regeling inzake luchtkwaliteit; Nederland op slot?*, Vereniging voor Milieurecht, BJu, 2006, nr. 1, pp. 61–66.
DE LEEUW & RUYSSENAARS (2011)
F. de leeuw & P. Ruyssenaars, Evaluation of Current Limit and Target Values as Set in the EU Air Quality Directive, ETC/ACM Technical Paper 2011/3, available at: http://acm.eionet.europa.eu/ (last accessed April 2012).
DE ROOIJ (2004)
R.A.A. de Rooij, 'Den Haag' onder druk? Over de relatie tussen de EU, gemeenten en provincies, in *Bestuurskunde*, 2004, nr. 6, pp. 279 ff.
DE SADELEER (2003)
N. De Sadeleer, Procedures for Derogations from the Principle of Approximation of Laws under Article 95 EC, in *Common Market Law Review*, 40, 2003, pp. 889.
DE SADELEER (2005)
N. De Sadeleer, *Habitat Conservation in EC Law – from Nature Sanctuaries to Ecological Networks, Yearbook of European Environmental Law*, 5, Oxford University Press, 2005, p. 215–252.
DE SAVORNIN LOHMAN (2007)
A.F. De Savornin Lohman, De afweging tussen economie en natuurbescherming in jurisprudentie en beleid', *Milieu & Recht* 2007, p. 2–6.
DE SMEDT (2008)
K. De Smedt, Environmental Liability in a Federal System: A Law and Economics Analysis, in *European Energy and Environmental Law Review*, 2008, vol. 17, pp. 106–117.
DE SMEDT (2009)
K. De Smedt, Is Harmonisation Always Effective? The Implementation of the Environmental Liability Directive, in *European Energy and Environmental Law Review*, 18, 2009, pp. 2–18.
DE VILLEMEUVE (1993)
C.H.V. de Villeneuve, Legal Aspects of Prevention by Technologies, Products and Management, in Wiggers-Rust e.o. (eds.), *Waste Prevention in the EEC*, Tjeenk Willink Zwolle, 1993, pp. 21–38.
DE VRIES (2005)
J.S. de Vries, De totstandkoming van de Richtlijn Milieuaansprakelijkheid, in Mellenberg R. & Uylenburg R. (eds.), *Aansprakelijkheid voor schade aan de natuur*, Europa Law Publishing, 2005, pp. 23–30.

DE WITTE (2012)
B. De Witte, Using International Law for the European Union's Domestic Affairs, in E. Cannizzaro, P. Palchieri & R.A. Wessel (eds.), *International Law as Law of the European Union*, Martinus Nijhof Publishers, 2012, pp. 133–156.
DENYS (1999)
C. Denys, Case C-203/96: Chemische Afvalstoffen Dusseldorp v. Minister van Vlkshuisvestiging, Ruimtelijk Ordening en Milieubeheer, 25 June 1998 (not yet published), Case Report, in *European Environmental Law Review*, 1999, pp. 21–30.
DESCAMPS (2005)
H. Descamps, Liability for Environmental Damage in Belgium (Flemish Region) in 2005, *ERA Forum*, 6(3), 2005, pp. 401–414.
DIJKSEN (1994)
A.J. Dijkens, Natuurbescherming op Texel, in *Het Vogeljaar*, 1994, nr. 1, pp. 15–16.
DIJKMANS, DE JONGE & POST (2011)
B.J. Dijkman, M. de Jonge & A. Post, Koppen in de E&G Wet – Eindrapport, Verslag van het onderzoek naar de nationale kop in de Elektriciteits- en Gaswetgeving ten opzichte van Europese richtlijnen en de afwijkingen in de Electriciteitswet 1998 en in de Gaswet ten opzichte van nationale generieke wetten.
DIMITRAKOPOULOS (2001)
D.G. Dimitrakopoulos, The Transposition of EU Law: 'Post-Decisional Politics' and Institutional Autonomy, in *European Law Journal*, 7(4), 2001, pp. 442–458.
DIMITRAKOPOULOS (2001)
D.G. Dimitrakopoulos, Unintended Consequences: Institutional Autonomy and Executive Discretion in the European Union, *Jnl Publ. Pol*, 2001, 21/2, pp. 107–131.
D'OLIVEIRA (1988)
U.J. d'Oliveira, Single European Act (SEA) and Environmental Policy – Some Questions, in Schwarze J. & Schermers H.G. (eds.), *Structure and Dimension of European Community Policy – Structure et dimensions des politiques communautaires*, Nomos Verlagsgesellschaft, 1988, pp. 123–125.
DONELAND (1997)
E. Doneland, The Role of the Office of the Parliamentary Draftsman in the Implementation of European Union Directives in Ireland, in *Statute Law Review*, 18(1), 1997, pp. 1–20.
DOPPELHAMMER (2000)
M. Doppelhammer, More Difficult than Finding The Way Round Chinatown? The IPPC Directive and Its Implementation, in European Environmental Law Review, 2000, vol. 9, pp. 199–206.
DOUGAN (2000)
M. Dougan, Minimum Harmonisation and the Internal Market, in *Common Market Law Review*, 2000, vol. 37, pp. 853–885.

DRESDEN (1997)
M.J. Dresden, Afval: een nationaal probleem?, in Dresden e.o. (eds.), *Afval: provinciaal, landelijk of Europees probleem?*, Tjeenk Willink, 1997, pp. 2–12.
DRESDEN (2005)
M.J. Dresden, Afvalstoffen in een nieuwe jas, in *Milieu & Recht*, 2005, pp. 2–8.
DREWRY (1995)
G. Drewey, The Case of the United Kingdom, in Pappas S.A. (ed.) *National Administrative Procedures for the Preparation and Implementation of Community Decisions*, European Institute of Public Administration, 1995, pp. 468 ff.
DRUPSTEEN (1999)
Th. G. Drupsteen, Integrated Pollution Prevention and Control: The Dutch Experience, in Backes Ch. & Betlem G. (eds.), *Integrated Pollution Prevention and Control*, Kluwer Law International, 1999, pp. 81–90.
DURVILLE (2003)
A.J. Duville, De hete soep van de FFW, in *Milieu & Recht* 2003/6, pp. 176–178.
DWARKING (1977)
R.M. Dwarkin, *Taking Rights Seriously*, Harvard University Press, 1977.
EISBOUTS, JANS, & VOGELAAR (2006)
W.T. Eisbouts, J.H. Jans & F.O.W. Vogelaar, *Europees Recht*; Algemeen Deel, Europa Law Publishing, 2006.
EISBOUTS ET AL. (2010)
W.T. Eisbouts, J.H. Jans, L.A.J. Senden & A. Prechal (eds.), *Europees Recht; Algemeen Deel*, Europa Law Publishing, (Groningen 2010).
EKINS & MACLEOD (2009)
P. Ekins & M. MacLeod, Conclusions and Recommendations, in MacLeod et al. (eds.), *Understanding the Costs of Environmental Regulation in Europe*, Edward Elgar 2009, pp. 230–246.
EKINS & VENN (2009)
P. Ekins & A. Venn, Assessing Innovation Dynamics Induced by Environmental Policy, in MacLeod et al. (eds.), *Understanding the Costs of Environmental Regulation in Europe*, Edward Elgar 2009, pp. 193–229.
EMILIOU (1996)
N. Emiliou, *The Principle of Proportionality in European Law*, Kluwer Law International, 1996.
EMMOTT (1999)
N. Emmott, An Overview of the IPPC Directive and Its Development, in Backes Ch. & Betlem G. (eds.), *Integrated Pollution Prevention and Control*, Kluwer Law International, 1999, pp. 23–41.
EMMOTT & HAIGH (1996)
N. Emmott & N. Haigh, Integrated Pollution Prevention and Control: UK and EC Approaches and Possible Next Steps, in *Journal of Environmental Law*, 8(2), 1996, pp. 301–311.
ENCHELMAIER (2013)
S. Enchelmaier, Alpine Transport Restrictions Reconsidered: Commission v. Austria, in *Common Market Law Review*, 50(1), 2013, pp. 183–202.

ENDRES (2011)
A. Endres, *Environmental Economics*, Theory and Policy, Revisited and extended English edition, Cambridge University Press, 2011.
EPINEY (2005)
A. Epiney, *Omweltrecht in der Europäischen Union*, 2nd edition, Nomos, 2005.
EPINEY (2006)
A. Epiney, European Principles, in Macroy (ed.), *Reflections on 30 Years of EU Environmental Law*, Europa Law Publishing, 2006, pp. 19–39.
ERASMUS (1993)
H. Erasmus, Priority Waste Streams, in Wiggers-Rust e.o. (eds.), *Waste Prevention in the EEC*, Tjeenk Willink, 1993, pp. 77–80.
ERMACORA (1998)
F. Ermacora, Community Legislation and Jurisprudence in the Area of Waste Management: Recent Developments, in *Review of European, Comparative and International Environmental Law*, 3(3), 1998, pp. 274282.
EZROJ (2009)
A. Ezroj, Extended Producer Responsibility Programmes in the European Union: In Search of the Optimal Legal Basis, in *Colorado Journal of International Environmental Law and Policy*, 2009, vol. 20, pp.199–223.
FABBRINI & DONÁ (2003)
S. Fabbrini & A. Doná, Europeanisation as Strengthening of Domestic Executive Power? The Italian Experience and the case of the 'Legge Comunitaria', in *Journal of European Integration*, 25, pp. 31 ff.
FARMER, TEN BRINK & KETTUNEN (2006),
A. Farmer, P. Ten Brink & M. Kettunen, Taking Advantage of Flexibility in Implementing EU Environmental Law, in *Journal for Environmental & Planning Law*, 2006, 3(5), pp. 395–405.
FAURE (1998)
M.G. Faure, Harmonisation of Environmental Law and Market Integration: Harmonising for the Wrong Reasons?, in *European Environmental Law Review*, 7, 1998, pp. 169–175.
FAURE (2000)
M.G. Faure, Defining Harmonization, Codification and Integration, in *European Environmental Law Review*, 9 2000, p. 174–182.
FAURE (2005)
M.G. Faure, De Europese Richtlijn Milieuaansprakelijkheid: Kritische inleidende bedenkingen, in Mellenberg R. & Uylenburg R. (eds.), *Aansprakelijkheid voor schade aan de natuur*, Europa Law Publishing, 2005, pp. 3–20.
FAURE AND DE SMEDT (2013)
M.G. Faure & K. De Smedt, The ELD's Effects in Practice, in L. Bergkamp and B. Goldsmith (eds.) *The EU Environmental Liability Directive a Commentary*, Oxford University Press, 2013, pp. 299–314.
FAURE & LEFEVERE (1996)
M.G. Faure & J.G.J. Lefevere, The Draft Directive on Integrated Pollution Prevention and Control: An Economic Perspective, in *European Environmental Law Review*, 1996, pp. 112–122.

FIETEN & DRAHMANN (2010)
R.M. Fieten & A. Drahmann, 'Nieuw beoordelingskader voor Ffw-ontheffingen: probleem opgelost?', *Bouwrecht* 2010, p. 181 e.v.
FLEURKE (2008)
F.M. Fleurke, What Use for Article 95(5) EC? An Analysis of Land Oberösterreich and Republic of Austria v Commission, in *Journal of Environmental Law*, 20(2), 2008, pp. 267–278.
FLEURKE & TROUWBORST (2011)
F.M. Fleurke & A. Trouwborst, Kolencentrales, robuuste verbindingen en EU-milieurichtlijnen: balanceren tussen nationale en Europese doelstellingen, *NtEr*, 2011 (12), p. 95–103
FLORIJN (2009)
L.T. Florijn, De Europees richtlijn luchtkwaliteit en de veehouderij: een mission impossible, in *Milieu & Recht*, 2005, nr. 5, pp. 278–284.
FOGLEMAN (2006)
V. Fogleman, Enforcing the Environmental Liability Directive: Duties, Powers and Self-Executing Provisions, in *Environmental. Liability,* 2006, pp. 127–146.
FOIS (2008)
P. Fois, Il Diritto Ambientale nell'Ordinamento dell'Unione Europea, in Cordini G, Fois P. and Marchisio S, *Diritto Ambientale, Profili Internazionali, Europei e Comparati*, Giappichelli, 2008, 6th edition, pp. 51–97.
FRANSEN (2008),
D.S.P. Fransen, Wet luchtkwaliteiteisen, in *Tijdschrift Bouwrecht*, 2008, nr. 2, pp. 96 ff.
FRERIKS (2005),
A.A. Freriks, (Herziene) Natuurbeschermingswet 1998 in werking; implementatie van de Vogel- en Habitatrichtlijnen nader voltooiing, in *Tijdschrift voor Milieuschade en Aansprakelijkheidsrecht*, 2005, nr. 6, pp. 207–213.
GARCIA-URETA (2005)
A. Garcia-Ureta, Nature Conservation, in *The Yearbook of European Environmental Law*, Oxford, 2005, pp. 371–394.
GASPARINETTI (2009)
M. Gasparinetti, Air Quality: A Breathtaking Directive?, in *The protection of ambient air in international and European law*, Eleven, 2009, pp. 123–134.
GERADIN (1994)
D. Geradin, Trade and Environmental Protection, in *Yearbook of European Law*, Oxford University Press, 1994, pp. 151–199.
GILHUIS (1993)
P.C. Gilhuis, Tussen verandering en continuïteit: het hoofdstuk over vergunningen en algemene regels, in *Milieu & Recht*, 1993, nr. 2, pp. 86–96.
GILHUIS (2006)
P.C. Gilhuis, Algemene aspecten, in Ch.W. Backes, P.C. Gilhuis & N.S.J. Koeman (eds.), *Milieurecht*, Kluwer, 2006, pp. 1–42.
GILHUIS & VERSCHUUREN (2007)
Gilhuis P.C. & Verschuuren J.M., Is er nog verschil en moet er nog verschil zijn?, in Gilhuis & Verschuuren (eds.), *Is er nog verschil tussen Europa en Nederlands milieurecht*, Boom Juridische uitgevers, 2003, pp. 125–133.

GORISSEN (2008)
N.H.A Gorissen, *Gewekt vertrouwen in Europees perspectief*, Ph.D. dissertation University of Maastricht 2008, Sdu, 2008.
GORMLEY (2010)
L.W. Gormley, Free Movements of Goods and Their Use – What Is the Use of It?, in *Fordham International Law Journal*, 33, 2010, pp. 1589–1628.
GORMLEY (2015)
L. W. Gormley 2015. Inconsistencies and Misconceptions in the Free Movement of Goods, *European Law Review*, 40(6), 925–939.
GRIMEAUD (2001),
D. Grimeaud, Reforming EU Water Law: Towards Sustainability?, in *European Environmental Law Review*, 2001, vol. 10, pp. 41–51.
GROEN (1988)
R.H. Groen, De provicie in het nieuwe stelsel van de afvalstoffenwetgeving, in *Milieu & Recht*, 1988, nr. 6, pp. 245–250.
GROOTHUIJSE (2007)
F. Groothuijse, De nakoming van de gebiedsbeschermende verplichtingen uit de Vogel- en Habitatrchtlijn: een spoedonderzoek, in *Van Utrecht via Brussel naar Maastricht*, Kluwer, 2007, pp. 121–139.
GROUSSOT (2005)
X. Groussot, *Creation, Development and Impact of the General Principles of Community Law: Towards a Jus Commune Europaeum?* 2005 Ph.D. dissertation, Lund University.
GROUSSOT (2006)
X. Groussot, *General Principles of Community Law*, Europa Law Publishing, 2006.
GUADEMENT (2001)
Y. Guadement, *Traité de Droit Administratif*, Tome 1, Droit administratief general, 16th edition, 2001.
GUIZZI (1990)
V. Guizzi, La Legge La Pergola N. 86/89: Una impostazione nuova del circuito decisionale e operative Italia-Comunitá, in *Rivista di Diritto Europeo*, 1990, pp. 3 ff.
HAIGH (1984)
N. Haigh, *EEC Environmental Policy & Britain. An Essay and a Handbook*, Environmental Data Services, 1984.
HAMPTON (2005)
P. Hampton, Reducing Administrative Burdens: Effective Inspection and Enforcement, March 2005.
HARDENBERG & VAN DE PEPPEL (1997)
E. Hardenberg & R.A. van de Peppel, Coördinatie van verguningen in het milieurecht, in *Milieu & Recht*, 1997, nr. 2, pp. 39–43.
HENSELMANS (1988),
J.V. Henselmans, Afval 2000, in *Milieu & Recht* 1988, nr. 6, pp. 215–222.
HAYTHORNTHWAITE (2007)
R. Haythornthwaite, Better Regulation in Europe, in Weatherill (2007), *Better Regulation*, SOIECL, 2007, pp. 19–26

HAYWARD (2000)
T. Hayward, Constitutional Environmental Rights: A Case for Political Analysis, in *Political Studies*, 48, 2000, pp. 558–572.
HERTIN, JACOB AND VOLKEY (2008)
J. Hertin, K. Jacob & A. Volkery, Policy Appraisal, in A. Jordan and A. Lenschow (eds.), *Innovation in Environmental Policy? Integrating Environment or Sustainability*, Edward Elgar, 2008, pp. 114–133.
HERTIN ET AL. (2009a)
J. Hertin, J. Turnpenny, A. Jordan, M. Nilsson, D. Russel & B. Nykvist, Rationalising the Policy Mess? Ex ante policy assessment and the utilisation of knowledge in the policy process, in *Environmental and Planning*, 2009 41(5), pp. 1185–1200.
HERTIN ET AL. (2009b)
J. Hertin, K. Jacob, U. Pesch & C. Pacchi, The production and use of knowledge in Regulatory Impact Assessment: An empirical analysis, in *Forest Policy and Economics*, 2009 11(5–6), pp. 413–421.
HERTIN (2016)
J. Hertin, Making Government More Reflexive: The Role of Regulatory Impact Assessment, Ph.D. dissertation, Wageningen University.
HEYES (2009)
A. Heyes, Is Environmental Regulation Bad for Competition? A survey, in *Journal of Regulatory Economics*, 2009, 26, pp. 1–28
HILLEGERS, LAM & NIJMEIJER (2006)
S. Hilleger, T.E.P.A. Lam, & A.G.A. Nijmeijer, Het wetvoorstel luchtkwaliteit nader beschouwt, in *Milieu & Recht*, 2006, nr. 10, pp. 597–605.
HINTON (1997)
E.F. Hinton, 'Balancing Justice, Expediency, and Legal Certainty: The Free Movement of Goods in the European Union' (1997) 5 *Willamette Journal of International Law and Dispute Resolution*, 1–28.
HOFHUIS (2006)
Y. Hofhuis, *Minimumharmonisatie in het Europees recht*, s.n., Ph.D. dissertation, University of Amsterdam, 2006.
HOITINK (1998)
J.E. Hoitink, *Bestaande rechten in het milieurecht*, Tjeek Willink, 1998.
HOLWERDA (2011)
J.M. Holwerda, Deploying Carbon Capture and Storage 'Safely': The Scope for Member States of the EU to Adopt More Stringent CO2 Stream-Purity Criteria under EU Law, [2011] *Climate Law*, nr. 2, pp. 37–61.
HORDIJK (1993)
M.G. Hordijk, Een nieuwe wet voor het milieubeheer, *Milieu & Recht*, 1993, nr. 2, pp. 66–74.
JACOB ET AL. (2008)
Klaus Jacob et al., *Improving the Practice of Impact Assessment* (EVIA 2008)
JACOBS (1988)
F.G. Jacobs, The Protection of the Environment under the Single European Act, in Schwarze J. & Schermers H.G. (eds.), *Structure and Dimension of European*

*Community Policy – Structure et dimensions des politiques communautaires*, Nomos Verlagsgesellschaft, 1988, pp. 117–122.
JACOBS (2006)
F.G Jacobs, The Role of the European Court of Justice in the Protection of the Environment, in *Journal of Environmental Law* (18)2, 2006, pp. 185–205.
JACQUÉ (1986)
P. Jacqué, The 'Single European Act' and Environmental Policy, in *Environmental Policy and Law*, 1986, vol. 16, pp. 122–124.
JANS (1989)
J.H. Jans, Europeesrerchtelijke grenzen aan nationaal milieubeleid, in *Sociaal-Economische Wetgeving*, 1989, pp. 217–240.
JANS (1991)
J.H. Jans, *Europees Milieurecht in Nederland*, Wolters-Noordhoff, 1991.
JANS (1992a)
J.H. Jans, Evenredigheid: ja, maar waartussen?, in *Sociaal-Economische Wetgeving*, 1992, pp. 751–770.
JANS (1992b)
J.H. Jans, Wat staat er nu in 100A lid 4 EEG-Verdrag?, in *NJB*, 1992, No. 19, p. 616.
JANS (1993)
J.H. Jans, Zelfvoorziening: beginsel van milieubescherming?, in *Milieu & Recht*, 1993, nr. 12, pp. 708–713.
JANS (1996a)
J.H. Jans, The Development of EC Environmental Law, in Winter (ed.), *European Environmental Law. A Comparative Perspective*, Dartmouth, 1996, pp. 271–276.
JANS (1996b)
J.H. Jans, Objectives and Principles of EC Environmental Law, in Winter (ed.), *European Environmental Law. A Comparative Perspective*, Dartmouth, 1996, pp. 276–296.
JANS (1996c)
J.H. Jans, The Competences for EC Environmental Law, in Winter (ed.), *European Environmental Law. A Comparative Perspective, Dartmouth*, 1996, pp. 317–340.
JANS (1998)
J.H. Jans, Hof van Justitie EG, 25 juni 1998; C-203/96, Noot, in *Milieu & Recht*, 1998, No. 11, pp. 292–293.
JANS (1999a)
J.H. Jans, The Status of the Self-Sufficiency and Proximity Principles with Regard to the Disposal and Recovery of Waste in the European Community, in *Journal of Environmental Law*, 11(1), 1999, pp. 121–156.
JANS (1999b)
J.H. Jans, The Relationship between the IPPC Directive and Other EC Environmental Law, in Backes Ch. & Betlem G. (eds.), *Integrated Pollution Prevention and Control*, Kluwer Law International, 1999, pp. 43–50.
JANS (2000a)
J.H. Jans, Annotatie bij ECJ C-318/98 Fornasar, in *Milieu & Recht*, 2000, pp. 208–211.

JANS (2000b)
J.H. Jans, Evenredigheid Revisited, in *Sociaal-Economische Wetgeving*, 2000, pp. 270–282.
JANS (2000c)
J.H. Jans, Boekbespreking R.H. van Ooik, De keuze der rechtsgrondslag voor besluiten van Europese Unie, in *Sociaal-Economische Wetgeving*, 2000, p. 471.
JANS (2000d)
J.H. Jans, *European Environmental Law*, Europa Law Publishing, 2000.
JANS (2005)
J.H. Jans, Noot aan Deponiezweckverband Eiterköpfe, in *Milieu & Recht*, 2005, pp. 440–443.
JANS (2007)
J.H. Jans, Minimum Harmonisation and the Role of the Principle of Proportionality, in *Umweltrecht und Umweltwissenschaft: Festschrift für Eckard Rehbinder*, 2007, pp. 705–717.
JANS (2008a)
J.H. Jans, HvJ EG 19 juni 2008, nr. C-219/07, Noot, in *Milieu & Recht*, 2008, vol. 35, No. 7, pp. 446–447.
JANS (2008b)
J.H. Jans, Richtlijn 96/62/EG inzake de beordeling en het beheer van de luchtkwaliteit art. 7 lid 3, HvJ EG 25 julie 2008 C-237/07, in *Milieu & Recht*, 2008, nr. 8, pp. 511–515.
JANS (2010)
J.H. Jans, Stop the Integration Principle, in *Fordham International Law Journal*, 33(5), 2010, nr. 5, 1533 ff.
JANS (2011)
J.H. Jans, Who Is the Referee? Access to Justice in a Globalised Legal Order, in *Review of European Administrative Law*, 4(1), 2011, pp. 85–97.
JANS ET AL. (2007)
J.H. Jans, R. De Lange, S. Prechal & R.J.G.M. Widdershoven, *Europeanization of Public Law*, Europa Law Publishing, 2007.
JANS, SEVENSTER & JANSSEN (2007)
J.H. Jans, H.G. Sevenster & J.M.P. Janssen, Environmental Spill-Overs into General Community Law, in *Fordham International Law Journal*, 31(5), 2007, pp. 1360–1386.
JANS, SQUINTANI ET AL. (2009)
J.H. Jans, L. Squintani with A. Aragao, R. Macrory & B.W. Winter, 'Gold Plating' of European Environmental Measures, in *Journal for European Environmental & Planning Law*, 6(4), 2009, pp. 417–435.
JANS & VEDDER (2008)
J.H. Jans & H.H.B. Vedder, *European Environmental Law*, Europa Law Publishing, 2008.
JANS & VEDDER, (2012)
J.H. Jans & H.H.B. Vedder, *European Environmental Law*, Europa Law Publishing, 2012.

JEFREYS (1991)
R. Jefreys, The Role of Legislative Draftsman in the UK in Making and Implementing EC Law, in *RegelMaat*, 1991, pp. 39 ff.
JENDROSKA (2006)
J. Jendroska, Public Information and Participation in EC Environmental Law, in Macroy (ed.), *Reflections on 30 Years of EU Environmental Law*, Europa Law Publishing, 2006, pp. 61–84.
JENKINS (1998)
R. Jenkins, Environmental Regulation and International Competitiveness: A Review of Literature and Some European Evidence, The United National University, INTECH, Discussion Paper Series,#9801, 1998.
JONGMA (2002)
M.P. Jongma, De mileuvergunning, Kluwer, 2002.
JONGMA (2003)
M.P. Jongma, De IPPC-richtlijn als inspiratiebron, in: P.C. Gilhuis & J.M. Verschuuren, *Is er nog verschil tussen Europees en Nederlands milieurecht?*, Den Haag: BJu 2003, p. 57–77.
JONGMAN & KAMPHORST (2002)
R. H. Jongman, D. Kamphorst, *Council of Europe. Committee for the Activities of the Council of Europe in the Field of Biological and Landscape Diversity*, Council of Europe Publishing, Strasburg 2002.
JORDAN (2001)
A. Jordan, National Environmental Ministries: Managers or Ciphers of European Union Environmental Policy?, in *Public Administration*, 2001, vol. 79, No. 3, pp. 643–663.
KAT (2005)
W. Kat, Effects on the Integrated Pollution Prevention and Control Directive on Environmental Protection, in *Revue de Métallurgie*, 2005, nr. 6, pp. 55–58.
KEADING (2007)
M. Keading, Administrative Convergence Actually, in *Journal of European Integration*, 2007, vol. 29, pp. 425 ff.
KIIVER (2007)
P. Kiiver, The Treaty of Lisbon, the National Parliaments and the Principle of Subsidiarity, in *Maastricht Journal of European and Comparative Law*, 15, 2007, pp. 77–83.
KLABBERS (2001)
J. Klabbers, International Law in Community Law: The Law and Politics of Direct Effect, in *Yearbook of European Law*, 2001, vol. 21, pp. 263–298.
KLATTE (1983)
E.R. Klatte, Tien jaar Europees milieubeleid (1973–1983), een balans, in *Milieu & Recht* 1983, vol. 10, pp. 298–312.
KNEGTERING (2009)
E. Knegtering, The Featheries and the Furries, Species Characteristics and Tendencies in Public Species Conservation, Ph.D. dissertaion, University of Groningen, 2009.

KNIFF (2010)
C.L. Kniff, Beste beschikbare technieken, in *Milieu & Recht*, 2010, nr. 2, pp. 150–158.
KOELEMEIJER ET AL. (2005)
R.B.A. Koelemeijer, Ch.W. Backes, W.F. Blom, A.A. Bouwman & P. Hammingh, *Consequenties van de EU-luchtkwaliteitrichtlijnen voor ruimtelijk onwikkelingsplannen in verschillende EU-landen, Report 500052001/2005*, Centrum voor Omgevingsrecht en Beleid/NILOS, Universiteit Utrecht, 2005.
KOEMAN (1991)
N.S.J. Koeman, Publiek-private samenwerking en afvalstoffen, in Jans & Van Acht (eds.), *Afvalstoffenrecht*, Tjeenk Willink, 1991, pp. 47–55.
KOEMAN (2005),
N.S.J. Koeman, Het Besluit Luchtkwaliteit: hoe nu verder?, in *Tijdschrift Bouwrecht*, 2005, nr. 6, pp. 504 ff.
KOEMAN & TEN VEEN (2006)
N. Koeman & A. Ten Veen, Netherlands, in AA.VV. 273–279.The International Comparative Legal Guide to: Environmental Law 2006, Global Legal Group, 2006, Chapter 35.
KOLE (1996)
R.A. Kole, Naar een aanvaarbare Flora- en Faunawet?, in *Het Vogeljaar*, 1996, nr. 4, pp. 171–174.
KONSTADINIDES (2009)
T. Konstadinides, Division of Powers in European Union Law: *The Delimitation of Internal Competence between the EU and the Member States*, Kluwer Law International, 2009.
KOOPMANS (1993)
A.J.C. Koopmans, Enkele kritische opmerkingen uit het oogpunt van Faunabescherming en Natuurbescherming over wetsontwerp 23 147 voor een nieuwe Flora- en Faunawet, in Backes & Koopmans, *Flora- en faunawet*, Tjeenk Willing, 1993, pp. 19–34.
KORTMANN (1991)
C.A.J.M. Kortmann, De vorm van implementatie van EEG-recht, in *RegelMaat*, 1991, pp. 47 ff.
KRÄMER (1987)
L. Krämer, The Single European Act and Environmental Protection: Reflection on Several New Provisions in Community law, in *Common Market Law Review*, 1987, vol. 24, pp. 659–688.
KRÄMER (1990)
L. Krämer, *EEC Treaty and Environmental Policy*, Sweet & Maxwell, 1990.
KRÄMER (1992)
L. Krämer, The implementation of Environmental Laws by the European Economic Communities, *German Yearbook of International Law*; 34, 1992, pp. 9–53.
KRÄMER (1993a)
L. Krämer, The Interdependency of Community ad Member States Activity on Nature Protection within the European Community, *Ecological Law Quarterly*, 1993, vol. 20, pp. 25–45.

KRÄMER (1993)
L. Krämer, Economic, Fiscal and Other Financial Measures to Contribute to Waste Prevention, in Wiggers-Rust e.o. (eds.), *Waste Prevention in the EEC*, Tjeenk Willink, 1993, pp. 163–174.
KRÄMER (1996)
L. Krämer, The Elaboration of EC Environmental Legislation, in Winter (ed.), *European Environmental Law: A Comparative Perspective*, Dartmouth, 1996, pp. 297–316.
KRÄMER (1996b)
L Krämer, Public Interest Litigation in Environmental Matters before European Courts, *Journal of Environmental Law*. 8, 1996, pp. 1–18.
KRÄMER (1997)
L. Krämer, *Focus on European Environmental Law*, Sweet & Maxwell, 1997.
KRÄMER (2000)
L. Krämer, Differentiation in EU Environmental Policy, in *European Environmental Law Review*, 2000, pp. 133–140.
KRÄMER (2002)
L. Krämer, *Casebook on EU Environmental Law*, Hart Publishing, 2002.
KRÄMER. (2005a)
L. Krämer, Directive 2004/35 on Environmental Liability and Environmental Principles, in *Tijdschrift voor Milieuschade en Aansprakelijkheidsrecht*, 2005, vol. 4, pp. 131–134.
KRÄMER (2005b)
L. Krämer, De positie van de milieuorganisaties als gevolg van de Richtlijn Milieuaansprakelijkheid, in Mellenberg R. & Uylenburg R. (eds.), *Aansprakelijkheid voor schade aan de natuur*, Europa Law Publishing, 2005, pp. 75–91.
KRÄMER (2006)
L. Krämer, Thirty Years of Environmental Governance in the European Union, in Macroy (ed.), *Reflections on 30 Years of EU Environmental Law*, Europa Law Publishing, 2006, pp. 555–576.
KRÄMER (2007)
L. Krämer, *EC Environmental Law*, Sweet & Maxwell, 6th edition, 2007.
KRÄMER (2011)
L. Krämer, *EC Environmental Law*, Sweet & Maxwell, 7th edition, 2011.
KROMAREK (1988)
P. Kromarek, Commentaire de l'Acte unique européen en matière d'environnement, *Revue juridique de l' environnement* 1988 (1), pp. 75–92.
KWISTHOUT (2002)
J.K.B.H. Kwisthout, Van afval naar stoffen, in Dresden & Uylenburg (eds.), *Afvalstoffen: Actuele thema's rond afval en stoffen*, Kluwer aan den Rijn, 2002, pp. 67–83.
LAAN (2002)
R.G.J. Laan, Grenzen voor Afval, in Dresden & Uylenburg (eds.), *Afvalstoffen: Actuele thema's rond afval en stoffen*, Kluwer aan den Rijn, 2002, pp. 25–38.

LEYLAND & ANTHONY (2008)
P. Leyland & G. Anthony, *Textbook on Administrative Law*, 6th edition, Oxford University Press, 2008, pp. 215–218.
LAMBERTS (1977)
C. Lamberts, *Milieurecht*, Kluwer, 1977.
LANGLET & SAID MAHMOUDI (2016)
D. Langlet & S. Mahmoudi, *EU Environmental Law and Policy*, Oxford University Press, 2016.
LANOIE, PATRY & LAJEUNESSE (2008)
P. Lanoie, M. Patry & R. Lajeunesse, Environmental regulation and Productivity: Testing the Porter Hypothesis, in *Journal of Productivity Analysis*, 30, 2008, pp. 121–128.
LAVRANOS (2010)
N. Lavranos, Protecting European Law from International Law, in *European Foreign Affairs Review*, 2010, vol. 20, pp. 265–282.
LAVRYSEN & THEUNIS (2007)
L. Lavrysen & J. Theunis, The Right to the Protection of a Healthy Environment in the Belgian Constitution: Retrospect and International Perspective, in Larmuseau I., *Constitutional rights to an ecologically balanced environment*, Vlaamse-Vereniging voor Omgevingsrecht, 2007, pp. 9–29.
LEE (2003)
M. Lee, Public Participation, Procedure, and Democratic Deficit in EC Environmental Law, in *The Yearbook of European Environmental Law*, Oxford University Press, 2003, vol. 3., pp. 193–226.
LEE (2005)
M. Lee, *EU Environmental Law: Challenges, Change and Decision-Making*, Hart Publishing, 2005.
LEEMANS (2007)
T.C. Leemans, De Nederlandse milieurichtlijnen en BBT: de toetsing door de rechter, in N. Teesing (ed.), *Nederlandse milieurichtlijnen en beste beschikbare technieken, Verslag van de 95ª ledenvergadering van de Vereniging voor Milieurecht op 28 maart 2007*, Boom Juridisch Uitgevers, 2007, pp. 47–61.
LEEMANS (2008)
T.C. Leemans, *De toetsing door de bestuursrechter in milieugeschillen* (diss. Leiden), Den Haag: BJu 2008.
LEENEN (1976)
H.J.J. Leenen, *Milieuhygiënerecht*, 2de drukt, Samson, 1976.
LEFEVERE (1997)
J.G.J. Lefevere, The New Directive on Ambient Air Quality Assessment and Management, European Environmental Law Review; 6(7), 1997, pp. 210–213.
LEIJENDEKKER-VAN KAAM (1988)
H.P.H.M. Leijendekker-van Kaam, Integratie van de afvalstoffenwetgeving, in *Milieu & Recht*, 1988, nr. 6, pp. 206–214.

LENAERTS (1994)
K. Lenaerts, The Principle of Subsidiarity and the Environment in the European Union: Keeping the Balance of Federalism, in *Fordham International Law Journal*, 1994, vol. 17, pp. 864–895.
LENAERTS & NUFFEL (2005)
K. Lenaerts & P. van Nuffel, *Constitutional Law of the European Union*, Thomson, Sweet & Maxwell, 2005.
LENAERTS & VAN NUFFEL (2011)
K. Lenaerts & P. van Nuffel, *European Union Law*, 3rd edition, Sweet & Maxwell, 2011.
LENSCHOW (2010)
A. Lenschow, Chapter 13 – Environmental Policy, in H. Wallace, M.A. Pollack & A.R. Young, *Policy-Making in the European Union*, Oxford University Press, 2010, pp. 307–330.
LENZ & BORCHARDT (EDS.) (2003)
C.O. Lenz & K.D. Borchardt (eds.), *EU- und EG-Vertrag*. Kommentar, Helbing & Lichtenhahn, 2003.
LOOPUYT-VAN DEN BERG (1988)
L.M. Loopuyt-van den Berg, Constructief overleg tussen overheid en bedrijfsleven noodzakelijk, in *Milieu & Recht* 1988, nr. 6, p. 222–229.
LIEFFERINK & ANDERSEN (1998a)
D. Liefferink & M.S. Andersen, Greening the EU: National Positions in the Run-Up to the Amsterdam Treaty, in *Environmental Politics*, 7(3), 1998, pp. 66–93.
LIEFFERINK & ANDERSEN (1998b)
D. Liefferink & M.S. Andersen, Strategies of the 'Green' Member States in EU Environmental Policy-Making, in *Journal of European Public Policy*, 5(2), 1998, p. 254–270.
LOUKA (2004)
E. Louka, *Conflicting Integration: The Environmental Law of the European Union*, Intersentia, 2004.
LÜBBE-WOLFF (2001)
G. Lübbe-Wolff, Efficient Environmental Legislation – On Different Philosophies on Pollution Control in Europe, in *Journal of Environmental Law*, 13(1), 2001, pp. 79–87.
LÜBBE-WOLFF (2011)
G. Luebbe-Wolff, Who Has the Last Word? National and Transnational Courts – Conflict and Cooperation, *Yearbook of European Law*, 30, 2011, pp. 86 ff.
LUST (2007)
S. Lust, Administrative Law in Belgium, in René Seerden (ed.), *Administrative Law of the European Union, its Member States and the United States: A Comparative Analysis*, Metro, 2007, pp. 5–60.
MACLEOD ET AL. (2009)
M. MacLeod, D. Moran, S. Hussain & K. Bevan, The Origins and Appraisal of Regulation, in MacLeod et al (eds.), *Understanding the Costs of Environmental Regulation in Europe*, Edward Elgar, 2009, pp. 8–31.

MACRORY (1999)
R. Macrory, Integrated Prevention and Pollution Control: The UK Experience, in Backes Ch. & Betlem G. (eds.), *Integrated Pollution Prevention and Control*, Kluwer Law International, 1999, pp. 53–64.
MAES (2006)
Maes G., Het Standstillbeginsel in Verdragsbepalingen en in Art. 23 G.W.: Progressieve (sociale) Grondrechtenbescherming, in *Rechtskundig Weekblad* 2005–2006, nr. 28, pp. 1081–1094.
MAK (2004)
P.J. Mak, Luchtkwaliteiteisen: niet nieuwe wel hot, in *Milieu & Recht*, 2004, nr. 5, pp. 322–328.
MALLENBERG (2005)
R. Mallenberg, Verslag van de Eerste paneeldiscussie, in Mellenberg R. & Uylenburg R. (eds.), *Aansprakelijkheid voor schade aan de natuur*, Europa Law Publishing, 2005, pp. 153–163.
MANDERS ET AL. (2009)
A.M.M. Manders, M. Schaap, M. Jozwicka, F. van Arkel, E. Weijers & J. Matthijsen, The contribution of sea salt to PM10 and PM2.5 in the Netherlands, Netherlands Research Programme on Particulate Matter, 2009.
MANT (1995)
H. Mant, The Proposed Directive on Ambient Air Quality Assessment and Management, in *European Environmental Law Review*, 4(2), 1995, pp. 50–52.
MASTENBROEK (2007)
E. Mastenbroek, The Politics of Compliance, University of Leiden, Ph.D. Thesis, 2007.
MASTENBROEK (2009)
E. Mastenbroek, Surviving the Deadline, in *European Union Politics* 2009, pp. 371 ff.
MEIJER DREES (1990)
F.J. Meijer Drees, Afvalstoffenbeleid, toegespits op de regelgeving in Nederland, in Meijer Drees & Van Velzen (eds.), *Afvalstoffenbeleid*, Tjeenk Willink 1990, pp. 3–11.
MEIJER & ZWIER (2012)
E. Meijer & W. Zwier, Voorjaarsschoonmaak in het natuurbeschermingsrecht: minder geld, minder regels, minder bescherming, in *Milieu & Recht*, 2012, jaargang 39, afl.3, pp. 160–171.
MCMANUS (2006)
F. McManus, European Noise Law, in Macroy (ed.), *Reflections on 30 Years of EU Environmental Law*, Europa Law Publishing, 2006, pp. 371–382.
MICHIELS (2007)
L. Michiels, Doorbreking en verhaal van handhavingkosten, in *Van Utrecht via Brussel naar Maastricht*, Kluwer, 2007, pp. 185–202.
MISONNE (2011)
D. Misonne, *Droit Européen de l'environnement et de la santé. L'embition d'un niveau élevé de protection*, Anthemis, 2011.

MONTINI (2009)
M. Montini, EC Legislation on Air Pollution: From Guidelines to Limit Values, in Post H. (ed.), *The Protection of Ambient Air in International and European Law*, Eleven, 2009, pp. 73–88.
MORENO (2006)
A.G. Moreno, Environmental Impact Assessment in EC Law, in *Reflections on 30 Years of EU Environmental Law*, Macroy (ed.), Europa Law Publishing, 2006, pp. 41–59.
MORTELMANS (1990)
K.J.M. Mortelmans, Afvalverwerking en de interne markt, in *Nederlandsch Juristenblad*, 1990, pp. 1118–1119.
MORTELMANS (1992)
K.J.M. Mortelmans, EEG-Minimum-harmonisatie en consumentenrecht, in *Tijdschrift voor Consumentenrecht*, 1992, pp. 170–186.
MORTELMANS (1994)
K.J.M. Mortelmans, De interne markt en het facettenbeleid na het Keck-arrest: nationaal beleid, vrij verkeer of harmonisatie, in *Sociaal-Economische Wetgeving* 1994, Vol. 4 pp. 236–250.
MORTELMANS (2008)
K.J.M. Mortelmans, Chapter VIII – The Functioning of the Internal Market: The Freedoms, in Kapteyn et al. (eds.), *The Law of the European Union and of the European Communities*, 4th edition, Kluwer Law International, 2008.
NAGL, MOOSMANN & SCHNEIDER (2006)
C. Nagl, L. Moosmann & J. Schneider, Assessment of Plans and Programmes Reported under 1996/62/EC – Final Report Service Contract to the European Commission – DG Environment Contract No. 070402/2005/421167/MAR/C1.
NAO (2006)
National Audit Office, Evaluation of Regulatory Impact Assessments 2005–06, NAO.
NASH (2009)
H.A. Nash, The Revised Directive on Waste: Resolving Legislative Tensions in Waste Management?, in *Journal of Environmental Law*, vol. 21, 2009, pp. 139–149.
NEFRAMI (2012)
E. Neframi, Mixed Agreements as a Source of European Union Law, in E. Cannizzaro, P. Palchieri & R.A. Wessel (eds.), *International Law as Law of the European Union*, Martinus Nijhof Publishers, 2012, pp. 325–349.
NELSON (1993)
E. Nelson, Waste prevention: products, in Wiggers-Rust e.o. (eds.), *Waste Prevention in the EEC*, Tjeenk Willink, 1993, pp. 39–44.
NEUERBURG & VERFAILLE (1991)
E.N. Neuerburg & P. Verfaille, *Schets van het Nederlands milieurecht*, Samsom/Vuga, 1991.

NEVEN (2005)
M.G.G. Neven e.o. Eurosites Insights. Image, implementation, Interpretation and Integration of Natura 2000 in European Perspective, Alterra Rapport 2005.
NICOLAYSEN (1988)
G. Nicolaysen, Environmental Policy before the Single European Act, in Schwarze J. & Schermers H.G. (eds.), *Structure and Dimension of European Community Policy – Structure et dimensions des politiques communautaires*, Nomos Verlagsgesellschaft, 1988, pp.111–115.
NOTARO (1999)
N. Notaro, Case C-203/96, Chemische Afvalstoffen Dusseldorp BV and Others v. Minister van Volkshuisvesting, Ruimtelijke Ordening en Milieubeheer, Judgment of the Sixth Chamber of the Court of 25 June 1998, [1998] ECR I-4075, in *Common Market Law Review*, 1999, Vol 36, pp. 1309–1323.
O'REILLY (1996)
J.Sc. O'Reilly, Coping with Community Legislation – A Practitioner's Reaction, in *Statute Law Review*, 17(1), 1996, pp. 15–26.
ONG (1998)
D.M. Ong, The Convention on International Trade in Endangered Species (CITES, 1973): Implications of Recent Developments in International and EC Environmental Law, *Journal of Environmental Law*, 1(2), 1998, pp. 291–305.
OOSTERHAGEN (1989)
M.T. Oosterhagen, Doelmatig inzamelen in de zin van rtikel 3 lid 2 AW, in *Milieu & Recht* 1989, nr. 4, pp. 157–163.
OOSTERHUIS ET AL. (2006)
F. Oosterhuis, V. Monier, C. Görlach, A. Jarvis, J. Medhurst, O. Kuik, R. Vanner, P. Ekins, J. Jantzen, H. van der Woerd, P. Vercaemst, D. Huybrechts and E. Meynaerts, Ex post Estimates of Costs to Business of EU environmental Legislation, Final Report to DG Environment, April 2006.
OOSTERHUIS (2006)
F. Oosterhuis, *Substitution of Hazardous Chemicals*, 2006 IVM, Vrij Universiteit Amsterdam.
OOSTERHUIS, PEETERS & UYLENBURG (2007)
F.H. Oosterhuis, M.G.W.M. Peeters & R. Uylenburg, Het beordelingskader an de IPPC Rihtlijn: implementatie, interpretatie en toepassing, STEM publictie 2007/1.
OUWENEEL (1996),
G. Ouweneel, Vogels beschermen in Nederland over 10, 25 en 75 jaar, in *Het Vogeljaar*, 1996, nr. 5, pp. 193–195.
PAGH (1996)
P. Pagh, *EU-miljøret. København* : Christian Ejlers, 1996.
PAGH (2006)
P. Pagh, The Battle of European Policy Competences, in Macroy (ed.), *Reflections on 30 Years of EU Environmental Law*, Europa Law Publishing, 2006, pp. 3–16.

PALLEMAERTS (1994)
M. Pallemaerts, Van de stranden van blackpool tot de moerassen van Santona: plaatsgebonden verplichtingen in het milieurecht, *Milieu & Recht*, 1994, p.19.
PALLEMAERTS (1996)
M. Pallemaerts, The Proposed IPPC Directive: Re-Regulation or De-Regulation?, in *European Environmental Law Review*, 1996, vol. 5, pp. 174–177.
PEETERS, VAN DER WOERD & IN DE BRAEK (2006)
M. Peeters, F. van der Woerd & G. in de Braek, Evaluatie van het Besluit Financiële Zekerheid – Kwalitatieve Ervaringen 2003–2006, STEM publicatie 2006/2.
PEETERS (2016)
M. Peeters, Greenhouse Gas Emissions Trading in the EU, in D.A. Farber and M. Peeters (eds.), *Climate Change Law*, 2016 Edward Edgar, chapter 2.
PERFETTI ET AL. (2007)
L. Perfetti et al., *Manuale di Diritto amministrativo*, CEDAM 2007.
PESCATORE (1987)
P. Pescatore, Some Critical Remarks on the 'Single European Act., in *Common Market Law Review*, 1987, pp. 9–18.
PETERS (1999)
J.A. Peters, Environmental Framework Directives of the European Union – Ideas on Coherence and Suggestions for a Logical Basic Structure, in Backes Ch. & Betlem G. (eds.), *Integrated Pollution Prevention and Control*, Kluwer Law International, 1999, pp. 11–22.
PETRICCIONE (1989)
R.M. Petriccione, Italy: A New Mechanism for the Implementation of Community Law, in *EURLR*, 1989, pp. 456 ff.
PIJNACKER HORDIJK (1991)
E.H. Pijnacker Hordijk, Zaak C-169/89, Gurmetterie Van den Burg, arrest van 23 mei 1990, in *Sociaal-Economische Wetgeving*, 1991, No. 4, pp. 261–271.
PISANI (1998)
C. Pisani, Chemische Afvalstoffen Dusseldorp BV and Others v. Minister van Volkshuisvestiging, Ruimtelijke Ordening en Milieubeheer – Case C-203/96, in *Review of European Community & International Law*, 7(3), 1998, pp. 312–313.
POLAK (1990)
J.M. Polak, Uitvoering EG-richtlijnen, in *Nederlandse Juristenblad*, 1990, afl. 5, p. 194.
PORTER (1991)
M.E. Porter, America's Green Strategy, in *Scientific American*, 264(4), 1991, p. 96.
PORTER & VAN DER LINDE (1995a)
M.E. Porter & C. Van der Linde, Toward a New Conception of Environment-Competitiveness Relationship, in *The Journal of Economic Perspectives* 1995, 9 (4), pp. 97–118.
PORTER & VAN DER LINDE (1995b)
M.E. Porter & C. Van der Linde, Green and Competitive: Ending the Stalemate, in *Harvard Business Review*, 1995, vol. 73, pp. 120–134.

POST (2009)
H. Post, The Future of Ambient Air Management: Concluding Remarks, in Post H. (ed.), *The protection of ambient air in international and European law*, Eleven, 2009.
PRECHAL & DE LEEUW (2008)
S. Prechal & M.E. de Leeuw, Transparency: A General Principle of EU Law?, in U. Bernitz, et al. (eds,), *General Principles of EC Law in a Process of Development*, Kluwer Law, 2008, pp. 201–242.
PRIEUR (2012),
M. Prieur, Non-Regression in Environmental Law, in SAPIENS Online, URL: http://sapiens.revues.org/1405
PRIEUR & SOZZO (2012),
M. Prieur & G. Sozzo, *La non régression en droit de l'environnement* [La non-regression in environmental law.], Brussels: Bruylant, 2012.
RAMNEWASH-OEMRAWSINGH (2005)
S.T. Ramnewash-Oemrawsingh (ed.) *IPPC: in wetgeving en praktijk*, Boom Juridische Uitgevers, 2005.
RAMSEY (1996)
L.E. Ramsey, The Copy Out Technique: More of a 'Cop Out' than a Solution?, in *Statute Law Review*, 17(3), 1996, pp. 218–228.
RASMUSSEN (2007)
A. Rasmussen, Early conclusions in the Co-Decision Legislative Procedure, EUI Working Papers, MWR 2007/31, European University Institute.
REHBINDER (2007)
E. Rehbinder, Implementation of the Environmental Liability Directive in Germany, in *Environmental Liability* 5, 2007, pp. 199–203.
REICHEL (2008)
J. Reichel, Between Supremacy and Autonomy – Applying the Principle of Good Administration in the Member States, in U. Bernitz et al. (eds.), *General Principles of EC Law in a Process of Development*, Kluwer Law, 2008, pp. 243–271.
REIJNHOUT (1988)
A. Reijnhout, Gemeentelijk visie op de afvalverwijdering in Nederland, nu en in de toekomst, in *Milieu & Recht*, 1988, nr. 6, pp. 238–244.
RENSON & VERDURE (2009)
A.S. Renson & Ch. Verdure, Déchets et sous-produits à l'aune de la directive 2008/98/CE, in *Revue du Droit de l'Union Européenne*, 2009, nr. 4, pp. 1–23.
REVESZ (2000)
R.L. Revesz, Environmental Regulation in Federal Systems, in H. Somsen et al. (eds.), *Yearbook of European Environmental Law*, vol. 1, Oxford University Press, 2000, pp. 1–35.
RIDEAU (1994)
J. Rideau, *Droit Institutionnel de L'Union et des Communitautés Européennes*, Lgdj 1994.
RIJN (1989)
T.P.J.N. Rijn, *Europese Milieuwetgeving en de interne markt, in Europees milieurecht: praktische problemen bij de totstandkoming en uitvoering*, T.M.C. Asser Instituut, 1989, pp. 21–32.

ROBESIN (2008)
M.A. Robesin, From IPPC to IED: Heath and Environment in Europe Need a Stronger Directive, in *Environmental Law Network International Review*, 2, 2008, pp. 54–59.
ROBESIN, JAGER & FRANSSEN (2009)
M.A. Robesin, H. Jager & J. Franssen, Environmental Effects of the Proposal for the Directive on Industrial Emissions (IED), Stichting Milieu & Natuur, 2009.
ROETTEMAN (2004)
J. Roetteman, Verontreinigde lucht: niet meer te zien, nog steeds te voelen, in *Milieu & Recht*, 2004, nr. 5, p. 321.
ROOD ET AL. (2005)
J. Rood, M. van Keulen, S. Nollen & G. Arts, Nederland en de totstandkoming van EU-milieurichtlijnen, Eindrapport, Nederlandse Instituut voor Instituut voor Internationale Betrekkingen, Clingendael, 2005.
ROSENDAAL (2005)
P.W.T. Rosendaal, Reactie uit de praktijk, in Ramnewash-Oemrawsingh S.T. (ed.), *IPPC: in wetgeving en praktijk*, Boom Juridische Uitgevers, 2005, p. 73.
RUITER (1971)
C.J.S. Ruiter, *Vogelwet 1936*, Tjeenk Willink, 1971.
RUTTEMAN (2011)
L. Rutteman, Koppen, in *Milieu & Recht*, Issue 4, 2011, p. 211.
SAMUELS (1998)
A. Samuels, Incorporating, Translating or Implementing European Union Law into UK Law, in *Statute Law Review*, 19(2), 1998, pp. 80–92.
SBRAGIA (2000)
Sbragia, A.M., Environmental Policy: The 'Push-Pull' of Policy-Making. In Wallace & Wallace (eds), *Policy-Making in the European Union*, Oxford University Press, 2000, pp. 293–316.
SCHERMERS (1975)
H. Schermers, Community Law and International Law, in *Common Market Law Review*, 1975, vol. 12, pp. 77–90.
SCHEUER (2005)
S. Scheuer (ed.), *EU Environmental Policy Handbook. A Critical Analysis of EU Environmental Legislation*, Brussels: European Environmental Bureau 2005.
SCHIPPERS & BESSELINK (2005)
E.C.M. Schippers & H.J.M. Besselink, Luchtkwaliteit, in *De Gemeentestem*, 2005, nr. 7233, pp. 110 ff.
SCHIPPERS & BESSELINK (2006)
E.C.M. Schippers & H.J.M. Besselink, Luchtkwaliteit. Een tussenstand, in *De Gemeentestem*, 2006, nr. 7256, pp. 107 ff.
SCHIPPERS & BESSELINK (2007),
E.C.M. Schippers & H.J.M. Besselink, Luchtkwaliteit, in *De Gemeentestem*, 2007, nr. 7282, pp 121 ff.

SCHIPPERS & BESSELINK (2009),
E.C.M. Schippers & H.J.M. Besselink, Luchtkwaliteit, in *De Gemeentestem*, 2009, nr. 7321, pp. 75 ff.
SCHLEMMINGER & MARTENS (2004)
H. Schlemminger & C.P. Martens, *German Environmental Law for Practitioners*, 2nd edition, Kluwer Law International, 2004.
SCHOUKENS (2017)
Schoukens, H. 2017. Ecological Restoration as the New Environmental Paradigm: Is EU Environmental Law Up to the Task?, *Georgetown Environmental Law Review*, vol. 30, pp. 1–74.
SCHOUWENBERG (2007)
E.P.A.G. Schouwenberg, Huidige en toekomstige stikstofbelasting op de Natura 2000-gebieden: achtergronddocument ex ante evaluatie van de Vogel- en Habitatrichtlijnen in Nederland Wettelijke Onderzoekstaken Natuur & Milieu / 2007 (aangevraagd IBL).
SCHRAUWEN (2005)
A. Schrauwen, Case C-320/03R and (03), Commission v. Republic of Austria, Order of the President of the Court on 2 October 2003 and Order of the President of the Court on 27 April 2004, in *Common Market Law Review*, 42, 2005, pp. 851–858.
SCHUTTE-POSTMA (2004a)
E.T. Schutte-Postma, Verkeer en luchtkwaliteit, in *Milieu & Recht*, 2004/6, pp. 337–344.
SCHUTTE-POSTMA (2004b)
E.T. Schutte-Postma, Luchtkwaliteit en EU; Europese achtergronden van het Besluit luchtkwaliteit, in Ramnewash-Oemrawsigh S.T. (ed.), *Regeling inzake luchtkwaliteit; Nederland op slot?*, Vereniging voor Milieurecht, BJu, 2006, nr. 1, pp. 11–20.
SCHUTTE-POSTMA (2005)
E.T. Schutte-Postma, Het Besluit luchtkwaliteit in discussie, in *NJB*, 2005, nr. 8, pp. 401–402.
SCHUTTE-POSTMA (2005-bis)
E.T. Schutte-Postma, De Nederlandse worsteling met de Europese richtlijnen voor luchtkwaliteit, in *NTER*, 2005, nr. 6, pp. 134–139.
SCHUTTE-POSTMA (2007)
E.T. Schutte-Postma, De Wet luchtkwaliteit: redding voor gestrande bouwprojecten?, in *Tijdschrift Bouwrecht*, 2007, nr. 1, pp. 1 ff.
SCHUTZE (2006)
R. Schutze, Cooperative Federalism Constitutionalised: The Emergence of Complementary Competences in the EC Legal Order, in *Europa Law Review*, 31 (2), 2006, pp. 167–184.
SCOTT (1998)
J. Scott, *EC Environmental Law*, European Law Series, Longman, 1998.
SCOTT (2000)
J. Scott, Flexibility in the Implementation of EC Environmental Law, in H. Somsen et al. (eds.) *Yearbook of European Environmental Law*, Vol. 1, Oxford University Press, 2000, pp. 37–60.

SCOTT (2004)
J. Scott, The Precautionary Principle before the European Courts, in R. Macrory (ed.), *Principles of European Environmental Law*, Europa Law Publishing, 2004, pp. 51–72.
SCOTT (2011)
Scott, J. Multi-Level Governance of Climate Change, in *Carbon and Climate Law Review*, 2011/1, pp. 25–33.
SENDEN (2005)
L.A.J. Senden, General Report, in Senden and Hirsch Ballin, *Co-Actorship in the Development of European Law-Making*, Asser Press, 2005.
SEPE (1995)
O. Sepe, The Case If Italy, in Pappas S.A. (ed.) *National Administrative Procedures for the Preparation and Implementation of Community Decisions*, European Institute of Public Administration, 1995.
SEVENSTER (1992)
H.G. Sevenster, *Milieubeleid en gemeenshapsrecht. Het interne juridische kader en de praktijk*, Kluwer, 1992.
SEVENSTER (1999)
H.G. Sevenster Het lozingsbegrip en de gevolgen van harmonisatie, in *Nederlandse Tijdschrift voor Europees Recht*, 1999, No. 12, pp. 323–326.
SEVENSTER & JANSSEN (2006)
H.G. Sevenster & J.M.P. Janssen, Zaak C-6/03, Deponiezweckverband Eiterköpfe t. Land Rheinland-Pfalz, in *Sociaal-Economische Wetgeving* 2006, pp. 117–121.
SEVENSTER & VAN MEIJENFELDT (2003)
H.G. Sevenster & H.G. van Meijenfeldt, Bijdrage aan de forumdiscussie, in Gilhuis & Verschuuren (red.), *Is er nog verschil tussen Europa en Nederlands milieurecht*, Boom Juridische uitgevers, 2003, pp. 119–124.
SEWANDONO (1992)
I. Sewandono, De Italiaanse wet voor de uitvoering van Communautaire verplichtingen, in *RegelMaat*, 1992, pp. 31 ff.
SEWANDONO (1992)
I. Sewandono, Wetvoorstel tot versnelling van de implementatie can EG-richtlijnen, in *NJB* 1992, pp. 1172 ff.
SMIDT (2010)
E. Smidt, Creatief denken loont, in: Natuur(lijk) met recht beschermd: Naar een effectieve en hanteerbare natuurbescherming, Vereniging voor Milieurecht 2010–2, pp. 119–123.
SMIT ET AL. (2008)
A.A.H. Smit et al., Een onmogelijk opgave? Een onderzoek naar de wijze waarop wetenschappen invulling geven aan de regionale wateropgaven en de spanningen die zich daarbij voordoen, Utrecht: Centrum voor omgevingsrecht en – beleid/ NILOS 2008.
SMORENBURG-VAN MIDDELKOOP & UYLENBURG (2012)
L. Smorenburg-van Middelkoop & R. Uylenburg, Redactioneel, in L. Smorenburg-van Middelkoop & R. Uylenburg (eds.), *De beste beschikbare technieken, van IPPC*

*naar IED, Ontwikkeling, toepassing en toetsing van BBT*, Europa Law Publishing, Groningen 2012, pp. v–xvi.

SOMSEN (1995)

H. Somsen, Case C-131/93, Commission v Federal Republic of Germany; Trade and Environment: Free Movement of Goods – Prohibition of Importation of Live Freshwater Crayfish 13 July 1994 (not yet reported), in *European Environmental Law Review*, 1995, pp. 214–217.

SPAANS (2000)

L.A.J. Spaans, De stilte rond het standstill beginsel, in *Milieu & Recht*, Issue 10, 2000, pp. 252–257.

SQUINTANI (2011)

L. Squintani, HvJ EG 15 april 2010, Van autowrakken tot energiecentrales; een algemene regel met betrekking tot verdergaande maatregelen ter bescherming van het milieu, *Milieu & Recht* 2011, pp. 381–386.

SQUINTANI (2012)

L. Squintani The Development of Ecological Corridors: Member States' Obligation under the Habitats and Birds Directives?, in *Journal for European Environmental & Planning Law*, 2 (2012), pp. 180–200.

SQUINTANI, HOLWERDA & DE GRAAF (2012)

L. Squintani, J.M. Holwerda & K.J. de Graaf, Regulating Greenhouse Gas Emissions from EU ETS Installations: What Room Is Left for the Member States?, in M. Peeters, M. Stallworthy & J. de Cendra de Larragán, *Climate Law in EU Member States, towards National Legislation for Climate Protection*, Edward Elgar, 2012, pp. 67–88.

SQUINTANI (2013)

L. Squintani, Gold-Plating of European Environmental Law, Ph.D. dissertation, University of Groningen 2013.

SQUINTANI (2013b)

L. Squintani, The Dutch Policy on Gold-Plating and the Transposition of Directive 2008/98/EC on waste, *Environmental Law Network International Review*, 1(2), 2013, pp. 44–50.

SQUINTANI & ZIJLMANS (2013)

L. Squintani & J. Zijlmans, 'Nationale koppen' en de doorwerking van natuurbeschermingsverdragen, *Milieu & Recht* 2013/35.

SQUINTANI & VAN RIJSWICK (2016)

L, Squintani and Van Rijswick 2016. L. Squintani & H.F.M.W. van Rijswick, Improving Legal Certainty and Adaptability under the Programmatic Approach, Journal of Environmental Law 2016 (3), DOI:10/1093/jel/eqw022.

STEPHEN (2004)

D. Stephen, Regulation by Brussels? The Myths and The Challenges, European Movement Policy Paper 2, November 2004.

STEUNENBERG & VOERMANS (2006)

B. Steunenberg & W. Voermans, *The transposition of EC directives: A Comparative Study of Instruments*, Techniques and Processes in Six Member States, Leiden, 2006.

STEUR, DE GOEDE EN SCHMEETS (2004)
B.F. Steur, P.J.M. de Goede & H.H.J. Schmeets, Nationale Coördinatie van Europees Beleid, 'Best Belangrijk', in *Bestuurskunde,* 2004, nr. 6, pp. 255 ff.
STOOP (2012)
J. Stoop, Nationale Koppen op EU-regelgeving; een relevante discussie?, *NtEr,* juli 2012, nr. 6, p. 229-237.
SCHWARZE (2006)
J. Schwarze, *European Administrative Law*, Revisited 1st edition, Sweet and Maxwell, 2006.
TAAL (2005)
M.T. Taal, Het ontwikkelien en gebruik van de BREFs, in Ramnewash-Oemrawsingh S.T. (ed.), *IPPC: in wetgeving en praktijk*, Boom Juridische Uitgevers, 2005, pp. 67–71.
TAKÁCS (2009)
T. Takács, *Participation in EU Decision Making, Implications on the National Level*, T.M.C. Asser Press, The Hague, 2009.
TANGEA, PORTUESE & GOUGH (2014)
J.A. Tangea, A. Portuese & O. Gough The Principle of Legal Certainty as a Principle of Economic Efficiency, *European Journal of Law and Economics* 2014, vol. 42, pp. 1–26.
TANNER (2006)
E. Tanner, Clear, Simple, and Precise Legislative Drafting: How Does a European Community Directive Fare?, in *Statute Law Review*, 27(3), 2007, pp. 150–175.
TEEKENS (2005)
J. Teekens, Wetsvoorstel 29 711: IPPC en milieuzorrg geïntegreerd in de Wet milieubeheer, in Ramnewash-Oemrawsingh S.T. (ed.), *IPPC: in wetgeving en praktijk*, Boom Juridische Uitgevers, 2005, pp. 11–29.
TEUNE (1993)
H.A.L. Teuna, Het hoofdstuk Afvalstoffen Wm: nieuwe impulsen voor provinces, blijvende onzekerheden voor afvalorganisaties, in *Milieu & Recht*, 1993, nr. 12, pp. 688–699.
THOMAS & LYNCH-WOOD (2008)
R. Thomas & G. Lynch-Wood, Transposing European Union Law in the United Kingdom: Administrative Rule-Making, Scrutiny and Better Regulation, in *European Public Law*, 14(2), 2008, pp. 177–211.
THOMPSON & JONES (2007)
K. Thompson & B. Jones, Administrative law in the United Kingdom, Administrative Law of the European Union, Its Member States and the United States: A Comparative Analysis, René Seerden (ed.), Metro, 2007.
TIEMAN (2003),
J.R.C. Tieman, *Naar een nuttige toepassing van het begrip afvalstof*, Kluwer, 2003.
TIEMAN (2006)
J.R.C. Tieman, *Afvalstoffen*, WLP, 2006.

TIMMERMANS (1980)
C.W.A. Timmermans, EEG harmonisatie en Nederlandse recht: een beeld van bewogen beweging, in *RM Themis*, 1980, vol. 4/5, pp. 406–431.
TIMMINK (1995)
H.A.G. Timmink, Minimumnormen in EG-richtlijnen, in *Sociaal-Economische Wetgeving*, 1995, pp. 79–106.
TIZZANO (1999)
A. Tizzano, I meccanismi della Legge La Pergola: una radiografia dei problem di funzionamento, in *Il Foro Italiano*, 1999, pp. 303 ff.
TOLSMA (2010)
H.D. Tolsma De toekomst van de Wabo: een omgevingsvergunning met integrale belangenafweging, in *Milieu & Recht*, 2010, nr. 2, p 146–150.
TONNAER (1994)
F.P.C.L. Tonnaer, *Handboek van het Nederlands Milieurecht*, Boek 1 en 2, Lemma, 1994.
TRIDIMAS (2005)
T. Tridimas, The Rule of Reason and Its Relation to Proportionality and Subsidiarity, in Schrauwen A. (ed.), *Rule of Reason*, Europa Law Publishing, 2005, pp. 109–128.
TRIDIMAS (2006)
Takis Tridimas, *The General Principles of EU law*, 2nd edition, Oxford University Press 2006.
TRIDIMAS (2007)
T. Tridimas, *The General Principles of EU Law*, Oxford University Press, 2007.
TRIDIMAS (2011)
T. Tridimas, Constitutional Review of Member State Action: The Virtues and Vices of an Incomplete Jurisdiction, 2011, 9 *International Journal of Constitutional Law*, pp. 737 ff.
TROMANS (2001)
S. Tromans, EC Waste Law – A Complete Mess? 2001, *Journal of Environmental Law*, 13(2), 2001, pp. 133–156.
TROOSTWIJK (1991)
H. Troostwijk, De planologische aspect van het afvalstoffenbeleid, in Jans & Van Acht (eds.), *Afvalstoffenrecht*, Tjeenk Willink, 1991, pp. 27–41.
TROUWBORST (2009)
A. Trouwborst, International Nature Conservation Law and the Adaptation of Biodiversity to Climate Change: A Mismatch?, in *Journal of Environmental Law* Advanced Access, 2009, pp. 1–24.
TRÜE (2005)
C. Trüe, The German Drinks Can Deposit: Complete Harmonisation or a Trade Barrier Justified by Environmental Protection?, *Journal for European Environmental & Planning Law*, 2(2), 2005, pp. 142–148.
USHER (1988)
J.A. Usher, *General Principles of EC Law*, Longman, 1988.

VAN BERGEN (2008)
R. van Bergen, *Wegwijzer Afvalstoffenrecht* 2008/2009, Kluwer 2008.
VAN CALSTER (1997)
G. van Calster, EC Noise Legislation and Policy, in *European Environmental Law Review*, 1997, vol. 6, pp. 174–181.
VAN CALSTER (1999)
G. van Calster, Case Comment, Court Criticises Restrictions on Free Movement of Waste, in *European Law Review*, 24(2), 1999, pp. 178–184.
VAN CALSTER (2000)
G. van Calster, The Legal Framework for the Regulation of Waste in the European Union, in Somsen et al. (eds.), *Yearbook of European Environmental Law*, 2000, vol. 1, pp. 161–224.
VAN CALSTER (2002a)
G. van Calster, Afval: Markt en overheid?, in Dresden & Uylenburg (eds.), *Afvalstoffen: Actuele thema's rond afval en stoffen*, Kluwer aan den Rijn, 2002, pp. 39–66.
VAN CALSTER (2002b)
G. van Calster, Case Comment, The Free Movement of Waste after DaimlerChrysler, in *European Law Review*, 25(5), 2002, pp. 610–617.
VAN CALSTER (2002c)
G. van Calster, De Europees afvaltrein rolt lekker voort, in *Nederlands tijdschrift voor Europees recht*, 2002, No. 6, pp. 162–167.
VAN CALSTER & LEE (2002)
G. van Calster & M. Lee, European Case Law Report September 2001 – March 2002, ECJ 13 December 2001, Case C-324/99, DaimlerChrysler AG v. Land Baden-Würteemberg, Not yet Reported in ECR, in *Review of European Community & International Environmental Law*, 11(2), 2002, pp. 240–244.
VAN DEN BRINK (2002)
A. Van den Brink, Versnelde implementatie en de Grondwet, in *NTER* 2002, pp. 222 ff.
VAN DEN BRINK (2004)
A. Van den Brink, *Regelgeving in Nederland ter implementatie van EU-recht*, Kluwer, 2004.
VAN DEN BROEK (1997)
J.H.G. Van den Broek, IPPC in werking getreden, in *Milieu & Recht*, 1997, nr. 1, pp. 7–15.
VAN DEN BROEK (2005)
J.H.G. van den Broek, De Kroonjuweel van VROM, Herijking, omgevinsvergunning en omgevingswetboek, *NJB*, 2005, nr. 11, pp. 578–584.
VAN DEN BROEK (2007)
G.M. van den Broek, Een gemeenschappelijk kader voor het herstel van milieuschade, in *Van Utrecht via Brussel naar Maastricht,* Kluwer, 2007, pp. 45–60.
VAN DEN HOUD (2004)
K.D. van den Houd, Meten, rekenen en voorspellen, in *Milieu & Recht*, 2004, nr. 6, pp. 345–349.

VAN DER FELTZ (2004a)

G.C.W. van der Feltz, Rechtspraak naar aanleiding van het Besluit luchtkwaliteit, in Ramnewash-Oemrawsigh S.T. (ed.), *Regeling inzake luchtkwaliteit; Nederland op slot?*, Vereniging voor Milieurecht, BJu, 2006, nr. 1, pp. 21–54.

VAN DER FELTZ (2004b)

G.C.W. van der Feltz, Luchtkwaliteit in planologie en milieurecht, in *Milieu & Recht*, 2004, nr. 5, pp. 329–336.

VAN DER FLIER & VAN DEN OOSTERKAMP (1994)

P.J. Van der Flier & J.S. Van den Oosterkamp, Voortvarende implementatie van EG-recht, mede in het licht van de Algemene wet bestuursrecht en de Annwijzigengen voor de regelgeving, in *Sociaal-Economische Wetgeving* 1994, pp. 727 ff.

VAN DER GRONDEN (1998)

J.W. van der Gronden, *De implementatie van het EG-milieurecht door Nederlandse decentrale overheden*, Kluwer, 1998.

VAN DER GRONDEN & MORTELMANS (2002)

J.W. van der Gronden & K.J.M. Mortelmans, Afval, een vruchtbare voedingsstof voor ontwikkeling van het Europese recht, in *Ars aequi*, 2002, No. 3, pp. 180–198.

VAN DER POT (2006)

Van der Pot *Handboek van het Nederlandse Staatsrecht*, bewerkt door: prof. mr. D.J. Elzinga, prof. mr. R. de Lange en m.m.v. mr. H.G. Hoogers, Kluwer 2006.

VAN DER VEEN (2005)

G.A. van der Veen, De EU-Richtlijn Milieuaanspraelijkheid in verhuiding tot de Wet milieubeheer en de Wet bodembescherming, in *Tijdschrift voor Milieuschade en Aansprakelijkheidsrecht*, 2005, vol. 4, pp. 141–149.

VAN DER VEEN (2007)

G.A. van der Veen, De implementatie van de Richtlijn Milieuaansprakelijkheid in de Wet milieubeheer: publiekrechtelijke lacunes plus te voortvarend einde van privaatrechtelijk kostenverhaal, in *Tijdschrift voor Milieuschade en Aansprakelijkheidsrecht*, 2007, vol. 3, pp. 67–71.

VAN DER VLIST (1991)

J. van der Vlist, Knelpunten in het Nederlandse afvalstoffenbeleid, in Jans & Van Acht (eds.), *Afvalstoffenrecht*, Tjeenk Willink, 1991, pp. 5–10.

VAN DER WAL & VAN SCHAIK (2007)

G. van der Wal & F.Y. van Schaik, 'De Nederlandse toepassing van de Habitatrichtlijn: een te grote rem op de bedrijvigheid?', *Bouwrecht* 2007, p. 652 e.v.

VAN GEILSWIJK (2003)

M. van Geilswijk, Ontheffingen van de verbodsbepalingen in de Flora- en faunawet, in *Milieu & Recht*, vol. 30 2003, afl. 2, pag. 42–48.

VAN GEILSWIJK (2004)

M. van Geilswijk Uitgesproken: Artikel 68 Flora- en faunawet, in *Milieu & Recht*, vol. 31 2004, afl. 10, pag. 608–612.

VAN GEILSWIJK & FRERIKS (2005)
M. van Geilswijk & A.A. Freriks, Wijzigingen Besluit beschermde dier- en plantensoorten op gespannen voet met Europese natuurbeschermingsrichtlijnen, *JFf* 2005, p. 45 ff. (aangevraagd).
VAN GEILSWIJK (2006)
M. van Geilswijk, Gedragscodes onder de Flora- en faunawet: een versterking van de soortenbescherming of het zwaard van Damocles?, in *Milieu & Recht*; vol. 33 2006, afl. 8, pag. 478–485.
VAN GEILSWIJK (2009)
M. van Geilswijk, Ruimtelijke ontwikkeling onder de Flora- en faunawet: terug bij af?, *Bouwrecht* 2009, p, 296 e.v.
VAN GESTEL (2005)
R.A.J. van Gestel, Geïntegreerde preventie en flexibele bestrijding van verontreiniging. Op naar een hoog niveau van bescherming? in Ramnewash-Oemrawsingh S.T. (ed.) *IPPC: in wetgeving en praktijk*, Boom Juridische Uitgevers, 2005, pp. 32–65.
VAN GESTEL & VERSCHUUREN (2000)
R.A.J. van Gestel & J. Verschuuren, Alara: minimumregel of beginsel met aspiraties?, in *Milieu & Recht*, 2000, nr. 3, pp. 56–63.
VAN KEULEN (2004)
M. van Keulen, Nederlandse EU-belangenbehartiging. Van consensus naar confrontatie?, in *Bestuurskunde,* 2004, nr. 6, pp. 263 ff.
VAN KREVELD (1991)
J.H. van Kreveld, De rol van de Nederlandse wetgevingsjurist bij de implementatie van het EG-recht, in *RegelMaat* 1991–1992, pp. 42–46.
VAN MIDDELKOOP & UYLENBURG (2002)
L. van Middelkoop & R. Uylenburg, Interventies en verslag van de discussies, in Dresden & Uylenburg (eds.), *Afvalstoffen: Actuele thema's rond afval en stoffen*, Kluwer aan den Rijn, 2002, pp. 85–100.
VAN OEVEREN (1984)
Ch. Van Oeveren, De juridische status van het afvalstoffenplan, in *Milieu & Recht*, 1984, nr. 4, pp. 105–109.
VAN OOIK (1999)
R.H. van Ooik, *De keuze der rechtsgrondslag voor besluiten van de Europese Unie*, Kluwer, 1999.
VAN OPHEM (1993)
H.V. van Ophem, Company Management and Waste Prevention, in Wiggers-Rust e.o. (eds.), *Waste Prevention in the EEC*, Tjeenk Willink, 1993, pp. 45–58
VAN RIJ & ANNEMA (2010)
H.E. van Rij & J.A. Annema, Luchtkwaliteitregels verplichten ten onrechte tot schijnzekerheid bij rekenmodellen, *Milieu & Recht*, 2010, nr. 4, pp. 208–212.
VAN RIJSWICK (1999)
H.F.M.W. van Rijswick, De consequenties van een ruime uitleg van het lozing uit richtlijn 76/464, in *Milieu & Recht*, 1999, No. 12, pp. 291–296.

VAN RIJSWICK (2000)
H.F.M.W. van Rijswick, Hoe nu verder met het lozingenbegrip? in *Milieu & Recht*, 2000, No. 10, pp. 258–262.
VAN ROSSEM (1998)
A. van Rossem, Nieuwe ontwikkelingen in het Europese afvalstoffenrecht?, in *Nederlandse Tijdschrift voor Europees Recht*, 1998, No. 3, pp. 20–23.
VAN ROSSEM (2000)
A. van Rossem, Hof geeft uitleg aan het (gevaarlijke-) afvalstoffenbegrip, in *Nederlandse Tijdschrift voor Europees Recht*, 2000, No. 9, p. 203–209.
VAN ROSSEM (2012)
J.W. van Rossem, The EU at a Crossroads: A Constitutional Inquiry into the Way International Law Is Received within the EU Legal Order, in E. Cannizzaro, P. Palchieri & R.A. Wessel, *International Law as Law of the European Union*, Martinus Nijhof Publishers, 2012, pp. 59–89.
VAN ROSSEM & SEVENSTER (1998)
A. van Rossem & H.G. Sevenster, Hof beantwoord vragen Afdeling over afvalregime, in *Nederlandse Tijdschrift voor Europees Recht*, 1998, No. 9, pp. 196–201.
VAN ROSSEM & VEDDER (2000)
A. van Rossem & H.H.B. Vedder, Sydhavnens: Dusseldorp revisited?, in Nederlands tijdschrift voor Europees recht, 2000, nr. 9, pp. 209–216.
VAN'T LAM, JURGENS & MICHIELS (2002)
V.M.Y. van 't Lam, G.T.J.M. Jurgens, F.C.M.A. Michiels, Het begrip 'inrichting' in de Wet milieubeheer: een onderzoek naar het begrip 'inrichting' als aangrijpingspunt voor milieuregelgeving, Ministerie van VROM (Den Haag 2002).
VAN'T LAM & UYLENBURG (2006)
V.M.Y. van't Lam& R. Uylenburg, Modernisering van VROM-Pseudowetgeving, STEM publicatie 2005/2006.
VAN VELZEN (1990)
C.J. Van Velzen, Afvalstoffenbeleid, in Meijer Drees & Van Velzen, *Afvalstoffenbeleid*, Tjeenk Willink, 1990, pp. 12–18.
VAN WIJK, KONIJNENBELT & VAN MALE (2008)
H.D. Van Wijk, W. Konijnenbelt & R. Van Male, *Hoofdstukken van bestuursrecht*, Elsevier Juridisch, 2008.
VAN WIJMEN (2002)
P.C.E. van Wijmen, Openingstrede, in Dresden & R. Uylenburg (eds.), *Afvalstoffen: Actuele thema's rond afval en stoffen*, Kluwer aan den Rijn, 2002, pp. 1–6.
VAN WIJMEM (2005)
P.C.E. van Wijmen, 'Eerst natuur, dan overig ruimtebeslag', *Bouwrecht* 2005, p. 554 e.v.
VAN ZOEST (1993)
A.J. van Zoest, Gemeenten tussen wet en nadere regelgeving, in *Milieu & Recht*, 1993, nr. 12, pp. 700–707.

VANDERMEERSCH (1987)
D. Vandermeersch, The Single European Act and the Environmental Policy of the European Economic Community, in *European Law Review*, 12(6), 1987, pp. 407–429.
VANPRAET & VAN DE HEYNING (2010)
J. Vanpraet & C. van de Heyning, Hoe fundamentele rechten het leefmilieu beschermen. Overzicht van het instrumentarium, *Nieuw Juridisch Weekblad* 227, 2010, pp. 562–576.
VEDDER (2003)
H.H.B. Vedder, Ontwikkelingen in het Europese afvalstoffenrecht, in *Sociaal-Economische Wetgeving* 2003, nr. 7/8, pp. 234–250.
VELTKAMP (1998)
B.M. Veltkamp, *Implementatie van EG-milieurichtlijnen in Nederland*, Kluwer, 1998.
VELTMAN (2002)
J. Veltman, De Natuurbeschermingswet opnieuw op de helling, Milieu & Recht, 2002, nr. 4, pp. 100–107.
VERDURE (2009)
Ch. Verdure, Gestion des déchets, protection de l'environnement et responsabilité, in *Revue Générales des Assurances et des Responabilités*, Issue 4, 2009, pp. 14449.
VERSCHUUREN (1993)
J. Verschuuren, Europese eisen aan de integrale milieuvergunning, in *Milieu & Recht*, 1993, nr. 2, pp. 104–109.
VERSCHUUREN (2003)
J.M. Verschuuren, De Vogelrichtlijn en de Habitatrichtlijn: nieuwe impuls voor achtergebleven rechtsgebied, in Gilhuis & Verschuuren (red.), *Is er nog verschil tussen Europa en Nederlands milieurecht*, Boom Juridische uitgevers, 2003, pp. 99–117.
VERSFELD (2005)
R.A. Versfeld, Reactie vanuit het bedrijfsleven, in Ramnewash-Oemrawsingh S.T. (ed.), *IPPC: in wetgeving en praktijk*, Boom Juridische Uitgevers, 2005, pp. 75–77.
VERSLUIS & HOOGENBOEZEM (2004)
E. Versluis & J. Hoogenboezem, Uitvoering van Europees Beleid in Nederland, in *Bestuurskunde*, 2004, nr. 6, pp. 271 ff.
VLEMMINX & BOEKHORST (2000)
F.M.C. Vlemminx & M.G. Boekhorst, Inleiding Artikelen 90–95: De Internationale Rechtsorde, Hoofdstuk 5, § 2, in Koekkoek A.K. (ed.), *De Grondwet*, Tjeenk Willink, 2000. pp. 442–482.
VOERMANS (2001)
W. Voermans, Objects trouvés, Adviscollege toetsing administrative lasten (Actal), in *RegelMaat*, 2001/6, pp. 24–228.
VOERMANS (2009)
W. Voermans Gold-Plating and Double Banking: An Overrated Problem?, in Snijders H. & Vogenauer H. (eds.), *Content and Meaning of National Law in the Context of Transnational Law*, Sellier European Law Publishers, 2009, pp. 79–88.

VOGELEZANG-STOUTE ET AL. (2009)
E.M. Vogelezang-Stoute, M.N. Boeve, N.M. van der Grijp, F.A.G. Groothuijse, mr. N.S.J. Koeman, L. van Middelkoop, mr. M.G.W.M. Peeters & R. Uylenburg, De Wet milieubeheer als kader voor implementatie van Europese wetgeving, een verkennende studie naar de mogelijkheden en knelpunten voor een correcte implementatie, STEM-repport 2009–02.
VOS (1989)
E.I.L. Vos, De Italiaanse wijze van implementeren, in *Ars Aequi* 1989, pp. 979 ff.
WAGNER (2000)
M. Wagner, *Das Konzept der Mindestharmonisierung*, Duncker & Humblot, 2000, pp. 307–308.
WAGNER (2003)
M. Wagner, *The Porter Hypothesis Revisited: A Literature Review of Theoretical Models and Empirical Tests*, Center for Sustainability Management, Universität Lüneburg, 2003.
WASSEL (2012)
R.A. Wessel, Reconsidering the Relationship between International and EU Law: Towards a Content-Based Approach?, in E. Cannizzaro, P. Palchieri & R.A. Wessel, *International Law as Law of the European Union*, Martinus Nijhof Publishers, 2012, pp. 7–34.
WEATHERILL (2005)
S. Weatherill, Harmonisation: How Much, How Little?, in *European Business Law Review*, 16(3) (2005) pp. 533–545.
WEATHERILL (2017)
S. Weatherill, *The Internal Market as a Legal Concept*, Oxford University Press, 2017.
WENNERÅS (2005)
P. Wenneràs, A Progressive Interpretation of the European Liability Directive in Conformity with EC Law, in Mellenberg R. & Uylenburg R. (eds.), *Aansprakelijkheid voor schade aan de natuur*, Europa Law Publishing, 2005, pp. 135–150.
WIDDERSHOVEN (2007)
R. Widdershoven, Het ABC van de doorwerking van richtlijnen, in Blomber et al., *Van Utrecht via Brussel naar Maastricht*, Kluwer, 2007, pp.235–252.
WIERS (2002)
J. Wiers, *Trade and the Environment in the EC and WTO*, Europa Law Publishing, 2002.
WIGGERS-RUST (2005)
L.F. Wiggers-Rust, De rol van niet-gouvernementele organisaties (NGOs) volgens de Richtlijn milieuaansprakelijkheid, *Tijdschrift voor Milieuschade en Aansprakelijkheidsrecht*, 2005, vol. 5, pp. 177–183.
WILS (2000)
W. Wils, The Birds Directive 15 Years Later: a Survey of the Case Law and a Comparison with the Habitat Directive, *Journal of Environmental law*, 6(2), 1994, p. 220.
WINTER (1994)
G. Winter, *German Environmental Law: Basic Texts and Introduction*, Nijhoff/Graham & Trotman, 1994.

WINTER (1999)
G. Winter, The IPPC Directive: a German Point of View, in Ch. Backes & G. Betlem (eds.), *Integrated Pollution Prevention and Control*, Kluwer Law International, 1999, pp. 65–79.
WINTER (2000a)
G. Winter, Die Sperrwirkung von Gemeinschaftsskundärrecht für einzelstaatliche Regulerung des Binnenmarkts mit besonderer Berücksichting von Art.130t EGV, 1998, 51, Die öffenliche Verwaltung, pp. 377 ff, at p. 380.
WINTER (2000b)
G. Winter, Die Steuering grenzüberschreitender Abfsllströme, in *DVBL*, 2000, pp. 657–669.
WINTER (2006)
G. Winter, Matching Task and Competences in the EC Multi-Level Environmental Administration, in Macroy (ed.), *Reflections on 30 Years of EU Environmental Law*, Europa Law Publishing, 2006, pp. 399–414.
WINTER ET AL. (2008)
G. Winter, J.H. Jans, R. Macrory & L. Krämer, Weighing up the EC Environmental Liability Directive, in *Journal of Environmental Law*, 2008, vol. 20, pp. 163–191.
WOERDMAN (2015)
E. Woerdman, 'The EU Greenhouse Gas Emissions Trading Scheme', in E. Woerdman, M.M. Roggenkamp and J.M. Holwerda (eds.), *Essential EU Climate Law*, Edward Elgar, 2015, pp. 43–75.
WOLDENDORP (2004)
H.E. Woldendorp, Regeren per decreet; natuurbescherming, milieubeheer en ruimtelijke ordening on de Nederlandse EEZ, in *Milieu & Recht*, 2004, nr. 5, pp. 266–272.
WOLDENDORP (2005)
H.E. Woldendorp, Wettelijke kader voor natuurbescherming, in *Bouwrecht* 2005, pp. 269–280.
WOLDENDORP (2006)
H.E. Woldendorp, Gebiedsbescherming volgens de Natuurbeschermingswet 1998, *Bouwrecht*, p.199 e.v.
WOLDENDORP (2007)
H.E. Woldendorp, Het Europese Hof oer natuurbescherming, in *Bouwrecht* 2007, pp. 223–231.
WOLDENDORP (2008a)
H.E. Woldendorp, 'De toepassing van de Europese natuurbeschermingsregelgeving: Nederland het braafste jongetje van de klas?', *Bouwrecht* 2008, p. 8 e.v.
WOLDENDORP (2008b)
H.E. Woldendorp, 'Vogelbescherming: de wettekst als vogelverschrikker', *Milieu & Recht* 2008/2, p. 71–78.
WOLDENDORP (2009)
H.E. Woldendorp, 'Waar is de gek die de normen heeft vastgesteld? (1)', *Bouwrecht* 2009, p. 481 e.v.

WOLDENDORP (2010)

H.E. Woldendorp, Kroniek Flora- en faunawet, recente ontwikkelingen in het soortenbescherming, in *Milieu & Recht*, 2010, pp. 425–433.

WOLDENDORP (2011)

H.E. Woldendorp H.E., Kroniek Natuurbeschermingswet, in *Milieu & Recht*, 2011, Afl. 3, pp. 138–155.

WYATT & MACRORY (2010)

D. Wyatt & R. Macrory, Does the EU's Proposed Directive On Industrial Emissions (IPPC) Preclude Member States From Imposing Emission Limits for Co2 Under National Rules Other Than Those Implementing the Proposed Directive?, 2010, Legal Advice, www.ucl.ac.uk/cclp/ccsnews.php?rn=988, accessed November 2011.

ZIJLMANS (2011)

J. Zijlmans, *De doorwerking van natuurbeschermingsverdragen in de Europese en Nederlandse rechtsorde*, Sdu uitgevers, 2011.

ZÖTTL (2000)

J. Zöttl, Towards Integrated Protection of the Environment in Germany?, in *Journal of Environmental Law*, 12(3), 2000, pp. 281–291.

# Index